Neoliberalism and Environmental Education

This timely book situates environmental education within and against neoliberalism, the dominant economic, political, and cultural ideology impacting both education and the environment. Proponents of neoliberalism imagine and enact a world where the primary role of the state is to promote capital markets, and where citizens arc defined as autonomous entrepreneurs who fulfill their needs via competition with, and surveillance of, others.

These ideas interact with environmental issues in a number of ways and *Neoliberalism and Environmental Education* engages this interplay with chapters on how neoliberal ideas and actions shape environmental education in formal, informal, and community contexts. International contributors consider these interactions in agriculture and gardening, state policy enactments, environmental science classrooms, ecoprisons, and in professional management and educational accountability programs. The collection invites readers to reexamine how economic policy and politics shape the cultural enactment of environmental education.

This book was originally published as a special issue of *Environmental Education Research*.

Joseph Henderson is a Research Scientist at the University of Delaware, DE, USA. Trained as an anthropologist of environmental and science education, his research investigates how sociocultural, political, and economic factors influence teaching and learning in emerging energy and climate systems.

David Hursh is a Professor at the Warner Graduate School of Education and Human Development, University of Rochester, NY, USA. His research situates education policy and reform in the United States and globally within the context of a neoliberal social imaginary.

David Greenwood is Associate Professor and Canada Research Chair of Environmental Education at Lakehead University in Thunder Bay, Ontario, Canada. His scholarship, teaching, and activism revolve around place-based, environmental, holistic, and sustainability education.

Neoliberalism and Environmental Education

Edited by
Joseph Henderson, David Hursh and
David Greenwood

LONDON AND NEW YORK

First published 2017
by Routledge
2 Park Square, Milton Park, Abingdon, Oxon, OX14 4RN, UK

and by Routledge
711 Third Avenue, New York, NY 10017, USA

Routledge is an imprint of the Taylor & Francis Group, an informa business

© 2017 Taylor & Francis

All rights reserved. No part of this book may be reprinted or reproduced
or utilised in any form or by any electronic, mechanical, or other means,
now known or hereafter invented, including photocopying and recording,
or in any information storage or retrieval system, without permission in
writing from the publishers.

Trademark notice: Product or corporate names may be trademarks or
registered trademarks, and are used only for identification and
explanation without intent to infringe.

British Library Cataloguing in Publication Data
A catalogue record for this book is available from the British Library

ISBN 13: 978-1-138-22957-0

Typeset in Times New Roman
by RefineCatch Limited, Bungay, Suffolk

Publisher's Note
The publisher accepts responsibility for any inconsistencies that may have
arisen during the conversion of this book from journal articles to book chapters,
namely the possible inclusion of journal terminology.

Disclaimer
Every effort has been made to contact copyright holders for their permission to
reprint material in this book. The publishers would be grateful to hear from any
copyright holder who is not here acknowledged and will undertake to rectify
any errors or omissions in future editions of this book.

Contents

Citation Information	vii
Preface *Michael A. Peters*	ix
Introduction: Environmental education in a neoliberal climate *David Hursh, Joseph Henderson and David Greenwood*	1
1. Education policy mobility: reimagining sustainability in neoliberal times *Marcia McKenzie, Andrew Bieler and Rebecca McNeil*	21
2. Nature is a nice place to save but I wouldn't want to live there: environmental education and the ecotourist gaze *Robert Fletcher*	40
3. Entrepreneurial endeavors: (re)producing neoliberalization through urban agriculture youth programming in Brooklyn, New York *Evan Weissman*	53
4. Sustainability science and education in the neoliberal ecoprison *Peter C. Little*	67
5. Refusing to settle for pigeons and parks: urban environmental education in the age of neoliberalism *Michael W. Derby, Laura Piersol and Sean Blenkinsop*	80
6. Supporting youth to develop environmental citizenship within/against a neoliberal context *Alexandra Schindel Dimick*	92
7. Negotiating managerialism: professional recognition and teachers of sustainable development education *Hamish Ross*	105
8. Neoliberalism, new public management and the sustainable development agenda of higher education: history, contradictions and synergies *Sophie E.F. Bessant, Zoe P. Robinson and R. Mark Ormerod*	119
9. The promise and peril of the state in neoliberal times: implications for the critical environmental education movement in Brazil *Nicolas Stahelin, Inny Accioly and Celso Sánchez*	135

CONTENTS

10. Towards a political ecology of education: the educational politics of scale in southern Pará, Brazil   149
David Meek

11. Against neoliberal pedagogies of plants and people: mapping actor networks of biocapital in learning gardens   162
Clayton Pierce

12. Community organizing, schools, and the right to the city   180
Gregory A. Smith

13. The UN Decade of Education for Sustainable Development: business as usual in the end   193
John Huckle and Arjen E.J. Wals

Index   209

Citation Information

The chapters in this book were originally published in *Environmental Education Research*, volume 21, issue 3 (April 2015). When citing this material, please use the original page numbering for each article, as follows:

Editorial
Environmental education in a neoliberal climate
David Hursh, Joseph Henderson and David Greenwood
Environmental Education Research, volume 21, issue 3 (April 2015), pp. 299–318

Chapter 1
Education policy mobility: reimagining sustainability in neoliberal times
Marcia McKenzie, Andrew Bieler and Rebecca McNeil
Environmental Education Research, volume 21, issue 3 (April 2015), pp. 319–337

Chapter 2
Nature is a nice place to save but I wouldn't want to live there: environmental education and the ecotourist gaze
Robert Fletcher
Environmental Education Research, volume 21, issue 3 (April 2015), pp. 338–350

Chapter 3
Entrepreneurial endeavors: (re)producing neoliberalization through urban agriculture youth programming in Brooklyn, New York
Evan Weissman
Environmental Education Research, volume 21, issue 3 (April 2015), pp. 351–364

Chapter 4
Sustainability science and education in the neoliberal ecoprison
Peter C. Little
Environmental Education Research, volume 21, issue 3 (April 2015), pp. 365–377

Chapter 5
Refusing to settle for pigeons and parks: urban environmental education in the age of neoliberalism
Michael W. Derby, Laura Piersol and Sean Blenkinsop
Environmental Education Research, volume 21, issue 3 (April 2015), pp. 378–389

CITATION INFORMATION

Chapter 6

Supporting youth to develop environmental citizenship within/against a neoliberal context
Alexandra Schindel Dimick
Environmental Education Research, volume 21, issue 3 (April 2015), pp. 390–402

Chapter 7

Negotiating managerialism: professional recognition and teachers of sustainable development education
Hamish Ross
Environmental Education Research, volume 21, issue 3 (April 2015), pp. 403–416

Chapter 8

Neoliberalism, new public management and the sustainable development agenda of higher education: history, contradictions and synergies
Sophie E.F. Bessant, Zoe P. Robinson and R. Mark Ormerod
Environmental Education Research, volume 21, issue 3 (April 2015), pp. 417–432

Chapter 9

The promise and peril of the state in neoliberal times: implications for the critical environmental education movement in Brazil
Nicolas Stahelin, Inny Accioly and Celso Sánchez
Environmental Education Research, volume 21, issue 3 (April 2015), pp. 433–446

Chapter 10

Towards a political ecology of education: the educational politics of scale in southern Pará, Brazil
David Meek
Environmental Education Research, volume 21, issue 3 (April 2015), pp. 447–459

Chapter 11

Against neoliberal pedagogies of plants and people: mapping actor networks of biocapital in learning gardens
Clayton Pierce
Environmental Education Research, volume 21, issue 3 (April 2015), pp. 460–477

Chapter 12

Community organizing, schools, and the right to the city
Gregory A. Smith
Environmental Education Research, volume 21, issue 3 (April 2015), pp. 478–490

Chapter 13

The UN Decade of Education for Sustainable Development: business as usual in the end
John Huckle and Arjen E.J. Wals
Environmental Education Research, volume 21, issue 3 (April 2015), pp. 491–505

For any permission-related enquiries please visit:
http://www.tandfonline.com/page/help/permissions

Preface

Michael A. Peters

University of Waikato

In their introduction the editors begin with the unequivocal statement 'Environmental education is political' and as Joe Henderson made clear in a personal note: 'We found environmental education research and practice to be distressingly apolitical and moving away from issues of economics and government. Given the dominance of neoliberal statecraft and subjectivity, we felt the need to interject political economy back into the conversation'. It is with some relief that I read this because I have always entertained a kind of anxiety about the ease with which environmentalism as a movement, and environmental education (EE) as its political expression, fits with neoliberalism and its green washing of the market and the adoption of market mechanisms as solutions to buying-off carbon emissions. Raising eco-consciousness through the market with the organics movement, local sourcing, child-free labour, free range chickens and eggs – green consumerism sits well with an enhanced neoliberal green citizenship; a form of neoliberal 'green politics' all without having to go outside the supermarket.

Joe also emphasized to me the collective intent for the volume: 'We all saw the harm that the larger neoliberal project was doing as both a cause of, and impediment to, addressing ecological issues. We wanted to both describe its negative influence and discuss how not dealing with it hinders the ability to address such issues'. In words that nicely express their combine purpose he elaborated: 'We wanted to challenge the "common sense" neoliberal notion that markets and market subjectivities exist in a state of nature' – exactly the task they set here for a more politically-informed EE.

To release EE and modern environmental politics from the suffocating embrace of neoliberalism it is necessary to ask with Jedediah Purdy (2015) 'What would an environmentalism of the left look like?' His answer is an emphatic and resounding endorsement of the need for democracy and democratic debate:

> It would first of all have to change its attitude to "nature." Environmentalism is the youngest generation of a longer-running politics of nature. This politics pivots on contested visions of nature's value, humanity's place in it, and what, in fact, "nature" even is. From the preservationist movement that helped create national parks and wilderness areas to the awareness of ecological interconnection that inspired the anti-pollution laws of the 1970s, the politics of nature has often been democratic and creative in advancing the notion of the living world as part of a human ecology. But the politics of nature has also been an anti-politics, appealing to "nature" to shut down democratic debate (p. 46).

He goes on to argue: 'The first task for left environmentalists is to own up to this history and ask how today's green mainstream still lacks, or even blocks, democratic and egalitarian projects' (p. 47). By 'this history' he means a white history that has occluded indigenous peoples and has been fed by a 'progressive' democratic technocracy. As an environmental law professor it is perhaps not unexpected that Purdy would also come to emphasize 'a democratic version of environmental justice' (p. 47) with attention to the distributive effects of environmental harms and injustices. In one sense this is a move that is designed also to rescue an environmentally nuanced notion of social democracy that thrives on 'deliberation' in the space of green reason. We might even prematurely talk of 'ecological democracy' that forgets its Romantic links to focus in a tough-minded way on who gets to speak, who sets the agenda and who is invited to participate as a means of addressing questions of the absence of power from deliberative models of democracy. More importantly, while recognizing the enduring force of the educative and pedagogical potential of deliberative democracy we might ask 'what biases are masked by the norms of deliberation? how do "hegemonic" impediments shape which perspectives do and do not count?' (Kadlec and Freeman 2007).

Purdy (2015) finishes with what he thinks is the most vexing question 'between environmentalism and the left tradition: the problem created by natural limits to economic growth' (p. 48). While the Left – social democratic or Marxist – has mostly 'sought emancipation through growth' 'there is no getting around the planet's finitude'. There may be no getting around 'easing the demand for growth' (p. 48). While I do not disagree, I do want to emphasize that 'easing the demand for growth' is an educational and pedagogical project not merely confined to waste management but that also involves the fundamental reorganization of productive forces away from monopolistic and global scales and toward the model of the local market – a decentralization and simultaneously a greater regionalism that is also synonymous with local assemblies and local government.

John Dewey (1916) as perhaps the arch defender of participatory democracy proposed an 'ecological' system over a hundred years ago that was based on a form of Darwinian naturalism that understood that knowledge arises from the experience of the human organism in the process of adapting to its environment. For Dewey democracy is not just a means of protecting our interests or expressing our individuality but also a forum for *determining our interests*. It was above all an account of democracy *as social inquiry* that emphasized the importance of discussion and debate as a mechanism of decision-making with the institution of education at its heart. Joseph Henderson, David Hursh and David Greenwood have done a splendid job in editing the collection *Neoliberalism and Environmental Education* that both enables and enhances a politically informed EE which disturbs the cosy accommodations with neoliberalism and points to a new pedagogy and political economy of environmentalism.

References

Dewey, John (1916) *Democracy and Education: An Introduction to the Philosophy of Education.* New York: Macmillan.

Kadlec, Alison and Friedman, Will (2007) "Deliberative Democracy and the Problem of Power," *Journal of Public Deliberation*: Vol. 3: Iss. 1, Article 8. Available at: http://www.public deliberation.net/jpd/vol3/iss1/art8

Purdy, Jedediah (2015) "An Environmentalism for the Left," *Dissent*, October 1: 48–50. Available at: https://www.dissentmagazine.org/article/after-nature-left-environmentalism-jedediah-purdy

INTRODUCTION

Environmental education in a neoliberal climate

David Hursh[a], Joseph Henderson[a] and David Greenwood[b]

[a]*Warner School of Education, University of Rochester, Rochester, NY, USA;* [b]*Faculty of Education, Lakehead University, Thunder Bay, Canada*

> This introduction to a special issue of *Environmental Education Research* explores how environmental education is shaped by the political, cultural, and economic logic of neoliberalism. Neoliberalism, we suggest, has become the dominant social imaginary, making particular ways of thinking and acting possible while simultaneously discouraging the possibility and pursuit of others. Consequently, neoliberal ideals promoting economic growth and using markets to solve environmental and economic problems constrain how we conceptualize and implement environmental education. However, while neoliberalism is a dominant social imaginary, there is not one form of neoliberalism, but patterns of neoliberalization that differ by place and time. In addition, while neoliberal policies and discourses are often portrayed as inevitable, the collection shows how these exist as an outcome of ongoing political projects in which particular neoliberalized social and economic structures are put in place. Together, the editorial and contributions to the special issue problematize and contest neoliberalism and neoliberalization, while also promoting alternative social imaginaries that privilege the environment and community over neoliberal conceptions of economic growth and hyper-individualism.

Environmental education is political. In one sense, this is obvious. People disagree about environmental issues, and this spills over into how we conceptualize and contest such matters as the goals, methods, and curriculum of environmental education. A critical, timely and telling example, according to Stage et al. (2013), can be found in the United States: Some states are refusing to implement the Next Generation Science Standards (NGSS Lead States 2013) because the standards include the requirement to teach about climate change.

As Stevenson (2013) points out, as much as local to international environmental educators have sought to achieve consensus regarding various purposes, thematics, and features of environmental education, including through various declarations and conferences at Belgrade and Tbilisi, tensions remain and are ongoing between 'scholars in the field and policy makers inside and outside the field' (151). The tensions exemplified in our opening example often arise, notes Stevenson, because of differing and irreconcilable 'educational ideologies,' underscoring the need, we suggest, for environmental educators and researchers to understand the broader social and educational concerns that shape teaching, learning, and inquiry.

Environmental education is also political in a less obvious but perhaps more crucial sense. In this special issue of *Environmental Education Research*, we focus on how over the last four decades environmental education has been shaped by and interacts with the context of the dominant political and economic logic in the West, namely that of neoliberalism. As we and the contributors to this collection variously show, neoliberal ways of thinking about and acting in the world have become so prevalent, naturalized, and internalized that we are often unaware of how neoliberalism constrains our thinking and practice, such that it is difficult in both thought and deed to imagine a society proceeding on different principles. How did it come to be this way?

Our point of departure and return is Rizvi and Lingard's (2010) description of neoliberalism as the dominant social imaginary of contemporary society, understood as 'a way of thinking shared in a society by ordinary people, the common understandings that make everyday practices possible, giving them sense and legitimacy' (34). This leads us through the following arguments regarding neoliberalism in this editorial, and collection.

First, there is not one neoliberalism, but rather neoliberalisms that differ depending on how it is instantiated and experienced in diverse contexts, settings, and countries. For example, neoliberal education policies in England are similar to but also different from those in the United States or New Zealand, for well-rehearsed reasons (see Thrupp and Hursh 2006). Furthermore, neoliberalism is not fixed in form or effect: It is always in flux as it is made and remade, and new effects are being felt across contexts, settings, and countries.

Second, as Block and Somers (2014) write: 'the project of creating self-regulating markets is ultimately impossible' and 'has never – and cannot ever – actually exist' (10). As sociologists who focus on the political economy aspects and prefer the term 'market fundamentalism' over neoliberalism to reflect the neoliberal's faith in markets, Block and Somers have examined how 'markets are always organized through politics and social practices' (2014) and what this means for contemporary debate. Most importantly, they argue, market fundamentalists are not setting 'the market free from the state but [are] instead *re-embedding* it in *different* political, legal, and cultural arrangements, ones that mostly disadvantage the poor and the middle class, and advantage wealth and corporate interests' (9, italics in original). In fact, recognizing that neoliberalism is necessarily political and that it privileges some groups over others helps refute the notion that we can and should use markets to make all decisions. Equally, we might begin to resist the drift 'from *having* a market economy to *being* a market society' (Sandel 2012, 10, emphasis in original). We have no choice, therefore, but to engage in the political process of re-embedding markets into civil society and interrogating their relationship to both education and the environment, including in one of their intersections, *environmental education.*

In this editorial, then, we aim to achieve the following: We begin by examining the claim that neoliberalism is not primarily an economic but a political project, which counters what many – including ourselves – have previously argued (see, e.g. Hursh 2008; Hursh and Henderson 2011). In essence, we suggest that neoliberals as typified by Hayek ([1944] 2007, 1960), Friedman (1962), and Friedman and Friedman (1980) and their followers, falsely portray neoliberalism as an apolitical economic project, in which we need only have faith that markets will solve our economic, educational, and environmental problems. Consequently, we resist the notion held by neoliberals that we do not need to engage in collective – including bipartisan, that is, socially and economically inclusive – political work to find solutions to questions such as how we are to sustainably live together on this finite planet.

Next, we explore why describing neoliberalism primarily as a political project better explains the conundrum of how it is that an economic philosophy that calls for a smaller role for government or the state and therefore reducing or eliminating governmental regulations can (more often than not) promote governmental *re-regulation* supporting market-based decision-making. Such re-regulation occurs, for example, in environment policy via the promotion of cap-and-trade schemes, and in education policy with legislation supportive of publicly funded private education (Benn 2011, 4).

We then submit that neoliberal political and economic policies not only undermine our ability to respond to current economic and environmental crises, but are, in fact, the primary cause of them, because they promote re-regulating society to privilege market transactions and reject pursuit of other collective solutions. We also argue this requires a further response: resurrection of a positive conception of the political. This is because, while stating that something is 'political' is often used pejoratively to suggest a process abused by those in positions of power, be that politically and/or economically, to say that something is political can also suggest the need to (re)build those social institutions and processes that help solve our collective problems. Returning to Block and Somers (2014), who promote a view of economics as necessarily political, they advocate an approach, rooted in scholarship that:

> analyzes the varied means by which people cooperate to sustain the kinds of institutions, allocations, and social practices that support collective livelihood. From this perspective, understanding how to best meet the needs of livelihood requires anthropological and historical analysis of actual social practices rather than abstract assumptions and economic axioms. (226)

Block and Somers conclude their analysis of market fundamentalism by stating that we need 'to deepen and enlarge democratic governance at the local, national, and global levels' (240). Their views strongly echo those of the US philosopher of education, John Dewey, who wanted both schools and workplaces to contribute to human development rather than 'a senseless pursuit of profits' (Wirth 1977, 169). Likewise, we note environmentalist Berry (2012) suggests we conceptualize economics in relation to 'nature and one another' (20), a view we have expanded on elsewhere (Greenwood 2013; Henderson and Hursh 2014).

Writing both before and against neoliberal imaginaries, Dewey and Berry raise questions about the contours and realities of neoliberalism, which we conclude, are both messy and contradictory, and need to be understood carefully by environmental educators and researchers. Neoliberals often portray themselves as apolitical, while at the same time using politics to promote markets solutions to our social, educational, and environmental problems. Such an approach, we show, severely limits how we can respond to our environmental and educational problems, including via environmental education. Therefore, we argue that educators and researchers need to analyze how neoliberalism undermines education in general, and environmental education, in particular.

We begin, unsurprisingly, with an all-too-brief description of neoliberalism.

Neoliberalism

Defining neoliberalism is not easy, in part because its roots and meanings are not immediately straightforward. Some of the confusion lies in the meaning and connotation of the word, *liberal*. As the historian, Judt (2010) describes:

> a liberal is someone who opposes interference in the affairs of others: who is tolerant of dissenting attitudes and behavior. Liberals have historically favored keeping other people out of our lives, leaving individuals the maximum space in which to live and flourish as they choose. In their extreme forms, such attitudes are associated with self-styled 'libertarians.' (5)

In the United States, liberalism is most closely associated with the characteristics of the social welfare state (exemplified by Franklin Roosevelt's New Deal), which, as a theory of the state, substantially differs from neoliberalism. Neoliberals vary in their view of the state, with all, in comparison to Roosevelt's social democratic liberals, envisioning a smaller state, and a few, as in the case of Milton Friedman, almost no state at all. However, the point we make below is that, in general, neoliberals envision the state as key to re-regulating the economy to promote markets, primarily to the exclusive of other forums for decision-making about public matters.

Given the above, briefly defining neoliberalism may be a fool's errand, but attempt it we must (many histories and disquisitions exist on its various aspects, including: Brown 2005; Harvey 2005; Judt 2010; Peck 2010; Stedman Jones 2012; Verhaeghe 2014). In short, neoliberalism arose in the 1930s in response to increasing governmental intervention in the economic and political system, whether via authoritarian dictatorships and their command-and control systems (e.g. Stalin's communism), or the social democratic liberalism of the United States and Great Britain, which neoliberals feared would lead to authoritarianism too. Hayek, in his Nobel Prize speech and best-selling book *The Road to Serfdom* ([1944] 2007), 'evoked the fear of "slavery" by insisting that it was just a matter of time before social democracies like Britain's would inevitably slide down the slippery slope from "planning" to "serfdom"' (Block and Somers 2014, 224). However, since we assume that authoritarian dictatorships have little attraction to environmental educators or researchers, we do well to contrast neoliberal policies with social democratic liberalism that gained influence before, during, and just after World War II. Social democratic liberalism, particularly that indexed to the economic theory of Keynes (1936), emphasized that government had a responsibility to reduce the size of economic booms and busts and to provide for the general welfare through health care, education, mass transit, and housing.

In the United States, these goals are first and primarily reflected in Roosevelt's policies in response to the Great Depression. Rather than trust that the economy would fix itself, Roosevelt instituted policies that would transform the relationship between the federal government and the economy – and by extension, how we think about economy, government, and economic models of various stripes. Some of Roosevelt's initiatives included the Public Works Administration and Civilian Conservation Corps (both 1935), Social Security (1935), the Glass-Steagall Act (1932), which regulated banking, and the Federal Deposit Insurance Corporation (1934), which insured depositors' savings and reduced banking panics.

On 11 January 1944, in his State of the Union Address, Roosevelt proposed a second Bill of Rights, which, if adopted, would have greatly increased government responsibility for security and prosperity. These rights included 'the right to a useful remunerative job ... to a decent home ... adequate medical care ... [and] a good education' (Sunstein 2004, ix). Social democratic liberal policies in the US and elsewhere improved living conditions in the industrialized world, and such policies gained dominance in many countries from World War II up to the administrations of Reagan and Thatcher, the first international leaders to fervently roll back social democratic liberalism[1] and roll out neoliberalism (Peck 2010; for a very accessible history, see Judt 2010).

Reagan and Thatcher adopted the ideas of two prominent groups of economists: The Mont Pelerin Society led by Hayek (1944, 1960), and those at the University of Chicago led by Friedman (1962). Briefly, Hayek, Friedman, and other neoliberals differ significantly from social democratic liberals in how they conceptualize and model the relationship between society and the individual. Rather than the vision provided by social democratic liberals where society is responsible for promoting the common good, under neoliberalism the individual is responsible for providing for his or her own needs, and it is through individuals working to fulfill those needs that society is created.

Consequently, both proponents and critics of neoliberalism often state that neoliberalism aims to reduce or eliminate government, such as Grover Norquist, of Americans for Tax Freedom, in blatantly declaring that he 'doesn't want to abolish government. I simply want to reduce it to the size where I can drag it into the bathroom and drown it in the bathtub' (cited in Klein 2007, 446). However, scholars also note that certain neoliberals embrace the notion that government has a key role in *re-regulating*, not de-regulating, the economy in favor of corporations. We see this in how governments organize markets and society for a variety of 'human activities, including the private provision of core public goods' (Wacquant 2010, 213). To illustrate, in the United States, the neoliberal ideology of privatization and choice forms the basis for publicly funded privately operated primary and secondary charter schools. In New York State, charter schools would not exist if the state government did not (i) create the legal framework for establishing and operating charter schools, (ii) grant charter school operators public funding and the right to free space in public schools buildings, and (iii) provide tax deductions and other benefits to investors. Similarly, in Canada and Australia, neoliberal regulation favors an economy of extractivism where economic and environmental policies and tax codes favor the concentration of corporate wealth from oil, gas, and mineral development. In short, neoliberals expect governments to replace a social democratic notion of the public good with a version in which competitive markets provide for the public good (Judt 2010).

Recent governmental actions favoring corporations include United States Supreme Court decisions equating corporate cash contributions to political campaigns with free speech, as in the *Citizens United v. Federal Election Commission* case, and exempting corporations from federal laws based on religious freedom, as in the recent *Burwell v. Hobby Lobby* case (Milbank 2014). In both cases, the Court conceptualized corporations as having the same rights as persons, including the freedom of speech and religion. Therefore, following Wacquant (2012), we understand neoliberalism as a political activity that 'wishes to reform and refocus the state so as to actively foster and bolster the market as an ongoing political creation' (72).

We note too that neoliberalism transforms not only the role of the state, but also the nature of individuals in society. Under neoliberalism, individuals best operate within markets and within these occupy what is akin to the subject position of entrepreneurs, fulfilling their own needs and pursuing their own goals in competition with others. In the same way, Adam Smith's 'invisible hand' (*The Wealth of Nations,* [1776] 1976) argues that individual decisions made within markets result in manufacturers meeting the consumers' needs, for neoliberals, individuals should make entrepreneurial decisions within markets to ensure economic growth that best serves the interests of society. But as Olssen, Codd, and McNeill (2004) fear:

> Every social transaction is conceptualized as entrepreneurial, to be carried out purely for personal gain. The market introduces competition as the structuring mechanism through which resources and status are allocated efficiently and fairly. The 'invisible hand' of the market is thought to be the most efficient way of sorting out what competing individual gets what. (137–138)

For Hayek, markets are much more efficient at allocating resources and goods than individuals. In fact, Hayek goes as far as to describe the market as having knowledge that individuals could not possibly possess; as Mirowski (2013) writes, Hayek believed that 'the market really does know better than any one of us what is good for ourselves and society' (54). Furthermore, because markets are purportedly the most efficient way to make societal decisions, any resulting economic and political inequality is not only necessary but also beneficial. Again, Mirowski (2013), writing on Hayek, observes that inequality is 'a necessary functional characteristic of their ideal market system' (79). But in contrast to some other forms of economic liberalism, for neoliberals, any economic, social, or political attempts to alter the outcomes of markets are necessarily counterproductive, for these would violate the 'natural order' of the market. As Block and Somers (2014) observe, such 'market fundamentalism' rests upon the idea of social naturalism, which is 'a way of viewing the world built on the assumption that the laws governing natural phenomenon also govern human society' (102).

The belief that markets are actually nature's preferred way of making decisions helps explain neoliberal resistance to developing 'interventionist policies' in response to environmental issues, such as climate change. As Sandbu (2014), a columnist for the *Financial Times* (London), recently explicated regarding climate change, 'the increased risk to the planet is exactly offset by the value of the extra growth,' that is, if the environmental harm exceeds the benefits to economic growth, markets will adjust to reduce the environmental harm. There is no need for policies; markets can be left alone to solve everything.

Assuming such a positive outcome to the workings of markets seems increasingly untenable given the empirical evidence that corporations have inadequately reduced pollution or carbon emissions or have yet to fully acknowledge the limits of the industrial growth paradigm (see Klein's recent summary 2014). In fact, while neoliberals steadily advance their faith in markets and private property within and beyond the corridors of government, including via the privatization of public services that necessarily include education and natural resources, others have pointed out that this results in money becoming the prime 'mediator of our relationships with the non-human world' (Sullivan 2010, 25). In both vivid and contrasting terms to the prevailing discourse, we can also note the words of Pope Francis – himself a strong critic of neoliberalism and currently writing an encyclical on climate change and the environment – who posits that the current neoliberal variant of global capitalism has become an ecologically destructive form of idol worship:

The thirst for power and possessions knows no limits. In this system, which tends to devour everything which stands in the way of increased profits, whatever is fragile, like the environment, is defenseless before the interests of a deified market, which become the only rule. (Francis 2013, Evangelii Gaudium, 56)

However, even when the neoliberal agenda has been revealed for its flaws from a range of perspectives, neoliberals have largely retained their sway. They continue to frame economic, educational, and environmental problems through assertions that the market (still) knows best, and, at the same time, intervene in politics. This is why understanding neoliberalism as a political rather than economic process alone helps explain why neoliberal economics have continued to dominate Western economies despite the 2007 global financial collapse. Lest one forgets, the economic damage brought on by neoliberal tenets such as promoting deregulation in home lending (among other financial actions) led many economists to conclude that neoliberalism was dead, at least for a time. *Newsweek*, a weekly US news magazine, boldly stated on its cover and lead story that 'we were all socialists now' (Meacham 2009) – or at least Keynesians, able to appreciate the valuable role that governments can play in protecting society from economic manipulation. Joseph Stiglitz, winner of the Nobel Prize in economics, went so far as to proclaim:

Neoliberal market fundamentalism was always a political doctrine serving certain interests. It was never supported by economic theory. Nor, it should be clear, is it supported by historical experience. Learning this lesson may be a silver lining in the cloud now hanging over the global economy. (2008a, 2)

Elsewhere, Stiglitz stated that 'neoliberalism ... is dead in most western countries ... The US has lost its role as the model for others' (Stiglitz 2008b, 1). But, in fact, as Stiglitz and others have since pointed out, financiers and politicians allied themselves to intervene in the markets, saving the banks and their executives, but not those mortgage holders who could no longer finance their homes (Crouch 2011; Johnson and Kwak 2010; Krugman 2008). Consequently, the stock market has rebounded, the banks have earned record profits, but most working and unemployed people are worse off than before a recession brought on by neoliberal policies (Saez and Zucman 2014). For many, a return to the social democratic liberalism of Keynesian policies, even though it would fall short of radically transforming capitalism, would be a welcome, albeit inadequate improvement on the present (Mazzucato, 2013).

Given these broad brushstrokes, it is probably of no surprise to hear that under neoliberalism, our economic, educational, and environmental crises continue. But before we turn to these, we note that the articles included in this collection both illuminate some of the failures of neoliberalism, and how we might use some of its logical contradictions to create alternatives.

For example, while some neoliberals such as Norquist (2008) desire to eliminate the state, even Hayek, in *The Road to Serfdom* ([1944] 2007), reminded readers that functioning markets 'rely, above all, on the existence of an appropriate legal system, a legal system designed both to preserve competition, and to make it operate as beneficially as possible' (43–45). Therefore, many neoliberals, and even those, who like Hayek, have an almost unquestioning faith in markets, acknowledge that the state must play a role. When we combine that realization with Wacquant's (2012) observation, reform becomes possible, because:

> 'The state' is neither *a* monolith, coherent actor (whether operating autonomously or as the diligent servant of the dominant) or a single lever liable to being captured by special interests or movements springing from civil society. Rather, it is a *space of forces and struggles* over the very perimeter, prerogatives and priorities of public authority, and in particular over what 'social problems' deserve its attention and how they are to be treated. (73, emphasis in original)

As we and others have argued, neoliberalism can be understood as both an economic philosophy and a political project. As a political project, it can also be described as a kind of ideology or metaphor for ordering social and material relationships (Connolly 2013). In so doing, we recognize that the scholarly literatures of sociology and education use many other labels to describe and understand the phenomenon of social ordering and associated patterns of domination and control that lead to movements of resistance. A brief list of terms in use could include the following: capitalism, patriarchy, (neo)colonialism, (neo)imperialism, white supremacy and privilege, governmentality, extractivism, and biopolitics. Terms such as these, and the social conditions they mark concerning power, authority, and rights, share many conceptual points of purchase as those with analyses of the project of neoliberalism. For example, many neoliberal economic configurations take a particular brand of laissez-faire capitalism for granted and, because of its emphasis on individualism at the expense of the collective, tend to reinforce colonial or even imperialistic social and economic inequities based on race, class, and gender under industrial extractivism.

Equally, like most large-scale political movements, neoliberal ideologies also function through what Foucault and others have called 'governmentality,' that is, the biopolitical control of populations (Burchell, Gordon, and Miller 1991; Dean, 1999). It is important to note here that neoliberalism has much in common with other large-scale political projects and that by making neoliberalism our focus, we do not wish to disconnect it from other critical and necessary – and what we view as parallel and complementary – conversations about the politics of education, economy, and environment. We feel, however, that neoliberalism deserves special attention, including in this special issue, because of the way its features have been normalized and reified in the discourses and practices of social institutions in contemporary societies worldwide. Its practices and ways of ordering thought and behavior have simply become embedded into the assumptions governing many aspects of social life – including how many people think about education and/or environment.

Neoliberalism and environmental education

It can be readily shown that neoliberal tenets have formed the core principles for primary, secondary, and higher education reform in many countries over the last two decades (Hursh 2008; Hursh and Wall 2011; Lave 2012). Leading Finnish educator Sahlberg (2011) writes that these countries adopt 'management and administrative models brought to schools from [the] corporate world' (203). Teaching, for example, is constrained by prescribed curriculum, and learning, evaluated through standardized tests. Evaluating students and teachers through standardized tests reflects a neoliberal faith in the fact that those key features of the world worth measuring can be objectively evaluated and expressed numerically in this 'age of accountability' (Henderson and Hursh 2014). Further, the neoliberal belief in privileging private over public institutions offers ideological and political support to efforts to privatize the management of schools, such as charter schools in the US, and free schools and academies in England (Benn 2011; Buras 2014). Lastly, much like markets are conceived as operating free of their social context, schools are increasingly evaluated as failing or passing regardless of the communities, contexts, and places in which they exist (Lipman 2011).

Such features to the contemporary climate for education typically result in a narrowed and restricted curriculum with students as receivers for pre-determined knowledge, particularly in the public school system (Gruenewald and Manteaw 2007). Consequently, it is difficult to develop and practice extensive approaches to teaching and learning that emphasize the interdisciplinary nature of knowledge, that are problem and issues based, and that perceive teachers and students as co-creators of knowledge. In short, environmental education, which is often necessarily interdisciplinary, problem centered, and emergent, is often marginalized or becomes non-existent (Martina, Hursh, and Markowitz 2009).

Beyond these educational concerns though, we also need to revisit how neoliberalism negatively impacts how humans relate to one another and to their environments, and thus, in this section, we start to develop a more specific critique of the relationship between neoliberalism and the environment, before bringing in environmental education again.

Neoliberalism, with its emphasis on markets, aspires to assigning a monetary value to everything, including environment, understood as 'nature.' As Büscher, Dressler, and Fletcher (2014) describe, such commodification can occur in several ways: (1) as part of eco-tourism, (2) as a '"nature-culture unity" to counter the sense of alienation produced by capitalism,' and (3) as an 'ecosystem service provider' (18). Equally, Sullivan (2010) observes the increasing prevalence of environmental discourse conceptualizing nature as an 'ecosystem service provider,' or as a suite of resources to be brought under control via supposedly efficient quantitative and increasingly technological management techniques (Gabrys 2014).

Another example of the commodification, marketization, and management of the environment is the way in which the potentially radical systemic critique of sustainability has been captured within the logic of industrialized capitalism and then as yet another way to generate profits. As Dauvergne and Lister (2013) proclaim regarding the evolution of the sustainability concept:

> Turning sustainability into eco-business, moreover, is altering the nature of environmentalism, increasing its power to accelerate some forms of change, but limiting what is on the table to question, challenge, and alter. Sustainability as an idea can be radical: not just calling for changes in the rules of the game (i.e. market dynamics), but also to the game itself (i.e. the global economy). (25)

(As some of the papers in this special issue evidence, the sustainability concept itself has become a useful tool for further creating value and extracting profits in the name of environmentalism and education.)

Other environmental concepts can be similarly vested with capitalist and neoliberal logics and histories. In their genealogy of resilience theory, Walker and Cooper (2011), for example, argue that Holling's (1973, 1986, 2001) work on the ecological crisis dovetails most obviously with neoliberal rhetoric, to justify creative destruction and entrepreneurialism as preferred forms of systematic reorganization. Similarly, recently released Intergovernmental Panel on Climate Change documents (Fifth IPCC 2013) leverage both resilience theory and language in describing and promoting particular action strategies to mitigate the deleterious effects of climate change and to further justify sustainable development. As Walker and Cooper write, such a form of 'neoliberal environmentalism addresses the depletion of ecosystems as a global security problem, the only solution to which is the securitization and financialization of the biosphere' (2011, 155).[2]

Crises, both real and manufactured, can be configured to not only promote neoliberal responses to questions of economy, identity, and education, but also those of the environment (Berliner and Biddle 1999; Brown 2005; Klein 2007). In the face of an impending future climate crisis, neoliberals are ramping up calls for entrepreneurial geo-engineering and the imposition of more markets into environmental areas in the form of cap-and-trade schemes (Hamilton 2013; Klein 2014; Mirowski 2013). In each case, technological and marketized solutions are proffered as seemingly apolitical fixes to what are really sociopolitical constructions. By rendering the solutions to environmental and educational problems within the realm of techno-science, the underlying political and economic rationalities and ideologies remain intact (Li 2007).

In short, neoliberalism seeks to transform environmental issues into economic ones, stripping them of other possible senses and ways of thinking and acting in response to them. The environment, when conceptualized as a commodity, can be assessed in terms of its monetary and exchange value (no matter how we might hesitate over such notions as 'natural capital').[3] Environmental issues and crises are turned into opportunities for entrepreneurialism and technological innovation, rather than a systematic political and cultural rethinking and reworking of our relationships with the environment, including our fellow earthbound inhabitants, human, and otherwise. What then, of contemporary environmental education practice and research, and what next?

Environmental education practice and research

The trajectory of environmental education practice and research has frequently mirrored larger sociopolitical movements over time, as it has evolved from origins rooted, e.g. in key curricular concepts in those of conservation and ecosystem science to recent manifestations addressing concepts of sustainability, resilience, and sustainable development. While we do not wish to rehash the entire history of the field (see e.g. Gough and Gough 2010; for a short history, and Gough 2013 for one linking practice and research), we note that environmental education, such as economics and politics, has been contested and will remain so. Like any educational activity, environmental education is contextualized, often contradictory, and certainly complicated. Even the same activity can shift between opposing conceptions depending on the context. For example, how one interprets the famous 'reduce-reuse-recycle triangle' depends upon the sociocultural context within which they exist. The issue of recycling, while seemingly mundane, points to the way in which neoliberal notions of environmentalism can infuse their way into our thinking. Which point of the triad is culturally preferred in the educational activity? The one that continues the consumptive market logic or the one that radically critiques consumption in the first place?[4] Similarly, just as environmental thought tends to become absorbed by the assumptions of political economy, environmental education tends to become absorbed by general education paradigms rooted in neoliberalism (Foster 2001). As Gruenewald (2004) and Stevenson (2007) have shown, the critical political content of environmental education tends to be muted when it intersects – as it so often does – with the constraining regularities of the prevailing 'grammar of schooling,' privileging as this does, work predominately taking place in school, that is assessable and ultimately credential bearing as a form of education.

In other words, the practice of environmental education, like all forms of education, can't escape questions of political economy and philosophy of education. For example, the politics of personal consumption might embody or deflect a critique of capitalist consumption, as in ecological modernization as a contemporary response to the eco-crisis in green politics and economics, and pedagogies (see O'Donoghue and Russo 2004). This contrasts markedly with the early global environmental movements of the 1970s, which were typically political in orientation and often contained a strong critique of consumptive capitalism, in particular its requirement of never-ending growth (e.g. Meadows et al. 1972), and views also expressed in the UNESCO documents from that time, including Belgrade and Tbilisi. Increasingly, however, in the industrialized world, the moralities of environmental education and environmentalism can be embodied in one's consumptive choices, as a restricted form of curriculum: from questions and inquiries of locally sourced organic food to hybrid vehicles and efficient light bulbs, valuable as those are. The concern here is that these actions may be used to signify moral righteousness to others (Barendregt and Jaffe 2014) and reduce the political to the personal. As Jensen (2009, n.p) warns, such cultural actions are problematic, for they tend to 'substitute(s) acts of personal consumption (or enlightenment) for organized political resistance,' thereby producing more individual responses to collective action problems as an acritical or post-critical environmental education (Gough 2013). However, even individual action is complicated, as Willis and Schor (2012) found: Individualistic consumptive activities, while limited in their ecological impact, were able to stimulate political activism toward environmental issues in other spheres of life. Therefore, it is important to note that neoliberal ideology and processes are neither hegemonic nor totalizing and remain contested, variegated, and often contradictory (Brenner, Peck, and Theodore 2010).

As to the papers in this special issue, these do show how neoliberal notions of environmental education have gained traction in the field, including how these sometimes work to crowd out more critical views and expectations. But this process has not been monolithic, and while conveyors and relays of instrumental neoliberal rationalities can be identified in environmental education practice, we can note too these often coexist in tension with more humane and non-commodified forms (Henderson 2014). The point here however is not about mapping the landscape or imagining blind spots and blank spots, but asking questions of how we understand, signify and value nature and community, and then act accordingly, in terms of how these affect the material dimension of our existence. In other words, how we think, represent, converse, and ultimately act on these constructed understandings affects our species and our surrounding environments, including the more-than-human, and one of the means for producing these is, of course, education. Put bluntly, environmental education, as a form of knowledge production and legitimation, is directly implicated in such cultural and material practices, and hence, so are environmental educators.

As we stated at the beginning of this introduction, environmental education is inherently political, whether we realize it or not. Moreover, as we have tried to show, environmental educators must be aware of the ways in which neoliberal ideologies and practices underpin the way in which we can think about, implement and develop environmental education. Education then, such as economics and the environment, always remains open to problematization and contestation at various levels: from the local level – school and communities – to the national and global (McKenzie 2012) – but are those involved in these, including at their intersections, also open too? This plea for reflexivity, we also acknowledge, is one thing to advance on paper. It is another thing entirely to develop as ways of being and practicing education that make these challenges possible and worthwhile, from within, not just beyond, the institutions and roles imbued with, if not wrestling with, neoliberal ideologies (Ball 2012b).

The articles collected in this issue exemplify and expand on these issues and challenges. They show how various forms of neoliberalism affect environmental education across the globe in different ways and at different scales, ranging from the local to the national and the global. Most importantly, the studies show how neoliberal policies are not simply transferred or adopted without modification from one site to another, but instead, policies are contested and modified, including in the lives of the researched and researchers. As Ball (2012a) writes:

> Policies move through and are adopted by, networks of social relations or assemblages, involving diverse participants, with a variety of interests, commitments, purposes and influence, which are held together by subscription to a discursive ensemble, which circulates within and is legitimated by these network relations. (11)

Moreover, as we have pointed out, neoliberal policies are contradictory, such as claiming that the market can regulate itself and solve our environmental problems such as climate change – when it has clearly failed to do so thus far. In response to the failures of neoliberalism, Rizvi and Lingard (2010) argue we need to identify and build on a 'new imaginary' that provides us with an alternative way of imagining what the world might look like. Authors of these papers offer various lines of analysis, critique, reflection, and vision, contributing in a range of ways, we hope, to the seeding and shaping of such a new imaginary. In brief,

McKenzie, Bieler and McNeil examine recent literature on neoliberal policy mobility and use this to engage sustainability as a 'vehicular idea', in order to understand how the three pillars model of sustainability is differentially contextualized. Their analysis demonstrates how neoliberal policies are taken up differently in diverse places, therefore allowing neoliberalism to become mobile and ubiquitous (Peck 2011a, 2011b; Peck and Theodore 2010a). Such a process reminds us that there is no one neoliberalism but instead variations of neoliberalism that are created in processes of neoliberalization. Their paper also shows how neoliberal environmental policies adopt the principles of free enterprise, competitive markets, individualism, and technological fixes to accommodate the specific histories of a particular place and time. In this way, approaches to environment might be reconceptualized as 'sustainable development' and 'sustainability,' allowing economic development to proceed 'despite economic' and 'ecological crises.' Finally, by taking up the ways in which sustainability policies move from one place to another, they also reveal the varied processes of globalization, showing how the relationship between neoliberalism and environmental education plays out in each context.

Fletcher's article 'Nature is a nice place to save but i wouldn't want to live there: environmental education and the ecotourist gaze' ably illustrates the way that many of the contributions seem at first to describe instances in which more progressive social democratic practices have been implemented: eco-tourism, urban youth agriculture, and horticulture in prisons; but these can just as equally perpetuate a neoliberal agenda in which nature is used as a commodity or to control populations. Ecotourism, Fletcher writes, exemplifies one of the ways in which the environment is commodified as an 'ecosystem service,' as the wilderness provides both an escape from industrial civilization and economic benefits for not only the local communities but also investors in tourism industries. Given the concerns outlined above, even more distressing, as his analysis shows, is that ecotourism may do little to further human understanding of the relationship between humans and non-humans. Similarly, Weissman's article on urban youth farming reveals how what initially appears as a wholly beneficial practice also harbors contradictory characteristics. Weissman examines urban youth agriculture programs to show how the programs promote 'market based – specifically entrepreneurial – solutions … to building alternatives to conventional agro-food' (p. 351). Weissman suggests that urban markets should incorporate political organizing and training with their youth programs, giving as one example, a project where youth mapped food access in their neighborhood and sought to understand how inequality is structured.

As tourists depart for what they hope is a therapeutic nature experience, and youth work in urban gardens to reconnect with 'nature,' prisoners may also 'experience nature' through such initiatives as the Sustainability in Prisons Project. Little's article demonstrates the contradictory aspects of environmental education in neoliberal times, strongly echoing the Foucauldian themes mentioned earlier. Little shows how gardening, environmental education, and sustainability science, while seeming to embody progressive policies, can also act as a disciplinary technology within a hyper-incarcerated society like the United States.

The difficulty of interrogating our relationship with nature during education is reflected upon in the contributions that specifically focus on workshops and classrooms that focus on environmental education. In both instances, Derby, Piersol and Blenkinsop, and Schindel Dimick reveal how difficult it is to problematize human relationships with nature in a society in which consumption and modernity are assumed. Derby, Piersol and Blenkinsop, for example, point out how the adult participants in a workshop in Canada were unable to visualize an alternative to the built environment in which they existed. While Schindel Dimick's research takes us into the secondary school environmental education classroom in the United States, to reveal how the neoliberal emphasis on the entrepreneurial individual undermines various attempts to develop students as critical citizens. As we described above regarding the contradictions regarding recycling, developing a sustainable lifestyle and society requires more than just consuming more intelligently; it requires interrogating neoliberal and capitalist economic assumptions, including the assumption that increased consumption (calculated, for example, as gross domestic product) is always good and has no viable (let alone, credible) alternative. Further, focusing on 'right consumption' fails to question whether environmental decisions should be governed by market-based criteria and considerations alone. In response, Schindel Dimick suggests various ways to infuse more critical practices into school classrooms.

In contrast to the previous two papers, the next two by Ross, and Bessant, Robinson and Ormerod examine how current education practices relate to New Public Management managerialism and managerialist technologies (Clarke and Newman 1997). Ross' article focuses on how faculty involved in sustainable development education negotiate their own professionalism within schools that increasing assess educators based on neoliberal management models that emphasize efficiency and that see 'teachers as unquestioned supporters and implementers of a competency-based, outcome oriented pedagogy' (Ryan and Bourke 2012, 3). Bessant, Robinson and Ormerod's study suggests that the contradictions in neoliberal policies enable some 'steering and nudging' toward education toward sustainable development. For example, in the United States, faculty at Columbia University have capitalized on student interest in the environment and sustainability to build The Earth Institute, directed by Jeffrey Sachs, with over 1000 employees. While one might debate how to define and operationalize sustainable development, at least The Earth Institute provides a place for these debates to occur.

The next two papers shift the focus away from formal educational institutions and toward community-based, non-formal education as it occurs at a national level. Brazil, note Stahelin, Accioly and Sánchez, is notable for infusing environmental education into its policy discourse, including the new constitution of 1988. They describe how these critical policies were an outcome of extensive social movements that incorporated both explicit Marxist and post-structuralist Marxist theories. Environmental education in Brazil holds the promise of being both theoretically and practically sophisticated. However, Stahelin, Accioly and Sánchez's case study of the Environmental Education in Family Agriculture Program shows how the transformative rhetoric of an environmental education program can be undermined by the national and international neoliberal economy in which corporations and the government seek to supply raw materials and cheap surplus labor to their internal elite and the rest of the globe.

Meek also examines environmental education in the agricultural sector as he conducted fieldwork with the Brazilian Landless Workers' Movement. He develops a political ecology of education that analyzes the conflict between neoliberal and anti-neoliberal forces in Brazil. Meek shows how anti-neoliberal educational opportunities have been developed at various scales and combined the efforts of worker and university (professor) activists. Anti-neoliberal education has connected environmental education with the political and economic process. He also demonstrates how, even within the neoliberal state described by Stahelin, Accioly and Sánchez, resistance and alternatives to neoliberalism are possible.

Political resistance to neoliberal ideology as reflected in agricultural practices forms the basis for the next paper, where Pierce examines the impact of the transnational capitalist food industry on our own bodily existence. Taking a Latourian approach to neoliberal practices, Pierce seeks to demonstrate how life (both food and people) are captured and remade in neoliberal society. His article complements Weissman's by demonstrating how we might engage in an analysis of food, but one that is also situated within critical understandings and responses to global, bio-engineered, industrial agriculture.

While Stahelin, Accioly and Sánchez and Meek look at possibilities of informal education within the nation state, in our penultimate paper, Smith looks at the possibilities for critical education within a US city receiving much critical attention at present, namely, Detroit. Smith shows how neoliberal rationalities created an educational system that devalues relationships with both one another and nature, and, instead, has emphasized efficiency and accountability. But neoliberals face resistance from those who want schools in Detroit to be public sites for organizing and dialog. Like other contributors to this collection, Smith sees neoliberalism as constraining, and also, because of its contradictions and negative educational, economic, and environmental consequences, as a failed concept writ large throughout Detroit's recent history.

Lastly, Huckle and Wals shift us to considerations at the global level, showing how efforts such at the United Nation's Decade of Education for Sustainable Development fail, largely because they do not confront the way in which neoliberal rationalities are embedded in many social and educational practices. With the UN Decade, rather than critical education for sustainability promoted and developed around the world, its practice and legacy are better described as 'business as usual.' In response to this situation, Huckle and Wals distill much of what is subject to critique in the previous articles, namely, how neoliberal environmental education fails to question neoliberal ideologies and structures that promote an unsustainable economy, individualism, entrepreneurialism, and consumerism. In its place, they advocate for a global education for sustainability citizenship that includes 'radical and transformationalist approaches … cosmopolitan global education, environmental global education, and global critical justice education' (p. 494).

In summary, this collection illustrates how neoliberalism currently dominates how we think about the world, including what is and is not (dreamed or deemed) possible in and as an environmental education. As the papers show, this happens to such an extent that we are often unaware of how neoliberalism constrains our thinking, feeling, and doing, as educators and researchers. Approaches such as environmental education risk increasing marginalization in politics and practice, simply because they are not tested in schools, and therein lie the rub in the 'age of accountability': are the horizons for that the very terms and conditions of neoliberal agendas, or past, current and future generations, the more-than-human world, or … ? As the papers show in their arguments and alternatives, it is possible that educators' and educational responses to the neoliberal hold on contemporary institutions can lead to a politics that releases – or at least reconfigures – the grip of neoliberalism on contemporary decision-making, be that in politics, economics, environment, education, or their various intersections. And it is our hope in signaling and communicating the possibilities and sites for change that this issue can contribute to a growing conversation regarding environmental education in a neoliberal climate.

Acknowledgements

The authors would like to thank the contributors to the special issue and the numerous reviewers who provided constructive feedback at all stages of development. Special thanks to Lyle Jeremy Rubin for comments on the historical development of neoliberalism, to Claire Drake for supporting the refereeing process, and to Alan Reid for providing guidance along the way.

Notes

1. The contrasts here, as typified by debates in newspaper lead articles, Op-Ed columns and blog postings, usually concern the qualities of economic resilience, personal and collective lifestyle, life chances across the social spectrum, and the relatively environmentally benign and culturally inclusive features of societies found in the Nordic states (yet often by those not living there); see too Wilkinson and Pickett (2009).
2. Readers should note that *Environmental Education Research* dedicated a special issue to resilience theory and environmental education (Krasny, Lundholm, and Plummer 2010). As environmental educators working within these paradigms and programs, we need to

be critically aware of the ideological underpinnings of our work and how they interact with broader conceptions of political economy. To ignore this dimension risks, the further colonization of alternative epistemologies and ontologies that may, or may not, be more sustainable and just.

3. As with the previous note, see for example, the special issue on 'Natural capital in education and economics: predicaments and potential', 2005, Volume 11 (1) of *Environmental Education Research*.
4. Some readers may recall a flow circle version too, or the square that introduces Refuse into the 'waste hierarchy', and the 'Recovery' option, allied to 'lifecycle thinking'.

Notes on contributors

David Hursh is a professor in the Warner Graduate School of Education, University of Rochester. His research focuses on neoliberalism, environmental education, and education policy. He has published numerous journal articles including in the Journal of Education Policy, the American Educational Research Journal, Policy Futures in Education, Educational Studies, and Discourse: Studies in the Cultural Politics of Education. His best-known book is *High-Stakes Testing and the Decline of Teaching and Learning: The Real Crisis in Education* (Rowman & Littlefield). His forthcoming book is *The End of Public Schools: The Corporate Reform Agenda to Privatize Education* (Routledge).

Joseph Henderson is a recent PhD graduate from the University of Rochester, where he specialized in sociocultural and political studies of environmental and science education. His research engages sustainability education, the emergent energy and climate systems, and education policy. He has recently accepted a Learning Sciences Researcher position at the University of Delaware, where he will join the multi-disciplinary NSF MADE CLEAR (Maryland-Delaware Climate Change Education, Assessment, and Research) Project. He has published in the *Journal of Environmental Sciences and Studies, Cultural Studies of Science Education, Educational Studies*, and *Discourse: Studies in the Cultural Politics of Education*.

David A. Greenwood (formerly Gruenewald) is an associate professor and Canada Research Chair in Environmental Education at Lakehead University in Thunder Bay, Ontario, where he also directs the Centre for Place and Sustainability Studies. He has published widely on critical place-based, environmental and sustainability education, and is best known for his theorizations of critical pedagogies of place. His current interests revolve around exploring the institutional dynamics of sustainability in higher education as well as making connections through the arts between these external dynamics of a place and the internal and relational dynamics of being in the world as a mindful and embodied agent of change.

References

Ball, Stephen J. 2012a. *Global Education Inc.: New Policy Networks and the Neo-liberal Imaginary*. New York: Routledge.

Ball, Stephen J. 2012b. "Performativity, Commodification and Commitment: An I-spy Guide to the Neoliberal University." *British Journal of Educational Studies* 60 (1): 17–28.

Barendregt, Bart, and Rivke Jaffe, eds. 2014. *Green Consumption: The Global Rise of Eco-chic*. New York: Bloomsbury.

Benn, Melissa. 2011. *School Wars: The Battle for Britain's Education*. London: Verso.

Berliner, David C., and Bruce J. Biddle. 1995. *The Manufactured Crisis: Myths, Fraud, and the Attack on America's Public Schools*. Reading, MA: Addison-Wesley.

Berry, Wendell. 2012. *It All Turns on Affection: The Jefferson Lecture and Other Essays*. Berkeley, CA: Counterpoint.

Block, Fred, and Margaret Somers. 2014. *The Power of Market Fundamentalism*. Cambridge, MA: Harvard University Press.

Brenner, Neil, Jamie Peck, and Nik Theodore. 2010. "Variegated Neoliberalization: Geographies, Modalities, Pathways." *Global Networks* 10: 182–222.

Brown, Wendy, ed. 2005. "Neoliberalism and the End of Liberal Democracy." In *Edgework: Critical Essays on Knowledge and Politics*, 37–59. Princeton: Princeton University Press.

Buras, Kristen. 2014. *Charter Schools, Race, and Urban Space: Where the Market Meets Grassroots Resistance*. New York: Routledge.

Burchell, Graham, Colin Gordon, and Peter Miller, eds. 1991. *The Foucault Effect: Studies in Governmentality*. Chicago: University of Chicago Press.

Büscher, Bram, Wolfram Dressler, and Robert Fletcher. 2014. *Nature™ Inc: Environmental Conservation in the Neoliberal Age*. Tuscon: University of Arizona Press.

Clarke, John, and Janet Newman. 1997. *The Managerial State: Power, Politics, and Ideology in the Remaking of Social Welfare*. Thousand Oaks, CA: Sage.

Connolly, William. 2013. *The Fragility of Things*. Durham, NC: Duke.

Crouch, Colin. 2011. *The Strange Non-death of Neo-liberalism*. Malden, MA: Polity Press.

Dauvergne, Peter, and Jane Lister. 2013. *Eco-business: A Big-brand Takeover of Sustainability*. Cambridge, MA: MIT Press.

Dean, Mitchell. 1999. *Governmentality. Power and Rule in Modern Society*. London: Sage.

Foster, John. 2001. "Education as Sustainability." *Environmental Education Research* 7 (2): 153–165.

Francis. 2013. *Apostolic Exhortation Evangelii Gaudium of the Holy Father Francis to the Bishops, Clergy, Consecrated Persons and the Lay Faithful on the Proclamation of the Gospel in Today's World*. http://w2.vatican.va/content/francesco/en/apost_exhortations/documents/papa-francesco_esortazione-ap_20131124_evangelii-gaudium.html.

Friedman, Milton. 1962. *Capitalism and Freedom*. Chicago: University of Chicago Press.

Friedman, Milton, and Rose Friedman. 1980. *Free to Choose*. San Diego, CA: Harcourt.

Gabrys, Jennifer. 2014. "Programming Environments: Environmentality and Citizen Sensing in the Smart City." *Environment and Planning D: Society and Space* 32 (1): 30–48.

Gough, Annette. 2013. "The Emergence of Environmental Education Research: A 'History' of the Field." In *International Handbook of Research on Environmental Education*, edited by Robert B. Stevenson, Michael Brody, Justin Dillon, and Arjen E. J. Wals, 13–22. New York: Routledge.

Gough, Noel, and Annette Gough. 2010. "Environmental Education." In *Encyclopedia of Curriculum Studies*, edited by Craig Kridel, Vol. 1, 339–343. Thousand Oaks, CA: Sage.

Greenwood, David A. 2013. "A Critical Theory of Place-conscious Education." In *International Handbook of Research on Environmental Education*, edited by Robert B. Stevenson, Michael Brody, Justin Dillon, and Arjen E. J. Wals, 93–100. New York: Routledge.

Gruenewald, David A. 2004. "A Foucauldian Analysis of Environmental Education: Toward the Socioecological Challenge of the Earth Charter." *Curriculum Inquiry* 34 (1): 71–107.

Gruenewald, David A., and Bob O. Manteaw. 2007. "Oil and Water Still: How No Child Left behind Limits and Distorts Environmental Education in US Schools." *Environmental Education Research* 13 (2): 171–188.

Hamilton, Clive. 2013. *Earthmasters: The Dawn of the Age of Climate Engineering*. New Haven, CT: Yale University Press.

Harvey, David. 2005. *A Brief History of Neoliberalism*. Oxford: Oxford University Press.

Hayek, Friedrich A. [1944] 2007. *The Road to Serfdom*. Chicago: The University of Chicago Press.

Hayek, Friedrich A. 1960. *The Constitution of Liberty*. Chicago: The University of Chicago Press.

Henderson, Joseph A. 2014. "'Not for Everyone, but Kind of Amazing': Institutional Friction and the Nature of Sustainability Education." PhD diss., University of Rochester.

Henderson, Joseph A., and David Hursh. 2014. "Economics and Education for Human Flourishing: Wendell Berry and the Oikonomic Alternative to Neoliberalism." *Educational Studies* 50 (2): 167–186.

Holling, Crawford S. 1973. "Resilience and Stability of Ecological Systems." *Annual Review of Ecology and Systematics* 4: 1–23.

Holling, Crawford S. 1986. "Resilience of Ecosystems: Local Surprise and Global Change." In *Sustainable Development of the Biosphere*, edited by W. C. Clark and R. E. Munn, 292–317. Cambridge: Cambridge University Press.

Holling, Crawford S. 2001. "Understanding the Complexity of Economic, Ecological and Social Systems." *Ecosystems* 4: 390–405.

Hursh, David W. 2008. *High-stakes Testing and the Decline of Teaching and Learning: The Real Crisis in Education*. Lanham, MD: Rowman and Littlefield.

Hursh, David W., and Joseph Henderson. 2011. "Contesting Global Neoliberalism and Creating Alternative Futures." *Discourse: Studies in the Cultural Politics of Education* 32 (2): 171–185.

Hursh, David W., and Andrew Wall. 2011. "Re-politicizing Higher Education Assessment within Neoliberal Globalization." *Policy Futures in Education* 9 (5): 561–573.

IPCC (Intergovernmental Panel on Climate Change) 2013. *Climate Change 2013: The Physical Science Basis*. www.ipcc.ch/report/ar5/wg1/#.UuK5QGQo7-Y.

Jensen, Derrick. 2009. "Forget Shorter Showers." *Orion Magazine*. http://www.orionmagazine.org/index.php/articles/article/4801/.

Johnson, Simon, and James Kwak. 2010. *13 Bankers: The Wall Street Takeover and the Next Financial Meltdown*. New York: Random House.

Judt, Tony. 2010. *Ill Fares the Land*. New York: Penguin Books.

Keynes, John Maynard. 1936. *The General Theory of Employment, Interest, and Money*. Basingstoke: Palgrave Macmillian.

Klein, Naomi. 2007. *The Shock Doctrine: The Rise of Disaster Capitalism*. New York: Metropolitan Books.

Klein, Naomi. 2014. *This Changes Everything: Capitalism vs. the Climate*. New York: Simon & Schuster.

Krasny, Marianne E., Cecilia Lundholm, and Ryan Plummer. 2010. "Special Issue: Resilience in Social-ecological Systems: The Roles of Learning and Education." *Environmental Education Research* 16 (5–6): 463–474.

Krugman, Paul. 2008. *The Return of Depression Economics and the Crisis of 2008*. New York: Penguin.

Lave, Rebecca. 2012. "Neoliberalism and the Production of Environmental Knowledge." *Environment and Society* 3 (1): 19–38.

Li, Tania Murray. 2007. *The Will to Improve*. Durham, NC: Duke University Press.

Lipman, Pauline. 2011. *The New Political Economy of Urban Education: Neoliberalism, Race, and the Right to the City*. New York: Routledge.

Martina, Camille, David Hursh, and Dina Markowitz. 2009. "Contradictions in Educational Policy: Implementing Integrated Problem-based Environmental Health Curriculum in a High Stakes Environment." *Environmental Education Research* 15 (3): 279–297.

McKenzie, Marcia. 2012. "Education for Y'all: Global Neoliberalism and the Case for a Politics of Scale in Sustainability Education Policy." *Policy Futures in Education* 10 (2): 165–177.

Meacham, Jon. 2009. "We are All Socialists Now." *Newsweek*, February 6. http://www.newsweek.com/we-are-all-socialists-now-82577.

Meadows, Donella H., Dennis L. Meadows, Jorgen Randers, and William W. Behrens III. 1972. *The Limits to Growth*. London: Earth Island Limited.

Milbank, Dana. 2014. "In Hobby Lobby Ruling, the Supreme Court Uses a 'Fiction'." *The Washington Post*, June 30. http://www.washingtonpost.com/opinions/dana-milbank-in-hobby-lobby-ruling-the-supreme-court-uses-a-fiction/2014/06/30/37663c72-009b-11e4-8572-4b1b969b6322_story.html.

Mirowski, Philip. 2013. *Never Let a Serious Crisis Go to Waste: How Neoliberalism Survived the Financial Meltdown*. Brooklyn, NY: Verso Press.

Mazzucato, Mariana. 2013. *The Entrepreneurial State: Debunking Public vs. Private Sector Myths*. London: Anthem Press.

NGSS Lead States. 2013. *Next Generation Science Standards: For States, By States*. Washington, DC: The National Academies Press.

Norquist, Grover. 2008. *Leave Us Alone: Getting the Government's Hands off Our Money, Our Guns, Our Lives*. New York: William Morrow.

O'Donoghue, Rob, and Vladimir Russo. 2004. "Emerging Patterns of Abstraction in Environmental Education: A Review of Materials, Methods and Professional Development Perspectives." *Environmental Education Research* 10 (3): 331–351.

Olssen, Mark, John Codd, and Anne-Marie O'Neill. 2004. *Education Policy: Globalization, Citizenship, and Democracy*. Thousand Oaks, CA: Sage.

Peck, Jamie. 2010. *Constructions of Neoliberal Reason*. Oxford: Oxford University Press.

Peck, Jamie. 2011a. "Geographies of Policy: From Transfer-diffusion to Mobility-mutation." *Progress in Human Geography* 35 (6): 773–797.

Peck, Jamie. 2011b. "Global Policy Models, Globalizing Poverty Management: International Convergence or Fast-policy Integration?" *Geography Compass* 5 (4): 165–181.

Peck, Jamie, and Nik Theodore. 2010. "Mobilizing Policy: Models, Methods, and Mutations." *Geoforum* 41: 169–174.

Rizvi, Fazal, and Bob Lingard. 2010. *Globalizing Education Policy*. New York: Routledge Press.

Ryan, Mary, and Terrie Bourke. 2012. "The Teacher as Reflexive Professional: Making Visible the Excluded Discourse in Teacher Standards." *Discourse: Studies in the Cultural Politics of Education* 34 (3): 411–423.

Saez, Emmanuel, and Gabriel Zucman. October, 2014. *Exploding Wealth Inequality in the United States*. Washington, DC: Washington Center for Equitable Growth. http://equitable growth.org/research/exploding-wealth-inequality-united-states/.

Sahlberg, Pasi. 2011. *Finnish Lessons: What Can the World Learn from Educational Change in FInland?* New York: Teachers College Press.

Sandbu, Martin. 2014. "'Seventeen Contradictions and the End of Capitalism'; 'Utopia or Bust'." *The Financial times*, May 2, 1. http://www.ft.com/cms/s/2/eec08048-d117-11e3-9f90-00144feabdc0.html#axzz3K1fxrTMm.

Sandel, Michael J. 2012. *What Money Can't Buy: The Moral Limits of Markets*. New York: Farrar, Straus and Giroux.

Smith, Adam. [1776] 1976. *An Inquiry into the Nature and Causes of the Wealth of Nations*. Edited by R. H. Campell and A. S. Skinner. Oxford: Carlendon Press.

Stage, Elizabeth K., Harold Asturias, Tina Cheuk, Phil A. Daro, and Sally B. Hampton. 2013. "Opportunities and Challenges in Next Generation Standards." *Science* 340 (6130): 276–277.

Stedman Jones, Daniel. 2012. *Masters of the Universe: Hayek, Friedman and the Birth of Neoliberal Politics*. Princeton: Princeton University Press.

Stevenson, Robert. 2007. "Schooling and Environmental Education: Contradictions in Purpose and Practice." *Environmental Education Research* 13 (2): 139–153.

Stevenson, Robert. 2013. "Researching Tensions and Pretensions in Environmental/Sustainability Education Policies: Form Critical to Civically Engaged Policy Scholarship." In *International Handbook on Research in Environmental Education*, edited by Robert B. Stevenson, Michael Brody, Justin Dillon, and Arjen E. J. Wals, 147–155. New York: Routledge.

Stiglitz, Joseph. E. 2008a. "The End of Neo-liberalism?" *Project Syndicate*, July 7. https://www.project syndicate.org/commentary/the-end-of-neo-liberalism-

Stiglitz, Joseph. E. 2008b, October 17. "The Philosophies of Deregulation and Neoliberalism Are Dead in the West." Urbana-Champaign Independent Media Center. http://www.ucimc.org/content/phi8losophies-deregulation-and-neoliberalism-are-dead-west-joseph-sti glitz. Interview Originally Published in German in Berliner Zeitung (October 9, 2008) at www.berlinonline.de.

Sullivan, Sian. 2010. "Green Capitalism, and the Cultural Poverty of Constructing Nature as Service-provider." *Radical Anthropology* 3: 18–27.

Sunstein, Cass R. 2004. *The Second Bill of Rights: FDR's Unfinished Revolution and Why We Need It More than Ever*. New York: Basic Books.

Thrupp, Martin, and David Hursh. 2006. "The Possibilities and Limits of Managerialist School Reform: The Case of Target-setting." In *Education, Globalization and Social Change*, edited by H. Lauder, P. Brown, J.-A. Dillabough, and A. H. Halsey, 642–653. Oxford: Oxford University Press.

Verhaeghe, Paul. 2014. *What about Me? The Struggle for Identity in a Market-based Society*. Brunswick, VIC: Scribe Publications.

Wacquant, Loic. 2010. "Crafting the Neoliberal State: Workfare, Prisonfare, and Social Insecurity1." *Sociological Forum* (25) 2: 197–220.

Wacquant, Loic. 2012. "Three Steps to a Historical Anthropology of Actually Existing Neoliberalism." *Social Anthropology* 20 (1): 66–79.

Walker, Jeremy, and Melinda Cooper. 2011. "Genealogies of Resilience: From Systems Ecology to the Political Economy of Crisis Adaptation." *Security Dialogue* 42 (2): 143–160.

Wilkinson, Richard G., and Kate Pickett. 2009. *The Spirit Level: Why More Equal Societies Almost Always Do Better*. London: Allen Lane.

Willis, Margaret M., and Juliet Schor. 2012. "Does Changing a Light Bulb Lead to Changing the World? Political Action and the Conscious Consumer." *The Annals of the American Academy of Political and Social Science* 644 (1): 160–190.

Wirth, Arthur G. 1977. "Philosophical Issues in the Vocational-liberal Studies Controversy (1900–1917): John Dewey vs. the Social Efficiency Philosophers." In *Curriculum and Evaluation*, edited by A. A. Bellack and H. Kliebard, 161–172. Berkeley, CA: McCutchan.

Education policy mobility: reimagining sustainability in neoliberal times

Marcia McKenzie[a], Andrew Bieler[b] and Rebecca McNeil[c]

[a]Department of Educational Foundations, University of Saskatchewan, Saskatoon, SK, Canada; [b]College of Education, University of Saskatchewan, Saskatoon, SK, Canada; [c]Independent consultant, Vancouver, BC, Canada

This paper is concerned with the twinning of sustainability with priorities of economic neoliberalization in education, and in particular via the mobility or diffusion of education policy. We discuss the literature on policy mobility as well as overview concerns regarding neoliberalism and education. The paper brings these analyses to bear in considering the uptake of sustainability in education policy. We ask to what extent sustainability as a vehicular idea may be twinning with processes of neoliberalization in education policy in ways that may undermine aspirations of, and action on, environmental sustainability. Toward the end of the paper, we draw on data from an empirical study to help elucidate how the analytic frames of policy mobility can inform our analyses of the potential concerns and possibilities of sustainability as a vehicular idea. In particular, we investigate how sustainability and related language have been adopted in the policies of Canadian post-secondary education institutions over time. The paper closes by suggesting the potential implications of the proceeding analyses for policymakers, practitioners, and researchers concerned with sustainability in education policy.

This paper is informed by trajectories of work in critical policy scholarship or policy sociology in education (e.g. Ball 1994, 1997; Dale 1999; Ozga 2000; Rizvi and Lingard 2010), as well as by interdisciplinary research on policy diffusion and transfer, and in particular, policy mobility (e.g. Peck and Theodore 2010a; Peck 2011a; Temenos and McCann 2013). We explore the shifts in theoretical perspective and methodological orientation that are required to analyze neoliberalism and sustainability as 'vehicular ideas' (Temenos and McCann 2012) and follow the uptake and mobility of policy concerned with sustainability[1] in Canadian post-secondary education institutions.

Our understanding of policy includes policy texts, but also broadly considers the contexts and consequences influencing their development and enactment. As Lingard and Ozga (2007) suggest, a process/text definition of educational policy 'indicates the politics involved in the production and implementation of a policy and in the actual purposes and language of the policy text' (2). We are concerned with these politics and their potentially productive and/or constraining effects on how sustainability is being conceived and mobilized in and through educational policy.

In this paper, we focus particularly on factors that may be influencing where and how sustainability is being taken up in post-secondary education policy, including in relation to processes of neoliberalization. We appreciate the cautions made against uses of 'neoliberalism' as a 'blunt, omnibus category' that can 'reproduce a narrowed analytical and political gaze;' as well as the arguments for nonetheless considering its distinctive hegemonic aspects across diverse settings and variations (Peck 2013, 17, 10). Analyses of the impacts of neoliberalization on education policy within specific locations and across sites have been ongoing over the past several decades (e.g. Ball 1994, 1998, 2013; Olssen and Peters 2005), with many concerned about 'the increasing colonization of educational policy by economic policy imperatives,' including neoliberalism (Ball 1998, 122).

Some researchers have also examined the shift to the language of 'sustainable development' or 'sustainability' in relation to economic policy priorities. For example, While, Jonas, and Gibbs (2004) have suggested the uptake of this lexicon in policy can provide a 'sustainability fix,' or in other words, support an 'organization of economic interests, institutional capacities, and political positions that allows development to proceed despite economic and ecological crises and in the face of growing popular concerns about the state of the environment' (Temenos and McCann 2012, 4). There seems little doubt that sustainability is a 'vehicular idea' (McLennan 2004; Temenos and McCann 2012) or a 'floating signifier' (Gonzalez-Gaudiano and Nidioa Buenfil-Burgos 2009), which can be taken up in different ways toward various means. Vehicular ideas are distinguished by their hermeneutic and contextual flexibility, by their ability to balance between discursive exclusivity and vague open-endedness, by their robust capacity to reabsorb opposition, evolve with the times, and move across sites (McLennan 2004, 488–489), which, more cynically, can serve to propel or greenwash economic interests. More optimistically, the terminology of sustainability can be powerful because of its ability to allow for coalition building and for 'moving things on' (Temenos and McCann 2012). The analysis of sustainability as a 'vehicular idea' requires consideration of both sides of this potentiality, which aligns with calls for both typological, observational analysis of such vehicular notions and attention to their normative characteristics (McLennan 2004, 494). For example, we can observe the uptake and use of various types of sustainability discourse, such as the three pillars definition, but we should not lose sight of the norms and ideologies that may be articulated with various types in particular policy-making contexts.

We bring these trajectories together in our concerns with the pairing of sustainability with priorities of economic neoliberalization in education, and in particular via the mobility or diffusion of education policy. We are interested in shifts from language of 'environment' to 'sustainable development' and 'sustainability' over the past several decades and explore the concerns and possibilities of the mobility of these terms and their associated meanings in education policy. We ask to what extent sustainability as a vehicular idea may be twinning with processes of neoliberalization in educational policy in ways that may undermine aspirations of, and action on, environmental sustainability. In doing so, we build on earlier work that has begun to examine the relationships among sustainability, neoliberalization, policy mobility, and education (e.g. Jickling and Wals 2008; Hursh and Henderson 2011; McKenzie 2012; Sylvestre, McNeil, and Wright 2013). Toward the end of the paper, we draw on data from an in progress empirical study to help elucidate how the analytic frames of policy mobility can inform our analyses of the potential concerns and possibilities of sustainability as a vehicular idea. In particular, we investigate how sustainability and related language have been adopted in the policies of Canadian post-secondary education institutions over time. The paper closes by suggesting the potential implications of the proceeding analyses for policymakers, practitioners, and researchers concerned with sustainability in education policy. We first begin with a discussion of sustainability as a 'vehicular idea' in relation to the developing literature on policy mobility.

The mobility turn and policy research

'It sometimes seems as if all the world is on the move' (Urry 2007, 3). The movement of vehicular ideas, like Richard Florida's creative city model or municipal sustainability fixes (Peck 2012; Temenos and McCann 2012), can be interrogated through the lens of the mobility turn in the social sciences and humanities. This 'turn' focuses on the immense scale of movement of objects, people, and ideas across the globe. It takes a stance that embraces epistemological exchange across disciplines and proposes a transformation of the social sciences away from static paradigms, where roots are favored at the expense of routes, in order to explore expanded metaphors of movement (Cresswell 2006; Frello 2008; Urry 2007). 'The term "mobilities" refers not just to movement but to this broader project of establishing a "movement-driven" social science in which movement ... as well as voluntary/temporary immobilities, practices of dwelling and "nomadic" place-making are all viewed as constitutive of economic, social and political relations' (Buscher, Urry, and Witchger 2011, 4). This project seeks to explain the complex relationships between mobilities, moorings (like airports or conference centers), spatial scales, and practices of place-making, in order to describe how social worlds, like sustainability policy-making, are in part 'made in and through movement' (Buscher, Urry, and Witchger 2011, 13). This paradigm marks a shift away from the historical focus of social scientific research on face-to-face relationships within spatially propinquitous communities, and toward an analysis of the multiple, the distributed, the fleeting, and the complex interdependencies between corporeal, communicative, and physical travel that variously shape what we have come to call 'globalization' (Buscher, Urry, and Witchger 2011). This turn is less defined by any overarching theoretical orientation than by a renewed empirical sensitivity to the movement of materials and ideas. This sensitivity attends not only to the global flow of vehicular ideas like 'sustainability,' but also to the flow of these ideas within and across national, regional, or local contexts.

This mobility turn is currently informing debates in critical policy research. The study of policy mobility and mutation is a relatively recent development in this field, partly building out of earlier scholarship in political science on policy diffusion and transfer. Providing an overview of various stages of the diffusion and transfer literature from the 1960s and onwards, Peck (2011a) suggests aspects of these literatures that continue to be relevant and useful in policy analysis and those which appear to have become outdated in more recent contexts of globalized networks of travel and technology. Table 1 provides an overview of differences identified by Peck (2011a) between the transfer–diffusion literatures and those developing, so far mainly within urban and economic geography, under the label of policy mobilities.

Table 1. Policy transfer vs. policy mobilities (adapted from Peck 2011a, 775).

	Policy transfer	Policy mobilities
Theoretical scale	Methodological nationalism	Mobility turn: global flow of policy across nations, regions, and places
Origins	Disciplinary: political science	Transdisciplinary: geography, political science, sociology, urban planning, and expanding, i.e. environmental education research
Epistemology	Positivist/rationalist	Postpositivist/constructivist
Privileged object	'Successful' transfers	Policies in motion/interconnection: continuous transformation and mutation
Social action	Instrumental: bounded rationality	Strategic: embedded calculation
Dynamic	Frustrated replication of best (or better) practices	Contradictory reproduction of connected but unevenly developing policy regimes
Spatiality	Sequential diffusion	Relational connection
Mode of explanation	Reification of essentialized design features	Contextually sensitive analysis of emergent capacities
Politics of knowledge	Abstracts from politics of knowledge and practice	Problematizes politics of knowledge and practice

Across these approaches, the interest is on how policies are instituted (i) over time, and (ii) over space, and (iii) which factors may be influencing temporal and spatial trends. Policy transfer–diffusion literatures have been concerned with how policy developed in one region or nation spreads to other locations over time, outlining geographic clustering (being influenced by one's neighbors) and networks (being influenced by the networks one participates in) as factors in the diffusion of a policy from its location of origin to other locations (Dale 1999; Weyland 2005). Temporally, diffusion has been suggested to occur on a bell curve, beginning with an innovation and slow uptake until policy uptake surges in popularity and eventually tapers off. The phase at which a government or institution may adopt a policy – either as an early adopter, within the peak of its popularity, or as a laggard – is suggested by the diffusion literature to be related to *why* the policy was adopted, or its mechanisms of uptake.

While a range of discussions of mechanisms of uptake exist in the transfer–diffusion literatures, a predominant approach is to consider the four classifications such as emulation, learning, competition, and coercion (Garrett, Dobbin, and Simmons 2008; Shipan and Volden 2008, 2012). 'Emulation' can be understood as the voluntary adoption of policy already in place elsewhere based on information passed through social channels. This may take the form of copying the strategies of powerful or successful actors or institutions, 'expert theorization' in which there is coalescence around favored solutions which are then 'sold' through various channels, or learning from peers where policy is borrowed from locations which share political or cultural affinities (Peck 2011a). 'Learning' describes circumstances where policies are adopted after observing their impact in another institution or jurisdiction (Shipan and Volden 2008). However, critical policy research has suggested that 'learning' is more prevalent among locations which share ideology and belief systems, making it difficult to isolate from emulation and other forms of transfer. As Peck (2011a) suggests: 'the near impossibility of rationally determining "success" or "failure" outside the framework of particular policy paradigms and belief systems means that learning behavior remains in the eye of the beholder' (787). The mechanism of 'competition' refers to cases where a policy is adopted due to a perception that it confers a competitive economic advantage, while 'coercion' can be understood as pressure or encouragement to adopt a policy from an outside source with some influence or power, such as a government funding body, and can take the form of required trade practices or economic sanctions (Shipan and Volden 2008). In his review of research in these areas, Peck (2011a) concludes that of the four mechanisms, emulation and competition appear to be the most prevalent, often acting in combination and operating through 'powersoaked epistemic networks' (788).

Indeed, such networks are a focus in the policy mobilities literature recently developing in urban and economic geography, which critiques frameworks of policy transfer–diffusion on the grounds that they focus on policies as discrete objects which can indeed be 'transferred' in whole to other locations (Prince 2012). Instead, the mobilities literature suggests that policies, in so far as they move from one location to another, often as bits and pieces, are also necessarily transformed through that process of movement and translation (Peck and Theodore 2010a). Rather than tracing policy from a particular point of origin to locations elsewhere, mobilities approaches also understand policy creation and mobilization as more dispersed or as not necessarily having a clear center or point of origin. This latter shift suggests the impacts of the globalization of policy practice, where policies are circulating globally with greater speed, 'aided by new communications technologies and a growing cadre of cosmopolitan policy advocates' (Peck and Theodore 2010a, 172).

We can analyze this globalization of policy practice by dissecting the relationships between five 'interdependent "mobilities" that produce social life organized across distance,' including corporeal travel, physical movement, imaginative travel, virtual travel, and communicative travel (Buscher, Urry, and Witchger 2011, 5). While inquiry may focus on any one of these areas, the mobility turn underlines the specific interdependencies between them, including corporeal travel of policy actors for meetings; imaginative travel effected through policy tourism or marketing campaigns; virtual travel via video conferences; communications via face-to-face meetings, social media, texts, mobile phone; and the actual movement of the bits and pieces of policy (Buscher, Urry, and Witchger 2011, 5). There has been some attention to the complex interrelationships between the multiple mobilities involved in the movement of policy. For instance, McCann (2011) outlines the role of local policy actors (policy professionals and civil society groups), the 'global policy consultocracy,' and informational infrastructures in policy mobilization processes (114). Conferences, seminars, fact-finding trips, 'policy tourism,' computer networks, blogs, social media, and other sites of connection provide venues of policy mobility, while measurement data such as indicators, storytelling, and related 'inscription devices' such as maps, charts, tables, and power point slides help policy 'carriers' or 'travelling technocrats' (Dale 1992; Larner and Laurie 2010) 'construct, legitimate, and propel specific policy models through and across scales' (Temenos and McCann 2012, 2).

The substance of the work undertaken by such carriers, traveling technocrats, and other mediator intellectuals is the 'facilitation' of spaces for dialog, like conferences, and platforms for selling ideas, like websites, so they become more accessible for particular policy-making networks (Osborne 2004, 441). Thomas Osborne (2004) argues that this style of intellectual labor is part of a broader shift away from the grand ideas and positivistic expertise of the ivory tower, and toward a more facilitative style of work that focuses on the production of flashy, vehicular ideas that are responsive to specific policy networks, think tanks, and media landscapes. Typically, this labor in ideas aims to exert political influence through networks and the creation of new networks, which marks a decisive shift away from the advisory policy expert who exerted influence through personal relationships with decision makers (Osborne 2004, 433).

This focuses on policy actors, locations, and techniques adds conditions of knowledge production and circulation to consider in examining the movement of policy and removes the nation state as the primary agent in the production and uptake of policies as in some earlier approaches to policy transfer–diffusion (Temenos and McCann 2013). This is part of a broader shift away from methodological nationalism within the new mobilities paradigm (Buscher, Urry, and Witchger 2011), wherein sociologist Ulrich Beck (2006) argues for a methodological cosmopolitanism to interrogate the contradictory and coerced effects of cosmopolitanization (or globalization) on everyday life and politics. This perspective directs our attention to the ways in which policy actors may be responding simultaneously to *both* regional *and* global policy-making networks and to the tensions and contradictions that come along with these blurred boundaries of cosmopolitanization (Beck 2006). This also suggests the significance of researching across multiple spatial scales and to the continuing significance of place-based contexts in the development of policy (McKenzie 2012). McCann (2011) emphasizes that a mobilities approach builds on longer standing traditions in geography (e.g. the work of David Harvey and Doreen Massey), which have understood place 'in terms of fixity and mobility; relationality and territoriality' (112). This suggests an attention to both the circulatory infrastructures and interconnections among 'somewhat "unbounded" state and state actors' while simultaneously focusing on the continued importance of territorial embeddedness (Temenos and McCann 2013, 346–347). Responding to critiques of the potential overemphasis on mobility in social analyses, Peck (2011a) likewise suggests that studies of policy mobility must embed understandings of mobility in the situated realities of policy-making frames, rule regimes, and institutional environments. We would add that the situated contexts need also to include longer histories of empire and the colonization of land and peoples (Tuck and McKenzie 2015).

Indeed, these situated contextual factors are understood to play a considerable role in policy uptake, with existing policy/politics suggested by some as largely determining new policy adoption. As every policy serves some interests more than others, there are no simple solutions of 'best' policy, but rather more complex underlying factors that influence which policies may be developed, emulated, or passed on (Temenos and McCann 2013). Discussing cross-national policy borrowing or transfer, Halpin and Troyna (1995) suggest that policy adoption has much more to do with legitimating other related policies within the country of adoption than to with the success, however defined, of the policy in other locations. Citing research by Whitty and Edwards (1992), they outline how elected politicians and officials are 'more likely to be interested in a borrowed policy's political symbolism than its details' (307). Likewise, Peck and Theodore (2010b) suggest how policy models that extend and affirm dominant paradigms and consolidate powerful interests are more like to travel. Furthermore, the style of ideas-work that supports the development of these kinds of models remains tied at the heels to ideologies of 'innovation' and 'enterprise' (Osborne 2004). Thus, the mobility of policy may have more to do with ideology than to do with rational or technical decision-making (Peck 2011b).

In sum, the study of policy mobilities is concerned with how policy is formed and modified through policy techniques and actors in situated and mobile locations and emphasizes the study of politics and power as they relate to policy.

Neoliberalization and mobile policies

Located within and spurring on these 'messier geographies' of 'fast policy' (Peck and Theodore 2010a, 2010b), neoliberalism is now part of the contextual landscape within which other policy considerations are undertaken in many regions of the world. If we hope to follow the networks or actors behind policy mobility, we will need to undertake an in-depth analysis of the politics of neoliberalism. We take four points from related work on processes of neoliberalization as central to our discussion here: (1) Neoliberalism is not dead: Despite discussions of what next 'after neoliberalism' following the 2008 financial crisis, it is clear that there has been further entrenchment of neoliberal rationalities in public policy, including educational policy, in Canada and elsewhere around the globe (Peck, Theodore, and Brenner 2012). (2) Neoliberalism is variegated: Or in other words, it takes specific forms in different locales, and thus, there is no one form of 'neoliberalism.' It is important to thus describe and analyze neoliberalization processes in relation to particular sites and situations, rather than discussing 'neoliberalism' in sweeping catchall ways (Brenner, Peck, and Theodore 2010; Peck 2013). (3) Thus, it is not as simple as to say 'neoliberalism did it:' As Peck (2013, 8) outlines, while 'analytically inconvenient,' neoliberalism should be understood to operate alongside of and in hybridity with a range of other forces, which may also, or more so, be influencing the policy contexts (for example, globalization). Part of the variation in neoliberalization in differing contexts is due to the other political and policy trajectories it comes into contact with. (4) Despite these caveats regarding approaching neoliberalism as a frame of analysis, it is also useful to understand the 'commonalities and connections across (local) neoliberalisms' in considering the political contexts into which other policies may be taken up (or not) (Peck 2013, 11), including those of sustainability in postsecondary education.

Common manifestations of neoliberalism include the extension of market-based competition as well as commodification processes into many realms of social life, including education (Peck, Theodore, and Brenner 2012; McKenzie 2012). The new 'competition state' or 'enterprise society' then operates strategically in relation to the globalization of economy through distributed forms of governance. Resulting impacts in education include a rescaling of political authority from an emphasis on the state to that of a 'global education policy field,' which is constituted through measures of comparative performance as well as via networks of politicians and policy makers with similar 'policy dispositions and related epistemic communities' (Lingard 2011, 368). A second impact of neoliberal governance on education is the turn to 'new public management,' or the application of private sector management practices in the public sector, including in administering education (Klees 2008; Lingard 2011). Reframing educational institutions and bodies as competitive entities, a focus of accountability and auditing enables oversight at a distance and fosters a culture of performativity. A third common aspect of neoliberal educational forms is increasing privatization of education, including of educational policy and policy processes. These trends are affecting post-secondary education specifically through new forms of management and auditing, the commodification of teaching and research, amplification of relations of competition, increasing privatization of campuses and research priorities, and an overall growing emphasis on measurable outputs (Davies, Gottesche, and Bansel 2006; Olssen and Peters 2005).

Returning to earlier discussions of policy mobility, one can see the ways in which neoliberalism both spreads through the circulatory systems of policy mobility as well as influences the situated institutional environments and rule regimes in which other 'mobile policies' may be developed or introduced. Indeed, Peck, Theodore, and Brenner (2012) suggest that the circulatory systems of policy operate 'across a now deeply neoliberalized terrain, from which promising local models are variously seeded, scaled up, and stylized for emulation, more often than not under the aegis of multilateral agencies, private consultancies, and expert networks' (279). Thus, neoliberalization acts as a filter for other policy initiatives or models, resulting in policies 'strongly skewed in favour of market-oriented rationalities and practices' (279). Such policy models are thus carriers of globally endorsed presumptions and are represented as replicable policy technologies, with both designs and outcomes viewed as transferable from place to place. This leads to the worry that:

> policy models pre-emptively disrupt what would otherwise be much more variegated, 'local' policy debates, (re)shaping the very terms in which such debates are con-structed. This has the (desired) effect of further depoliticizing the policy-making pro-cesses through the circulation of prefabricated solutions, traveling in the disarmingly, apparently 'neutral' and post-ideological form of evaluation techno-science and best practice pragmatism. (Peck, Theodore, and Brenner 2012, 283)

In these ways, we worry that neoliberalization is filtering not only how education is conceptualized and shaped through policy (Davies and Bansel 2007; Peters 2001), but also how sustainability in education is understood and addressed. In the follow-ing section, we discuss 'sustainability' as it articulates with neoliberalism and global policy flows.

The twinning and mobility of neoliberalism and sustainability in education policy

The 'pan global rhetoric' of sustainability[2] in education has been suggested to be deeply susceptible to neoliberal influence (Huckle 2008) in that it can maintain a façade of green politics while allowing for the persistence of neoliberal relations to the environment (Irwin 2007). The neoliberalization of sustainability in education policy has been suggested as evident in the failure to engage with the ecological limits to growth in the so-called sustainability focus of corporate social responsibil-ity work in schools (Manteaw 2008, 122), and in the curtailment of progress on sus-tainability education in particular national or regional contexts (Huckle 2008; McKenzie 2012). Some suggest that '[e]ducation is becoming more deeply con-nected to economic and security projects that are highly invested in projects pushing unrestricted economic growth ... in areas of science and technology, military/secu-rity apparatuses, and resource acquisition' (Pierce 2013, 17). To unpack this neolib-eralization of sustainability in education policy, we might learn from analyses of economistic framings of 'sustainability' in other areas of environmental policy. Coffey and Marston (2013) show how the reform agenda of ecologically modern discourses, where sustainability is at least still tied to environmental goals, may be co-opted by the neoliberal framing of sustainability in exclusively economic terms. They conclude that policy strategies that combine these discourses are 'flawed because, in commodifying nature, limiting the nature and magnitude of change required, and placing responsibility to act on to individuals, they offer a constrained understanding of the challenge of sustainability and what needs to be done' (196). This suggests how neoliberal framings of sustainability can be subtly masked through their ad hoc synthesis with other environmental policy discourses. The worry is that in these kinds of ways, the enterprise society of neoliberalism is bringing 'sustainability' into its fold at a moment when '[t]he tensions of capitalism are being played out on a global, biospheric scale and thus implicate the future of life on earth' (Cooper 2008, 49).

The global orientation of sustainability-related terminologies and the movement or stasis of various understandings (González-Gaudiano 2005; Irwin 2007) demand in-depth research into the mobilities, moorings, definitions, and policy routes that allow for the movement of particular understandings of sustainability and the immobility of others. Why do particular understandings of 'sustainability' get to move across nations and institutions, while other conceptualizations are immobilized? The complexity of this query may be interrogated by considering mobility not only as a physical and communicative phenomenon but, also, as a discursive and ideological process that shapes the kinds of ideas or actors that get to move and those which are rendered immobile (Frello 2008). This directs our attention to the ways in which language shapes the mobility or immobility of particular understandings of sustainability, which we interrogate by considering the competing or facilitatory discourses that variously shape its meaning in policy (Jørgensen and Philips 2002). Thus, if we are going to direct our research imaginations to a future beyond the high carbon societies of the neoliberal period (Urry 2011), we need to remain mindful of the versions of 'sustainability' that we draw upon to forecast preferable futures and remain vigilant to its' co-optation.

This can be explored further by considering sustainability as a vehicular idea, which foregrounds a number of interrelated concerns. First, the ways in which 'sustainability' gives substance to new kinds of cognitive labor in environmental policy-making, which we can analyze by following the facilitative labor (Osborne 2004) of various carriers and technocrats as they move through powerful epistemic networks (Peck 2011a). Second, its role as a 'floating signifier' (González-Gaudiano 2005; Gonzalez-Gaudiano and Nidioa Buenfil-Burgos 2009) with rather diffuse meanings across the discourses that gather under its name, which can potentially mask the persistence of powerful ideologies like the invisible hand of the free market under variegated conditions of neoliberalization (Irwin 2007; Peck 2013). The policy discourses through which this masking unfolds are incredibly complex, due to the disparate and diffuse connotations that have latched onto this floating signifier.

Third, we can analyze the role of sustainability policy goals in depoliticizing local policy debates. For instance, Temenos and McCann (2012) outline the ways in which mobile and neoliberal policies can frame thinking on local issues, including in relation to which solutions might be sought or developed in relation to sustainability policy. Other definitions of the problem and associated solutions can then be left outside the conversation to the point where they are unable to be thought or raised. They suggest how sustainability as a policy goal or concept can at times be used in these ways, to frame issues in a manner that is both open and at the same time delimits the range of possible ways forward (Temenos and McCann 2012, 1393). Temenos and McCann (2012) suggest that 'The utilization of vehicular ideas like sustainability allows sometimes sudden breaks in policy direction to appear almost seamless, natural, and inevitable, or alternatively, mask the fact that not much beyond the surface has changed' (1402). As a 'vehicular idea' or mobile policy goal, sustainability and related terms can be understood to be formulated with purposive ambiguity or mutability so as to be able to move quickly between policy-making sites. And unlike moral or theoretical vocabularies, vehicular ideas with their multiple interpretations have a more limited shelf life: 'They serve to make things happen at a particular time, after which their time may be up' (McLennan 2004, 435).

Finally, the notion of sustainability as a vehicular idea also highlights the ways in which the language and power of neoliberalism bring 'sustainability' on board in a variety of consensual and depoliticized ways that 'fix' the terms of debate around local environmental issues (Temenos and McCann 2012) and mask the persistence of market liberalization (Irwin 2007). This can be analyzed as part of a broader depoliticization of the policy process and politics generally, which Swyngedouw (2010) describes as 'structured around the perceived inevitability of capitalism and a market economy as the basic organizational structure of the social and economic order, for which there is no alternative' (215). In an analysis of the transition from environmental education to education for sustainability in New Zealand, Ruth Irwin (2007) argues that the framing of the 'invisible hand' of the free market by the metaphorical vehicle of 'sustainability' serves to perpetuate a calculative, instrumental relationship to the earth (Irwin 2007). She argues, 'the metaphor of the market gets subsumed in the rhetoric of 'sustainability' and *all factors* are absorbed into the enframing rubric of potential resource' (11). Thus, there is increasing evidence that certain types of sustainability discourse are depoliticized in policy-making processes, in ways that foreclose imagining or constructing a future that is more just and environmentally sustainable than what neoliberalism has to offer, including in education (Irwin 2007; Temenos and McCann 2012; Coffey and Marston 2013). The remainder of this paper suggests the ways in which sustainability may be functioning as a 'vehicular idea' in the context of initial data from a national study of sustainability in the educational policy of post-secondary institutions in Canada.

Researching sustainability in the education policy of post-secondary institutions

As part of the contextual dynamics of Canadian political and institutional factors, and in the context of this special issue, we are concerned with the extent to which processes of neoliberalization may be active in how sustainability is understood in education, and to what extent these two ideas may be traveling together in their global mobility and local uptake. Our discussion here draws on year one data collected from the 220 accredited post-secondary institutions in Canada[3] based on their publicly available policy documents and websites (see Beveridge et al. forthcoming). Of the 220 institutions, 110 had sustainability policies or plans (hereafter referred to jointly as 'policies'). In our analysis of the policies, the most frequent terms used in the policy titles were as follows: environment (49 uses), sustainable development (38 uses), and sustainability (41 uses).[4] For the purposes of this discussion, we are focusing on the language used in the titles and sustainability definitions in order to begin to examine the mobilities of the aims and language of the policies. Building on our discussion of sustainability as a vehicular idea, we ask to what extent the conceptions of sustainability in education policy texts may be keeping up with the neoliberal times.

Figure 1 shows temporal changes in the terms used in the sustainability policy titles, with earlier policies more commonly using the terminology of environment and sustainable development, with these terms decreasing in usage as the term sustainability emerged in the mid-2000s. The width of the bars indicates the relative number of policies developed in a given year, with most current policies developed after 2002. Sustainability is the most frequently used term in the titles of policies created over the past five years. Of the 110 institutions with sustainability policies, 69 policies included definitions of the terminology used in the policy titles. While a number of the definitions were environment-specific or specifically used the language of sustainable development in alignment with the policy titles, almost a third of the policies included a definition of sustainability which included a focus on the natural environment, society, and economy, or what is often called a 'three pillars' definition of sustainability (Sneddon, Howarth, and Norgaard 2006). Given the suggested emergence of sustainability as a dominant terminology, in what follows, we examine the definitions in the policies to extend an analysis of sustainability as a potential vehicular idea. In particular, we discuss three pillars definitions and ask how the priorities of neoliberalization may be shaping the construction of 'sustainability' as defined in these post-secondary education policies.

The three pillars are often introduced in the literature as a nested concept – the largest circle being the 'natural environment,' which the 'society' circle is then placed within, and 'economy,' is in turn, as part of society (Adams 2006, 2). They are placed in this hierarchy based on the understanding that without a natural environment human beings would not exist, and without a society to create it, there would be no economy. However, within the policies reviewed, there was no mention of any hierarchy or prioritization of these three elements. We might attend to the ideological

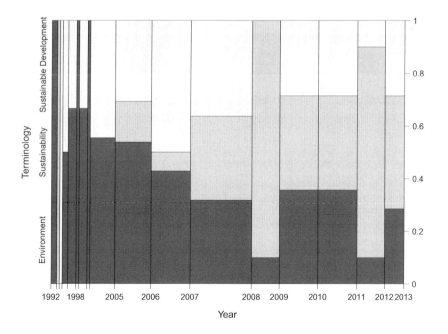

Figure 1. Policy title terminology by year and displaying relative number of policies per year (from Beveridge et al. forthcoming).

implications of this indeterminateness: Is an invisible hand supposed to organize coordination between the three pillars? The vagueness of this type of sustainability definition corroborates our understanding of it as a vehicular idea (McLennan 2004). We can read the elasticity of this three pillars definition as suggesting that sustainability, like environmental education before it, has become a 'floating signifier' with diverse meanings in each of the numerous discourses that gather under its umbrella (Gonzalez-Gaudiano 2005, 248). This purposive ambiguity is an important variable to consider in studying mobility, since it is the indeterminateness of vehicular ideas that allows them to travel quickly across policy-making sites (Temenos and McCann 2012) and 'move with the times' (McLennan 2004, 488–489).

In addition, we also want to draw attention to the segmentation of the 'pillars' and as a result, the boundaries that are established between them. As Gough and Scott (2006) write,

> it is important not to mistake a convenient representation of something for the thing itself. There are no clear boundaries between environment, society and economy, and each is fundamentally dependent on the other ... Thus, the solid lines by which this model is normally divided are very misleading. (276)

The division of sustainability into three spheres can thus also be read as a kind of boundary maintenance activity, wherein the blurry boundaries between these domains are hardened at the policy-making level. The segmentation of these areas as 'pillars' can reduce reflection on the meaning of sustainability in one of these areas from the perspective of the other: for example, reflection on the meanings of 'economic sustainability' from the perspective of 'environmental sustainability' or the latter in relation to 'social sustainability.' Whereas the nested hierarchy model implies at least some reflection on the interrelationship of the three pillars, the absence of any such model in the definitions themselves leaves open for any one area to take priority in moving toward 'sustainability.'

Returning to the discussion of the previous section regarding the potential twinning of sustainability with neoliberalism, three pillar definitions thus run the risk of enabling sustainability as a vehicular idea in problematic ways. It can function both as a floating signifier through its ambiguity (anything goes), as well as enabling sustainability to be 'fixed' in certain ways through the creation of the boundaries between pillars (i.e. giving priority to a particular pillar). This enables sustainability to get onto the policy-making table as it is seen as flexible and not in conflict with economic and political priorities of neoliberalization and practically can result in situations where, for example, a local administrator believes they can appropriately check off policy requirements to address sustainability if they have done work on economy, society, *or* environment. The boundaries of the three pillar definitions can thus insulate the economy pillar from those of social and environmental sustainability, enabling a form of neoliberal sustainability (Coffey and Marston 2013). If the boundaries around the three pillars are allowed to harden, and there are no structures for critical reflection on their interrelations, there runs the risk of a relative dominance of a neoliberal framing of sustainability within such policy definitions. While we recognize this discussion is based only on sustainability definitions in the policies and not on an analysis of the full policies or of practices in institutions,[5] it is intended to provide an example of concerns about the twinning of sustainability with neoliberalism in education policy, as well as to help generate further questions and modes of analysis for researching how such definitions of sustainability become prioritized and mobilized.

In closing the discussion of this research, the initial analysis suggests that increasing numbers of post-secondary institutions in Canada are developing sustainability-related policies and that increasingly frequently, the terminology used to name these policies is 'sustainability.' While this may appear promising on the surface, peeling back just one layer to look at how sustainability is defined in these policies, suggests that priorities of neoliberalization may travel with and into how sustainability is conceptualized. Further analysis is needed to determine the extent to which this may be borne out in the policies in their full, as well as to consider more nuanced questions of mobility and uptake, such as to what extent sustainability networks, policy actors, virtual communications, or other conduits of mobility are facilitating the ways in which sustainability is adopted in localized contexts as well as how regional or municipal policies and priorities may also be influencing the specifics of how sustainability is articulated and practiced. We see shifts in the language of sustainability-related policy over time as shown in Figure 1, but there are also trends in the language and definitions used regionally, as well as in the numbers of institutions within various provinces/territories which have policies (see Beveridge et al. forthcoming). The terminology used in international or national policies and declarations, assessment bodies such as the Association for the Advancement of Sustainability in Higher Education (AASHE) or Cégep-Vert in Québec, or the UN-affiliated Regional Centers of Expertise in Education for Sustainable Development, are some of the factors which may be influencing the movement and translation of particular versions of sustainability. Claims of a sustainability focus are also increasingly a selling point in attracting students, faculty, and funders (Kerr and Hart-Steffes 2012, 12), in an age where post-secondary institutes operate in conditions of commodification and market-based competition (Davies, Gottesche, and Bansel 2006). In the worst case scenario of institutional greenwashing, sustainability policies and related high level initiatives such as signing of declarations may function as 'sustainability fixes' (While, Jonas, and Gibbs 2004), in which there is an appearance of taking steps toward protecting the environment while the higher prioritization given to economic considerations in the institution as a whole means that little may have changed. In a better case scenario, the ever growing focus on sustainability in post-secondary education is an opportunity for 'moving things on' (Temenos and McCann 2012) through the institutional prioritization of environmental considerations.

Implications for research

Given these multiple potentialities of sustainability in education policy in current conditions of mobile neoliberal policy-making, we are left with questions of the possible implications for policy-making, practice, and research. Or more specifically, if we consider the mobility of both neoliberal and sustainability policy, how can we guard against their inevitable pairing? If neoliberal forms of capitalism are increasingly tied to biological life through our dependence on extractive science and technology (Castree 2007; Pierce 2013), disassociated three pillar versions of sustainability which do not require the disruption of the logics of neoliberalism seem wholly inadequate. In a national political context which has lost even the veneer of sustainability,[6] the elasticity of the three pillars definition with its ability to 'keep up with the times' is not promising.

We suggest that an exploration of policy mobility can be helpful in considering how and why certain ideas travel and in enabling more intentionality in which ideas are taken up, or possibly ruptured. Guarding against being mere neoliberal 'network dopesters' (Peck 2012, 25), we can then better ask which actors, associations, and policies we are mobilizing and why. Such analytic frames also enable us to better consider the value, not only of mobile policies, but those which are also community and place specific. With an orientation to policy which considers the contexts or origins of policy as well as its enactment through practice, we propose the following kinds of questions that may be asked about the origins and mobilities of education policy:

- Can the policy or policy mandate be traced to a beginning, and if so, who was responsible for its genesis and the writing of the text?
- What are the typical and unconventional routes followed by sustainability-related education policy in their movement from one institution to another or from one country to another?
- How are sustainability-related education discourses synthesized with other policy agendas and discourses, and what are the effects of such hybrid policy discourses?
- How is sustainability articulating in relation to neoliberalization in local contexts?
- How does the mobility of sustainability-related education policy intersect with community and place-based 'policies' of sustainability education?
- What are the most significant moorings (retreats, conference centers) and platforms (websites, magazines, journals, etc.) for the development, branding, and selling of sustainability-related education policy or alternatively for dissensus and dialog?
- What are the various roles played by different policy actors, both locally at an institutional level, but also across institutions and nations through global policy networks?
- How can environmental education researchers engage diverse communities in the process of reimagining the meaning and scope of sustainability-related policy in education?

Although beyond the scope of the current paper, another host of detailed questions surrounds the related sphere of policy enactment or practice – in what happens on the ground in particular institutions and communities as policies are adopted and interpreted in local contexts, including in relation to how policies are combined, modified, resisted, and otherwise informed by situated actors, places, and practices (Bowe, Ball, and Gold 1992; Ball, Maguire, and Braun 2012).

Much of the existing research on policy mobilities focuses on unique urban planning, social, or health policy initiatives which can then be traced in their uptake across different locales – for example, workfare policies in the US (Peck and Theodore 2010b) or urban design policies such as smart growth or business improvement districts as they have spread globally (McCann and Ward 2012). Likewise, the uptake of sustainability in educational policy can be studied to better understand when and where various terminology and models emerged and the means through which they have become more distributed and with what effects (Ball and Junemann 2012). Methodologies for studying policy mobilities are still nascent, but have tended toward qualitative ethnographic and case study approaches which 'follow the policy' within and across sites (McCann and Ward 2012; Peck and Theodore 2010a). McCann (2011) advocates for 'global ethnographies' that study relationships between sites while maintaining one site as the primary perspective (121). Temenos and McCann (2013) suggest that most policy mobilities work to this point has largely employed '"standard" qualitative case study methods' (351) and that there is additional need for more detailed empirical research. McCann (2011) also suggests the value of analyzing policy documents and websites to better understand the structural and historical contexts within which policy mobilities have emerged and are active, as well as the potential of quantitative methods in examining some data (122). Finally, mobile methods also involve following the actors and their techniques (Buscher, Urry, and Witchger 2011), honing a deep familiarity with the specific techniques used by actors to organize the movement of policy.

By better understanding how current sustainability policies in education emerge, travel and are adapted in particular national or regional contexts, including in convergence or divergence with processes and discourses of neoliberalization, we can perhaps offer more critical and imaginative interventions in how sustainability is mobilized in education (McKenzie 2009). Arguably, we need a rupture or dissensus with the limited terms of debate around 'sustainability' in education policy, which we might imagine as a widening and redistribution of those who have a say in the unfolding of depoliticized education policy (Stevenson 2013). Philosopher Rancière (2009) says 'dissensus brings back into play both the obviousness of what can be perceived, thought and done, and the distribution of those who are capable of perceiving, thinking and altering the coordinates of the shared world' (49). A dissensus with consensual understandings of sustainability would involve a radical reconfiguration of who is able to have a voice and of what is expressible in public discourse around 'sustainability' in education policy. It will require drawing upon many dynamic understandings and practices of social, cultural, and environmental sustainability (Stoekl 2007; Dillard, Dujon, and King 2009; Monani 2011) in order to move beyond these neoliberal times.

Acknowledgments

Our thanks to Kathleen Aikens, Laurie Lidstone, Philip Vaughter, and Tarah Wright for their contributions to the development of the methods and the collection of the data referred to in this paper and to project manager Nicola Chopin for her very capable and constant support.

Funding

This publication draws on research from the Sustainability and Education Policy Network (SEPN), supported by a Partnership Grant from the Social Sciences and Humanities Research Council of Canada [grant number 895-2011-1025], Principal Investigator Dr. Marcia McKenzie. For more information, visit www.sepn.ca.

Notes

1. We understand 'sustainability' here as any policy that takes up the natural environment in some capacity, including in relation to social, economic, culture, health, and other factors. While we are concerned with the various ways sustainability terminology is engaged, we have limited the scope to those cases which include some reference to and consideration of environment.

2. We focus on the terminology of sustainability in this paper; however, in some cases, similar issues arise and have been discussed in relation to 'sustainable development' and other sustainability-related terminology. We draw on this broader literature in our discussion of sustainability.
3. Data were collected in 2012 from all 220 post-secondary institutions in Canada accredited with the Association of Universities and Colleges of Canada (AUCC) and the Association of Canadian Community Colleges (ACCC).
4. Policies which focused on sustainability goals but did not include any of the above terms in their titles totaled 6. Some policy titles included more than one of the terms, and thus, the numbers add up to more than 110.
5. For a content analysis of the policy documents of 50 of the 220 post-secondary institutions in Canada, see Vaughter et al. (forthcoming).
6. The Canadian federal government under Prime Minister Stephen Harper has revoked the protection of 99% of Canada's waterways and dismantled federal agencies responsible for environmental science and environmental assessment over the last several years to facilitate oil and tar sands development (Land 2013).

Notes on contributors

Marcia McKenzie is an associate professor of Educational Foundations and director of the Sustainability Education Research Institute at the University of Saskatchewan, and principal investigator of the Sustainability and Education Policy Network.

Andrew Bieler is a postdoctoral fellow with the Sustainability and Education Policy Network at the University of Saskatchewan. His research probes the role of collaboration between the arts and sciences in learning for a sustainable future. He also curates engaging conversations between artists and other social groups and experiments with tactile ways of knowing place.

Rebecca McNeil recently completed her MES thesis on sustainability in higher education in the School for Resource and Environmental Science at Dalhousie University and is a communications strategist for the environmental sector in Vancouver, British Columbia.

References

Adams, W. M. 2006. *The Future of Sustainability: Re-thinking Environment and Development in the Twenty-first Century*. Report of the IUCN Renowned Thinkers Meeting, January 29–31, The World Conservation Union.
Ball, S. J. 1994. *Education Reform: A Critical and Post-Structural Approach*. Buckingham: Open University Press.
Ball, S. J. 1997. "Policy Sociology and Critical Social Research: A Personal Review of Recent Education Policy and Policy Research." *British Educational Research Journal* 23 (3): 257–274.
Ball, S. J. 1998. "Big Policies/Small World: An Introduction to International Perspectives in Education Policy." *Comparative Education* 34 (2): 119–130.
Ball, S. J. 2013. *The Education Debate: Policy and Politics in the Twenty-first Century*. 2nd ed. Bristol: Polity Press.
Ball, S. J., and C. Junemann. 2012. *Networks, New Governance, and Education*. Bristol: Policy Press.
Ball, S. J., M. Maguire, and A. Braun. 2012. *How Schools Do Policy: Policy Enactments in Secondary Schools*. London: Routledge.
Beck, U. 2006. *Cosmopolitan Vision*. Malden, MA: Polity.
Beveridge, D., M. McKenzie, P. Vaughter, and T. Wright. Forthcoming. "Sustainability in Canadian Post-Secondary Institutions: An Analysis of the Relationships among Sustainability Policy Initiatives and Geographic and Institutional Characteristics." *International Journal of Sustainability in Higher Education*.
Bowe, R., S. J. Ball, and A. Gold. 1992. *Reforming Education and Changing Schools: Case Studies in Policy Sociology*. London: Routledge.

Brenner, N., J. Peck, and N. Theodore. 2010. "After Neoliberalization?" *Globalizations* 7 (3): 327–345.

Buscher, M., J. Urry, and K. Witchger. 2011. *Mobile Methods*. New York: Routledge.

Castree, N. 2007. *Neoliberal Environments: A Framework for Analysis*. Manchester: Manchester University. http://www.socialsciences.manchester.ac.uk/PEI/publications/wp/documents/Castree.pdf.

Coffey, B., and G. Marston. 2013. "How Neoliberalism and Ecological Modernization Shaped Environmental Policy in Australia." *Journal of Environmental Policy & Planning* 15 (2): 179–199.

Cooper, M. 2008. *Life as Surplus: Biotechnology & Capitalism in the Neoliberal Era*. Seattle, WA: University of Washington Press.

Cresswell, T. 2006. *On the Move: Mobility in the Modern Western World*. New York: Routledge.

Dale, R. 1992. "Recovering from a Pyrrhic Victory? Quality, Relevance and Impact in the Sociology of Education." In *Voicing Concerns: Sociological Perspectives on Contemporary Education Reforms*, edited by M. Arnot and L. Barton, 201–207. Wallingford: Triangle Books.

Dale, R. 1999. "Specifying Globalization Effects on National Policy: A Focus on the Mechanisms." *Journal of Education Policy* 14 (1): 1–17.

Davies, B., and P. Bansel. 2007. "Neoliberalism and Education." *International Journal of Qualitative Studies in Education* 20 (3): 247–259.

Davies, B., M. Gottsche, and P. Bansel. 2006. "The Rise and Fall of the Neo-Liberal University." *European Journal of Education* 41 (2): 305–319.

Dillard, J., V. Dujon, and M. C. King. 2009. *Understanding the Social Dimension of Sustainability*. New York: Routledge.

Frello, B. 2008. "Towards a Discursive Analytics of Movement: On the Making and Unmaking of Movement as an Object of Knowledge." *Mobilities* 3 (1): 25–50.

Garrett, G., F. Dobbin, and B. A. Simmons. 2008. "Conclusion." In *The Global Diffusion of Markets and Democracy*, edited by B. A. Simmons, F. Dobbin, and G. Garrett, 344–360. New York: Cambridge University Press.

Gonzalez-Gaudiano, E. 2005. "Education for Sustainable Development: Configuration and Meaning." *Policy Futures in Education* 3: 243–250.

Gonzalez-Gaudiano, E., and R. Nidioa Buenfil-Burgos. 2009. "The Impossible Identity of Environmental Education: Dissemination and Emptiness." In *Fields of Green: Restorying Culture, Environment, and Education*, edited by M. McKenzie, P. Hart, H. Bai, and B. Jickling, 97–108. Cresskill, NJ: Hampton Press.

Gough, S., and W. Scott. 2006. "Education and Sustainable Development: A Political Analysis." *Educational Review* 58 (3): 273–290.

Halpin, D., and B. Troyna. 1995. "The Politics of Education Policy Borrowing." *Comparative Education* 31 (3): 303–310.

Huckle, J. 2008. "An Analysis of New Labour's Policy on Education for Sustainable Development with Particular Reference to Socially Critical Approaches." *Environmental Education Research* 14 (1): 65–75.

Hursh, D. W., and J. A. Henderson. 2011. "Contesting Global Neoliberalism and Creating Alternative Futures." *Discourse: Studies in the Cultural Politics of Education* 32 (2): 171–185.

Irwin, R. 2007. "'After Neoliberalism': Environmental Education to Education for Sustainability." Paper presented at the Philosophy of Education Society of Australasia, Wellington, New Zealand.

Jickling, B., and A. E. J. Wals. 2008. "Globalization and Environmental Education: Looking beyond Sustainable Development." *Journal of Curriculum Studies* 40 (1): 1–21.

Jørgensen, M. W., and L. J. Philips. 2002. *Discourse Analysis as Theory and Method*. London: Sage.

Kerr, K. J., and J. S. Hart-Steffes. 2012. "Sustainability, Student Affairs, and Students." *New Directions for Student Services* 137: 7–17.

Klees, S. J. 2008. "A Quarter Century of Neoliberal Thinking in Education: Misleading Analyses and Failed Policies." *Globalisation, Societies and Education* 6 (4): 311–348.

Land, L. 2013. *A Summary of Current Federal Legislative Amendments Affecting First Nations*. Accessed March 23. http://www.oktlaw.com/wp-content/uploads/2013/01/summaryconcerns.pdf.

Larner, W., and N. Laurie. 2010. "Travelling Technocrats, Embodied Knowledges: Globalising Privatisation in Telecoms and Water." *Geoforum* 41: 218–226.

Lingard, B. 2011. "Policy as Numbers: Ac/Counting for Educational Research." *The Australian Educational Researcher* 38: 355–382.

Lingard, B., and J. Ozga, eds. 2007. *The RoutledgeFalmer Reader in Education Policy and Politics*. New York: Routledge.

Manteaw, B. 2008. "When Businesses Go to School: Neoliberalism and Education for Sustainable Development." *Journal of Education for Sustainable Development* 2 (2): 119–126.

McCann, E. J. 2011. "Urban Policy Mobilities and Global Circuits of Knowledge: Toward a Research Agenda." *Annals of the Association of American Geographers* 101 (1): 107–130.

McCann, E. J., and K. Ward. 2012. "Assembling Urbanism: Following Policies and 'Studying Through' the Sites and Situations of Policy Making." *Environment and Planning A* 44 (1): 42–51.

McKenzie, M. 2009. "Scholarship as Intervention: Critique, Collaboration, and the Research Imagination." *Environmental Education Research* 15: 217–226.

McKenzie, M. 2012. "Education for Y'all: Global Neoliberalism and the Case for a Politics of Scale in Sustainability Education Policy." *Policy Futures in Education* 10 (2): 165–177.

McLennan, G. 2004. "Travelling with Vehicular Ideas: The Case of the Third Way." *Economy and Society* 33 (4): 484–499.

Monani, S. 2011. "At the Intersections of Ecosee and Just Sustainability: New Directions for Communication Theory and Practice." *Environmental Communication: A Journal of Nature and Culture* 5 (2): 141–145.

Olssen, M., and M. A. Peters. 2005. "Neoliberalism, Higher Education and the Knowledge Economy: From the Free Market to Knowledge Capitalism." *Journal of Education Policy* 20 (3): 313–345.

Osborne, T. 2004. "On Mediators: Intellectuals and the Ideas Trade in the Knowledge Society." *Economy and Society* 33 (4): 430–447.

Ozga, J. 2000. *Policy Research in Educational Settings: Contested Terrain*. Buckingham: Open University Press.

Peck, J. 2011a. "Geographies of Policy: From Transfer-diffusion to Mobility-mutation." *Progress in Human Geography* 35 (6): 773–797.

Peck, J. 2011b. "Global Policy Models, Globalizing Poverty Management: International Convergence or Fast-Policy Integration?" *Geography Compass* 5 (4): 165–181.

Peck, J. 2012. "Recreative City: Amsterdam, Vehicular Ideas and the Adaptive Spaces of Creativity Policy." *International Journal of Urban and Regional Research* 36 (3): 462–485.

Peck, J. 2013. "Explaining (with) Neoliberalism." *Territory, Politics, Governance* 10: 1–24.

Peck, J., and N. Theodore. 2010a. "Mobilizing Policy: Models, Methods, and Mutations." *Geoforum* 41: 169–174.

Peck, J., and N. Theodore. 2010b. "Recombinant Workfare, across the Americas: Transnationalizing "Fast" Social Policy." *Geoforum* 41: 195–208.

Peck, J., N. Theodore, and N. Brenner. 2012. "Neoliberalism Resurgent? Market Rule after the Great Recession." *South Atlantic Quarterly* 111 (2): 265–288.

Peters, M. 2001. "Education, Enterprise Culture and the Entrepreneurial Self: A Foucauldian Perspective." *Journal of Educational Enquiry* 2 (2): 58–71.

Pierce, C. 2013. *Education in the Age of Biocapitalism: Optimizing Educational Life for a Flat World*. New York: Palgrave Macmillan.

Prince, R. 2012. "Metaphors of Policy Mobility: Fluid Spaces of 'Creativity' Policy." *Human Geography* 94 (4): 317–331.

Rancière, J. 2009. *Aesthetics and Its Discontents [Malaise dans L'esthétique]*. English ed. Malden, MA: Polity Press.

Rizvi, F., and B. Lingard. 2010. *Globalizing Educational Policy*. London: Routledge.

Shipan, C. R., and C. Volden. 2008. "The Mechanisms of Policy Diffusion." *American Journal of Political Science* 52 (4): 840–857.

Shipan, C. R., and C. Volden. 2012. "Policy Diffusion: Seven Lessons for Scholars and Practitioners." *Public Administration Review* 72 (6): 788–796.

Sneddon, C., R. B. Howarth, and R. B. Norgaard. 2006. "Sustainable Development in a Post-Brundtland World." *Ecological Economics* 57: 253–268.

Stevenson, R. 2013. "Researching Tensions and Pretensions in Environmental/Sustainability Education Policies: From Critical to Civically Engaged Policy Scholarship." In *International Handbook of Research on Environmental Education*, edited by R. B. Stevenson, M. Brody, J. Dillon, and A. E. J. Wals, 147–155. New York: Routledge.

Stoekl, A. 2007. *Bataille's Peak: Energy, Religion and Postsustainability.* Minneapolis, MN: University of Minnesota Press.

Swyngedouw, Erik. 2010. "Apocalypse Forever? Post-political Populism and the Spectre of Climate Change." *Theory, Culture & Society* 27 (2–3): 213–232. doi:10.1177/026327640 9358728.

Sylvestre, P., R. McNeil, and T. Wright. 2013. "From Talloires to Turin: A Critical Discourse Analysis of Declarations for Sustainability in Higher Education." *Sustainability* 5 (4): 1356–1371.

Temenos, C., and E. McCann. 2012. "The Local Politics of Policy Mobility: Learning, Persuasion, and the Production of a Municipal Sustainability Fix." *Environment and Planning a* 44: 1389–1406.

Temenos, C., and E. McCann. 2013. "Geographies of Policy Mobilities." *Geography Compass* 7 (5): 344–357.

Tuck, E., and M. McKenzie. 2015. *Place in Research: Theory, Methodology, and Methods.* New York: Routledge.

Urry, J. 2007. *Mobilities.* Malden, MA: Polity Press.

Urry, J. 2011. *Climate Change and Society.* Malden, MA: Polity Press.

Vaughter, P., M. McKenzie, L. Lidstone, and T. Wright. Forthcoming. "Campus Sustainability Governance in Canada: A Content Analysis of Post-secondary Institutions' Sustainability Policies." *International Journal of Sustainability in Higher Education.*

Weyland, K. 2005. "Theories of Policy Diffusion Lessons from Latin American Pension Reform." *World Politics* 57 (2): 262–295.

While, A., A. E. G. Jonas, and D. C. Gibbs. 2004. "The Environment and the Entrepreneurial City: The 'Sustainability Fix' in Leeds and Manchester." *International Journal of Urban and Regional Research* 28: 549–569.

Whitty, G., and T. Edwards. 1992. "School Choice Policies in Britain and the USA: Their Origins and Significance." Paper Presented at the Annual Meeting of the American Educational Research Association, San Francisco, California, April.

Nature is a nice place to save but I wouldn't want to live there: environmental education and the ecotourist gaze

Robert Fletcher[1]

Department of Environment and Development, University for Peace P.O. Box 138-6100, Ciudad Colon, Costa Rica

This article explores the role of ecotourism in the neoliberalisation of environmental education. The practice of ecotourism is informed by a particular 'ecotourist gaze' in terms of which the 'education' that providers characteristically offer is implicitly framed, embodying a culturally specific perspective in which western society is depicted as alienating and constraining and immersion in 'wilderness' is understood as a therapeutic escape from the reputed ills of industrial civilisation. While in the past, these educational aspects of ecotourism delivery have often contradicted the activity's promotion as a quintessential neoliberal conservation mechanism, increasingly this education has become neoliberalised as well in its growing emphasis on the environment's role as an instrumental provider of 'ecosystem services' for human benefit. In conclusion, this analysis calls for transcendence of these limitations in pursuit of a more inclusive environmental education encompassing diverse ethnic and socioeconomic dimensions of the human community.

'Hiking isn't therapeutic, it just pisses me off'.

Anon.[1]

Introduction

This article explores the role of ecotourism in the neoliberalisation of environmental education. Defined by The International Ecotourism Society as 'responsible travel to natural areas that conserves the environment and improves the well-being of local people', ecotourism is among the fastest growing segments of a global tourism industry that, in 2011, recorded more than US $1 trillion in total receipts (Honey 2008; UNWTO 2012). Despite its substantial overlap with many aspects of outdoor and environmental education, however, to date, ecotourism has developed for the most part as an independent focus of research. This separation is perpetuated from both sides of the divide. Within the rapidly growing ecotourism literature, on the one hand, and notwithstanding important exceptions highlighted below, there is

---

[1]Current affiliation: International Development Studies, Department of Human Geography and Planning, Utrecht University, Utrecht, The Netherlands.

relatively little discussion of environmental education (Sander 2012), despite the fact that this is commonly considered one of the core components of sound ecotourism practice (Honey 2008). Honey (2008), indeed, asserts that '[e]cotourism means education, for both tourists and residents of nearby communities' (p. 30).

On the other hand, despite the activity's growing popularity and global reach, ecotourism has rarely been addressed as a specific modality within the large body of research addressing environmental and outdoor education (hereafter 'EE') (notable exceptions include Russell 1994, 1999; Russell and Hodson 2002). Stevenson et al.'s (2013a) 51-chapter compilation *Research on Environmental Education*, for instance, contains no listing for 'ecotourism' in the index and none of the individual chapters address the activity directly. Meanwhile, Saylan and Blumstein's (2011, p. 103) recent call to fix *The Failure of Environmental Education* does in fact mention ecotourism as a potential delivery system for education, observing that '[o]perators are increasingly making sure their programs teach ecotourists how not to "love animals and the habitat to death" and thus promote protection of the areas they frequent'. Yet this observation is not further developed, leaving the entire 'how' of this delivery unexplored.

The neoliberalisation of education in general within advanced liberal societies in recent years has become a growing focus of scrutiny (e.g. Klein 2007; Shore 2008, 2010; Giroux 2012), while a small body of work, upon which this special issue builds, has begun to address this same process within EE in particular (Gruenewald 2004; Hursh and Henderson 2011). At the same time, the practice of ecotourism has been characterised as a quintessential mechanism of neoliberal environmental governance in its promise to ascribe an economic value to *in situ* natural resources and thereby incentivize their preservation (e.g. West and Carrier 2004; Duffy 2008; Fletcher and Neves 2012). To date, however, no one has synthesised these various foci to analyse ecotourism's specific contribution to environmental education and the neoliberalisation thereof, a lacuna that this article seeks to fill.

It begins with the premise that the practice of ecotourism is informed by a particular cultural perspective characteristic of the white, upper-middle-class members of postindustrial societies who have historically comprised the majority of practitioners (Fletcher 2009a, 2014). While ecotourism developers commonly frame their interventions as a straightforward presentation of economic incentives by means of which local stakeholders will be induced to participate in the industry, my research indicates that ecotourism development commonly entails an implicit attempt to acculturate locals to the specific worldview informing the practice. Planners rarely acknowledge this dynamic explicitly; however, they often shorthand it as an effort to 'educate' locals, understood as a straightforward, neutral presentation of facts rather than the promotion a culturally specific point of view.

Meanwhile, as I explain further below, the specific cultural perspective that ecotourists bring to their practice informs a particular 'ecotourist gaze' by means of which they evaluate their experience and gauge whether or not it proves satisfying. The 'education' that providers characteristically offer to clients is implicitly framed in terms of this gaze as well, embodying a perspective on human–nonhuman relations in which western society is depicted as alienating and constraining and immersion in 'wilderness' is understood as a therapeutic escape from the reputed ills of industrial civilisation. This raises the possibility that much environmental education, particularly within the context of ecotourism delivery, is fundamentally ethnocentric in its promotion of a particular cultural perspective that is commonly misunderstood as a universal aspect of the human condition (Fletcher 2009a, 2014; Root 2010; Gough 2013).

While in the past, ecotourism's educational aspects have often contradicted the activity's promotion as a neoliberal[2] conservation mechanism, promoting instead a value-based commitment to conservation, increasingly this education has become neoliberalised as well in its growing emphasis – consonant with recent trends in environmental governance in general – on the environment's role as an instrumental provider of 'ecosystem services' for human benefit (Robertson 2006; Sullivan 2009, 2013). This illustrates the pervasive hegemony of neoliberal rationality in general (Peck 2010), in terms of which all environmental action must increasingly be justified in terms of cost-benefit analysis and its contribution to economic growth (Fletcher 2010).

Environmental education and ecotourism

Reviewing the now vast literature addressing environmental and outdoor education is beyond the scope of this article (but see Stevenson et al. 2013a for an exhaustive overview). Instead, I want to highlight what has been increasingly recognised as a significantly under-researched aspect of the field, namely the ways in which dynamics of cultural identity and background shape how environmental education is delivered and received. While Stevenson and colleagues (2013b, p. 513) claim that '[a]pproaches to environmental learning now recognise that worldviews and belief systems shape individuals' understanding and interpretation of environmental issues and mediate their environmental behaviour', they also acknowledge a relative lack of attention to the factors shaping worldviews, suggesting that '[t]he many different dimensions of identity offer fertile ground for future research on the nature of worldview-identity relationships' (Stevenson et al. 2013b, p. 515). Gough, similarly, observes that 'the vast majority of work in environmental education to date has been concerned with universalized subjects, rather than recognising multiple subjectivities' (2013, p. 376). In particular, Root (2010, p. 107) contends, most 'outdoor environmental education remains Eurocentric', failing to problematise the culturally specific perspective shaping its ostensibly universal subject. Hence, while 'issues of class, ethnicity, ability and sexuality have slowly trickled into environmental education research' (Fawcett 2013, p. 410) they remain quite marginal to the field (Root 2010; Gough 2013; Haluza-Delay 2013; Lowan-Trudeau 2013; Russell and Fawcett 2013).[3]

As a result, various researchers emphasise a 'need for environmental education to be self-critical, as well as socially critical' (Gough 2013, p. 379; see also Di Chiro 1987). In particular, Root (2010) asserts that 'there is a great need to decolonize the largely White, Western field of environmental education' (p. 104). At the same time, researchers highlight the continued marginality of political economy to environmental education (Gruenewald 2004, Haluza-Delay 2013), which may thereby lend implicit 'support to an individualistic, inequitable, and unsustainable growth economy' (p. 79). In order to correct for this neglect, Haluza-Delay (2013) calls for increased 'attention to the political-economic systems that negatively impact both natural environments and marginalize social groups' (p. 395).

Surveying the full array of scholarly research addressing ecotourism is likewise beyond the scope of this analysis (see Fletcher 2014 for a comprehensive overview). Suffice it to point out that the majority of literature thus far has focused on the production of ecotourism and/or its economic/environmental impacts in the places it is implemented. By contract, cultural dynamics of ecotourism consumption have been little explored to date. The work that has been done describes ecotourists as 'pushed' by a desire to escape 'overcrowded, unpleasant conditions' at home (Honey 2008, p. 12) and pulled by a variety of factors, including a quest for authenticity, transcendence, or sense of connection with nonhuman nature (see e.g. Munt 1994; Ryan, Hughes, and Chirgwin 2000; Duffy 2002; West and Carrier 2004; Cater 2006).

A small body of research has begun to analyse the educational component of ecotourism delivery as well (e.g. Orams 1997; Kimmel 1999; Russell 1994, 1999; Russell and Hobson 2002; Gilbert 2003; Zanotti and Chernela 2008; Sander 2012; Zanotti 2012). Yet, how cultural dynamics of ecotourism consumption influence this educational delivery has been largely unexamined. In what follows, then, I seek to synthesize these various discussions to describe the ways in which environmental education in ecotourism delivery is shaped by both the particular cultural perspective informing the activity's practice and the neoliberal capitalist political economy of which it is part and parcel.

The ecotourist gaze

My long-term research concerning the cultural dimensions of ecotourism (see Fletcher 2009a, 2014 for details) suggests that ecotourism, like environmental education in general, as noted above, is profoundly Eurocentric, drawing the majority of practitioners from the ranks of the white, upper-middle-classes in postindustrial, predominantly western societies[4] (Fletcher 2009a, 2014). This is due, in part, to the fact that the activity resonates strongly with aspects of the particular cultural perspective characteristic of, and largely peculiar to, this demographic. Even among this demographic, of course, views and orientations vary significantly, yet my research documents a relatively coherent body of values and beliefs characteristic of upper-middle-class culture that ecotourists tend to share. Below, I briefly summarize the most significant dimensions of this perspective for purposes of the present discussion (for more detailed treatments, see Fletcher 2008, 2009a, 2014).

First, the practice of ecotourism is grounded in a characteristically western dichotomy between opposing realms of 'nature' and 'culture', compelling a quest to cross the line from 'culture' into 'nature' in pursuit of a romanticized 'wilderness' space (West and Carrier 2004). Second, ecotourism embodies a 'postmaterial' desire, predominant among the wealthier segments of postindustrial populations, to sacrifice physical and material security in pursuit of a 'self-actualizing' experience (Inglehart 1990). Third, ecotourism fulfills a characteristically upper-middle-class imperative to continually progress and achieve through an active, physical, outdoor experience that contrasts with this class group's characteristic occupation in sedentary, indoor mental labour (Fletcher 2008). Fourth, ecotourism tends to draw for inspiration on narratives of colonial exploration through identification with the white, European protagonists of such narratives (Braun 2003).

All of this is attended by a further aspect of this particular cultural perspective, namely a common self-conception of the individual as divided into opposing elements of mind and body, where the latter is understood as a vicious, wild animal that must be kept tamed and subdued through vigorous self-discipline if one is to be accepted within 'civilised' society (Fletcher 2009b, 2014). From this point of view, ostensibly uninhabited 'wilderness' is experienced as a liminal space where one can be freed for a time from this self-constraint and is thus perceived as transcendent and liberating.

In order to achieve this liberating liminal experience, ecotourists need to perceive signs indicating that they have left industrial civilisation behind and entered a 'natural', 'wilderness' space. The result is a particular aesthetic, lampooned by both Brooks (2000) and Lander (2008), in terms of which ecotourists – like the white upper-middle-class in general – desire all that is ostensibly natural and undeveloped, for such signs help to alleviate one's subjective sense of oppression provoked by the perception of confinement within industrial civilisation. Similarly, ecotourists desire intense, physical, visceral experiences that give them a sense of completion and achievement – especially those involving (limited) hardship and suffering – in order, simultaneously, to fulfill their class conditioned need to continually progress through self-discipline and deferral of gratification, on the one hand, and to escape this same conditioning through a liminal experience diametrically opposed to the sedentary mental activity dominating their everyday reality, on the other (Fletcher 2008, 2009a).

This all coalesces in a particular 'gaze' by means of which ecotourists evaluate their experience and adjudicate to what extent it is fulfilling (Fletcher 2014). The concept of a 'tourist gaze' was developed by Urry (2001), drawing on Foucault (1973), who contends that tourists are typically motivated by a desire to view exotic sights, the anticipation of which is a strong source of the pleasure they derive from their experience. He cautions, however, 'There is so single tourist gaze as such. It varies by society, by social group, and by historical period' (2001, p. 1), depending upon such factors as 'class, gender, [and] generational distinctions of taste within the potential population of tourists' (p. 3). Following from this, my research suggests that ecotourism, in particular, embodies its own peculiar gaze with a specific set of expectations in terms of the exotic signs it seeks to collect as well as its demand for a certain form of bodily experience, as described above. Again, there are obviously variations in terms of how the gaze is embodied by different ecotourists but I believe that the preceding attributes hold true for the majority.

The particular cultural perspective informing ecotourism influences its deployment as a sustainable development strategy in rural areas of less-developed societies throughout the world (Fletcher 2009a, 2014). As one of the most widespread supports for conservation globally, ecotourism commonly promotes what Honey (2008) calls the 'stakeholder theory', the assertion that 'people will protect what they receive value from' (p. 3). By generating sufficient revenue that natural resources will be worth more *in situ* than extracted, in other words, ecotourism seeks to incentivize resources' conservation by local people. This, as I explain elsewhere (Fletcher 2010), is a quintessential neoliberal form of environmental governance, grounded in: (1) efforts to direct actors' behaviour through manipulation of incentive structures; (2) calculation in terms of the cost–benefit ratio of alternative forms of actions; and (3) reliance on economic growth to generate resources for conservation. In this sense, ecotourism represents a growing trend toward neoliberalisation within the global conservation movement as a whole that has become an increasing focus of research in the last several years (see e.g. Brockington, Duffy, and Igoe 2008; Büscher et al. 2012).

On the other hand, my research shows that in their actual practice, planners often promote ecotourism development in precisely the opposite manner: as an ethical practice that local stakeholders will adopt due primarily to recognition of its intrinsic aesthetic and affective value (Fletcher 2009a, 2014). In this, I have shown, developers often implicitly promote the particular cultural perspective informing the practice of ecotourism for adoption by the local stakeholders whom they hope to involve in the industry. It is this surreptitious promotion that they commonly shorthand as 'education', presenting it as a straightforward demonstration of the objective facts of the situation and the inherent appeal of outdoor recreational experience rather than a value-laden and context-specific practice shaped by a particular regime of cultural conditioning.

All of this, then, influences the 'education' ecotourism providers are urged to provide to clients and local stakeholders alike. In this paradoxical promotion of ecotourism grounded in economic incentives, on the one hand, and ethical injunction, on the other, one can identify the operation of distinctive approaches to governance in general – what Foucault (1991, 2007, 2008) calls 'arts of government' or 'governmentalities'. Framing ecotourism as an incentive for conservation can be seen as an expression of what Foucault identified as a novel form of neoliberal governmentality – or when applied to environmental governance, an 'environmentality' (Luke 1999; Agrawal 2005a, 2005b; Fletcher 2010) – one that 'will act on the environment and systematically modify its variables' (Foucault 2008, p. 260). The educational aspects of ecotourism delivery, by contrast, generally embody a far different approach to environmental governance than this neoliberal form, seeking, instead, to create what Agrawal (2005b) calls 'environmental subjects – people who care about the environment' (p. 162). This, indeed, is what most proponents consider the main end of EE in general, as when Gruenewald (2004) asserts that 'the purpose of environmental education is to provide people with the experience and knowledge needed to care for our environments' (p. 73). This approach embodies what might be called a more a conventional *disciplinary* form of governmentality/environmentality seeking to influence actors' behaviour through inculcation of norms and values. The chief difference between neoliberal and disciplinary forms of governmentality, Foucault (2008) explains, is that the former constitutes an 'environmental type of intervention instead of the internal subjugation of individuals characterising a disciplinary approach' (p. 271).

Neoliberalisation in ecotourism education

This distinction between neoliberal and disciplinary aspects of ecotourism promotion, however, is diminishing at present as the increasing hegemony of neoliberal rationality within contemporary environmental governance (see e.g. Buscher et al. 2012; Fletcher 2010, 2012; Sullivan 2013) ensures that environmental education itself becomes more neoliberalised over time (Gruenewald 2004; Hursh and Henderson 2011). As Gruenewald (2004) describes, 'Currently, in order to legitimize itself, EE is (1) claiming to enhance standards-based achievement in traditional disciplines and (2) developing its own standards and conventions' ,(p. 80) – reflecting a paradigmatic neoliberal preoccupation with 'measurementality' (Turnhout, Neves, and de Lijster 2014) in general as well as reproducing the 'rationality of the market' (Gruenewald 2004, p. 87) in its emphasis on EE's instrumental contribution to students' overall productivity. EE can also contribute to neoliberalism's emphasis on individuated responsibility by encouraging environmental action via 'ethical consumption' and other market-based mechanisms (see Carrier 2010). Of course, this is not universally the case, and EE can still present significant challenges to neoliberal trends when utilized, for instance, as a tool for environmental justice (Haluza-Delay 2013).

Neoliberalisation within environmental education is also expressed, most profoundly I believe, in the growing popularity of the framing of nonhuman nature as a provider of so-called 'ecosystem services' (see Robertson 2006; Sullivan 2009, 2013). While the concept of ecosystem services has been in use among ecologists for some time, it was given new impetus in global environmental governance by Robert Costanza and colleagues' (1997) famous effort to calculate the total value of the world's ecosystem services ($16–54 trillion) and the concept's subsequent promotion in the 2005 Millennium Ecosystem Assessment (Sullivan, 2009). Since that time, the concept has become pervasive in environmental circles (Sullivan 2013) and seems destined to expand still further via such dynamics as the UN Environment Programme's newfound TEEB (The Economics of Ecosystems and Biodiversity) initiative (see MacDonald and Corson 2012). In terms of this perspective, proper valuation of ecosystem services is commonly promoted as the key to environmental protection, ostensibly reversing the 'market failure' caused by externalization of environmental damage and thus incentivizing producers to consider the full costs of natural resources in their business calculations (see esp. Sullivan 2013).

Two examples of this dynamic in ecotourism education from my recent research both concern bats. In two separate presentations at different ecotourism facilities (one in Costa Rica, the other in Peru), researchers highlighted the important 'services' bats ostensibly provide to rainforest ecosystems in order to emphasise the need for bat conservation. These services were characterised as regulating insect (primarily mosquito) populations, contributing to seed dispersal, plant pollination, and so forth. One researcher described his long-term goal as seeking to quantify the total value of ecosystem services provided by bats to humans so as to develop a stronger case for the importance of bats' conservation – an aim pursued by other ecologists as well (e.g. Kunz et al. 2011). The key point here is to emphasise how different this ecosystem service approach is in terms of justifying conservation efforts (i.e., based in cost–benefit calculation) – an exercise of neoliberal as opposed to disciplinary environmentality – whereas conservation in the past would be more commonly justified based on organisms' aesthetic and intrinsic value (e.g. McCauley 2006). This type of neoliberal framing, my research suggests, is becoming increasingly common in ecotourism education and elsewhere (see also Sullivan 2013).

The rise of the ecosystem services perspective is representative of increasing neoliberalisation within the global conservation movement in general noted above, which, 'simply put, comes down to making environmental conservation compatible with capitalism' (Büscher and Arsel 2012, p. 129; see also Brockington, Duffy and Igoe 2008; Brockington and Duffy, 2010). Yet, it is precisely a capitalist system predicated on continual growth that is in no small part responsible for the very environmental problems it is now increasingly called upon to resolve, leading Büscher (2012) to describe neoliberal conservation as 'the paradoxical idea that capitalist markets are the answer to their own ecological contradictions' (p. 29). Emphasising ecosystem services, then, not only fails to highlight the political-economic dimensions of ecological degradation commonly neglected in environmental education, as noted above, but actually contributes to obfuscation of this dynamic by promoting a capitalism-friendly approach to conservation.

Nature deficit disorder?

The preceding analysis has intriguing implications in relation to the growing concern among environmental educators that lack of direct experiential contact with nonhuman nature is contributing to the 'death of environmentalism' (Shellenberger and Nordhaus 2004) by diminishing many people's sense of connection with – and hence regard for the future of – this nature (Adams 2004; Louv 2005; Kareiva 2008; Brockington 2009). After all, one of the main goals of environmental education is to encourage 'pro-environmental behaviour' on the part of recipients (Saylan and Blumstein 2011). As Russell (1999) observes, this goal is commonly grounded in a line of reasoning holding that

NATURE EXPERIENCE → CARING → COMMITTMENT → ACTION (p. 123)

In his best-selling, *Last Child in the Woods*, for instance, Louv (2005) laments the 'nature deficit disorder' increasingly afflicting the US population. This condition is attributed to growing urbanization, to an increase in 'videophilia' (reliance on electronic media for virtual nature experiences) and to decreasing opportunities for experiential environmental education in school curricula (Louv 2005; Pergams and Zaradic 2006, 2008; Kareiva 2008). The problem is evidenced, ostensibly, by research demonstrating a dramatic decline in per capita visitation to national parks and other protected areas in several postindustrial societies in the last several decades (Pergams and Zaradic 2006, 2008).

Contrary to this type of reasoning, the analysis developed here supports Russell's (1999) contention that the 'proper' concern for nonhuman nature inspiring the type of environmentalism inclusive of a desire to visit national parks and other protected areas may be the function of a particular cultural perspective rather than of an objective relationship with 'nature' per se. In other words, for contact with nonhuman nature to have the desired effect of inspiring support for environmentalism may necessitate the capacity to see and know nature in a particular way (Argyrou 2005). Hence, when Kareiva (2008) laments that 'humans are becoming seriously disconnected from nature' (p. 2757), he may be expressing a culturally specific viewpoint concerning humans' relationship with the rest of the world rather than an objective, universal condition.

Indeed, this analysis suggests that a broad-based, aesthetic environmentalism may require not intimate contact with nonhuman nature but rather, on the contrary, a certain distance, both physical and conceptual, from this very nature, allowing one, in a sense, to 'look at the nature from a safe distance' (Barry 2003, p. E5) that affords a level of romanticisation that would be difficult to maintain were one to live primarily within 'wilderness' spaces. Howells (2001), having spent a week on an extreme ecotour in the Peruvian Amazon sleeping on the rainforest floor while subsisting on grubs and other foraged foods, subtitles his account of the experience 'The Rainforest is a Nice Place to Save, But I Wouldn't Want to Live There'. Hence, while critics worry that the type of aestheticised, virtual nature experiences found in video games and television documentaries may diminish people's concern for more mundane 'real' nature (Pergams and Zaradic 2008; Brockington 2009; Igoe 2010), in point of fact, the opposite may be true: encounters with spectacular, hyperreal, virtual environments may actually enhance support for conservation more than sustained contact with a 'real' nature that is far more messy, dirty, and inconvenient.

Conclusion

In this article, I have sought to advance discussion of EE in ecotourism delivery by complicating the widespread conviction that straightforward provision of a direct encounter with nonhuman nature will necessarily prove transformative for either inbound clients or local hosts, inspiring the creation of 'environmental subjects'. Rather, I have suggested that what is commonly termed 'education' in this process is often an implicit attempt to propagate a culturally specific perspective on both human subjectivity and human–nonhuman relations that mediates actors' experience of the 'nature' they encounter. At the same time, I have observed that neoliberalisation within ecotourism education, as expressed among other aspects in the growing advancement of the 'ecosystem services' concept, problematically contributes to the promotion of neoliberal capitalism as the solution to the environmental and social problems that it itself exacerbates. In opposition to the contention, increasingly common among conservationists and environmental educators, that more direct nature experience will inspire pro-environmental behaviour, I have suggested with Russell (1999) that the interrelationship between 'experience' and prior 'stories' that participants in environmental education activities carry with them helps to determine how they are affected by their participation and hence that substantial conceptual work is necessary in order to invoke the proper experience inspiring the type of action environmentalists desire.

At present, however, this is merely an untested hypothesis, requiring further research to explore how participants of different backgrounds respond to a given environmental education curriculum based on the divergent 'stories' that they bring to their common experience. As Russell and Hobson (2002) assert, more research is also needed to assess how best to communicate via EE an understanding of the political economy influencing ecological degradation over and above the actions of discrete individuals. This is particularly important with respect to the growing trend toward neoliberalisation within environmental management noted above, which, as previously described, promotes precisely the type of individual responsibility and action via market consumption fundamentally at odds with an appreciation of the significance of capitalist forces in contributing to the degradation they are increasingly called upon to redress. In this way, tools can be developed to ensure that EE contributes to a more inclusive environmental politics that encompassing diverse ethnic and socioeconomic dimensions of the human community, as well as critically reflecting on the overarching political-economic milieu in terms of which it occurs, in order to keep EE – and the ecotourism through which it often delivered – from functioning as merely 'an ineffectual band-aid on the wounds of the earth and its inhabitants' (Haluza-Delay 2013, p. 394).

Notes

1. Quotation printed on T-shirts distributed at 2008 Association of Outdoor Recreation and Education (AORE) Conference in Boise, Idaho. Ostensibly from a young participant in an unidentified wilderness therapy program.

2. While the term 'neoliberalism' has been defined in various ways (see Flew 2011), it is most commonly characterised as the overlapping processes of commodification, marketisation, privatisation, deregulation, and decentralisation implemented via 'free market' reform policies throughout the world beginning in earnest in the 1980s (Castree 2008; Harvey 2005).
3. Unfortunately, due to space limitations, issues of gender and sexuality will be neglected by this analysis, as will a further important issue, namely the 'continued marginalisation of animal others in environmental education research' (Fawcett 2013, p. 412).
4. Of course, this is not entirely so, and even this demographic bias is changing rapidly at present as ecotourism practice becomes increasingly globalized (see Fletcher 2014).

Notes on Contributor

Robert Fletcher is assistant professor of International Development Studies at Utrecht University in the Netherlands. His research interests include ecotourism, conservation, environmental governance, climate change and resistance and social movements. He is the author of *Romancing the Wild: Cultural Dimensions of Ecotourism* (Duke University Press, 2014) and co-editor of *Nature^{TM} Inc: Environmental Conservation in the Neoliberal Age* (University of Arizona Press, 2014).

References

Adams, W. M. 2004. *Against Extinction: The Story of Conservation*. London: Earthscan.

Agrawal, A. 2005a. *Environmentality: Technologies of Government and the Making of Subjects*. Durham, NC: Duke University Press.

Agrawal, A. 2005b. "Environmentality: Community, Intimate Government, and the Making of Environmental Subjects in Kumaon, India." *Current Anthropology* 46 (2): 161–190.

Argyrou, V. 2005. *The Logic of Environmentalism: Anthropology, Ecology, and Postcoloniality*. New York: Berghahn.

Barry, D. 2003. "Row, Row, Row Your Kayak, Frantically down the Stream." *Seattle Times,* September 22, p.E5.

Braun, B. 2003. "'On the Raggedy Edge of Risk': Articulations of Race and Nature after Biology." In *Race, Nature, and the Politics of Difference*, edited by D. S. Moore, A. Pandian, and J. Kosek, 175–203. Durham, NC: Duke University Press.

Brockington, D. 2009. *Celebrity and the Environment: Fame, Wealth and Power in Conservation*. London: Zed Books.

Brockington, D., and R. Duffy, Eds. 2010. Antipode 42, No. 3, Special Issue on "Capitalism and Conservation."

Brockington, D., R. Duffy, and J. Igoe. 2008. *Nature Unbound: Conservation, Capitalism and the Future of Protected Areas*. London: Earthscan.

Brooks, D. 2000. *Bobos in Paradise: The New Upper Class and How They Got There*. New York: Simon & Schuster.

Büscher, B. 2012. "Payments for Ecosystem Services as Neoliberal Conservation: (Reinterpreting) Evidence from the Maloti-Drakensberg, South Africa." *Conservation and Society* 10 (1): 29–41.

Büscher, B., and M. Arsel. 2012. "Introduction: Neoliberal Conservation, Uneven Geographical Development and the Dynamics of Contemporary Capitalism." *Tijdschrift Voor Economische En Sociale Geografie* 103 (2): 129–135.

Büscher, B., S. Sullivan, K. Neves, J. Igoe, and D. Brockington. 2012. "Towards a Synthesized Critique of Neoliberal Biodiversity Conservation." *Capitalism Nature Socialism* 23 (2): 4–30.

Carrier, J. G. 2010. "Protecting the Environment the Natural Way: Ethical Consumption and Commodity Fetishism." *Antipode* 42 (3): 672–689.

Castree, N. 2008. "Neoliberalising Nature: The Logics of Deregulation and Reregulation." *Environment and Planning A* 40 (1): 131–152.

Cater, E. 2006. "Ecotourism as a Western Construct." *Journal of Ecotourism* 5 (1&2): 23–39.

Costanza, R., R. d'Arge, S. de Groot, M. Farber, B. Grasso, K. Hannon, S. Limburg, et al. 1997. "The Value of the World's Ecosystem Services and Natural Capital." *Nature* 387: 253–260.

Di Chiro, G. 1987. "Environmental Education and the Question of Gender: A Feminist Critique." In *Environmental Education: Practice and Possibility*, edited by I. Robottom, 23–48. Geelong, Victoria: Deakin University Press.

Duffy, R. 2002. *Trip Too Far: Ecotourism, Politics, and Exploitation*. London: Earthscan.

Duffy, R. 2008. "Neoliberalising Nature: Global Networks and Ecotourism Development in Madagascar." *Journal of Sustainable Tourism* 16 (3): 327–344.

Fawcett, L. 2013. "Three Degrees of Separation: Accounting for Nature Cultures in Environmental Education Research." In *International Handbook of Research on Environmental Education*, edited by R. B. Stevenson, M. Brody, J. Dillon, and A. E. J. Wals, 409–417. New York: Routledge.

Fletcher, R. 2008. "Living on the Edge: The Appeal of Risk Sports for the Professional Middle Class." *Sociology of Sport Journal* 25 (3): 310–330.

Fletcher, R. 2009a. "Ecotourism Discourse: Challenging the Stakeholder Theory." *Journal of Ecotourism* 8 (3): 269–285.

Fletcher, R. 2009b. "Against Wilderness." *Green Theory and Praxis: The Journal of Ecopedagogy* 5 (1): 169–179.

Fletcher, R. 2010. "Neoliberal Environmentality: Towards a Poststructuralist Political Ecology of the Conservation Debate." *Conservation and Society* 8 (3): 171–181.

Fletcher, R. 2012. "Using the Master's Tools? Neoliberal Conservation and the Evasion of Inequality." *Development and Change* 43 (1): 295–317.

Fletcher, R. 2014. *Romancing the Wild: Cultural Dimensions of Ecotourism*. Durham, NC: Duke University Press.

Fletcher, R., and K. Neves. 2012. "Contradictions in Tourism: The Promise and Pitfalls of Ecotourism as a Manifold Capitalist Fix." *Environment and Society: Advances in Research* 3 (1): 60–77.

Flew, T. 2011. "Michel Foucault's *the Birth of Biopolitics* and Contemporary Neo-liberalism Debates." *Thesis Eleven* 108 (1): 44–65.

Foucault, M. 1973. *The Birth of the Clinic: An Archaeology of Medical Perception*. New York: Vintage.

Foucault, M. 1991. "Governmentality." In *The Foucault Effect: Studies in Governmentality*, edited by G. Burchell, C. Gordon, and P. Miller, 87–104. Hemel Hempstead: Harvester Wheatsheaf.

Foucault, M. 2007. *Security, Territory, Population*. New York: Picador.

Foucault, M. 2008. *The Birth of Biopolitics*. New York: Palgrave MacMillan.

Gilbert, R. 2003. "Ecotourism and Education for Sustainability: A Critical Approach." *International Review of Environmental Strategies* 4 (1): 75–83.

Giroux, H. A. 2012. *Education and the Crisis of Public Values: Challenging the Assault on Teachers, Students, and Public Education*. New York: Peter Lang Publishing.

Gough, A. 2013. "Researching Differently: Generating a Gender Agenda for Research in Environmental Education." In *International Handbook of Research on Environmental Education*, edited by R. B. Stevenson, M. Brody, J. Dillon, and A. E. J. Wals, 375–383. New York: Routledge.

Gruenewald, D. 2004. "A Foucauldian Analysis of Environmental Education: Toward the Socioecological Challenge of the Earth Charter." *Curriculum Inquiry* 34: 71–107.

Haluza-Delay, R. 2013. "Education for Environmental Justice." In *International Handbook of Research on Environmental Education*, edited by R. B. Stevenson, M. Brody, J. Dillon, and A. E. J. Wals, 394–403. New York: Routledge.

Harvey, D. 2005. *A Brief History of Neoliberalism*. Oxford: Oxford University Press.

Honey, M. 2008. *Ecotourism and Sustainable Development: Who Owns Paradise?* 2nd ed. New York: Island Press.

Howells, R. E. 2001. The Teachings of Gerineldo 'Moises' Chavez. *Outside*, January.

Hursh, D., and J. Henderson. 2011. "Contesting Global Neoliberalism and Creating Alternative Futures." *Discourse: Studies in the Cultural Politics of Education* 32 (2): 171–185.

Igoe, J. 2010. "The Spectacle of Nature in the Global Economy of Appearances: Anthropological Engagements with the Spectacular Mediations of Transnational Conservation." *Critique of Anthropology* 30 (4): 375–397.

Inglehart, R. 1990. *Culture Shift in Advanced Industrial Society.* Princeton: Princeton University Press.

Kareiva, P. 2008. "Ominous Trends in Nature Recreation." *PNAS* 105 (8): 2757–2758.

Kimmel, J. 1999. "Ecotourism as Environmental Learning." *Journal of Environmental Education* 30 (2): 40–44.

Klein, N. 2007. *The Shock Doctrine: The Rise of Disaster Capitalism.* New York: Metropolitan Books.

Kunz, T. H., E. Braun de Torrez, D. Bauer, T. Lobova, and T. H. Fleming. 2011. "Ecosystem Services Provided by Bats." *Annals of the New York Academy of Sciences* 1223: 1–38.

Lander, C. 2008. *Stuff White People Like.* New York: Random House.

Louv, R. 2005. *Last Child in the Woods: Saving Our Children from Nature-Deficit Disorder.* Chapel Hill, NC: Algonquin.

Lowan-Trudeau, G. 2013. "Indigenous Environmental Education Research in North America: A Brief Review." In *International Handbook of Research on Environmental Education,* edited by R. B. Stevenson, M. Brody, J. Dillon, and A. E. J. Wals, 404–408. New York: Routledge.

Luke, T. 1999. "Environmentality as Green Governmentality." In *Discourses of the Environment,* edited by E. Darier, 121–151. Oxford: Blackwell.

MacDonald, K. I., and C. Corson. 2012. "'TEEB Begins Now': A Virtual Moment in the Production of Natural Capital." *Development and Change* 43: 159–184.

McCauley, D. J. 2006. "Selling out on Nature." *Nature* 443 (7): 27–28.

Munt, I. 1994. "Eco-tourism or Ego-tourism?" *Race and Class* 36: 49–60.

Orams, M. B. 1997. "The Effectiveness of Environmental Education: Can We Turn Tourists into 'Greenies'?" *Progress in Tourism and Hospitality Research* 3: 295–306.

Peck, J. 2010. *Constructions of Neoliberal Reason.* Oxford: Oxford University Press.

Pergams, O. R. W., and P. A. Zaradic. 2006. "Is Love of Nature in the US Becoming Love of Electronic Media? 16-Year Downtrend in National Park Visits Explained by Watching Movies, Playing Video Games, Internet Use, and Oil Prices." *Journal of Environmental Management* 80: 387–393.

Pergams, O. R. W., and P. A. Zaradic. 2008. "Evidence for a Fundamental and Pervasive Shift Away from Nature-based Recreation." *PNAS* 105: 2295–2300.

Robertson, M. M. 2006. "The Nature That Capital Can See: Science, State, and Market in the Commodification of Ecosystem Services." *Environment and Planning D: Society and Space* 24: 367–387.

Root, E. 2010. "This Land is Our Land? This Land is Your Land: The Decolonizing Journeys of White Outdoor Education Educators." *Canadian Journal of Environmental Education* 15: 103–119.

Russell, C. L. 1994. "Ecotourism as Experiential Environmental Education" *Journal of Experiential Education* 17 (1): 16–22.

Russell, C. L. 1999. "Problematizing Nature Experience in Environmental Education: The Interrelationship of Experience and Story." *Journal of Experiential Education* 22 (3): 123–128.

Russell, C. L., and L. Fawcett. 2013. "Moving Margins in Environmental Education Research." In *International Handbook of Research on Environmental Education,* edited by R. B. Stevenson, M. Brody, J. Dillon, and A. E. J. Wals, 369–374. New York: Routledge.

Russell, C. L., and D. Hodson. 2002. "Whalewatching as Critical Science Education?" *Canadian Journal of Science, Mathematics and Technology Education* 2 (4): 485–504.

Ryan, C., K. Hughes, and S. Chirgwin. 2000. "The Gaze, Spectacle and Ecotourism." *Annals of Tourism Research* 27 (1): 148–163.

Sander, B. 2012. "The Importance of Education in Ecotourism Ventures: Lessons from Rara Avis Ecolodge, Costa Rica." *International Journal of Sustainable Society* 4 (4): 389–404.

Saylan, C., and D. T. Blumstein. 2011. *The Failure of Environmental Education (and How We Can Fix It).* Berkeley: University of California Press.

Shellenberger, M., and T. Nordhaus. 2004. *The Death of Environmentalism: Global Warming Politics in a Post-environmental World*. San Francisco: The Breakthrough.

Shore, C. 2008. "Audit Culture and Illiberal Governance: Universities and the Politics of Accountability." *Anthropological Theory* 8 (3): 278–298.

Shore, C. 2010. "Beyond the Multiversity: Neoliberalism and the Rise of the Schizophrenic University." *Social Anthropology* 18 (1): 15–29.

Stevenson, R. B., M. Brody, J. Dillon, and A. E. J. Wals, eds. 2013a. *International Handbook of Research on Environmental Education*. New York: Routledge.

Stevenson, R. B., A. E. J. Wals, J. Dillon, and M. Brody. 2013b. "Introduction: An Orientation to Environmental Education and the Handbook." In *International Handbook of Research on Environmental Education*, edited by R. B. Stevenson, M. Brody, J. Dillon, and A. E. J. Wals, 1–12. New York: Routledge.

Sullivan, S. 2009. "Green Capitalism, and the Cultural Poverty of Constructing Nature as Service-provider." *Radical Anthropology* 3: 18–27.

Sullivan, S. 2013. "Banking Nature? The Spectacular Financialisation of Environmental Conservation." *Antipode* 45 (1): 198–217.

Turnhout, E., K. Neves, and E. de Lijster. 2014. "Measurementality in Biodiversity Governance: Knowledge, Transparency and the Intergovernmental Science-policy Platform on Biodiversity and Ecosystem Services (IPBES)." *Environment and Planning A* 46: 581–597.

UNWTO (United Nations World Tourism Organization). 2012. *Tourism Highlights 2011*. Madrid: UNWTO.

Urry, J. 2001. *The Tourist Gaze*. 2nd ed. London: Sage.

West, P., and J. G. Carrier. 2004. "Ecotourism and Authenticity: Getting Away from It All?" *Current Anthropology* 45 (4): 483–498.

Zanotti, L. 2012. "Folk Knowledge, Interactive Learning, and Education: Community-based Ecotourism in the Amazon." In *Anthropology of Environmental Education*, edited by H. Kopnina. New York: Nova Publishers.

Zanotti, L., and J. Chernela. 2008. "Conflicting Cultures of Nature: Ecotourism, Education and the Kayapó of the Brazilian Amazon." *Tourism Geographies* 10 (4): 495–521.

Entrepreneurial endeavors: (re)producing neoliberalization through urban agriculture youth programming in Brooklyn, New York

Evan Weissman

Department of Public Health, Food Studies, and Nutrition, Syracuse University, Syracuse, NY, USA

Driven by social and environmental criticism of the neoliberalization of agro-food systems, urban agriculture today enjoys renewed interest throughout the United States as a primary space to engage the politics of food. Using Brooklyn, New York as a case study, I employ mixed qualitative methods to investigate the contradictions that arise in tensions between the goals of urban agriculture and its practice. Education and youth development programming figure prominently in Brooklyn's urban agriculture movement and provide insights into understanding the neoliberalization of food politics, especially an emphasis on market mechanisms as central to human well-being and the disciplining of youth in the skills and modes of conduct required by the neoliberal economy. Although current trends indicate that urban agriculture youth programming works to (re)produce neoliberalism and undercuts the political efficacy of Brooklyn's urban agriculture, these projects simultaneously produce openings for building political solidarities.

Introduction

A lot of the [urban agriculture] projects around the country that have gotten the most attention have youth components. Whether it's Growing Power [the most widely recognized urban farm program in the United States] or the work here [in Brooklyn] with Added Value and East New York Farms! [two well known urban farm projects] ... they all have strong youth programs. And I think they've been contagious because people see it changes the way people eat, it provides education, it provides entrepreneurial skills and job training. (Personal interview, June 3, 2010)[1]

In this statement, the director of a state agency supporting the expansion of urban food production offered her views on the emerging urban agriculture movement in the United States. This representative quote identifies both a common characteristic of urban agriculture efforts in Brooklyn and an underlying assumption of urban agriculture's role in addressing the contradictions of conventional agro-food: individuated, youth-focused efforts that enact market-based – specifically entrepreneurial – solutions are keys to building alternatives to conventional agro-food.

Agriculture and food (agro-food[2]) have become the focus of societal intrigue throughout the United States in recent years. Concerns over food safety, expanding American hunger, the social and environmental impacts of food, and the human health-related consequences of the American diet are on the forefront of the popular conscience like never before in American history. We could reasonably assert a 'food movement' is emerging to address the multitude of issues now placed squarely on the shoulders of America's agro-food system. Food is now understood to be more than its standard dictionary definition – 'nourishment in solid form' – but is recognized to embody a whole host of politically negotiated decisions. In this context, interest in urban agriculture – broadly defined as any production of food within cities – is growing across the US as a space to engage food politics.

In this article, I explore the contemporary period of urban agriculture expansion in Brooklyn, New York as a case study. I focus explicitly on the youth programming and educational components of urban farm projects because, as illustrated in the introductory quote, the data indicate that youth programs and education are understood as being of the utmost importance for urban agriculture projects. Youth programs support tangible and readily documented program successes (e.g. numbers of students reached, youth enrolled in programs, and/or other documented instances of youth involvement) and are key funding opportunities (i.e. funding is often more readily available to projects with youth components). More importantly, it is widely understood that the real impacts of urban agriculture are found within educating youth about food en route to learning healthy eating habits, creating an ethic of consumption, and for developing actors to participate in alternative food networks (AFNs) (Personal interviews, June 24, 2008; June 26, 2008; May 10, 2010; June 3, 2010).

Through a focus on urban agriculture youth and education programs, I employ mixed qualitative methods to investigate the ways in which urban agriculture youth programming is working to challenge the problems produced by conventional agro-food. I examine the contradictions that arise in the real and important tensions between the goals of urban agriculture and its practice in Brooklyn. Accordingly, I ask: in what ways is urban cultivation a struggle against neoliberalization, and conversely, how does Brooklyn's urban agriculture youth programming (re)produce neoliberalization?

A brief overview of neoliberalization

Neoliberalism, as defined by Harvey (2005, 2), is a 'theory of political economic practices that proposes that human well-being can best be advanced by *liberating individual entrepreneurial freedoms* and skills within an institutional framework characterized by strong private property rights, free markets, and free trade' (emphasis added). Accordingly, the role of the neoliberal state is to maintain 'an institutional framework appropriate to such practices' (Harvey 2005, 2). A 'free' market is assumed to be the best path to individual freedoms that presuppose human welfare. Whereas classic liberalism prioritizes individual liberties, neoliberalism prioritizes free enterprise.

The wide variety of ways in which the ideology of neoliberalism is mobilized by capital has pushed critical scholars to understand neoliberal*ization* as a *process*, not neoliberalism as a 'thing' (Bakker 2007; Brenner and Theodore 2002; Castree 2006, 2007a, 2007b; Harvey 2005; Heynen and Robbins 2005; Heynen, Kaika, and

Swyngedouw 2006; Mansfield 2004; Peck and Tickell 2002). Scholars explore the ways in which neoliberal theory has been actuated through various processes including: state restructuring, privatization, enclosure, deregulation, monetization, and commodification. Importantly, as shifts in the urban cultivation of Brooklyn highlight, neoliberalization is historicized through the distinction between an earlier 'roll-back' period of dismantling the state and a later period of 'roll-out' neoliberalization, characterized by the development of new forms of governance (Peck and Tickell 2002, 384).

Brenner and Theodore (2002, 351) employ the concept of 'creative destruction' to distinguish between the dialectically related but analytically distinct *destruction* of institutions through neoliberal market reform and the *creation* of 'a new infrastructure for market-oriented economic growth, commodification, and the rule of capital' (362). Peck and Tickell (2002) explain this shift from destruction to creation as an evolution of neoliberalism from its earliest form in the 1970s through established neoliberalism in the 1980s to the 'deep neoliberalisms' of today. These deep neoliberalisms are often unimposing and entirely hegemonic; the ideology often goes unnamed and unnoticed.

Agro-food alternatives

Social efforts and inherent contradictions both work to expose the harmful health, safety, and environmental impacts of the contemporary agro-food system. Consequently, some agro-food activists pressure the agro-technology industry, the farming industry, and the food industry (inter-related sectors of the system) for healthy, nutritious, and safe food. These agro-food efforts often manifest in the development of AFNs, broadly defined as 'networks of producers, consumers, and other actors that embody alternatives to the more standardized industrial mode of food supply,' that emerge in response to the exposed contradictions of conventional agro-food (Renting, Marsden, and Banks 2003, 394). AFNs, such as farmers' markets, fair trade producer cooperatives, community supported agriculture (CSA), and urban agriculture, work to build alternatives to conventional agro-food (Allen 2004; Goodman, DuPuis, and Goodman 2012; Guthman 2008b; Koc and Dahlberg 1999; Watts 2000).

Many AFNs emerge as educational programs and/or explicitly focus on youth as a response to concerns about the public health outcomes of the American diet. These efforts include curriculum to teach youth about food production and nutrition (Lautenschlager and Smith 2007). Much focus has been on hands-on learning opportunities tied to food, especially through cooking and growing, and linking the two through a systems perspective. For example, the 'Edible School Yard' program was created in Berkeley, California to teach kids about food through growing and cooking as a tool for agro-food transformation (Allen and Guthman 2006; Pudup 2008). There is thus an emphasis on engaging youth in food production through school gardens, community gardens, and other urban agriculture projects.

Within the literature, there is a longstanding debate that explores the tendencies of AFNs – especially those that focus on youth development – to either be *alternative*, creating small substitutes to conventional agro-food that do not challenge the overall functioning of the system, or *oppositional*, posing fundamental political challenges to the status quo (Allen et al. 2003). In many ways, the academic literature itself follows suit and is either celebratory or critical of AFNs. On the one hand are scholars who explore the work done by AFNs within current material realities while recognizing their own limitations. On the other hand are critical scholars who high-light the mainstreaming of agro-food alternatives and the highly racialized and classed characteristics of AFNs and the 'ideological influence of neoliberalism on movement ambition' (Goodman, DuPuis, and Goodman 2012, 3).

Some scholarship (e.g. Donald and Blay-Palmer 2006) examines AFNs as producing 'spaces of possibility' through the creation of 'alternative economic spaces' within a broader capitalist political economy. Contrary to growing critiques, Donald and Blay-Palmer (2006, 1903) argue: 'it is premature to conclude that the industrial food system has colonized the alternative.' Alternative agro-food networks have the potential to bring about more just, inclusive urban development models despite the ever-present threat of cooptation. However, 'the extent to which these practices contain the seeds of a successor to "actually existing neoliberalism" is also not known' (Donald and Blay-Palmer 2006, 1917).

More critical scholarship on agro-food politics (e.g. Guthman 2003, 2004, 2007, 2008a, 2008b, 2008c) argues that contemporary food politics are actually *anti*-politics that 'devolves regulatory responsibility to consumers via their dietary choices' (2003, 264). Much of what passes as agro-food politics is esthetic, Guthman (2003) explains, creating binary frames between 'good' and 'bad' food and thus ignoring the extensive links between the privileged participation in alternative agro-food networks and impoverished eating. It is the inequality itself that makes possible an esthetic of food. Guthman (2008b) argues that understanding agro-food politics vis-à-vis neoliberalization is necessary because 'it is precisely the neoliberalization of food and agriculture that many activists are opposing' (1172).

Scholars have specifically criticized claims made by Guthman (2003, 2004, 2007, 2008a, 2008b, 2008c) and others (Allen 2004, 2008; Allen and Guthman 2006; Pudup 2008) regarding the relationships between neoliberalization and agro-food alternatives for the lack of empirical evidence supporting said claims (Hayes-Conroy 2010; Kloppenburg and Hassanein 2006). Kloppenburg and Hassanein (2006) succinctly explain that critical scholarship provides 'a useful counterpoint to those of us who have enthusiastically embraced the wide range of [AFN] initiatives and projects', but the scholarship 'has not always been informed by an adequate recognition of the achievements and potentials of such approaches' and is 'inadequately supported by data' (417).

Indeed, we need fuller, more complex understandings of alternative agro-food that focuses on the material work of the many diverse efforts that fall under the broad agro-food movement umbrella. Scholarship is needed that focuses 'not so much on what [agro-food alternatives] *represent* ... but rather what they *do*' (Hayes-Conroy 2010, 66, emphasis added). This research, then, works to intervene in the literature using the data collected on urban agriculture in Brooklyn to weigh in on the distinction between AFN discourses and their material work. I also work to transcend this binary by explaining the disconnect materially through an understanding of urban agriculture emerging *within* the context of rollout neoliberalization.

Research design and methods

The relationship between agro-food alternatives and contemporary capitalism serves as the entry into my research: how does contemporary capitalism shape the political possibilities of urban agriculture as a struggle to address inequalities produced by conventional agro-food? To address this question, I used participatory observation and in-depth interviews to explore the relationship between urban agriculture and neoliberalization.

I study urban agriculture in Brooklyn as a case study, teasing out the complexities of the case through the triangulation of data (Naumes and Naumes 1999; Orum, Feagin, and Sjoberg 1991). Data were primarily collected through participatory observation, a method that provides opportunity to systematically observe and document behaviors and activities through active participation at research sites (Hennink, Hutter and Bailey 2011). I conducted two months of preliminary research to establish contacts and set up research sites (June–July 2008) and then conducted eight continuous months of qualitative fieldwork (January–August 2010).

Data for this article were collected at six distinct research sites of production, including three commercial farms and three not-for-profit farms. All six urban farms have paid staff, ranging at the time from one to four regular, full-time employees. The farms ranged in size from a 6,000 square foot rooftop commercial venture to a three acre spread on a former asphalt lot. One of the farm projects is actually multiple farm sites, including a 60 hen egg CSA, a one acre farm, and multiple backyard CSA sites.

Participant observation helped me to fully appreciate the lived spaces of urban farmers and the political positioning of their work. Participation also provided opportunity for me to develop reciprocal relationships in the field. While collecting data, I engaged fully in every aspect of food production and marketing activities, including composting, caring for hens and harvesting eggs, working the soil, harvesting, weeding, gathering resources throughout the city, retail marketing, and delivering produce to restaurants. I participated in the regular daily activities of urban agriculture at two of my research sites, including one commercial operation and one not-for-profit project. At these two sites, I completed weekly assigned chores. Additionally, I participated in workshops, trainings, meetings, conferences, and public hearings on urban agriculture policy (e.g. related to bee keeping and land access). I engaged in advocacy and activist efforts. At all six urban farm sites I attended regular volunteer workdays, whereby the farms were open to the public in exchange for voluntary labor. Through all of these experiences I engage in discussions with countless individuals, including ongoing conversations with urban farmers, regular exchanges with long-term farm volunteers, and brief encounters with market customers. These conversations included many discussions with high school aged youth participants in urban agriculture projects.

This participation provided access to Brooklyn's urban agriculture in ways not possible through other methods and provided me with first-hand experience to draw on for data. Through participant observation I was well positioned to gather data that would not have been available through other qualitative methods. This approach provided me with unique access opportunities and I was able to gain a full understanding of urban cultivation, including motivations for urban farming, views on the expansion of agro-food alternatives, and the politics of this work.

I kept detailed fieldnotes during my time in the field and transcribed them immediately after collection, including verbatim recordings of conversations when and where possible. Data collection and analysis were cyclical, whereby preliminary analysis informed ongoing research. I analyzed my fieldnotes through open coding and the identification of patterns, themes, and variations (Emerson, Fretz, and Shaw 1995).

During the entire research process, and after exiting the field, I collected a wide variety of documentary materials, including information from websites, newsletters, emails, listservs, brochures, leaflets, and workshop and conference programs. These materials helped to contextualize the urban farm projects, indicating, for example, the political orientation of projects through mission statements and highlighting the specific material work of the different farms through program descriptions, especially youth and education programs.

Interviews augmented data collected through participant observation (Babbie 1990; Dunn 2000). I conducted face-to-face, semi-structured interviews with 28 key informants in Brooklyn's growing urban agriculture movement, including urban farmers ($n = 5$), urban agriculture activists ($n = 9$), political leaders ($n = 5$), and project participants ($n = 9$). Of the 28 interviewees, 17 were women and 11 men; 20 were Caucasian and 9 African-American; all were between 25 and 50 years of age; and there was a widespread range of the years of experience with urban farming, one woman had been involved in some form of urban food production for 30 years whereas another interviewee was engaged in urban agriculture for only a few months.

Interviews were conducted at various points during fieldwork, but most occurred after data were collected through participant observation and preliminary analysis was underway. Interviewees were identified through snowball sampling based on initial contact information provided by two key organizations. This was a particularly useful approach to identifying potential interviewees within the tight social network of Brooklyn's urban agriculture movement (Hennink, Hutter, and Bailey 2011).

My goal in the interviews was to substantiate data collected through participant observation and to better understand the politics of urban agriculture through indepth conversations. I used an interview guide to gather perspectives and insights from leaders and other actors in Brooklyn's urban agriculture. I collected information on the rationales and outcomes of urban farming, including project motivations, program specifics, impacts of urban agriculture, barriers to both individual projects and the movement overall, and thoughts on the future of urban farming in Brooklyn. I used a conversational approach to my interviews, providing interviewees opportunity to focus on topics most relevant to the person and/or urban agriculture project (Babbie 1990; Dunn 2000; Hennink, Hutter, and Bailey 2011). Thus, each interview was co-constructed, whereby data were co-produced through conversation and through the interviewing process (Heyl 2002). Interviews were audio recorded and transcribed verbatim. Transcripts were closely read multiple times to gain a broad overview of the interviews and to develop an understanding of the key themes in relation to existing literature. Transcripts were then open coded and analyzed using HyperRESEARCH 2.8 software (www.researchware.com) to develop a detailed understanding of interviewee perspectives (Cresswell 2003). Direct quotes used in this article highlight particularly salient points or are otherwise illustrative of collected data.

Urban agriculture and youth programming in Brooklyn

Urban agriculture is any agricultural production – including the cultivation of crops and animal husbandry – both within and on the fringe of a metropolitan area. Urban agriculture is distinguished from rural agriculture in that it is embedded in an urban political ecology.

Scholars debate the precise definition of urban and peri-urban, but the definitions are always relational, depending on such things as population density and infrastructure development (particularly transit). As a result, 'urban agriculture' itself is loosely defined. Within dense city centers such as Brooklyn, urban agriculture is readily apparent. Urban agriculture may be found in a variety of locations, including backyard, patio, and rooftop gardens, commercial operations of all sizes, vacant lot cultivation, institutional gardens (e.g. schools, hospitals, and prisons), and community gardens. Urban agriculture takes place on private, public, and quasi-public (e.g. schoolyards) land, on residential property, and on proper commercial farms. Popular perceptions often view urban agriculture as a transitory redress for specific social, political, and economic problems, but advocates of urban agriculture insist on its permanence (Hodgson, Campbell, and Bailkey 2011; Mougeot 2006).

Urban farming has many potential benefits. Chief among them are (1) educational opportunities for youth; (2) subsistence production aimed at reducing urban hunger; (3) income generation and the development of employment opportunities; (4) social benefits including social integration, recreation, and community health; and (5) overall contributions to a city's ecology and to urban sustainability through the creation of green space, waste reduction, and resource conservation (Hodgson, Campbell, and Bailkey 2011; Mougeot 2006).

The many forms of urban agriculture detailed above are all found throughout contemporary Brooklyn. Indeed, Brooklyn is at the forefront of the emerging urban agriculture movement and thus provides an important research opportunity. Although Brooklyn's urban agriculture occurs mostly in community gardens, the urban agriculture renaissance in Brooklyn today is driven by the development of urban market farms, commercial projects (either entrepreneurial or not-for-profit initiatives) that operate on private property and are cultivated by paid farmers or professionals. In large part, the growth of market-oriented urban farming may be interpreted as an attempt to 'scale up' urban agriculture, an effort to produce greater quantities of food for wider distribution.

Youth programming figures prominently in the urban agriculture efforts emerging throughout Brooklyn today. Three of the six urban farms examined for this research focus *exclusively* on youth and another two have significant youth components to their farm projects. One farm is simply working to develop an economically viable model of urban agriculture. The urban farm projects work with youth by both partnering directly with neighborhood schools and through engagement of neighborhood youth in educational programs and employment opportunities. One farm is actually on public school grounds.

Projects focus on 'youth empowerment' programming that facilitates skills acquisition and fosters community engagement. As one interviewee notes:

> For this project, it's specifically using urban agriculture as a way to [support] young people in [neighborhood] as [neighborhood] has a particularly high population of youth ... So, for us ... wanting to address community need, parents wanted to see their children engaged in something positive and so when they were weighing in on what kind of program they wanted to create it definitely involved youth. (Personal interview, June 15, 2010)

Neighborhood youth is provided much-needed summer employment opportunities to create positive changes in their communities. Youth learn about the food system, about agricultural production, and examine neighborhood problems and solutions through first-hand perspectives. Through hands-on gardening and farming, students learn horticulture, environmental stewardship, nutrition, and health. There is a great deal of emphasis placed on 'leadership development,' whereby young persons learn how to lead work crews, develop communication skills, and enhance their problem-solving capabilities. Much focus is on the broad development of 'soft skills', the basic skills required of all employment opportunities, especially appropriate social interactions with colleagues and customers. One farm project director discusses the tangible outcomes of his efforts as evident in the visible changes in how his neighborhood is known to outsiders:

> And so [the farm is] a space where we could take the common phrase: 'kids these days and neighborhoods like these' and flip the script pretty easily. So all of a sudden the 'communities like these' were very interesting and the 'kids these days' were teaching you something and also providing you your basic food needs. (Personal interview, June 29, 2010)

Collected observational data and interviews indicate that education opportunities are the most import outcome of urban agriculture projects (Personal interviews, May 10, 2010; June 3, 2010; June 24, 2010; June 26, 2010; June 29, 2010). As one political leader notes: 'urban agriculture ... and school gardening and farm-to-school are on the map with Michelle Obama and with the farm at the White House [because] so much of that is driven by youth' (Personal interview, June 3, 2010).

This belief is also evident in the workings of the urban farm projects themselves, all of which have youth components. Programs include on-farm field trips, in-class lessons, paid internships, volunteer workdays, extra-curricular activities, and cooking and nutrition classes. Teaching kids about gardening and food, the argument goes, will teach them to make better choices as food consumers.

Youth programs support tangible and readily documented program successes (e.g. numbers of students reached, youth enrolled in programs, and/or other documented instances of youth involvement) and are key funding opportunities (i.e. funding is often more readily available to projects with youth components). As one urban farm project manager explains while discussing her new partnerships with schools: 'So, the other thing that's available for schools is a lot of grants ... [and] we started making money doing tours and other educational programs with other schools on our farm' (August 6, 2010). Another urban farmer notes: 'Our goal is to create funding resources through ... school gardening and farm-to-school [programming]' (Personal interview, June 3, 2010).

More importantly, it is widely understood that the most important impacts of urban agriculture are found within educating youth about food en route to learning healthy eating habits, creating an ethic of consumption, and for developing actors to participate in AFNs.

> [M]y god those kids don't know what a tomato is ... the educational components of [urban farms] are really the invaluable parts. (Personal interview, May 10, 2010)

> The kids will come off the basketball courts and walk right by food growing ... This is an important thing, just getting kids to *see* food growing around them. (Personal interview, June 15, 2010)

> It's kids asking me for lemon sorrel on the street 'cause that's what they tasted. It's our staff getting called 'Farmer X' and 'Farmer Y' and 'Farmer Z' on the street. It means the kids have an understanding of what it means to be a farmer, what it means to grow

food, what food tastes like. In the neighborhood those are some of the tangible impacts. (Personal interview, June 29, 2010)

Urban agriculture and the (re)production of neoliberalization

Urban agriculture can be an important source of food, especially in poor and working class neighborhoods[3] and can be a valuable tool for educating youth about food, nutrition, and the environment. But the provisioning emerges through focus on agrarian self-help approaches insisted upon by much neoliberal ideology. Although project participants all recognized the need for systemic agro-food changes, in practice solutions focused on teaching youth to create small, independent alternatives. After discussing problems associated with conventional agro-food, one urban agriculture activist notes: 'I realized I need to actually *work* the land' in order to effect change (Personal interview, June 21, 2010). Or as a project director explains: 'it's hard to find a good store or market [in our community] so we have to do it ourselves' (Personal interview, June 8, 2010). And while this is inspiring in many ways, the sentiment also shifts focus from the need to address fundamental inequalities that create food access disparities.

These statements illustrate the belief that the solution to agro-food problems lies with the individual, framed, as Callinicos (1999) explains, by the language of 'empowerment' but still defining problems as resulting from individual shortcomings. Urban agriculture programs operate under the assumption that individual agrarian efforts can improve consumption choices through education and hands-on learning. A state program director explains her job as primarily education within urban geographies of hunger/obesity:

> I tend to do a lot of work in the communities with the greatest of need in terms of access to healthy produce, highest rates of obesity and diabetes. Our job here at the Department is to try to get local food in to those communities and make connections with education programs and other programs that mean people will actually eat the local foods that end up there. (Personal interview, June 3, 2010)

This Department does the material work of trying to improve 'local' food availability and teaching people how to eat. There is no focus on expanding normal forms of food access taken for granted by many Americans (i.e. grocery stores), the material needs that transcend the lack of 'local' food, or class relations that shape food access. This state initiative works to expand access and thus addresses an important limiting feature of neoliberal agro-food. But the goal is still to change personal consumption habits, itself a neoliberal solution, rather than to directly confront structural inequalities that produce food disparities.

The neoliberal shaping of urban agriculture is embedded in the assumption that knowledge and individualized efforts, and overcoming the shortcomings in each, will yield systemic change. 'If only people knew where their food comes from' has become an unquestioned belief within food activist circles, the assumption being that people experience violence at the hands of capitalist agro-food because of limitations in *their* knowledge base. The accepted wisdom is that imparting knowledge on consumer choice to the uneducated masses will drive the agro-food revolution. As one urban farmer noted: 'The purpose of growing a good tomato in this town is to get people talking about where good food comes from',[4] as in: 'if only people knew' ... then young Brooklynites would make better food choices. That same farmer concluded: 'the real question is can we tap into ourselves again [and grow food]?' The implication being that agro-food system changes rely on individualized bootstrap efforts. Although more transparency in the agro-food system is needed, the implication of this thinking is that consumption patterns are shaped by individual choices made by consumers who ought to know better than to opt for unhealthy food-like options. There is nothing wrong with knowing where your food comes from, per se, and this is certainly better than the industrial capitalist alternative, but this view overlooks the broader structures shaping patterns of food consumption.

One leader of a well-known urban farm project explains: 'What we say is: "we are not growing farmers, we are growing ... conscious producers and consumers of both food and knowledge" and if we get a farmer out of one that's great' (Personal interview, June 29, 2010). Statements like these raise a very important question regarding the role of urban production: when does urban farming pose a challenge to neoliberalization?

Although this is an open question to a certain degree, in Brooklyn much urban agriculture is less a challenge to neoliberalization and more a form of entrepreneurialism. On the one hand, the youth involvement provides much-needed jobs in neighborhoods sorely lacking economic opportunities, engages youth in educational projects that build knowledge, and help youth to develop important skills. On the other hand, the youth projects are all framed as 'entrepreneurial', disciplining youth to be good neoliberal subjects, trained in the skills and modes of conduct required by the neoliberal economy and its 'cult of entrepreneurship'.[5]

Building local alternatives is the goal of agro-food efforts aimed at the very visible problems produced by the neoliberalization of agro-food. At the same time, however, the focus of the efforts on local alternatives is itself (re)producing neoliberalization in many ways. This focus matters precisely because as my observational data indicate, the urban agriculture programs examined through this research themselves view urban cultivation as an *inherently* political act, and this is clearly not always the case. Urban agriculture and other food projects address some socio-ecological contradictions of agro-food (e.g. hunger, human health impacts, environmental destruction) without fully struggling against the processes of neoliberalization that produce these contradictions, and are themselves a form of rollout neoliberalization (Allen 2004; Guthman 2008a, 2008b, 2008c).

Neoliberalism emerges in the dialectic between the discursive and the material. Urban agriculture projects work with youth to 'build the next generation of leaders' (Personal interview, June 29, 2010) or to address food system problems that materialize most acutely in young bodies. But the projects do not develop leaders of social struggle. Political awareness and activist tools are not developed. Instead, the urban agriculture youth programs help to form neoliberal subjects who will not challenge the status quo but instead focus on individual responsibility. Participants in urban agriculture efforts focus on self-improvement, via dietary choices, or entrepreneurial efforts to expand food options instead of political action.

The sentiment that individual agrarian efforts will save America and the agro-food system will be changed one slow meal at a time was repeated throughout my research. As one interview with a project coordinator explained about her neighborhood, located in a recognized food desert: 'it's hard to find a good food store or market so we have to do it ourselves' (Personal interview, June 8, 2010). And there may be something to the focus on personal effort if collectivized. As reflected in the lack of food options, the market has indeed failed many neighborhoods in Brooklyn, and the solution might lie in 'do[ing] it ourselves' (Personal interview, June 8, 2010). This notion recognizes political economic failures and calls for engaged social action to address these failures. Yet these efforts simply materialize in a do-it-yourself (DIY) esthetic.

Through rollout forms, neoliberal ideology is entrenched in everyday consciousness and emerges in material form. As a result, neoliberal subjectivity is as prevalent as ever. Within AFNs and movements, as the data illustrate, neoliberal ideology is so pervasive that Margaret Thatcher's truism 'there is no alternative' takes on new dimensions as alternative projects literally (re)produce neoliberalization. 'In a sense', Guthman (2008b) argues, 'activists produce neoliberal forms not because they embrace a particular discourse, but because neoliberalism is in many ways *characterized* by these emergent forms' (1, emphasis added).

I do not want to undermine the emancipatory potentials of *all* agro-food efforts. Brenner and Theodore (2002, 376) remind us that neoliberalization may also provide political openings:

> At the present time, it remains to be seen whether the powerful contradictions inherent within the current urbanized formation of roll-out neoliberalism will provide openings for more progressive, radical democratic appropriations of city space, or whether, by contrast, neoliberal agendas will be entrenched still further within the underlying institutional structures of urban governance.

The data indicate that for now, Brooklyn's urban agriculture works to entrench neoliberal urban governance rather than exploit political openings through social struggle. Notably, however, many urban farm projects are starting to incorporate explicit political organizing and training work into their youth programs. For example, one organization recently completed a mapping project with youth to understand systems of inequality shaping food access. Another organization conducted a political organizing training for their youth. Thus, as the data also illustrate, there are clear exceptions to patterns of rollout neoliberalization and/or political openings created by urban agriculture that could be exploited.

Cultivating the city is itself claimed by my research participants to be a political act. Indeed, there are many excellent examples of efforts working toward emancipatory goals, toward the formation of a politics of food justice. The role played by urban farm projects in creating agro-food alternatives is necessary but not sufficient for the transformation of capitalist agro-food. Brooklyn's urban agriculture is creating political openings that may pave the way for subsequent politics of justice, but we should not fool ourselves into reading more into urban agriculture than currently exists; urban agriculture in Brooklyn is not yet poised to help spark an agro-food revolution. Significantly, many working within an alternative food framework recognize the limitations of this approach for failing to wage a larger battle:

> It's a pretty critical point right now for [food and agriculture] in the U.S. ... I think there are a lot of promising trends that are going to help people have access to better food ... programs like this [youth farming project] are hopefully changing people's attitudes, but it's not going to be enough if people buy some of their produce at their farmers' market or they support a few local farmers. It's going to take a lot more to really make a big impact. (Personal interview, June 15, 2010)

Concluding thoughts

Building local alternatives is the goal of agro-food efforts aimed at the very visible socio-ecological problems produced by the neoliberalization agro-food, including hunger, public health consequences of conventional food, and the negative environmental impacts of the system as a whole. In that way, urban agriculture emerges as a struggle against neoliberalization. At the same time, however, the focus of the efforts (re)produces neoliberalization in many ways. Many food initiatives cropping up today do not fully struggling against the processes of neoliberalization that are at the heart of socio-environmental contradictions (Allen 2004; Guthman 2008a, 2008b, 2008c). In fact, it is precisely the education and youth programming of Brooklyn's urban agriculture projects that highlight the neoliberalization of food politics whereby agro-food alternatives often embody key neoliberal characteristics that confine the politics of resistance. The anomaly that agro-food politics and the scholarship that supports it (re)produce neoliberalization rests in large part on the (often inadvertent) acquiescence to market logics.

Building on the work of Guthman (2003, 2004, 2007, 2008a, 2008b, 2008c) and others (Allen 2004, 2008; Allen and Guthman 2006; Pudup 2008), I employed a critical lens to examine urban cultivation within its neoliberal confines. I specifically did not want to produce a celebratory account in the vein of much current agro-food scholarship, and the alternative economic spaces literature more broadly, without fully exploring the extent to which urban farms are truly liberated forms of economic activity (Samers 2005). Indeed, the data indicate that urban agriculture youth projects are decidedly *not* liberated from capitalism. Yet there are spaces of hope, where the growing consciousness of food issues may serve as an entry into broader critiques of contemporary capitalism.

A growing body of scholarship now focuses on *diverse* economies and *alternative economic spaces* (e.g. Gibson-Graham 1996, 2006, 2008). This 'anti-essentialist' approach, as J.K. Gibson-Graham (2008, 615) calls it, eschews understanding structural logics in favor of a focus on the contingency of socioeconomic processes and the 'performative orientation to knowledge rather than a realist or reflective one'. Clearly, this approach *could* explain Brooklyn's urban agriculture. But my interests were to explore the limitations of urban farming as currently practiced in Brooklyn in order to understand the ways urban farming relates to capitalism rather than merely 'think capitalism away' (Castree 1999). And, as the specific examples of youth and educational programming highlight, capitalism directly confronts urban agriculture materially and thus curtails the emancipatory potentials of urban farming.

Notes

1. Author conducted all interviews; names and affiliations have been excluded to maintain anonymity.
2. Agro-food is shorthand for the agriculture and food system(s), signifying an understanding that food and agriculture and linked systems and need to be understood and analyzed as such. Used in the singular to denote the hegemonic industrialized, conventional, globalized, capitalist, etc. system (i.e. traditional big ag); agro-food systems can also include various alternatives.
3. Fieldnotes, 8 June 2010: urban farms provide the only decent option in poorer neighborhoods, this becomes *obvious* through field work.
4. Fieldnotes, *CSA in NYC*, Just Food Annual Conference, February 28 2010.

5. Mitchell's (2008, 11) endearing term for the insidious efforts to implement 'a certain kind of neoliberal capitalism in which ... accumulation – that is the chasing of money – is *always* a function of dispossession'.

Notes on contributor

Evan Weissman is an assistant professor of food studies in the Department of Public Health, Food Studies, and Nutrition in the David B. Falk College of Sport and Human Dynamics and Syracuse University. His research focuses on efforts to address food system inequalities within American cities, and he is a founding member and currently serves on the board of Syracuse Grows, a food justice network promoting urban agriculture and community gardening.

References

Allen, Patricia. 2004. *Together at the Table: Sustainability and Sustenance in the American Agrifood System*. University Park: Pennsylvania State University Press.

Allen, Patricia. 2008. "Mining for Justice in the Food System: Perceptions, Practices, and Possibilities." *Agriculture and Human Values* 25: 157–161.

Allen, Patricia, Margaret FitzSimmons, Michael Goodman, and Kurt Warner. 2003. "Shifting Plates in the Agrifood Landscape: The Tectonics of Alternative Agrifood Initiatives in California." *Journal of Rural Studies* 19: 61–75.

Allen, Patricia, and Julie Guthman. 2006. "From 'Old School' to 'Farm-to-school': Neoliberalization from the Ground Up." *Agriculture and Human Values* 23: 401–415.

Babbie, Earl. 1990. *Survey Research Methods*. 2nd ed. Belmont, CA: Wadsworth.

Bakker, Karen. 2007. "The 'Commons' versus the 'Commodity': Alter-globalization, Anti-privatization and the Human Right to Water in the Global South." *Antipode* 39: 430–455.

Brenner, Neil, and Nik Theodore. 2002. "Cities and Geographies of 'Actually Existing Neoliberalism'." *Antipode* 34: 349–379.

Callinicos, Alex. 1999. *Social Theory: A Historical Introduction*. Cambridge: Polity.

Castree, Noel. 1999. "Envisioning Capitalism: Geography and the Renewal of Marxian Political Economy." *Transactions of the Institute of British Geographers* 24: 137–158.

Castree, Noel. 2006. "From Neoliberalism to Neoliberalisation: Consolations, Confusions, and Necessary Illusions." *Environment and Planning A* 38: 1–6.

Castree, Noel. 2007a. "Neoliberalizing Nature: The Logics of Deregulation and Reregulation." *Environment and Planning A* 40: 131–152.

Castree, Noel. 2007b. "Neoliberalizing Nature: Processes, Effects, and Evaluations." *Environment and Planning A* 40: 153–173.

Cresswell, John. 2003. *Research Design: Qualitative, Quantitative, and Mixed Methods*. 2nd ed. Thousand Oaks, CA: Sage.

Donald, Betsy, and Alison Blay-Palmer. 2006. "The Urban Creative-food Economy: Producing Food for the Urban Elite or Social Inclusion Opportunity?" *Environment and Planning A* 38: 1901–1920.

Dunn, Kevin. 2000. "Interviewing." In *Qualitative Research Methods in Human Geography*, edited by I. Hay, 50–82. New York: Oxford University Press.

Emerson, Robert, Rachel Fretz, and Linda Shaw. 1995. *Writing Ethnographic Fieldnotes*. Chicago, IL: University of Chicago Press.

Gibson-Graham, J. K. 1996. *The End of Capitalism (As We Knew It)*. Cambridge, MA: Blackwell.

Gibson-Graham, J. K. 2006. *Postcapitalist Politics*. Minneapolis: University of Minnesota Press.

Gibson-Graham, J. K. 2008. "Diverse Economies: Performative Practices for 'Other Worlds'." *Progress in Human Geography* 32: 613–632.

Goodman, David, E. Melanie DuPuis, and Michael Goodman. 2012. *Alternative Food Networks: Knowledge, Practice, and Politics*. London: Routledge.

Guthman, Julie. 2003. "Fast Food/Organic Food: Reflexive Tastes and the Making of 'Yuppie Chow'." *Social and Cultural Geography* 4: 45–58.

Guthman, Julie. 2004. *Agrarian Dreams: The Paradox of Organic Farming in California*. Berkeley: The University of California Press.

Guthman, Julie. 2007. "The Polanyian Way? Voluntary Food Labels as Neoliberal Governance." *Antipode* 39: 456–478.

Guthman, Julie. 2008a. "Bringing Good Food to Others: Investigating the Subjects of Alternative Food Practice." *Cultural Geographies* 15: 431–447.

Guthman, Julie. 2008b. "Neoliberalism and the making of Food Politics in California." *Geoforum* 39: 1171–1183.

Guthman, Julie. 2008c. "Thinking Inside the Neoliberal Box: The Micro-politics of Agro-food Philanthropy." *Geoforum* 39: 1241–1253.

Harvey, David. 2005. *A Brief History of Neoliberalism*. Oxford: Oxford University Press.

Hayes-Conroy, Jessica. 2010. "School Gardens and 'Actually Existing' Neoliberalism." *Humboldt Journal of Social Relations* 33: 64–94.

Hennink, Monique, Inge Hutter, and Ajay Bailey. 2011. *Qualitative Research Methods*. Thousand Oaks, CA: Sage.

Heyl, Barbara. 2002. "Ethnographic Interviewing." In *Handbook of Ethnography*, edited by P. Atkinson, S. Delamont, A. Coffey, J. Lofland, and L. Lofland, 369–383. Thousand Oaks, CA: Sage.

Heynen, Nik, Maria Kaika, and Erik Swyngedouw. 2006. *In the Nature of Cities: Urban Political Ecology and the Politics of Urban Metabolism*. New York: Routledge.

Heynen, Nik, and Paul Robbins. 2005. "The Neoliberalization of Nature: Governance, Privatization, Enclosure and Valuation." *Capitalism, Nature, Socialism* 16: 5–8.

Hodgson, Kimberly, Marcia Campbell, and Martin Bailkey. 2011. *Urban Agriculture: Growing Healthy, Sustainable Places*. Chicago, IL: American Planning Association.

Kloppenburg, Jack Jr., and Neva Hassanein. 2006. "From Old School to Reform School?" *Agriculture and Human Values* 23: 417–421.

Koc, Mustafa, and Kenneth Dahlberg. 1999. "The Restructuring of Food Systems: Trends, Research, and Policy Issues." *Agriculture and Human Values* 16: 109–116.

Lautenschlager, Lauren, and Chery Smith. 2007. "Beliefs, Knowledge, and Values held by Inner-city Youth about Gardening, Nutrition, and Cooking." *Agriculture and Human Values* 24: 245–258.

Mansfield, Becky. 2004. "Rules of Privatization: Contradictions in Neoliberal Regulation of North Pacific Fisheries." *Annals of the Association of American Geographers* 94: 565–584.

Mitchell, Don. 2008. "The Insidious Work of the University." *Human Geography* 1: 9–11.

Mougeot, Luc J. A. 2006. *Growing better Cities: Urban Agriculture for Sustainable Development*. Ottawa, ON: International Development Research Centre.

Naumes, William, and Margaret Naumes. 1999. *The Art and Craft of Case Writing*. Thousand Oaks, CA: Sage.

Orum, Anthony, Joe Feagin, and Gideon Sjoberg. 1991. "Introduction: The Nature of Case Studies." In *A Case for the Case Study*, edited by J. Feagin, A. Orum, and G. Sjoberg, 1–26. Chapel Hill, NC: UNC Press.

Peck, Jamie, and Adam Tickell. 2002. "Neoliberalizing Space." *Antipode* 34: 380–404.

Pudup, Mary Beth. 2008. "It Takes a Garden: Cultivating Citizen-subjects in Organized Garden Projects." *Geoforum* 39: 1228–1240.

Renting, Henk, Terry Marsden, and Jo Banks. 2003. "Understanding Alternative Food Networks: Exploring the Role of Short Food Supply Chains in Rural Development." *Environment and Planning A* 35: 393–411.

Samers, Michael. 2005. "The Myopia of 'Diverse Economies', or a Critique of the 'Informal Economy." *Antipode* 37: 875–886.

Watts, Michael. 2000. "Agro-food System." In *The Dictionary of Human Geography*, edited by R. J. Johnston, D. Gregory, G. Pratt, and M. Watts, 15–17. Oxford: Blackwell.

Sustainability science and education in the neoliberal ecoprison

Peter C. Little

Department of Anthropology, Rhode Island College, Providence, RI, USA

> As part of the general 'greening' of prisons in the last decade of neoliberalization and the formation of institutionalized programs to provide science and environmental education opportunities for the incarcerated, the Sustainability in Prisons Project (SPP), a partnership between Evergreen State College and the Washington State Department of Corrections, has become the most vibrant partnership in the US to mesh the cultures and institutions of environmental science and corrections. Drawing attention to the SPP's anchoring mission, which is 'to bring science and nature into prisons,' this article looks at environmental science education in the contemporary prison in light of recent discussions of neoliberal science and eco-biopolitical theory, with the final aim of developing what amounts to a carceral political ecology of environmental education amid an ever expanding neoliberal penal State.

Introduction

Think about what Michel Foucault said about gardens: 'The garden is the smallest parcel of the world and then it is the totality of the world. The garden has been a sort of happy, universalizing heterotopia since the beginnings of antiquity' (Foucault 1984, 47). Now think about gardens, horticulture, environmental education, and sustainability science *within* the prison environment. Think of ecocarcerality and how sustainability science and education in the prison become a site of biopower, a disciplinary technology, to use Foucault's terminology. This is the thematic focus of what follows, an article that cracks open the emerging eco-prison, that is, the contemporary marriage of neoliberal sustainability and penality. The emergence of penal environmental science education, it will be argued, calls for an approach attentive to contemporary critiques of the 'penal State' (Wacquant 2002, 2010a, 2010b, 2012a, 2012b, 2012c), as well as nuanced perspectives on neoliberal science and environmental biopolitics.

The current neoliberal situation (Harvey 2005, 2007; Giroux 2008; Graeber 2010; Chomsky 2011), a political, economic, technological, scientific, social, and ecological age illustrated best by the growing surplus of intrusive privatization, marketization, and bureaucratization schemes to order and manage central domains of life and living (e.g. work, education, health care, and habitat), is also a moment of late industrial society marked by mass imprisonment or hyperincarceration (Alexander 2010). Prisons and prison policies today are symbolic markers of neoliberal state transformation or 'state crafting' (Wacquant 2010b) and the numbers help illustrate any discussion of so-called 'Lockdown America' (Parenti 1999) or our 'Prison Nation' (Herivel and Wright 2003). According to the most recent estimates provided by the US Department of Justice's Bureau of Prisons, there are over 2.2 million adults incarcerated in federal and state prisons in the US. With the highest incarceration rate in the world – for every 100,000 people, 743 are currently incarcerated, and the US beats the runner up Russia (with 577 inmates per 100,000) by a healthy margin. One in every 15 African–American men and one in every 36 Hispanic men are incarcerated in comparison to one in every 106 white men, and 16% of the adult prison population suffers from mental illness and 20% of inmates report sexual and other forms of abuse while in prison. Furthermore, roughly two-thirds of those released from US jails and prisons end up returning within three years, and one in three men of color can expect to go to prison in their lifetime (Alexander 2010).

This mass incarceration trend in the US and especially the jarring racial politics of our age of hyperincarceration, it has been argued, are a powerful signal of the rising penal State, of 'punitive governance' (Lancaster 2010) informed by neoliberal craftsmanship. As Wacquant (2012a) contends,

> we cannot understand policing and prison policies in advanced societies today unless we place them in the framework of a broader *transformation of the state*, a transformation that is itself linked to a makeover of wage work and a shift in the balance of power between the classes and assorted groups struggling over its control. In this struggle, transnational corporations and the 'modernising' factions of the bourgeoisie and state nobility have formed an alliance under the banner of neoliberalism, gained the upper hand and launched a sweeping campaign to revamp public authority on the labour, welfare and penal fronts. Economic deregulation, the rise of precarious wage work ... and the ascent of the punitive state, go hand in hand: the 'invisible hand' of the precarized labour market finds its institutional counterpart in the 'iron fist' of a state that redeploys its forces so as to suppress or contain the *dislocations and disorders generated by the spread of social insecurity.* (Wacquant 2012, 2, emphasis in original)

Such a neoliberal prison perspective, I will argue here, matters to eco-prison or eco-penality studies of the 'greener' sort, that is, studies tuning into the practices of 'ecologizing' 'factions of the bourgeoisie' and their emerging alliances with penal State nobility (e.g. state corrections personnel) and environmental scientists and educators (Ulrich and Nadkarni 2009). Bringing such critical discussions of the penal State into the 'green prison' movement (Judd 2008; Stohr and Wozniak 2014) – a movement also marked by a growing discourse of 'green criminology' (Lynch and Stretesky 2003; Beirne and South 2006, 2007; Benton 2007) addressing the criminality of environmental pollution and earthly destruction – is a wide open area of contemplation and interrogation that is, as will be discussed below, attracting environmental scientists and educators working to develop environmental or 'sustainability' programs in prisons.

The article will be organized as follows. First, I explore the recent work of the Sustainability in Prisons Project (SPP), a university-corrections partnership that is quickly creating the mold, the model for how to mesh sustainability science and practice with the aims of State corrections facilities. As an environmental anthropologist fascinated by this sustainability project (Little 2013), I will argue that the SPP provides a vibrant case of State–university alliance intended to fully integrate the logics of penality and sustainability expertise in our institutional age of environmental knowledge accumulation and neoliberal science. Next, I discuss how this move to what might be thought of in a variety of different terms, 'ecobiopolitics' (Olson 2010), carceral political ecology, ecocarcerality, and ecopenality, opens up new terrain for critical environmental education studies *of* and *in* prisons, as well as fertile ground for forging linkages between various fields, including the anthropology of prisons (Rhodes 2001, 2004; McCorkel 2013), environmental justice studies, political ecology, and science and technology studies. In what follows, I aim to both productively critique the greening of prisons and illustrate the constructive possibilities of sustainability science and education in prisons. While certainly a move that generates more questions than explanations, attending to both 'critique' and 'possibility' is a more genuine path toward honoring the complexities, conundrums, and deep contradictions at work in a neoliberal age of precarious synthesis between ecology and economy and, for the purposes here, between sustainability and penality.

The sustainability in prisons project

The SPP, a partnership between Evergreen State College and the Washington State Department of Corrections (DOC), has become the most vibrant project in the country to mesh the cultures of sustainability science and corrections. The SPP's goal is rather straightforward: 'Our mission is to bring science and nature into prisons. We conduct ecological research and conserve biodiversity by forging collaborations with scientists, inmates, prison staff, students, and community partners. Equally important, we help reduce the environmental, economic, and human costs of prisons by inspiring and informing sustainable practices' (LeRoy et al. 2012). Among its many accomplishments, the SPP's projects have saved correction facilities millions of dollars by creating recycling and energy-saving programs and they have made major progress in restoring populations of an endangered species of frogs (e.g. Oregon Spotted Frogs) and rearing endangered butterflies (e.g. Taylor's checkerspot butterflies). The SPP's partners continue to grow, but some prominent players include the following: The Nature Conservancy, the National Science Foundation, US Department of Defense, the US Fish and Wildlife Service, and the Center for Natural Lands Management.

Established in 2005 in Washington State, the SPP has already helped to develop sustainability projects in prisons in 14 states and is quickly gaining international attention, with three countries beginning to adopt SPP's ecological research and biodiversity conservation approach. Engaged in projects at minimum, medium, and maximum security prisons, the SPP works to forge collaborations with prison staff and inmates to carry out a variety of activities, including, but not limited, endangered species and ecological restoration, horticulture, water conservation, green purchasing and procurement, zero-waste garbage sorting and composting, as well as bicycle and wheelchair restoration. Recently, the SPP received funding from the National Institute of Corrections to develop a 'Sustainability 101' curriculum to be offered to Washington DOCs staff and prisoners, a curriculum aimed at addressing 'why and how sustainability can be improved and provide specific information about how to get involved with programs at the local facility' (LeRoy et al. 2012, 79). As this educational goal indicates, the SPP aims to provide environmental education opportunities for both prisoners and corrections staff.

The SPP is driven by meeting a diversity of interests. They adopt a multi-stakeholder commitment approach, seeking ways to make SPP programs meet the interests of offenders, the environmental education community, the science education community, as well as officers, administrators, and the general public (SPP 2012, 37). For prisoners, according to the SPP, their programs allow for 'increased opportunities for intellectual stimulation' and 'improvement in knowledge and workplace skills' (2012, 37). For the environmental education community, these programs lead to an 'improved understanding of the environment' and an 'increase in environmental stewardship' (37). For the science education community, SPP programs help increase 'interest and engagement in science-learning' (ibid.). And finally, for corrections administrators, officers, and the general public, the programs lead to 'cost-effective prison operations,' and have the capacity to lead to a 'reduction in behavioral infractions,' and a 'reduction in recidivism rates' (ibid.).

Much of the SPP's success, it should be added, is due to the fact that one of the cofounders is now the Director of Prisons for the Washington State DOCs, and as one SPP staff explained it to me, 'without him on board and being an advocate for this program, it would never have gotten off the ground.' Put another way, the very merger of the goals of sustainability science and corrections fit within what Foucault's biopower perspective has been about all along: 'it is precisely when these technologies [and knowledges] find a localization within specific institutions (schools, hospitals, prisons), when they "invest" these institutions, that biopower really begins its take-off' (Dreyfus and Rabinow 1982, 185). Moreover, the SPP has made sustainability science and education 'productive' by its very merger with the prison system, arguably the most powerful institution since antiquity. The implementation of environmental science and education in prisons, it will be argued below, is linked to the productive and reformative logic of prisons.

Toward eco-prisons

We might find it useful to think of the SPP as a faction of sustainability practitioners engaged in synthesizing sustainability science, environmental education, and penal functionality, a move rooted in earlier prison horticulture projects (Jiler 2006). The so-called 'green' prison movement (Judd 2008; Stohr and Wozniak 2014) has penetrated the major institutions of corrections, namely the National Institute of Corrections (NIC) and the American Corrections Association (ACA). For example, the NIC's recent development of a report entitled *The Greening of Corrections: Creating a Sustainable System* (NIC 2011) and holding of a national symposium on the topic in 2011 showcases the federal interest meshing sustainability and penality. The ACA is yet another institutional player in upholding the 'sustainability' turn in the US prison system. It has, for example, developed new accreditation standards requiring 'facilities seeking accreditation to demonstrate that they have examined, and where appropriate and feasible, implemented strategies that promote recycling, energy and water conservation, pollution reduction and utilization of renewable energy alternatives' (Atherton and Sheldon 2011, 3).

Washington State's SPP hosts environmental and conservation work programs that aim to inspire positive changes in prisoner attitudes, to help reduce recidivism, to provide educational and vocational training opportunities, therapeutic benefits, and 'opportunities to contribute' – a DOCs term – to the 'community' beyond prison walls. According to a recent study (Gallagher 2013) based on a statewide survey of inmates ($n = 293$) comparing inmates with sustainability-related jobs and a control group with non-sustainability-related jobs, found that offenders whose jobs involved more education and training, or who worked with 'living things,' or had 'opportunities to contribute' to the community, tended to score higher on the New Ecological Paradigm Scale (Dunlap and Van Liere 1978; Dunlap et al. 2000; Dunlap 2008), a questionnaire that assesses environmental attitudes and is commonly used in environmental education studies. Gallagher (2013) found that these high scores indicate that these elements of inmate participation in SPP programs are associated with more pro-environmental attitudes and that because pro-environmental attitudes have been correlated with pro-social attitudes (Hines, Hungerford, and Tomera 1987; Bamberg and Möser 2007), her research suggested that SPP and the Washington State DOCs consider incorporating more of these sustainability-related jobs into other work programs.

SPP staff are fully aware of the crux of meshing ecology and corrections, of meshing environmental science and prison culture, and they are also cognizant of the brittle political–economic dimensions of their 'sustainable practices,' even if, as Harvey (1996) famously put it, 'all ecological projects (and arguments),' whether within or outside prison walls, 'are simultaneously political–economic projects (and arguments) and vice versa' (Harvey 1996, 182). SPP scientists and educators are sensitive to the politics of prison labor and 'careful,' as one SPP staff put it, 'not to take advantage of inmates in the work we do.' This is where the so-called political ecology of prisons gets interesting, the point at which the SPP's mission 'to bring science and nature to prisons' is met with a culture of caring for inmate education and advocating for their involvement in sustainability and conservation projects, as well as in the production of environmental science and knowledge. SPP staff, in this sense, are in a continual navigation of possible exploitation, and they are careful to avoid, the best they can, any form of inmate disempowerment. 'It can get tricky,' as one SPP staff put it. SPP staff continually highlight the educational component of the SPP and view inmate involvement in SPP projects as 'opportunities to contribute' – again, a DOCs term – and not inmate exploitation. The educational focus, in this sense, counters the prison labor concern (Lafer 2003) which is ultimately an uneasiness with what has been termed 'carceral Keynesianism' (Parenti 1999) or how prison labor mimics 'public-work style stimulus' (Parenti 1999, 217). Wacquant offers a similar angle on prison labor, suggesting that it is a myth that prisons and prison labor have economic benefits:

> Putting convicts to work is not a practical proposition in contemporary society, for a host of legal and economic reasons. Contrary to the claims of the critics of the so-called 'prison-industrial complex', incarceration is not a profitable 'industry' for society because its costs are astronomical ($25,000 per inmate per year in a California state penitentiary and $70,000 in New York county jail) and it generates no wealth. It is a gross drain on the public coffers that is profoundly irrational from a capitalistic standpoint. The private operators that benefit from the prison boom are minor players who exploit the bureaucratic rigidities of the state downstream, not strategic actors that impact penal policy upstream. (Wacquant 2012a, 5)

While Wacquant is right to point out that we are witnessing a reintroduction of 'deskilled labor behind bars' (Wacquant 2012b, 215; see also Harcourt 2012), I find it less convincing to say that SPP-related work is 'deskilled' labor. It turns out that much of SPP prison labor is skilled 'scientific' work. In fact, one inmate involved in one of the SPP programs went on to get a PhD in biology after his release. Sure, it is a serious minority population with access to this 'skilled' labor, but it is happening and therefore should figure somewhere in our fields of penal critique.

Among SPP staff I have spoken with, there is also an orbiting ethos of 'ecohealth' and 'ecotherapy' (Frumkin 2012; Hasbach 2012) that informs much of the work that SPP and their partners do, that building inmate–earth relationships has some level of healing power. For example, in one interview, I was told 'I really feel that to have a physical connection with the planet, whether working with soil or working with frogs, it can only have a beneficial impact on your physical and mental health and wellbeing.' The work of the SPP illustrates how spaces of incarceration are becoming simultaneously spaces of environmental science production and sustainability practice, even neoliberal institutional arrangements where environmental identities can be made possible and where environmental education is carefully used to reduce recidivism. This transformation process, which the SPP is playing a central role and which one prisoner likened to the transformation that occurs during composting, is a vibrant example of what McCorkel (2013) calls 'habilitation,' or a social technology intended 'to "break down" a self that is incomplete and disordered' (McCorkel 2013, 17). In the words of one prisoner involved in an SPP program at the Cedar Creek Correctional Facility in Washington who posted his story of 'transformation' on the SPP Website:

> By utilizing this opportunity to participate in this program I have gained so much knowledge and wisdom in these fields. I feel as though the information I've accumulated from this experience is one of my most cherished possessions. And this is why: gardening is all about rebirth. You see, you plant a seed in the proper soil with the correct amount of nutrients and in the correct timing of year and up grows this beautiful plant full of life. This same concept I believe applies to my life situation. I have been reborn into a better individual. By no means am I saying that my incarceration is rebirth. More so, my positive and productive choices that I have made have been my rebirth process.

Much of this discourse on the transformative and even 'habilitative' effect of prisoner involvement in sustainability science and education gets at what Olson (2010) might call 'ecobiopolitics,' an extension of biopolitical theory which I explore further below. 'For now at least, this prisoner's narrative illustrates how rebirth and 'life itself' (Rose 2007) reflection is informed by his direct involvement in an SPP garden project.

Environmental knowledge and prison ecobiopolitics

As environmental education researchers have shown, the very institutionalization of environmental education can and often does undermine the transformative goals and logics of environmental education programs (Martin 1996; Gruenewald 2004). According to Gruenewald (2004), the issue comes largely down to the crux of education itself:

> The ultimate challenge for education, environmental or otherwise, is to prepare people [and prisoners] with the skills and knowledge needed to identify and shape the quality of the world we share with others – human and nonhuman; in a multicultural and political world, this means education for cultural competence and political participation. (Gruenewald 2004, 72)

As environmental education scholars have pointed out, one of the primary struggles of informing educational programs with ecological and environmental learning opportunities and curricula is that ecological knowledge itself was often marginalized from mainstream or general education (Gruenewald 2004). Until the SPP appeared on the corrections scene in 2004, environmental education in prisons basically did not exist, though the prison context, which the SPP has attempted to change, causes it to focus on two entangled questions: what happens when subjugated and neglected knowledge is brought into an environment of strict social subjugation and marginalization? How does environmental science education become hegemonic when deployed in spaces of human confinement and subjugation? Both questions re-anchor the discussion back to Foucault, who had much to say about 'subjugated knowledges.' He meant two things by this term. First, he contended, these knowledges were present in historic 'functional and systemic ensembles' – like the prison – but were dwarfed or excluded from exposure. Second, these knowledges were, as he puts it, 'disqualified as nonconceptual knowledges, as insufficiently elaborated knowledges: naïve knowledges, hierarchically inferior knowledges, knowledges that are below the required level of erudition or scientificity' (Foucault [1976] 2003, 7). In light of this perspective, the very environmental knowledge of prisoners working on SPP projects is largely 'qualified' by their relationship to and opportunity to work with SPP scientists. Prisoner environmental knowledges are far from 'inferior' when such knowledges are the outcome of SPP projects, that is, projects guided by scientific rigor.

The environmental science and education programs the SPP and its partners are engaging in are inter- and intra-institutional practices and transformations tightly wrapped up in the prison reform game that has typified the prison system for centuries. As Foucault put it,

> One should recall that the movement for reforming the prisons, for controlling their functioning is not a recent phenomenon. It does not seem to have originated in a recognition of failure. Prison "reform" is virtually contemporary with the prison itself: it constitutes, as it were, its programme. (Foucault 1979, 234)

As the SPP and its partners attempt to both improve the sustainability grade of corrections facilities (e.g. reducing costs via recycling and composting) and have a positive impact on prisoners' lives, they are engaging in a remedial practice of 'eco' prison reform or transformation. Again, Wacquant's pithy angle on the neoliberal prison–state relationship is a key. As Wacquant points out, the neoliberal penal state's attempts to 'improve prison conditions' are missing a heady moral storyline:

> The real challenge, to be specific, is not to improve prison conditions, although that is clearly a matter of immediate urgency, but to rapidly *depopulate the prison* by engaging a proactive policy of *decarceration* based on alternative sentencing and the social treatment of urban ills. For, whereas we no longer know why we lock people up, we do know very well that passing through the prison has destructive and demoralising effects on inmates as well as on their families and associates. (Wacquant 2012, 9)

What I am calling here *carceral political ecology* opens up new terrain for work already underway at the intersection of political ecology (Robbins 2011) – an environmental social theory that, in general, draws on political economy to expose complex power dynamics of human–environment relations – and science and technology studies, an interdisciplinary field that investigates the social, political, economic, and cultural dimensions of science, scientific knowledge production, and expertise (Goldman, Nadasdy, and Turner 2011; Lave 2012a, 2012b). While political ecology and STS are linkable in the case of carceral political ecology, the emerging field of 'carceral geography' (Moran 2013) seems equally relevant to the discussion. A field largely seeded in earlier discussions of the 'total institution'

(Goffman 1961) and biopower (Foucault 1979), 'carceral geography' (Moran 2013) 'has tended to foreground the carceral *space*, both in terms of the individual's movement into and out of that space and his or her experience within it, as well as the physical manifestation of the penal institution in space' (Moran 2013, 175, emphasis in original). In many ways, the prison becomes a new *space* of institutionalized sustainability science in a neoliberal age of both hyperincarceration and rising environmental knowledge production and environmental education programs. This new institutional space is, like all institutions, 'inhabited by a multitude of positions and voices' (Rhodes 2004, 223), which only adds to the complexities of studying SPP-corrections relations.

It is beyond the scope of this article to fully explore the following cascade of questions, but they are ones that can help guide both carceral political ecology and prison ecobiopolitical studies: How is sustainability science becoming a node or linkage between the neoliberal penal State and the neoliberal university? How, and to what extent, are prisoners actually 'becoming' sustainability scientists and environmental knowledge producers? How, and to what extent, are prisons becoming a microcosm for how sustainable living and sustainable practices are done and made possible? It is also important to engage the following questions inspired by Frickel and Moore (2006, 25) to help guide future investigations of the ecobiopolitical dimensions of SPP programs and perhaps even expose the very political nature of the neoliberal eco-prison itself: How do intersecting or overlapping logics of sustainability science and prison policy shape the content and conditions of environmental knowledge production and education? What are the primary formal and informal mechanisms of institutional change invoked by prison sustainability science and education? Which ones matter most in conditioning the trajectory of environmental science research and its broader dissemination and use within the prison system and among SPP partners? What impacts do SPP–corrections partnerships have on equitable access to sustainability science and education? In other words, critical social science research grappling with the intersecting logics of sustainability and penality, of ecobiopolitics and environmental science education, is a wide open field of interrogation.

Conclusion

This article aimed to explore and take a modest look at the practice of sustainability science and education in a spatial environment of incarceration. As stated earlier, my approach to studying the SPP is not meant to simply drag neoliberal sustainability science efforts and the 'greening' of the penal State through the mud to expose trenchant power relations, but instead to face the complexities, conundrums, and deep contradictions at work in attempts to pair neoliberal sustainability science and penality itself. Bringing 'nature' and 'science' into the environment of incarceration, the active educational goal of the SPP and its partners, puts an interesting twist on the very 'nature' of the contemporary prison as a stark example of an 'outlaw institution' crafting spaces for environmental education and learning: 'The prison is supposed to enforce the law but, by the very nature of its organisation, it operates *exlex*, in the manner of *an outlaw institution*. Promoted as a remedy for insecurity and marginality, it does little more than to concentrate and intensify them, but so long as it renders them politically *invisible*, we ask nothing more of it' (Wacquant 2012a, 7). If nothing else, a carceral political ecology perspective informed by ecobiopolitical theory helps make visible the political 'nature' of environmental science and educational goals emerging amid this contemporary outlaw institutional surge. It asks of the neoliberal eco-prison to adopt an eco-critical, eco-reflexive, and eco-justice approach that recognizes new synergies between bodies, ecologies, and emerging racial politics in our 'Age of Colorblindness' (Alexander 2010), an age of vibrant discourse on the 'end' of racial caste in America coupled with a redesigned or 'New Jim Crow' era reality informed by 'our current system of mass incarceration' (2010, 12).

The discussion of sustainability science and education unfolding in the neoliberal eco-prison brings us back to, or rightfully extends from, Foucault's original biopolitical thinking. 'Biopolitics,' he writes 'deals with the population, with the population as political problem, as a problem that is at once scientific and political, as a biological problem and as power's problem. And I think that biopolitics emerges at this time' (Foucault [1976] 2003, 245). If our times are marked by the emergence and growth of SPP programs in prisons, of eco-prison efforts and partnership, our times surely call for an 'ecobiopolitical' (Olson 2010) approach. In other words, a more laudable critique of the neoliberal eco-prison might be best served by a biopolitical theory that moves from the prison 'population' to the 'environment' itself as a 'political problem,' to use Foucault's phrasing. When environmental education and sustainability science are meshed with 'restoring' and rehabilitating inmates, this becomes a precarious ecobiopolitical move, a dual ethos move that synthesize caring for both the wellbeing of inmates and the 'environment.'

As Lemke (Lemke 2011, 120) points out, 'an analytics of biopolitics must … take into account forms of subjectivation, that is, the manner in which subjects are brought to work on themselves, guided by scientific, medical, moral, religious, and other authorities.' If this is the case, then ecobiopolitics takes into account forms of environmental subjectivation. Surely the ethos of sustainability is part of SPP training, even if such an environmental ethos is not the front-and-center objective of the SPP's environmental science education programs. In my experience talking to SPP staff and partners, the conversation usually includes comments about how inmate involvement in SPP programs 'transforms' them or 'makes them think differently,' as one SPP staff put it. This real or possible cognitive shift might even be understood as a 'science shift' for prisoners, a subjective transformation were scientific thinking is playing a greater role.

As Lave (2012a) points out, at the forefront of current neoliberal science studies is a strong emphasis on extramural science, that is, knowledge production rooted in citizen science (both activist and volunteer forms), amateur science, crowdsourcing, commercial science, indigenous knowledge, and local knowledge. Nowhere in emerging neoliberal science studies discussions is the prison, or inmate science, mentioned. One feature of what Lave (2012a) calls 'neoliberal science regimes' (Lave 2010, 2012a), is 'a new wave of appropriation of labor and knowledge. Both amateur and citizen scientists provide vast amounts of unpaid work for physical scientists' (Lave 2012a, 28). While inmate exploitation is a vocalized concern for SPP staff, the environmental science prisoners engage in 'unpaid' work. One can not dodge that fact, nor should one assume SPP staff and their partners are intentionally using prisoners as labor for expanding neoliberal science regimes. All SPP staff and partners I have spoken with remind me that prisoners who get to work on SPP programs are the 'best behaved,' as one SPP staff put it. These are highly coveted jobs in prisons that have SPP programs, so even though it is 'unpaid labor' in every definition of the term, the value placed on SPP work among prisoners, I was told, 'speaks for itself.'

In our neoliberal age, Hursh and Henderson (2011) write, 'education is increasingly contested, as the plutocracy promotes education as a means of producing productive, rather than critical, employees' (Hursh and Henderson 2011, 181). Adding topics such as political ecology and ecobiopolitics to the SPP's 'Sustainability 101' curriculum would likely be considered a slippery alternative sustainability education endeavor, even for SPP staff themselves who are interested in human–environment relations, the social and political dimensions of ecological restoration, and even critical pedagogy. While SPP education activities between 2011 and 2012 included numerous lectures at Washington corrections facilities, with topics ranging from fish, frogs, fires, wetland mitigation, biofuels, noxious weeds, streams, and animal track identification, environmental social science and humanities topics lacked attention. Among SPP staff I have spoken with, this is a recognized educational program gap, and an educational gap, that leads to a whirlpool of contentious environmental educational issues and questions. What effect an environmental education program in prisons emphasizing 'critical' environmental studies, such as political ecology or ecobiopolitics, would have, is, for now, anybody's guess. Is an 'eco-justice pedagogy' (Bowers 2001) in prisons possible? Can the neoliberal eco-prison even welcome such a possibility *without* rethinking and rehabilitating the ethical and moral barometer of the penal State itself? In light of Friere's central and enduring question, 'How can the oppressed, as divided, unauthentic beings, participate in developing the pedagogy of their liberation?' (Friere [1968] 2005, 48), how can the imprisoned engage in developing environmental education programs and eco-justice pedagogies for their own liberation?

Meaningfully engaging these questions calls for a radical shift or move toward SPP partnerships that dovetail with progressive programs like the Inside-Out Prison Exchange Program, a program based out of Temple University that aims to increase 'opportunities for men and women, inside and outside of prison, to have the transformative learning experiences that emphasize collaboration and dialog, inviting participants to take leadership in addressing crime, justice, and other issues of social concern.' Such a move would surely require a committed partnership between critical environmental educators, environmental social science and humanities scholars, corrections staff, and prisoners. An even steeper slope for both critical environmental educators and political ecologists to navigate in spaces of incarceration is how to fold in the rightful work of prison abolitionists and critical debates on the very topic of prison obsolescence (Davis 2003), a topic which, after all, might eventually become a front-and-center focus of any radical discussion of 'new' environmental justice (Stein 2004) dimensions of sustainability science and education efforts in prisons in our neoliberal climate.

Notes on contributor

Peter C. Little is an assistant professor in the Department of Anthropology at Rhode Island College. His research explores various topics in the field of political ecology and he is author of *Toxic Town: IBM, Pollution, and Industrial Risks* (NYU Press, 2014).

References

Alexander, Michelle. 2010. *The New Jim Crow: Mass Incarceration in the Age of Colorblindness*. New York: New Press.

Atherton, E. and P. Sheldon. 2011. "Plenary Address: How to save $1,000 per Inmate." *National Symposium on Sustainable Corrections*. Accessed June 6, 2012. http://www. GreenPrison.org

Bamberg, S., and G. Möser. 2007. "Twenty Years after Hines, Hungerford, and Tomera: A New Meta-analysis of Psycho-social Determinants of Pro-environmental Behaviour." *Journal of Environmental Psychology* 27: 14–25.

Beirne, P., and N. South, eds. 2006. *Green Criminology*. Hampshire: Ashgate.

Beirne, P., and N. South, eds. 2007. *Issues in Green Criminology: Confronting Harms against Environments, Humanity, and Other Animals*. Portland, OR: Willan.

Benton, T. 2007. "Ecology, Community, and Justice: The Meaning of Green." In *Issues in Green Criminology: Confronting Harms against Environments, Humanity, and Other Animals*, edited by P. Beirne and N. South, 3–31. Portland, OR: Willan.

Bowers, C. A. 2001. "Toward an Eco-justice Pedagogy." *Educational Studies* 32 (4): 401–415.

Chomsky, Noam. 2011. *Profit over People: Neoliberalism and Global Order*. New York: Seven Stories.

Davis, Angela Y. 2003. *Are Prisons Obsolete?* New York: Seven Stories.

Dreyfus, Hubert L., and Paul Rabinow. 1982. *Michel Foucault: Beyond Structuralism and Hermeneutics*. Chicago, IL: University of Chicago Press.

Dunlap, R. E. 2008. "The New Environmental Paradigm Scale: From Marginality to World-wide Use." *Journal of Environmental Education* 40 (1): 3–18.

Dunlap, R. E., and K. D. Van Liere. 1978. "A Proposed Measuring Instrument and Preliminary Results: The 'New Environmental Paradigm'." *Journal of Environmental Education* 9 (1): 10–19.

Dunlap, R. E., K. D. Van Liere, A. G. Mertig, and R. E. Jones. 2000. "New Trends in Measuring Environmental Attitudes: Measuring Endorsement of the New Ecological Paradigm: A Revised NEP Scale." *Journal of Social Issues* 56 (3): 425–442.

Foucault, Michel. 1979. *Discipline and Punish: The Birth of the Prison*. New York: Vintage.

Foucault, Michel. 1984. "Of Other Spaces, Heterotopias." *Architecture, Mouvement, Continuité* 5: 46–49.

Foucault, Michel. (1976) 2003. *"Society Must Be Defended": Lectures at the Collége De France, 1975–1976*. edited by Arnold I. Davidson. New York: Picador.

Frickel, Scott, Kelly Moore. 2006 "Prospects and Challenges for a New Political Sociology of Science." In *The New Political Sociology of Science: Institutions, Networks, and Power*, edited by Scott Frickel and Kelly Moore, pp. 3–31. Madison, WI: University of Wisconsin Press.

Friere, Paulo. (1970) 2005. *Pedagogy of the Oppressed*. 30th Anniversary Edition. Translated by Myra Bergman Ramos. New York: Continuum.

Frumkin, Howard. 2012. "Building the Science Base: Ecopsychology Meets Clinical Epidemiology." In *Ecopsychology: Science, Totems, and the Technological Species*, edited by Peter H. Hahn Jr. and Patricia H. Hasbach, 141–172. Cambridge, MA: MIT Press.

Gallagher, Brittany E. 2013. "Science and Sustainability Programs in Prisons: Assessing the Affects of Participation on Inmates." Unpublished MA Thesis, Environmental Studies Program, Evergreen State College.

Giroux, Henry A. 2008. *Against the Terror of Neoliberalism: Politics Beyond the Age of Greed*. Boulder, CO: Paradigm.

Goffman, Irving. 1961. *Asylums: Essays on the Social Situation of Mental Patients and Other Inmates*. New York: Anchor Books.

Goldman, Mara J., Paul Nadasdy, and Matthew D. Turner, eds. 2011. *Knowing Nature: Conversations at the Intersection of Political Ecology and Science Studies*. Chicago, IL: University of Chicago.

Graeber, David. 2010. "Neoliberalism, or the Bureaucratization of the World." In *The Insecure American*, edited by H. Gusterson and C. Besteman, 79–96. Berkeley: University of California Press.

Gruenewald, David A. 2004. "A Foucauldian Analysis of Environmental Education: Toward the Socioecological Challenge of the Earth Charter." *Curriculum Inquiry* 34 (1): 71–107.

Harcourt, Bernard E. 2012. "On the American Paradox of *Laissez Faire* and Mass Incarceration." *Harvard Law Review* 125: 54–68.

Harvey, David. 1996. *Justice, Nature, and the Geography of Difference*. Oxford: Blackwell.

Harvey, D. 2005. *A Brief History of Neoliberalism*. New York: Oxford University Press.

Harvey, D. 2007. "Neoliberalism as Creative Destruction." *The Annals of the American Academy of Political and Social Science* 610 (21): 22–44.

Hasbach, Patricia H. 2012. "Ecotherapy." In *Ecopsychology: Science, Totems, and the Technological Species*, edited by Peter H. Hahn, Jr. and Patricia H. Hasbach, 115–140. Cambridge, MA: MIT Press.

Herivel, Tara, and Paul Wright, eds. 2003. *Prison Nation: The Warehousing of America's Poor*. New York: Routledge.

Hines, J. M., H. R. Hungerford, and A. Tomera. 1987. "Analysis and Synthesis of Research on Responsible Environmental Behavior: A Meta-analysis." *The Journal of Environmental Education* 18 (2): 1–8.

Hursh, David W., and Joseph A. Henderson. 2011. Contesting Global Neoliberalism and Creating Alternative Futures. *Discourse: Studies in the Cultural Politics of Education* 32(2):171–185.

Jiler, James. 2006. *Doing Time in the Garden: Life Lessons through Prison Horticulture*. New York: New Village Press.

Judd, A. 2008. *The Green Prison Movement*. Accessed November 1, 2013. http://www.nowpublic.com/environment/green-prison-movement

Lafer, Gordon. 2003. "The Politics of Prison Labor." In *Prison Nation: The Warehousing of America's Poor*. edited by Tara Herivel and Paul Wright, 120–128. New York: Routledge

Lancaster, Roger N. 2010. "Republic of Fear: The Rise of Punitive Governance in America." In *The Insecure American*, edited by Hugh Gusterson and Catherine Besteman, 63–76. Berkeley: University of California Press.

Lave, Rebecca. 2012a. "Neoliberalism and the Production of Environmental Knowledge." *Annual Reviews in Environment & Society* 3 (1): 19–38.

Lave, Rebecca. 2012b. "Bridging Political Ecology and STS: A Field Analysis of the Rosgen Wars." *Annals of the Association of American Geographers* 102 (2): 366–382.

Lave, Rebecca, Philip Mirowski, and Samuel Randalls. 2010. "Introduction: STS and Neoliberal Science." *Social Studies of Science* 40 (5): 659–675.

Lemke, Thomas. 2011. *Biopolitics: An Advanced Introduction*. New York: New York University Press.

LeRoy, Carri, K. Bush, J. Trivett, and B. Gallagher. 2012. *The Sustainability in Prisons Project: An Overview (2004–2012)*. Olympia, WA: Evergreen State College, The Sustainability in Prisons Project.

Little, Peter C. 2013. Sustainability Science Advocacy in Lockdown America: New Terrain for Engaged Environmental Anthropology? *Anthropology News*. March Issue.

Lynch, M. J., and P. B. Stretesky. 2003. "The Meaning of Green: Contrasting Criminological Perspectives." *Theoretical Criminology* 7: 217–238.

Martin, P. 1996. "A WWF View of Education and the Role of NGOs." In *Education for Sustainability*, edited by J. Huckle and S. Sterling, 40–54. London: Earthscan.

McCorkel, Jill A. 2013. *Breaking Women: Gender, Race, and the New Politics of Imprisonment*. New York: New York University Press.

Moran, Dominique. 2013. "Carceral Geography and the Spatialities of Prison Visiting: Visitation, Recidivism, and Hyperincarceration." *Environment and Planning D: Society and Space* 31: 174–190.

National Institute of Corrections. 2011. *The Greening of Corrections: Creating a Sustainable System*. Report Accessed August 10, 2013. http://nicic.gov/Library/024914

Olson, Valerie A. 2010. "The Ecobiopolitics of Space Biomedicine." *Medical Anthropology* 29 (2): 170–193.

Parenti, Christian. 1999. *Lockdown America: Police and Prisons in the Age of Crisis*. London: Verso.

Rhodes, Lorna. 2001. "Towards an Anthropology of Prisons." *Annual Review of Anthropology* 30: 65–83.

Rhodes, Lorna A. 2004. *Total Confinement: Madness and Reason in the Maximum Security Prison*. Berkeley: University of California Press.

Robbins, Paul. 2011. *Political Ecology: A Critical Introduction*. 2nd ed. West Sussex: Wiley-Blackwell.

Rose, N. 2007. *The Politics of Life Itself: Biomedicine, Power, and Subjectivity in the Twenty-first Century*. Princeton: Princeton University Press.

Stein, R., ed. 2004. *New Perspectives on Environmental Justice: Gender, Sexuality, and Activism*. New Brunswick, NJ: Rutgers University Press.

Stohr, Mary K., and John F. Wozniak. 2014. "The Green Prison." In *The American Prison: Imagining a Different Future*, edited by Francis T. Cullen, Cheryl Lero Johnson, and Mary K. Stohr, 193–212. Los Angeles, CA: Sage.

Ulrich, C., and N. M. Nadkarni. 2009. "Sustainability Research in Enforced Residential Institutions: Collaborations of Ecologists and Prisoners." *Environment, Development and Sustainability* 11: 815–825.

Wacquant, Loïc. 2002. "The Curious Eclipse of Prison Ethnography in the Age of Mass Incarceration." *Ethnography* 3 (4): 371–397.

Wacquant, Loïc. 2010a. "Prisoner Reentry as Myth and Ceremony." *Dialectical Anthropology* 34: 605–620.

Wacquant, Loïc. 2010b. "Crafting the Neoliberal State: Workfare, Prisonfare, and Social Insecurity." *Sociological Forum* 25 (2): 197–220.

Wacquant, Loïc. 2012a. "The Prison is an Outlaw Institution." *The Howard Journal of Criminal Justice* 55 (1): 1–15.

Wacquant, Loïc. 2012b. "The Wedding of Workfare and Prisonfare Revisited." *Social Justice* 38 (1–2): 203–221.

Wacquant, Loïc. 2012c. "The Punitive Regulation of Poverty in the Neoliberal Age." *CJM* 89: 38–40.

Refusing to settle for pigeons and parks: urban environmental education in the age of neoliberalism

Michael W. Derby, Laura Piersol and Sean Blenkinsop

Simon Fraser University, Vancouver, BC, Canada

> The institutionalization of neoliberal reforms that began to take hold in the 1970s were by and large 'common-sense governance' by the 1990s. While the growing predominance of neoliberal discourse and marginalization of alternatives in environmental education is disconcerting on the level of policy, this paper explores an equally troubling phenomenon: the deepening of a neoliberal logic, such that it pervades the way we understand and relate with the world. Specifically, this paper draws upon an experience at a recent environmental education conference whereby participants were invited to explore three place-based inquiries inspired by Aldo Leopold in an urban environment: what is happening here? what has happened here? and what should happen here? Although the intention of the workshop was to explore some of the challenges involved in implementing a critical pedagogy of place, many of the participants seemed unwilling to criticize the way in which an urban downtown core suppresses the more-than-human aspects of place. We contend that environmental education is a key arena for debating the limits of neoliberalism and explore how these well-intentioned, but ultimately uncritical responses, run the risk of being appropriated by the ecologically destructive logic-informing neoliberal natures.

Introduction

At a recent environmental education conference, we organized a workshop to collaboratively and experientially consider the role of place as co-teacher (Blenkinsop and Beeman 2010) and explore some of the challenges in implementing a critical pedagogy of place (Gruenewald 2003). We invited workshop participants into a downtown urban environment and encouraged them to ask three questions inspired by Leopold (1949): What is happening here? What has happened here? and What should happen here? Specifically, we hoped that participants might experience and reflect upon some of the predicaments involved in establishing meaningful connections with the more-than-human aspects of place – including ways in which 'what-is' can work to obfuscate 'what has been' and prescribe 'what should be' – in densely urbanized environments.

Upon returning to reflect as a group, however, we were struck by how many participants expressed gratitude for the chance to simply get outside. One group commented on the soothing sounds emanating from an artificial fountain they encountered; another enjoyed sitting on a tiny strip of lawn running around a skyscraper. We were somewhat taken aback by the breezy, uncritical nature of these reflections; especially being that we had found something patently disconcerting about the manufactured waterfall and meticulously sculpted shrubs that adorned the frontages of the buildings. We struggled as visitors to imagine what the place had been like historically as it now resembled 'downtown anywhere America' – office towers, commercial logos bespattering every surface, and loud, rushing traffic that all but overwhelmed the senses. After sharing some of these more critical reflections with the group in an attempt to explore some of the ways in which the urban environment distorts its historical and ecological dimensions, one participant commented that it was like we were 'insulting his living room.' Another participant commented, 'I work with students in an urban environment … out there on the streets I could find the beauty in the leaves swaying in the wind, isn't that what environmental education is all about?' Another added,'Aren't *we* "nature"? Nature isn't something found far away, it's right here.'[1] Many in this group of environmental educators seemed determined to avoid engaging in any kind of critical analysis of this urbanized area. The idea that we might discuss what 'should' happen here was met with a particular sense of collective impropriety, as if the act of 'shoulding' itself was archaic and innately offensive.

There has long been a dangerous and false human/nature dichotomy that posits nature as 'pristine' and 'far and away' as well as an extensive literature that tracks changes in how we historically interpret 'nature' (Castree and Braun 2001; Cronon 1995; Evernden 1985). In this article, however, we take issue with an equally troubling assumption that 'nature,' or what we will call 'wilderness,' is ever-present and necessarily part and parcel of humanity regardless of context or ontological orientation. Our concern is that in responding cursorily to the false separation of nature and culture, environmental educators risk furthering a neoliberal agenda that appropriates our language in order to justify the colonized logic of urban spaces and continued exploitation of what remains of the 'wilderness.' We worry that in responding to the false dualism of nature and culture, we can swing into assuming that there is no distinction at all, such that the 'wild' becomes ubiquitously present and equally accessible regardless of context. We will suggest that positions that uncritically accept urban environments as ecologically rich, although generally coming from a sense of authentic concern, are potentially dangerous inclinations whereby neoliberal tropes may trickle into our 'common sense' presuppositions about human–world relationality. We seek to warn against a troubling hybridization of neoliberalism and environmentalism to the extent that environmental educators are in danger of abandoning critical analysis of urban spaces and thus aid and abet the ecologically destructive paradigm that is neoliberalism.

We want to suggest that the 'wilderness'[2] we encounter in cities *is* qualitatively different from what is encountered in predominantly undomesticated areas. Despite the procession of birds that might flock overhead, the coyotes that roam urban alleyways, or the families of raccoons that rummage through garbage bins, cities are not *wilderness on its own terms*. Cities are, by and large, colonized places. The ongoing process of colonization absolutely includes silencing, dehistoricizing, and violently dislocating indigenous and other marginalized populations over the course of its historical development, but it also includes a similar kind of suppression of the more-than-human world. We have, in a modern urban setting, violently altered, subdued, and mastered the natural world such that it is forced to conform to our anthropocentric, and we maintain neoliberal, visions and needs.

This is not to claim that wild elements and the potential for wilderness do not persist within city limits. There is a kind of continual negotiation between the wild aspects of place and the urban environment. As Cronon (1995) claims, 'wildness (as opposed to wilderness) can be found anywhere: in the seemingly tame fields and woodlots of Massachusetts, in the cracks of a Manhattan sidewalk, even in the cells of our own bodies' (19). But surely it is more difficult to encounter this wild(er)ness, paved over as it is, physically, culturally, politically, and intellectually from our urban, alienated, and culturally positioned existences. The wildness of urban settings is shaped by our desires, manicured and conformed to fit our needs. As we will describe going forward, this article is not a cry to retreat to some romanticized pristine wilderness, but a call to action that acknowledges the potential presence of the wild in an urban setting while demanding frank discussion with regard to its accessibility, integrity, and ability to flourish – along with a nuanced awareness as to how many cultural veils lie between our students and genuine encounters with that urban wild. Smith (2007), who has also attempted to navigate these dubious terms, sensibly reminds us that while radical environmentalists have a tendency to use the term wilderness uncritically, and while little of nature remains untouched, 'there are clearly places that are relatively wild in the sense of not being under constant human surveillance, regulation, and control, where non-human life continues *relatively* unhindered' (479).

A readily accessible and ubiquitous version of wilderness is, we maintain, essential to a neoliberal worldview predicated on unmitigated economic progress by means of manufacturing environmental conditions favorable to 'good business' (Harvey 2005; Hursh and Henderson 2011; McCarthy and Prudham 2004). Although troubling the human/nature dichotomy is an important discursive move in environmental philosophy, the neoliberal agenda has no qualms about appropriating our language and arguments in order to justify its exploitative telos. Although instrumental and anthropocentric orientations to human–world relationality are nothing new, we are concerned that the uncritical acceptance of colonized urban environments as equally 'wild' as the 'wilderness' among environmental educators represents a perturbing extension of the neoliberal agenda. In this article, we will begin with a short discussion centered on the historical development of neoliberalism as a 'common sense' inevitability within the public mind: its slow and invasive positioning as not only an economic theory of trade liberalization but a way of understanding the world. This will be followed by an exploration of how some of the common sentiments we have witnessed in environmental educators might be easily misconstrued and repurposed to confirm an ecologically destructive neoliberal position. From here, it will become possible for us to point toward the ways in which a neoliberal logic can be infused into the field of environmental education; we hope to reveal the troubling tint to the water in which we swim. The article ends by offering ways in which urban environmental educators might respond to the challenges of bringing urban students into more direct contact with wilderness and the potential for wildness in urban settings without sliding into perfunctory acceptance of what-is.

The neoliberalization of common sense

In what ways are the aforementioned common sentiments of environmental educators related to the ostensibly abstract economic imperatives of what has come to be known as *neoliberalism*? Or more to the point, does the lack of critical socio-ecological analysis indicate a dangerous neoliberal encroachment upon our 'common sense' as environmental educators? After all, one might reasonably expect a group of environmental educators to have a heightened sensitivity to the state of the more-than-human aspects of place and thus be willing to engage in critical reflection upon a highly industrial and corporatized downtown core.

Once again, we pose these questions not to needlessly disparage environmental educators, rather we wish to reiterate and reexamine how our field is being subsumed and threatened by a furtive neoliberal logic. Despite the predominance of neoliberal discourses in the United States and Canada, the ever-creeping privatization of education by a corporate and governmental elite, there is a sense, we feel, that most environmental educators simply do not 'buy it.' Given critical scholarship from the field on how neoliberalism 'exacerbates inequalities, damages the environment, and undermines education' (Hursh and Henderson 2011, 172; see also Gruenewald and Manteaw 2007; McKenzie 2012) and the commendable work of countless environmental educators engaged in diverse projects that contest wholesale neoliberalization, one must recognize the compelling power of environmental discourses to resist neoliberal enclosures (and admire the educators who sustain this struggle). The unique position of environmental education as a key arena for debating the limits, costs and consequences of neoliberalism, however, has not been lost on the power elite who target environmental discourses in education in order to marginalize alternative conceptions and limit debate (Kingsnorth 2013; McKenzie et al. 2009). As Hursh and Henderson (2011) have suggested, neoliberal policies have employed an all too familiar rhetoric of inevitability in order to limit public discourse, promote technical and market-based solutions to education, and decontextualize our knowledge and relationship to place. They suggest that educators develop a social democratic approach to education that promotes critical analysis, connects history to place, and encourages students to participate in dreaming and co-creating alternatives to neoliberalism. We concur and re-emphasize that environmental educators must recognize that a neoliberal logic is predicated upon the continued colonization, marginalization, and silencing of the more-than-human world, thus requiring us to develop and maintain a commitment to a reflexive practice that continually asks difficult questions and problematizes our cultural–historical 'common sense.' What is happening here? What has happened here? And, indeed, what *should* happen here?

McCarthy and Prudham (2004) have maintained that environmentalism holds the power to draw attention to the politically contested character of neoliberalism, but also the pervasive, taken-for-granted and apolitical presuppositions of neoliberal discourses and practices. This was in fact one of the primary objectives of our conference workshop: to draw critical attention to these taken-for-granted discourses, but also to the more tacit and habitual 'practices' of how we construct places, how we interact with and make sense of the colonized and corporatized architectonics of the city itself that stifle the senses and muffle more-than-human presences. What does it mean when essentially apolitical responses ensue from a circle of environmental educators? Do these responses represent a 'deepening' (Lysandrou 2005) of the neoliberal commodification of place? Or perhaps a hybridization of environmental education with an ahistorical and politically complacent neoliberal line of reasoning? Both Heynen et al. (2007) and Kingsnorth (2013) have warned of the dangers of such a hybridization illustrating the way in which powerful environmental groups have fallen prey to such tactics as: market-based incentives, commodity-like carbon permits, and the privatization of nature as a tool of conservation. 'That these measures tend to entrench a utilitarian and fetishistic disposition toward the biophysical world does not seem to trouble those groups willing to pursue clean-up and conservation at any cost' (Heynen et al. 2007, 12). We argue that a similar process of hybridization may be implacably wearing away at the ecological ethos of environmental educators: patient, tenacious, reasserting its taken-for-granted inevitabilities and quotidian experience of 'what-is' as the only possibility. The city is as it is, there are no alternatives. That said, we wonder, does *neoliberalization* actually offer us a useful way to name and make sense of this phenomenon?

Neoliberalism is a big term. And in recent years, it has only swelled as critical literature on the subject has proliferated – particularly within the field of critical geography (Bakker 2010; Harvey 2005; Heynen et al. 2007; Himley 2008) – where the word has come to describe a multiscalar and multifarious array of political, economic, environmental, and social experiences. This has invariably led some to believe the concept is too bloated to capture the diversity of projects labeled 'neoliberal' and actually acts to divert attention away from the syncretic ways in which neoliberal tropes are territorialized to particular places, contexts, and circumstances (Heynen et al. 2007). There is a legitimate concern here that critical scholars, in totalizing diverse neoliberal-inspired experiences, may be doing more to obfuscate than disclose (Peck and Tickell 2002). The desire to demarcate this fluid strategy (Bauman 2000) may in fact only divert attention away from neoliberalism's destructive adaptability and willingness to blend in, commingle, even concede some of its 'ideological foundations,' as long as resources and wealth are being 'redistributed' to the wealthy (Harvey 2005). That said, we share in the sentiments of Heynen et al. (2007) when they claim: 'And yet something is going on worth naming' (4). Let us briefly trace what happens historically when neoliberal discourses infiltrate multiple social, cultural, and ecological environments and begin to settle in the common lexicon and sensibility throughout the decades.

Broadly speaking, the institutionalization of neoliberal reforms began to take hold in the 1970s, swept through most of the world during the 1980s, and was considered 'common sense governance' by the 1990s (Heynen et al. 2007; Hursh and Henderson 2011).[3] For example, even left-of-center provincial governments, such as the one in Ontario in the early 1990s, had conceded to this 'consensus' and began introducing classic neoliberal policies. By the time the Progressive Conservatives were elected in 1995, steep spending cuts, liberalization of labor laws, and tax reductions for the wealthy were being hailed as part of a so-called 'Common Sense Revolution' (Prudham 2007). As Prudham has clarified, this new 'common sense,' of course, really stood for 'markets, markets and more markets, expanding the scope of private decision-making and accumulation via three familiar tropes of rollback neoliberalism: fiscal austerity; deregulation and re-regulation; and privatization.' (169). Although these tropes represent something of a revolutionary shift in our social–ecological relationality under a neoliberal paradigm, one might reasonably respond that capitalism has always been predicated on the consumption and exploitation of the 'natural world.' In other words, why not simply speak of capitalism? Surely, our conceptions of world–human relationality and sustainability were no further advanced under, say, a Keynesian economic model? Bakker (2010) has responded to this line of thinking claiming that the answer hinges, in part, on qualitative differences that characterize new practices of capital accumulation emerging throughout the past three decades:

> Simply put, whereas market principles were often viewed in opposition to environmental protection and conservation in the mid-twentieth century, they had by the end of the century become reconciled with economic growth and entrenched in mainstream environmental policy as emblematized in the doctrine of sustainable development (726).

The dominance of neoliberal ideas and policies has so firmly established itself since the 1970s, its 'revolutionary' logic is now situated as a common sense response. With regards to environmental conservation, this has profoundly impacted the ways in which environmental education is conceptualized and implemented (Hursh and Henderson 2011; McKenzie 2012).

In one sense, neoliberalism is just the latest manifestation of a long lineage of ecologically exploitative ideologies that renders the world an object of economic activity and yet, there is something deeply troubling about the increasing urbanity of our common sense and the seeming unwillingness of some environmental educators to problematize this reality. Environmental education represents a pivotal strategic territory in the struggle to either legitimize or contest neoliberal natures, and the very ways, we engage with the world as a result of these understandings, are key to the conflict. As Harvey (2005) has warned, '[Neoliberalism] has pervasive effects on ways of thought to the point where it has become incorporated into the common sense way many of us interpret, live in, and understand the world' (3). Or, in the words of Thatcher herself: 'Economics are the method, but the object is to change the soul' (as cited in Harvey 2005, 23).

Under the logic of neoliberalism, it becomes profitable to think of the wilderness and urban experience as equal, stripping the more-than-human world of its particularities, its affect, and its agency. For one, this helps to justify the continued and wholesale destruction of tracts of 'wild areas' in order to shape this thing called 'nature' to fit our narratives and needs. The nature we encounter in urban areas is one sculpted to our desires, stripped of context, colonized to meet our political and at times spiritual needs (MacKinnon 2012): isolated vestigial islands of what was once relationally wild, the lone tree in the parking lot, or the pigeon pecking away at garbage in the alley.

Appropriating the common sense of environmental education

Let us return to our workshop participants and re-examine how environmental education is being subsumed by the neoliberal agenda on the level of how we 'understand the world.' The participant who said the downtown core of the city was akin to his 'living room' appears to be avoiding critical reflection upon the place he calls home. A plausible and potentially dangerous appropriation of this stance is the idea that urbanization is already established and sprawling cities are inevitable; this is simply the way of progress. Therefore, the reasonable response is to adapt, identify with the positive aspects of the city, and rationalize one's complacency rather than critique it. As Sartre (1992) pointed out, there is no critique when there appears to be no other realistic possibility, the only response is to adapt. As we have seen, the common sense aspect of neoliberalism is now so entrenched that few, if any, alternatives seem plausible. It seems impractical and indecorous to question the billboards, the tidy fountain, the oddly sculpted hedges, because 'hey, people have to live and work somewhere.' The worrisome aspect of this kind of mentality is that it both narrows our capability to critique what-is and envision what could (or, dare we say, *should*) be; it reduces more holistic senses of social justice; and it marginalizes alternatives. This position, of course, also conveniently relegates us from any further action or responsibility. 'Oh, be realistic. It is going to happen anyway,' seems to be the rallying call, 'half of our world population lives in urban environments, we need to acknowledge this as environmental educators.'

We acknowledge the prevailing global drift (or rather push) toward urbanization, but we urge environmental educators to remain vigilant and critically question the way in which this industrial project proceeds and think carefully about the implications of relinquishing control over our 'living-rooms' to neoliberal designers. If, for instance, Leopold (1949) was correct in suggesting that 'wilderness is the raw material out of which man has hammered the artifact called civilization.' (188) and that his point was one of diversity, complexity, and subtlety such that wilderness has been the inspiration and impetus for the multitude of human cultures that now exist across the globe, then what are the implications of cultural possibility beyond neoliberalism if the only wilderness that remains is one that is colonized, domesticated, and manufactured in the neoliberal image? By refusing to take a critical stance when educating in such environments, we risk sliding along a slippery slope toward passive acceptance of the dominant modes of urbanization – the strip mall, the big box store, and the sprawl – as 'inevitable.' When we accept the lone, non-indigenous tree in its faux pot that doubles as a public ash tray, the panhandler that everyone ignores, the Styrofoam and flotsam in the fountain, and the walls plastered in corporate logos as our 'living room', something has gone terribly wrong with our sense of 'home.' We call to question the 'common sense' of accepting this commodified and commercialized version of the wild simply because it is the best that we assume we are going to get. Granted, it is tempting to adopt such a position because it helps us avoid some of the guilt and sadness for all that we have transmogrified and lost, however, we must not uncritically settle for the pigeon and the parkette. We must be wary of allowing students to assume that we live at the end of history, that we should never impose our 'utopian visions' upon other people's homes, that there really are no alternatives.

Another workshop participant argued that there is beauty and wildness in the leaves blowing in the wind or the flower in the cracks of the sidewalk. While this is true, we have found that in urban environmental education, we must take care not to over romanticize. Interestingly, what we are pointing toward here might be a reversal of the Romanticism that is so often critiqued when environmental educators speak of the false romantic dream of pristine wilderness. In this urban version, the romantic folly lies with the assumption that students can access or recognize the presence of wildness in the urban parkette in spite of the years of direct human sculpting and oppression. That environmental education is all about esthetic moments of transcendence with the occasional dandelion or butterfly that we happen to find in urban green spaces. Again, it seems that we may often be so desperate for any kind of positive connection with the more-than-human that to question the little voices and gestures that do whimper in an urban setting seems overly cynical. What we are trying to offer in response to either form of romance is that environmental educators should consider a kind of wilderness continuum – with 'on modern, neo-liberal, terms' at one end and 'on more-than-human terms' at the other. The former, at its extreme end, is a deeply anthropocentric and strictly economic relation, and it represents the backgrounding and silencing of anything that is non-human. Whereas, the latter, at its extreme end, understands that the more-than-human has an existence, independence, and agency of its own, that human/more-than-human relations are negotiated between and among equals, and where diversity, complexity, flexibility, and apex carnivores are present and flourishing. Obviously, the space in-between these extremes are filled by varying levels of both as we move along this continuum. It is essential that we learn to see ourselves as part of and in relationship with the broader ecology and not perpetuate anthropocentric lines of thought that seek to artificially separate humans; however, we also need to be thoughtful in the process that we do not conflate everything, including wild(er)ness, under the archaic and potentially dangerous umbrella of 'nature.'

Finally, we also take issue with the way in which a neoliberal agenda may appropriate some of the sentiments expressed in the statement: 'Aren't *we* "nature?" Nature isn't something found far away, it's right here.' It is true in the city that moisture still evaporates off the buildings carrying the scent of sea, for example, but that vapor now also carries exhaust fumes and heavy particulate matter. Yes, the moon still rises above the apartment buildings, but its shining forth is somewhat subdued by the starless purple sky and light pollution. One of the dangers of an 'anything goes' approach to defining nature and wildness is that it is easily manipulated by a neoliberal logic. We maintain that in our efforts to tackle the divide between nature and culture, we are ignoring the important differences that do exist among the range of human influenced spaces and also those which are still mostly beyond our reach. The 'wildness' that we encounter in cities is *predominantly* wild on our own terms, managed and transmogrified into tree-lined streets and flower-laden parkettes. The wilderness that we know of the backcountry is *predominantly* wild beyond our wanting and doing, it is self-arising and unpredictable; we have not tamed it or turned it into a delightful display of esthetics. It is messy and complex beyond our control and beyond easy understanding. It forces us to be humble and attentive in ways that seem more rare within an urban setting. As educators, we need to acknowledge such radical differences in the knowing and being that take place across locales, from the urban park to the arctic tundra and everything in-between.

Ethically speaking, it is also extremely worrisome to use the label 'natural' as a blanket term for everything that we do and are. As McClaren (2009) has written, 'Humans construct cities. If human constructions are not natural, then what does that make humans?' (303). Again, he is attempting to bridge the nature/culture divide, however, could we not similarly argue: 'Humans keep slaves and oppress other humans. If domination and colonization are not natural, then what does that make humans?' We have to become hypervigilant of our use and understanding of such terms as wide-scale ecocide can be justified as 'natural' and just what humans do on the way to a better more vibrant future.

Implications for Environmental Education

These slippery conflations of neoliberal ways of understanding with 'common sense' environmentalism have important implications for environmental educators, of which we would like to explore a few. To begin with, there is a need for hyperactive vigilance and critical questioning in regards to the kinds of encounters with the wild that *are* happening or even *can* happen in urban settings. What affordances does the urban provide and which does it preclude? What presuppositions about human–world relationality need to be highlighted in an urban environment in order that what-is does not position itself as the only way that things can be. We also need to turn a critical eye to our own practices as educators and attend to the insidious ways in which the neoliberal agenda has encroached upon the field. This means looking at every aspect: from the various organizations on which we rely for funding, to the ways in which we mediate understanding of a place to our students, to the questions we ask, the questions we ignore and why.

As Gruenewald (2003) points out, 'If place-based educators seek to connect place with self and community, they must identify and confront the ways that power works through places to limit the possibilities for human and non-human others. Their place-based pedagogy must in other words be critical.' (7). This also means thinking very carefully about how our students are oriented toward the urban encounters they experience. Clearly, many urban environmental educators can encounter a dandelion pushing up through a sidewalk crack and recognize in it the wildness of survivability, a will to overcome and live, beauty, freedom, and even the ephemeral reality of the human condition. But this is not and must not be the only possible reaction; in fact, it is not the most logical conclusion to reach unless one has a long history, knowledge, immersion in, and orientation toward the wilderness. Rather, deciding that humans are the dominant species, that 'wilderness' exists on the periphery or as a Romantic social construction, and that those wild spaces are of little value seems a much more obvious response for the thoroughly urbanized student – conclusions that obviously parallel a neoliberal agenda in unsettling ways.

If we settle for *only* teaching our students to appreciate the dandelion without challenging the hegemony of 'what-is' and the presuppositions being reified, we risk sliding unconsciously into neoliberal positions while also sacrificing the experience of being the one stared at, of coming into the wild on more of *its* own terms, a human presence subsumed in the polyphony of more-than-human presences. All of us need to have opportunities to encounter the power, independence, activity, and self-determining qualities of the wilderness. Without this understanding, we may lack the requisite humility necessary to overcome the destructive anthropocentric tendencies of neoliberalism. This is part of the deepest challenge to the urban environmental educator as they try to expose their students to wild(er)ness in a desiccated, context manipulated, human dominated situation, rather than trying to make sense of an 'arctic experience' by staring at a zoo-bound polar bear. There are likely many activities and discussions that might help to foster this process including: discussions about the design, structure, and layouts of parks by city-planners; noticing the choices made with regard to sight-lines, open spaces, and chosen species for planting; exploring the presence of non-fruiting cultivars or extended explorations; and discussions around concepts of alien and invasive species. Care must also be taken to avoid the potential sacrifice of tracts of autonomous wilderness as they can become too easily interchangeable and thus replaced by the city park. We argue that, in the end, they are not equivalent and that environmental educators must teach with this in mind: One acts as an extension of a modern capitalist ideology and the other potentially works to thrust the exploitative logic of such an ideology into question. It is imperative that environmental educators resist neoliberal hybridization and refuse to settle for a colonized environment as an easy substitute for either the wild (er)ness or significant encounters within it.

Part of this involves accepting feelings of sadness for what is lost or suppressed in urban environments and addressing this in our practice. In this time of ecological crisis, there is indeed much to mourn, and this is not something we should bravely ignore or attempt to pave over with uncritical positivity. We need to turn our attention to educators such as Macy and Brown (1998) who have a system in place for what they call 'despair work' (71). This does not mean dwelling in this place, it means acknowledging our involvement and letting this push us forward to act to mitigate the level of suffering. It is also time for environmental educators and advocates to actively think of their roles in the ways many feminist or First Nations educators and advocates tend to think of their projects – as centered around issues of oppression and colonization. What does it mean to work with students who are situated in the privileged anthropo-center; to support them in recognizing their role in the ongoing marginalization, destruction, and oppression of another culture; to help them to actually hear the voice of the other; and to recognize it as being of value and worth listening to? This shift in metaphor, to wilderness as 'oppressed community,' also means questioning where responsibility should indeed lie, is it fair to place the task of alleviating the destruction onto oncoming generations? We contend that most of the ecological destructive activities happening on the planet right now are rooted in the unconditional acceptance of the neoliberal paradigm. Individual feelings of guilt for the problems at hand should be tempered by a call for change in terms of the dominant modes and understandings of modern Western culture.

As environmental educators, we should actively explore attempts to 'reinhabit' (Gruenewald 2003) places, question our constructs of 'nature' (Bonnett 2004) and 'the wild' (Smith 2007), while also having an eye toward decolonization itself. Instead of shying away from asking what 'should' happen here, we need to have serious discussions around this question, along with 'what is happening' and 'what has happened.' This helps us to engender a position of decolonizer and reinhabitator simultaneously. We believe that this is a very active back and forth process as sacrificing one process for the other results in the inability to live well ecologically or socially within a place. An approach void of criticality perpetuates a shallow understanding of place leaving dominant cultural presuppositions intact and thus denying the possibility for deep reinhabitation as one ends up replicating many of the ecologically destructive/ignorant ways of being in the world. On the other hand, pursuing a purely critical approach potentially neglects thoughtful ways of connecting with place, while ignoring the need for relation and the active role the more-than-human can and must play in any decolonization process. After all, what marginalized group wants the end point determined for them by the historical oppressor, even if the intentions are good? Instead, we need to ensure our practices as educators are humble and that we are both actively engaged in listening to the more-than-human and pairing the twofold processes suggested by Gruenewald (2003). Reinhabitation and decolonization depend on each other, and a critical pedagogy of place is not possible without pursuing both processes in tandem.

This could mean, perhaps, a class spending meaningful time in the 'schoolyard,' letting the beetle that lives among the blades of grass crawl on the hand, working to listen and attend to the beetle and understand its context on its terms. At the same time, these classes can learn to question the meaning and historical development of 'a schoolyard' – the history and implications of 'lawns' – and then move to eventually restore some native plant species, creating tangled, hidden spaces where there once was clean cut lines. Again, we need to take a highly vigilant stance in this process assuming that colonization may still be present in the most, if not all, of the moves toward reinhabitation.

Finally, we should continue to fight for the preservation of wild spaces and insist on funding, time, and training to take our students out to experience relative 'wilderness' in low impact ways so there is a better sense of what is absent, or at least profoundly restricted, in that pocket of lawn or artificial waterfall, so the more-than-human voices that are silenced in the city can have a chance to be attended to again, so that wilderness might be encountered more on its own terms. It is not a rare experience anymore to encounter an urban student who has not entered a forest by the age of nine, they know nothing of the way the sun filters through the canopy or what it is like to be surrounded by voices and chatter much different from their own. And they may never if we do not insist that such experience is an essential part of understanding how to live in an ecologically just and conscious way in the face of ecological crises and neoliberal rationalizations.

Funding

This research was supported by a grant from the Social Sciences and Humanities Research Council of Canada.

Notes

1. Although the comments employed in this article are based on actual statements, we would like to address them as representative of 'common sentiments' that we have encountered within the field. This article is not aiming to single out any specific individuals, rather we are focused on thinking carefully about what we do and say while asking questions about our shared assumptions and practices.
2. We acknowledge that we are skirting a rather flummoxed distinction here between wilderness/wild/wildness and nature/natural world. Our sense is that the term 'nature/natural world' has become a nebulous catchall that often subsumes the term 'wilderness,' such that metropolitan parkettes, suburban 'green spaces,' the Gobi desert, and the great ice sheets covering Greenland are all bundled into a single convoluted and useless category.
3. Despite these sweeping historical generalizations and the establishment of neoliberalism as the most powerful ideological project to arise in recent decades, neoliberalism should not be considered either inevitable or necessarily hegemonic. As McCarthy and Prudham (2004) have reminded us, neoliberalism has been roundly criticized and resistance efforts have responded to its diverse strategies with equally context contingent and localized forms of refusal and dissent (for case studies see Heynen et al. 2007).

Notes on contributors

Michael W. Derby is a researcher with the Maple Ridge Environmental School Project and is presently working on his PhD at Simon Fraser University. His research seeks to develop eco-critical curriculum that imaginatively engages students and inspires caring relationships with the more-than-human world.

Laura Piersol is a PhD Candidate in Philosophy of Education at Simon Fraser University and a researcher with the Maple Ridge Environmental School Project. Her current research focuses on children's moral development regarding the natural world.

Sean Blenkinsop is a member of the Faculty of Education at Simon Fraser University. His research falls under the auspices of philosophy of education with a particular focus on the environment. He is currently involved with the Maple Ridge Environmental School Project, a publicly-funded K-7 school conceptualized with an ecological lens.

References

Bakker, Karen. 2010. "The Limits of 'Neoliberal Natures': Debating Green Neoliberalism." *Progress in Human Geography* 34 (6): 715–735.

Bauman, Zygmunt. 2000. *Liquid Modernity*. Cambridge: Polity.

Blenkinsop, Sean, and Chris Beeman. 2010. "The World as Co-Teacher: Learning to Work with a Peerless Colleague." *The Trumpeter: Journal of Ecosophy* 26 (3): 26–39.

Bonnett, Michael. 2004. "Lost in Space? Education and the Concept of Nature." *Studies in Philosophy and Education* 23: 117–130.

Castree, N., and B. Braun, eds. 2001. *Social Nature: Theory, Practice and Politics*. Oxford: Blackwell.

Cronon, William. 1995. *Uncommon Ground: Toward Reinventing Nature*. New York: Norton.

Evernden, Neil. 1985. *The Natural Alien: Humankind and Environment*. Toronto: University of Toronto Press.

Gruenewald, David. 2003. "The Best of Both Worlds: A Critical Pedagogy of Place." *Educational Researcher* 32 (4): 3–12.

Harvey, David. 2005. *A Brief History of Neoliberalism*. New York: Oxford University Press.

Heynen, Nik, James McCarthy, Scott Prudham, and Paul Robbins. 2007. "Introduction: False Promises." *Neoliberal Environments: False Promises and Unnatural Consequences*. New York: Routledge.

Himley, Matthew. 2008. "Geographies of Environmental Governance: The Nexus of Nature and Neoliberalism." *Geography Compass* 2 (2): 433–451.

Hursh, David W, and Joseph Henderson. 2011. "Contesting Global Neoliberalism and Creating Alternative Futures." *Discourse: Studies in the Cultural Politics of Education* 32 (2): 171–185.

Kingsnorth, Paul. 2013. "Dark Ecology: Searching for Truth in a Post-green World." *Orion* 32 (1): 18–29.

Leopold, Aldo. 1949. *A Sand County Almanac*. Toronto: Random House.

Lysandrou, P. 2005. "Globalisation as Commodification." *Cambridge Journal of Economics* 29 (5): 769–797.

MacKinnon, J. B. 2012. "False Idyll." *Orion* 31 (3): 42–47.

Macy, Joanna, and Molly Young Brown. 1998. *Coming back to Life: Practices to Reconnect Our Lives, Our World*. Gabriola Island: New Society Publishers.

McCarthy, James, and Scott Prudham. 2004. "Neoliberal Nature and the Nature of Neoliberalism." *Geoforum*, 35: 275–283.

McClaren, Milton. 2009. "The Place of the City in Environmental Education." In *Fields of Green*, edited by M. McKenzie, P. Hart, H. Bai, and B. Jickling, 301–306. Cresskill, NJ: Hampton Press.

Mckenzie, Marcia. 2012. "Education for Y'all: Global Neoliberalism and the Case for a Politics of Scale in Sustainability Education Policy." *Policy Futures in Education* 10 (2): 165–177.

McKenzie, Marcia, Paul Hart, Heesoon Bai, and Bob Jickling. 2009. *Fields of Green: Restorying Culture, Environment, and Education*. Cresskill, NJ: Hampton Press.

Peck, J., and A. Tickell. 2002. "Neoliberalizing Space." *Antipode* 34 (3): 380–404.

Prudham, Scott. 2007. "Neoliberalism and the Contamination of Municipal Water in Walkerton, Ontario." *Neoliberal Environments: False Promises and Unnatural Consequences*. New York: Routledge.

Sartre, Jean Paul. 1992. *Being and Nothingness: A Phenomenological Essay on Ontology*. Translated and edited by H. E. Barnes. New York: Washington Square Press.

Smith, M. 2007. "Wild-life: Anarchy, Ecology, and Ethics." *Environmental Politics* 16 (3): 470–487.

Supporting youth to develop environmental citizenship within/against a neoliberal context

Alexandra Schindel Dimick

Department of Learning and Instruction, University at Buffalo, Amherst, NY, USA

> What aspects of environmental citizenship do educators need to consider when they are teaching students about their environmental responsibilities within a neoliberal context? In this article, I respond to this question by analyzing the relationship between neoliberalism and environmental citizenship. Neoliberalism situates citizen participation as an individual concern that removes states from responsibility for public goods, such as the environment, while environmental citizenship scholarship runs the risk of promoting a diluted form of environmental engagement similar to that found within neoliberal ideology. This can result in negative consequences for the environment and for environmental participation among citizens. I conclude with a discussion of pedagogic and curricular practices that educators can use to support youth in developing forms of environmental citizenship that actively disrupt neoliberalism's privatization of responsibility for the environmental commons.

In response to the enormity of global environmental concerns, environmental education scholars contend that an educational aim of environmental education should be to develop students' civic capacities and dispositions to engage as participatory citizens[1] in relation to environmental issues and concerns (Chawla and Cushing 2007; Jensen and Schnack 2006; Schusler et al. 2009). This is often justified due to the seriousness of environmental concerns and their basis in human activity (Jensen and Schnack 2006).

Whatever the goals of environmental education, because it is like all education a social activity, its instructional form and content will be influenced by dominant social structures and ideologies. One of these is neoliberalism.[2] Neoliberalism – one of the most influential and widespread ideologies of our current political culture – is most commonly associated with economic and governing policies that attempt to maximize individual and corporate entrepreneurship through deregulation and competition (Harvey 2005). Neoliberalism has become such a pervasive and dominant way of thinking about our political and economic practices that it not only influences but also limits our commonsense understandings of the world and how we live in it (Harvey 2007; Hursh and Henderson 2011). Recent scholarship on neoliberalism and environmental education has demonstrated its influence on curriculum development and implementation (Jickling and Wals 2008; Marina, Hursh, and Markowitz 2009), discussed and explored resistance to neoliberal educational policy discourses (Gruenewald and Manteaw 2007), and analyzed the relationship between the economy and the environment (Hursh 2010; Hursh and Henderson 2011). The following vignette is illustrative of the latter case, in which high school students confront the complex ways that the economy and the environment are intertwined.

The vignette below occurred within a classroom where I was engaged in a larger study about the meanings of social justice within science education.

Vignette: reducing consumption

During a unit focused on garbage, recycling, and composting, a high school environmental science teacher, Mr Carson,[3] introduced his students to the idea that mass consumerism represents a significant environmental concern. The students in this classroom were frequently encouraged to consider the environment in their consumer purchases (e.g. purchasing energy saving household goods) and engage in pro-environmental actions such as recycling and taking public transportation or riding bicycles, but the environmental impact of consumerism had not been discussed prior to this lesson.

To teach this topic, Mr Carson showed his students a segment of a video about consumption: *The Story of Stuff* (http://www.storyofstuff.com/). In the video, the narrator briefly notes her own obsession with her iPod® and other 'stuff' and then describes the unjust and environmentally harmful aspects of consumption. She describes where stuff comes from and goes as a linear system involving extraction, production, distribution, consumption, and disposal and then describes 'another way' toward a system that 'doesn't waste resources or people' but instead focuses on sustainability and equity with processes such as green chemistry. The video asserts that consumption exploits the environment through the unfettered extraction of natural resources from the US and developing countries' soil. The video emphasizes the 'golden arrow of consumption,' which signifies consumer shopping and spending, and suggests the 'primary way our value is measured and demonstrated is by how much we contribute to this arrow, how much we consume.' After the video, Mr Carson led a class discussion and asked what students thought about the idea that 'you don't have value if you don't buy stuff.' One student, Wil, argued that he disagreed with this idea, because 'you don't have to do it,' or you do not have to consume. However, he later admitted feeling the pull of new gadgets. Other students agreed that they 'bought into' the need for the latest fashion (Field notes 2010).

A few days later, I held a group discussion with nine of the students in the class. I wanted to know what the students thought about reducing their own consumption as the video had proposed. The dialogue below was representative of two points that dominated students' responses:

Jason: No one wants to be left behind with a trend, so you got to keep up and not get left behind cause you don't wanna be made fun of.

Researcher: So is there any way that we can reduce those consumptions?

Jason: Technically you could do it, but we need the money to keep the economy going. The more stuff they come out with the more money we make. (Group Discussion 2010)

Students in this discussion group recognized the complicated nature of reducing consumption and questioned: should we consume *less* for the environment or consume *more* for the economy? The students struggled to make sense of their obligations toward the environment alongside their obligations toward the economy and their personal desires to consume more to keep up with trends. Within my research study, the teacher and students discussed consumption as a problem residing in individual choices, which I contend is symptomatic of a pervasive neoliberal ideology that makes it commonsense to view consumption – even though depicted in the video as a social problem – as merely an individual concern.

This question – consume *less* for the environment or consume *more* for the economy? – is inherently an economic concern that would be necessary regardless of additional ideological considerations. However, in the context of neoliberalism, this question reveals a significant point that merits larger consideration for environmental citizenship and its application within environmental education, namely the implications for private vs. public citizen participation and responsibility that are present in both neoliberal ideas and environmental citizenship scholarship.

Rather than having a ready solution to the consumption concerns of my students, current thought on environmental citizenship has yet to resolve them. Worse yet, some efforts to develop environmental citizenship make use of problematic neoliberal principles that are contradictory to environmental sustainability. In particular, there are inherent constraints to pursuing an idea of environmental citizenship that centers much of its attention on the private and individualized activities of citizens. Furthermore, the application of neoliberal ideology within environmental citizenship poses a significant constraint on environmental sustainability efforts. Given this concern, this article raises the following question: what aspects of environmental citizenship do educators need to consider when they are teaching students about their environmental responsibilities within a neoliberal context? I respond to this question by analyzing the relationship between neoliberalism and environmental citizenship. In the following pages, I first describe my study methods. Following this, I discuss the ways in which neoliberalism situates citizenship and the problems that this poses for environmental sustainability. Lastly, I explore how environmental education might foster more productive forms of environmental citizenship among youth in ways that seek to overcome the constraints and problems of neoliberalism.

Study methods

The data in this article derive from a qualitative case study (Stake 1995; Yin 2003) that sought to examine the possibilities and tensions in social justice science education. The study was conducted from September 2009 to January 2010 in an environmental science class in an urban public charter high school located on the East Coast of the US The class consisted of 24 African American and Black American[4] students and their White, male teacher, Mr Carson, in his fifth year of teaching. Mr Carson described himself as a social justice educator. Of the students in Mr Carson's class, five girls and four boys participated in my research.

I collected data from multiple sources to triangulate my research findings: participant observation within each class during the study; curricular texts and assignments; pre- and post-interviews and biweekly focused discussions with the teacher; and monthly focus groups with students. Focused discussions with the teacher explored how he put his understanding of teaching science for social justice into practice and how he reflected on his practice and the students' responses. Student focus group discussions occurred during lunch and after school and attempted to record students' voices and understandings of their classroom experiences. I also examined students' written assignments when applicable to the research.

Data analysis

Data analysis began at the start of my research because it influenced the questions I asked of participants in discussions. I wanted to understand the ways in which participants made sense of their classroom experiences and focused on issues raised during preliminary reconstruction analysis of the data (Carspecken 1996). After using open coding to assign initial meaning reconstructions to the data, I narrowed my focus on particular segments of the data for deeper analysis.

Neoliberal citizen-subjects

Neoliberal ideology represents a theory of political and economic practices that extend market rationality and values to nearly every sphere of human activity (Harvey 2007). Neoliberalism signifies an ideological shift in understandings of capitalism in which unregulated, competitive markets represent the most optimal and productive form of economic development (Brand 2007). The extension of the neoliberal project to the level of individuals occurs when individual citizen-subjects are positioned as entrepreneurs and consumers who strategize for their own well-being rather than as citizens of larger global communities within social and environmental contexts (Brown 2005).

Citizenship has historically been the subject of much debate in political science. Classic liberal and republican definitions of citizenship share a common interest in 'political relationships and activity in the public arena' (Dobson and Bell 2006, 7). Changes to this understanding have materialized relatively recently with the emergence of neoliberalism. For example, although there are distinctions between individual moral and economic activity in classical liberalism, neoliberalism blurs these distinctions by constructing individuals as entrepreneurs in all aspects of life (Brown 2005). According to Brown, the model neoliberal citizen-subject 'bears full responsibility for the consequences for his or her actions no matter how severe the constraints on this action' (43). The neoliberal citizen must navigate various options and strategize for herself rather than organizing with others. Examples of this strategizing can be seen across various international contexts: educational policies that promote charter schools and vouchers in the US and Great Britain (Hursh and Henderson 2011); environmental policies that promote individual behavior change for sustainable living (Kenis and Mathijs 2012); and policies that situate teachers as entrepreneurial strategists to obtain work (Robert 2013). In the neoliberal context, state policies and discourses situate citizenship in personal activity as individuals are expected to perform as 'individual "entrepreneurs" in every aspect of life … and citizenship is reduced to success in this entrepreneurship' (Brown 2005, 43–44).

Neoliberalism has influenced environmental sustainability through a shifting in responsibility for the environmental commons from the state to the individual. Neoliberal ideology actively seeks to disavow the state from responsibility for the common good (e.g. clean environment), while individuals are increasingly asked to do more for the environment (e.g. Hobson 2013). It is not surprising that movements such as environmentalism, which are potentially oppositional to capitalism, are transformed within a neoliberal ethos. Environmental action could potentially limit or constrain capitalist growth and accumulation through the radical political act of reducing or ceasing consumption (Barry 2006). Instead, strands or grains of environmental movements accommodate themselves to a neoliberal commonsense by focusing on individual, rather than collective, action. This can be seen in 'green lifestyle' movements. The logic of green lifestyles rests on the idea that individual entrepreneurs should accommodate environmental concerns in their household purchases and activities in order to reduce CO_2 emissions. As a result, the burden of responsibility for a clean environment increasingly rests with individual citizen-subjects making lifestyle choices for an environmentally sustainable future.

Under neoliberalism, failure to achieve environmental sustainability is equated with the aggregate failure of individuals to incorporate rationality into their private sphere environmental decision-making rather than with a failure of the state. Such attention to individual responsibility can also be seen within scholarship on environmental citizenship. The following section focuses on the problems that arise when environmental citizenship makes use of the neoliberal idea in which environmental responsibility resides in individual environmental activity.

Environmental citizenship in the context of neoliberalism

The concept of environmental citizenship has gained considerable traction among scholars over the past decade, as scholars have raised questions about the meaning of environmental citizenship, what locations it encompasses (local, state, international), and the means by which sustainability might be achieved, by whom (through the work of under paid labor), and under what circumstances (economic enticements, legal regulations, participatory democracy that emerges in the face of environmental injustices) (Dobson and Bell 2006; Hobson 2013). Environmental citizenship expands upon existing conceptions of citizenship to encompass individuals' responsibility to work toward environmental sustainability. In this section, I focus on a key claim of environmental citizenship that is important in analyzing the influence of neoliberalism – the argument that environmental citizenship requires some form of blurring between the traditional boundaries of public and private sphere rights and responsibilities in order to work for the common good of environmental sustainability (e.g. Dobson and Bell 2006; Dobson and Valencia Sáiz 2005; Scerri 2013). As Dobson (2007) contends, the environmental citizen is one who 'make[s] a commitment to the common good' because 'self-interested behaviours will not always protect or sustain public goods such as the environment' (280). Several problems with this conception of environmental citizenship can be illuminated when examined in the context of neoliberalism.

Scholarship on environmental citizenship echoes neoliberal logic in suggesting that responsibility for sustainability 'lies with the citizen' (Brand 2007, 624; Dobson and Bell 2006). This can be seen across various environmental sustainability endeavors: plastic bag taxes that attempt to encourage reusable bags, environmental health policies that provide education to increase sustainable lifestyle choices in private spheres of life, and public education that promotes sustainable lifestyles (e.g. reduction of greenhouse gas emissions through use of public or bike transportation, reducing domestic energy and water usage, recycling, etc.). While private sphere sustainability efforts are necessary, the privatizing of environmental sustainability signifies a shift in responsibility from the state and toward the individual.

One problem with the shift in privatizing responsibility for the environment lies in a contradiction – the environment is a public good that all are intended to share, yet individuals must independently take on responsibility for this good. Environmental sustainability holds the potential for collective and shared rights to be available for all, yet individuals must choose to independently take on the moral responsibility of sustainable living to produce this right for all to share. Under neoliberalism, moral responsibility is equated with rational action (Brown 2005). Although individuals bear the burden of responsibility, they do not necessarily benefit from their own pro-environmental activities. Many tangible benefits are dispersed (e.g. clean air and water) among all earth's inhabitants, while only some benefits may go to the individual actor (e.g. intrinsic or moral value, positive peer social value, or long-term monetary benefits). Unfortunately, as economic theorists contend, when benefits are collectively shared but individually born, there will be an inefficient or sub-optimal public good provided, because some individuals will 'free ride' off the goods produced by others (Olson 1971). Thus, private sphere environmental activities are unlikely to achieve the most favorable results for the environment.

A second significant problem with this shift lies in the cultural, structural, and other factors that may influence environmental decision-making. Environmental choices are influenced and constrained by such tangible factors as identity, habits, government services, and finances (Whitmarsh et al. 2009). For example, the presence of bicycle lanes to promote commuter biking may influence one's decision to drive or ride a bike to work just as much as one's cultural upbringing. In response to the unpredictability of private sphere environmental activity, Hobson (2013) suggests environmental citizenship may not be a state to be achieved or arrived at, but rather a 'contingent and conditional commitment, influenced strongly by contextual factors' (68).

We can view this privatization of responsibility as a failure in the application of neoliberal logic to protect the environmental commons, because it untethers the state from its responsibility to regulate and protect a common good. Scerri (2013) contends:

> This privatizing of responsibility for redressing socially created problems provides self-responsible individuals with opportunities to address the impacts of their own localized actions *as if* there were no legitimate authority charged with organizing the rules for life held in common. (emphasis in original, 297)

Thus, the variability in individuals' environmentally sustainable activities creates a vacuum of responsibility for the environmental commons.

While a neoliberal environmental citizen logic does not match with the fundamentally public nature of the environment, it also delimits the kinds of environmental activities people engage in. The application of neoliberal logic to environmental participation promotes a problematic conception of citizenship as a private moral obligation rather than as an activity that occurs with others in a political community. Within this logic, citizen engagement is solitary and individuals are situated as lone actors in relation to environmental concerns. Yet, collective endeavors and political communities do not evolve spontaneously, since 'private moral obligations do not automatically translate into political obligations' (Scerri 2013, 298). However, engagement in political communities is precisely what scholars advocate as potentially being able to foster greater environmental and societal benefits (Agyeman and Evans 2006; Barry 2006; Hobson 2013).

In summary, I have discussed multiple problems associated with the application of neoliberalism – specifically, the privatization of responsibility for the environmental commons – within environmental citizenship. Nevertheless, it is equally important to emphasize that individual pro-environmental activities are both significant and necessary. Environmental health can be viewed as a collective problem that arises, at least in part, 'from the sum of individual preferences and consumption' (Dovers and Handmer 1993, 219). However, reliance on individual pro-environmental activities runs the risk of promoting a diluted form of environmental engagement that, similar to neoliberal ideology, abrogates the state from its responsibility for the environmental commons. This can result in negative consequences for the environment, while it also presents a weakened form of environmental citizenship by forwarding a form of environmental engagement that is disconnected from the contexts in which environmental decisions are made and from broader political activities.

Supporting youth in the development of environmental citizenship

What does all this mean for the preparation of environmental citizens who are capable of addressing current and future environmental problems? Environmental education that seeks to develop environmental citizenship – or to assist students in understanding their roles in society and their obligations toward the environment – must do so in ways that overcome the problems outlined above. Prevailing neoliberal discourses about individual action and consumption position youth in ways that reinforce existing relationships of inequality rather than disrupt them. This occurs when citizenship is associated with private activity and individualized entrepreneurship and consumption rather than with broader, collective endeavors that can work to disrupt social and environmental injustices (Agyeman and Evans 2006). Yet, these relationships and patterns can be disrupted through pedagogical and curricular practices that attempt to support youth to develop forms of environmental citizenship that actively push against neoliberalism's privatization of responsibility for the environmental commons. In this section, I describe four such practices. The form of environmental citizenship that I advocate for here involves working against systems of oppression and domination and toward both social and environmental justice.

Identify and critique

A first step in this process involves assisting youth in identifying and critiquing dominant and normalized understandings of the environment and their environmental participation. Various educational theories that advocate for social change recommend both critically analyzing and taking action upon the social and economic systems that uphold inequalities in the educational system and in society (e.g. Freire 2000; Freire and Macedo 1987; North 2008; Shor 1992). Freire's 'critical consciousness' calls upon educators to help students 'read,' or understand and critique, and 'write,' or take action upon, injustices and modes of oppression in their lives and society. A few of the most environmentally devastating normalized understandings that youth can 'read' and 'write' include the following: the assumption that neoliberal free-market economics represents the most beneficial political and economic practices for societies (Booth 2004); the disconnect between economic and consumer practices and its affect on the environment (Booth 2004; Gruenewald 2004; Hursh 2010); the anthropocentric belief that situates all other lives inferior to that of humans and which prioritizes humans' right to manipulate and exploit natural resources (Martusewicz and Schnakenberg 2010; Peters 2013). Yet, developing critical consciousness always exists within situational contexts, and the space and place in which social transformations exist must be decolonized and reinhabited (Gruenewald 2003). Thus, Gruenewald challenges educators to embrace a 'critical pedagogy of place' in order to develop critical consciousness while incorporating 'critical social and ecological concerns into one's understanding of place' (9).

A particular challenge in the process of developing critical consciousness and situating it within place-based ecological concerns lies in assisting students with the development of dispositions toward social and environmental justice. Classroom practices that attempt this must recognize that entrenched feelings, such as mistrust of others or misalignment between competing values, might influence learning, actions, and feelings (North 2008). Post-structuralist scholars reflecting on classroom practices and inequality suggest that 'oppression originates in discourse, and in particular, in the citing of particular discourses, which frame how people think, feel, act, and interact' (Kumashiro 2000, 40). This perspective challenges us to consider the ways that particular environmental activities and discourses might reproduce oppression or exclude some youth who do not view themselves as fitting within the normalized perspective of environmental thinking or activity. For example, ecofeminists remind us that individualized pro-environmental activities, which are reflected in neoliberal discourses of environmental activity, may reproduce dominant modes of oppression among women or caregivers upon whom the unpaid labor of the household environmental duties may fall (MacGregor 2006).

Education that supports youth to develop as environmental citizens must recognize and challenge dominant discourses. In one study in which youth engaged in a habitat restoration community service event for Earth Day, one youth connected this activity to his cultural identity as a Mexican and linked this event to the kind of work for which one should receive payment (Tzou, Scalone, and Bell 2010). To disrupt dominant social hierarchies and patterns of oppression, the authors contend that youth's narratives must instead be placed at the center of environmental education to 'create empowering positions for youth' (116). However, Barrett (2008) challenges educators to recognize that centering youth's voices may 'still impose agendas that support particular versions of appropriate thought, behaviour, and action' (212–213). Competing discourses often influence what teachers and students conceive of as possible. To counterbalance this, Barrett suggests that educators, researchers, and students can examine student apathy, or lack of care, toward the environment by 'assisting [students] in deconstructing ways in which they have been discursively produced – ways they have been constituted, and constituted themselves as, for example, a good student' (220) or a good environmental science learner or activist. This may open possibilities for students and teachers to reposition themselves with greater possibility for social and environmental change and resistance.

In summary, environmental education that supports students to work toward an environmental citizenship that breaks with a neoliberal consciousness will foster a critical pedagogy of place while simultaneously examining normative beliefs and practices that may inhibit the work of social and environmental justice in various contexts. As youth engage in this process, they can form the knowledge and dispositions to consider and challenge the global social and environmental impact of current ways of living.

The context of decision-making

Supporting students to develop as environmental citizens within a neoliberal context that imposes features or problems, I have described above means that youth must learn that important individual actions exist within a broad context that can and should involve civic activities with others. A primary or sole reliance on individual sustainable lifestyles ignores the situated contexts in which people make choices and any cultural, structural, financial, or other factors that may influence environmental decision-making. Once these contexts are understood, students can also learn that there are limits and constraints to individual action and consumption when they occur in isolation (Whitmarsh et al. 2009). As Whitmarsh et al. explain:

> [W]e see individual cognitive decisions about consumption … as mediated through socially-shaped lifestyle choices, resulting in sets of practices which are in turn delimited by social systems of provision and the rules and resources of macro-level structures. That is, individual choices both shape and are shaped by wider social structures. (3)

As one example of this, a lack of infrastructure that would support recycling may limit or constrain many individuals in communities from engaging in this activity. Yet, recognizing that pro-environmental activities are related to a community's infrastructure means that students can learn that individual actions need not be considered solely as private sphere responsibilities, but, instead, that there are collective responsibilities associated with individual activities. This releases individuals from taking on the entire burden of responsibility for environmental sustainability – unlike in neoliberal thought where the burden of responsibility rests primarily with individual entrepreneurs.

Another significant mitigating factor to consider as part of students' decision-making is the role of developmental readiness (Sobel 1993, 1996). Sobel cautions that ecological commitments must begin in childhood with opportunities for children to explore and connect with their environments rather than focusing on abstract empathy and decision-making, such as caring for the plight of animals far from their communities. Over time, youth can develop critical reflection and social action. Equally important to such ecological readiness is the role of youth's identity formation and how this relates to their decision-making. For example, adolescence is a sensitive time period in youths' lives as they define their identities, which are very much intertwined with the fashion, products, and brands they wear, the music they listen to, and the icons they own (e.g. jewelry and music players). In examining consumption, for example, educators draw attention to the ways people and the environment are interwoven with students' personal choices. Thus, educators must take youth's developmental states into consideration and create thoughtful, supportive environments that affirm youth's identity formation in the midst of deeply personal political reflections.

Global political communities

Environmental citizenship can also confront the neoliberal privatization of the environmental commons. Environmental citizen participation must involve identifying governing authorities responsible for environmental concerns and holding them accountable for creating policies and engaging in practices that protect and restore the environment. To attain a global environmental commons, environmental citizens must build global political communities that stretch beyond our figurative and national borders and share in collective efforts to hold nation states accountable for the environment. Building global communities is never simple and has proven complicated even within local communities in which culture, socioeconomic status, ethnicity, gender, sexuality, and other factors too often interfere with communication and alliance-building (Dimick 2012; North 2008). Thus, the need for global communities means youth must develop the disposition to care critically about and for others' well-being (Antrop-González and De Jesús 2006).

Conclusion

The alternative viewpoint on consumerism that was presented in the vignette represents a critical and significant first step. However, stopping with this lesson left the students alone to grapple with a critique that situated the individual against a larger system of power. Individualized problems invite individual solutions. Given the dominance of neoliberal thought in our age, educators can easily find themselves focusing on important but narrow aspects of environmental citizenship, particularly how individual choices affect the environment. This is important, but purely individual action is insufficient to help achieve environmental sustainability and positions citizens as independent actors who must bear the burden of responsibility for the environment in isolated, private spheres of living. Although environmental sustainability necessitates individualized consumer and lifestyle choices, focusing too much on private responsibility for the environment within environmental education may curtail youths' abilities to understand the root causes of global environmental injustices or to conceive of solutions that 'change established systems and structures that reproduce patterns of injustice over time' (Westheimer and Kahne 2004, 240; see also Courtenay-Hall and Rogers 2002). Individual action and consumption show students only limited ways that they can interact with the environment, but there is another way – as the kind of environmental citizen this article has favored – in which they can act as members of a public that have shared obligations with others to address concerns about the environment and its resources for themselves, for the global community, for non-human life on earth, and for future generations.

Acknowledgements

I would like to thank the co-editors of this special issue – David Hursh, Joseph Henderson, and David Greenwood – and the reviewers for their generous and helpful guidance on this article. Thanks also to Matthew Dimick for his editing and feedback.

Notes

1. My use of the concept of 'citizen' in this article is not without significant reservations. Citizenship has been used in problematic ways by states and for political purposes in order to deny rights to education, health care, representation, and voting, particularly among indigenous, colonized, and migrating people. Thus, it is with reservation that I use the term citizenship in this article to engage in the environmental citizenship dialogue

within environmental education and environmental politics scholarship (e.g. Reid et al. 2008; Scerri 2013), who use it to signify educational outcomes for students who engage in social and political processes or to consider ways people work together to sustain and restore the environmental commons.
2. Other ideological constructs might be used to examine environmental citizenship, including individualism and consumerism. However, for my purposes such ideologies were not found as constructive as neoliberalism because they do not adequately address concerns for the common good and citizens' rights and responsibilities.
3. All names used for participants in this article are pseudonyms.
4. The students identify as both African American and Black American. Many students in the class identify with multiple cultures and histories, including African American, Filipino, Haitian, Dominican, West Indian, and Puerto Rican to name a few.

Notes on contributor

Alexandra Schindel Dimick is an assistant professor at the University at Buffalo. Her research interests include youth civic engagement, environmental participation, and social justice in science education.

References

Agyeman, J., and B. Evans. 2006. "Overcoming Obstacles to Ecological Citizenship: The Dominant Social Paradigm and Local Environmentalism." In *Environmental Citizenship*, edited by A. Dobson and D. Bell, 153–184. Cambridge, MA: The MIT Press.
Antrop-González, R., and A. De Jesús. 2006. "Toward a Theory of Critical Care in Urban Small School Reform: Examining Structures and Pedagogies of Caring in Two Latino Community-based Schools." *International Journal of Qualitative Studies in Education* 19 (4): 409–433.
Barrett, M. 2008. "Participatory Pedagogy in Environmental Education: Reproduction or Disruption?" In *Participation and Learning: Perspectives on Education and the Environment, Health and Sustainability*, edited by A. Reid, B. B. Jensen, J. Nikel, and V. Simovska, 212–224. Dordrecht: Springer.
Barry, J. 2006. "Resistance is Fertile: From Environmental to Sustainability Citizenship." In *Environmental Citizenship*, edited by A. Dobson and D. Bell, 21–48. Cambridge, MA: The MIT Press.
Booth, D. E. 2004. *Hooked on Growth: Economic Addictions and the Environment*. Lanham, MD: Rowman & Littlefield.
Brand, P. 2007. "Green Subjection: The Politics of Neoliberal Urban Environmental Management." *International Journal of Urban and Regional Research* 31 (3): 616–632.
Brown, W. 2005. *Edgework: Critical Essays on Knowledge and Politics*. Princeton, NJ: Princeton University Press.
Carspecken, P. 1996. *Critical Ethnography in Educational Research: A Theoretical and Practical Guide*. New York: Routledge.
Chawla, L., and D. F. Cushing. 2007. "Education for Strategic Environmental Behavior." *Environmental Education Research* 14 (3): 215–237.
Courtenay-Hall, P., and L. Rogers. 2002. "Gaps in Mind: Problems in Environmental Knowledge-behaviour Modelling Research." *Environmental Education Research* 8 (3): 283–297.
Dimick, A. S. 2012. "Student Empowerment in an Environmental Science Classroom: Toward a Framework for Social Justice Science Education." *Science Education* 96 (6): 990–1012.
Dobson, A. 2007. "Environmental Citizenship: Towards Sustainable Development." *Sustainable Development* 15: 276–285.
Dobson, A., and D. Bell. 2006. *Environmental Citizenship*. Cambridge, MA: The MIT Press.
Dobson, A., and Á. Valencia Sáiz. 2005. "Introduction." *Environmental Politics* 14: 157–162.
Dovers, S. R., and J. W. Handmer. 1993. "Contradictions in Sustainability." *Environmental Conservation* 20 (3): 217–222.

NEOLIBERALISM AND ENVIRONMENTAL EDUCATION

Freire, P. 2000. *Pedagogy of the Oppressed* (30th anniversary edition). New York: Continuum.

Freire, P., and D. Macedo. 1987. *Literacy: Reading the Word and the World*. New York: Continuum.

Gruenewald, D. 2003. "The Best of Both Worlds: A Critical Pedagogy of Place." *Educational Researcher* 32 (4): 3–12.

Gruenewald, D. 2004. "A Foucauldian Analysis of Environmental Education: Toward the Socioecological Challenge of the Earth Charter." *Curriculum Inquiry* 34 (1): 71–107.

Gruenewald, D., and B. O. Manteaw. 2007. "Oil and Water Still: How No Child Left behind Limits and Distorts Environmental Education in US Schools." *Environmental Education Research* 13 (2): 171–188.

Harvey, D. 2005. *A Brief History of Neoliberalism*. New York: Oxford University Press.

Harvey, D. 2007. "Neoliberalism as Creative Destruction." *Annals of the American Academy of Political and Social Science* 610: 22–44.

Hobson, K. 2013. "On the Making of the Environmental Citizen." *Environmental Politics* 22 (1): 56–72.

Hursh, D. 2010. "The Long Emergency: Educating for Democracy and Sustainability during Our Global Crisis." In *Critical Theories, Radical Pedagogies, and Social Education: New Perspectives for Social Studies Education*, edited by A. P. DeLeon and E. W. Ross, 139–150. Rotterdam: Sense.

Hursh, D., and J. Henderson. 2011. "Contesting Global Neoliberalism and Creating Alternative Futures." *Discourse: Studies in the Cultural Politics of Education* 32 (2): 171–185.

Jensen, B. B., and K. Schnack. 2006. "The Action Competence Approach in Environmental Education." *Environmental Education Research* 12 (3–4): 471–486.

Jickling, B., and A. Wals. 2008. "Globalization and Environmental Education: Looking beyond Sustainable Development." *Journal of Curriculum Studies* 40 (1): 1–21.

Kenis, A., and E. Mathijs. 2012. "Beyond Individual Behavior Change: The Role of Power, Knowledge and Strategy in Tackling Climate Change." *Environmental Education Research* 18 (1): 45–65.

Kumashiro, K. 2000. "Toward a Theory of Anti-oppressive Education." *Review of Education Research* 70 (1): 25–53.

MacGregor, S. 2006. "No Sustainability without Justice: A Feminist Critique of Environmental Citizenship." In *Environmental Citizenship*, edited by A. Dobson and D. Bell, 101–126. Cambridge, MA: The MIT Press.

Marina, C. A., D. Hursh, and D. Markowitz. 2009. "Contradictions in Educational Policy: Implementing Integrated Problem-based Environmental Health Curriculum in a High Stakes Environment." *Environmental Education Research* 15 (3): 279–297.

Martusewicz, R. A., and G. Schnakenberg. 2010. "EcoJustice, Community-based Learning, and Social Studies Education." In *Critical Theories, Radical Pedagogies, and Social Education: New Perspectives for Social Studies Education*, edited by A. P. DeLeon and E. W. Ross, 25–41. Rotterdam: Sense.

North, C. 2008. "What is All This Talk about 'Social Justice'? Mapping the Terrain of Education's Latest Catchphrase." *The Teachers College Record* 110 (6): 1182–1206.

Olson, M. 1971. *The Logic of Collective Action: Public Goods and the Theory of Groups*. Cambridge, MA: Harvard University Press.

Peters, M. 2013. "Greening the Knowledge Economy; Ecosophy, Ecology, and Economy." In *International Handbook of Research on Environmental Education*, edited by R. B. Stevenson, M. Brody, J. Dillon, and A. E. J. Wals, 498–506. New York: Routledge.

Reid, A., B. Jensen, J. Nikel, and V. Simovska. 2008. *Participation and Learning: Perspectives on Education and the Environment, Health and Sustainability*. Dordrecht: Springer.

Robert, S. A. 2013. "Incentives, Teachers, and Gender at Work." *Education Policy Analysis Archives* 21 (31): 1–25.

Scerri, A. 2013. "Green Citizenship and the Political Critique of Injustice." *Citizenship Studies* 17 (3–4): 293–307.

Schusler, T. M., M. E. Krasny, S. J. Peters, and D. J. Decker. 2009. "Developing Citizens and Communities through Youth Environmental Action." *Environmental Education Research* 15 (1): 111–127.

Shor, I. 1992. *Empowering Education: Critical Teaching for Social Change*. Chicago, IL: University of Chicago Press.

Sobel, D. 1993. *Children's Special Places: Exploring the Role of Forts, Dens, and Bush Houses in Middle Childhood*. Tuscon, AZ: Zephyr Press.

Sobel, D. 1996. *Beyond Ecophobia: Reclaiming the Heart in Nature Education*. Great Barrington, MA: The Orion Society and The Myrin Institute.

Stake, R. 1995. *The Art of Case Study Research*. Thousand Oaks, CA: Sage.

Tzou, C., G. Scalone, and P. Bell. 2010. "The Role of Narratives and Social Positioning in How Place Gets Constructed for and by Youth." *Equity & Excellence in Education* 43 (1): 105–119.

Westheimer, J., and J. Kahn. 2004. "What Kind of Citizen? The Politics of Educating for Democracy." *American Educational Research Journal* 24 (20): 237–269.

Whitmarsh, L., S. J. O'Neill, G. Seyfang, and I. Lorenzoni. 2009. Carbon Capability: What Does It Mean, How Prevalent is It, and How Can We Promote It? *Tyndall Centre for Climate Change Research*. Accessed February 2, 2013. http://www.tyndall.ac.uk/sites/default/files/twp132.pdf.

Yin, R. K. 2003. *Case Study Research: Design and Methods*. Thousand Oaks, CA: Sage.

Negotiating managerialism: professional recognition and teachers of sustainable development education

Hamish Ross

School of Education, The University of Edinburgh, Edinburgh, UK

Policy strategies to reward teachers for field-specific expertise have become internationally widespread and have been criticized for being manifestations of neoliberal globalization. In Scotland, there is political commitment to such strategies, including one to award recognition to teachers for expertise in sustainable development education (SDE). This study examined 22 application forms for that award, conducted face-to-face discussions with 8 successful teacher applicants, and with two policy-making actors and analyzed the websites of relevant policy institutions. The study asked how the concept of 'the professional teacher of SDE' was negotiated through the policy. In both policy and teacher discourse, there was a struggle to reconcile the constructions of the teacher as an individualized generic manager and as committed to SDE as a networked, disciplinary field of endeavor. Managerialism is a neoliberal technology, so these tensions are interpreted as traces of neoliberal ideology. Moreover, their negotiation is interpreted as de- and re-bordering engagements with globalization. The critical potential of these interpretations is in the revealed incompleteness of the engagements, leaving teachers and policy-makers with scope to manage responses to neoliberal globalization in SDE.

Introduction

This study of a teacher reward policy for sustainable development education (SDE) explored how the wider ideology of neoliberalism was mediated. It claims that this policy in Scotland can be seen as representative of a wider, international movement of teacher reward policy-making. While researchers have argued that such educational movements are ideologically neoliberal in character and globalizing in effect (Rizvi and Lingard 2010), few studies have examined the specific ideological work that takes place within individual cases. For the purposes of this study, neoliberal globalization was understood as strategy (Clarke 2004, 2008) enacted through various technologies including managerialism. Managerialism refers to the delivery of externally developed standards or objectives through processes such as auditing, planning, target-setting, monitoring, and quality-checking in order to constantly improve the flexibility of an institution and the quality of its services to its clients. Managerialism is one of several private-sector technologies that have redefined both public-sector service provision and the concept of professionalism (Clarke and Newman 1997).

The interpretation of interview and documentary data collected for this policy case suggested that the concept of 'the professional teacher of SDE' included tensions between seeing the teacher as an individual manager of an agenda and also as committed to a networked, disciplinary field of endeavor. These tensions are argued to be effects of neoliberal globalization. This is pertinent because the policy in question concerns SDE, which itself has been subject to critique in relation to neoliberal globalization (Jickling and Wals 2008). However, while the policy described here was linked to neoliberal ideology, it was not defined by it. The study concludes that to identify the work involved is more critical than either accepting or ignoring a dominant and globalizing neoliberal ideology.

The global context

There is an international focus on the development of minimum teacher competency standards (Larsen 2010) and rewards, which attracts metaphors such as Kriewaldt's 'policy juggernaut' (2012, 31). For mid-career teachers, more advanced teaching standards and awards (sometimes mandatory), and field-specific standards and awards (usually voluntary), can also be found worldwide. There are studied cases for example in Australia (Ingvarson 2010), the People's Republic of China (Ko and Adamson 2011), the USA (Andrews 2011), Jordan (Obeidat and Al-Hassan 2009), and Latin America (Vaillant and Rossel 2012).

The argument that such policies reflect neoliberal globalization is that they incentivize teacher learning and modernization, or up-skilling, in order that national schooling can continue to contribute to the competitive expansion of human capital and economic growth in the face of the changing global realities of the free-market (the global knowledge economy) and its effects (e.g. mass migration and climate change). Such policies are thus informed by neoliberalism as a 'theory of political economic practices proposing that human well-being can best be advanced by the maximization of entrepreneurial freedoms within an institutional framework characterized by private property rights, individual liberty, unencumbered free markets, and free trade' (Harvey 2007, 22). It is possible to cast that light upon the educational phenomena of standards, awards, and teacher education and development policies (Bates 2008; Beck 2008; Collinson et al. 2009; Sclafani 2009) although the argument is rarely central in studies of individual standards or award policies, even where the potential for such argument exists (Mackenzie 2007; Obeidat and Al-Hassan 2009; Andrews 2011; Vaillant and Rossel 2012).

There is also good reason to explore the relationships between neoliberalism, teaching standards, and SDE. Sterling (2001), Bassey (2002), and many others have observed that government emphases on the competitive development of human capital, through a range of education policies, involve unsustainable assumptions (such as continuous global economic growth or expanding inequality) and have detrimental effects on the prospects for sustainability through education. For example, the universalizing tendency of fields of performance comparison invoked by (some) articulations of educational standards or awards criteria can undermine the local-centric pedagogies of (some) approaches to SDE and related pedagogies (Cutter-Mackenzie, Clarke, and Smith 2008; Thomas and Kearney 2008; Bieler 2012). Such studies might accept the merits of standards – indeed, transformative standards have been proposed (Andrzejewski, Baltodano, and Symcox 2009) – but they highlight the need to take seriously the possibility of global neoliberal influence upon their construction and implementation.

The local context

The present study explores a specific policy site in Scotland, a country that demonstrates significant commitment to the teaching standards and awards agenda discussed internationally above. Scotland has a population of approximately 5.3 million, including 50,000 teachers working with 670,500 pupils in 2606 publicly funded schools.[1] All these teachers must be on a register maintained by the General Teaching Council for Scotland (GTCS). The GTCS is the long-standing, statutory but independent professional regulatory body that claims to maintain and enhance teaching standards in Scotland.[2] The GTCS defines minimum competency standards, which have recently been re-devised into a career-long continuum. Public school teachers are required to engage in 'professional update' to maintain their registration. This requires of all teachers: 'Engagement in professional learning; Self-evaluation against the appropriate GTC Scotland Professional Standard; Discussion of this engagement and the impact of this, as part of the [the employer's] professional review and development process; Maintain[ing] a professional learning record and portfolio of evidence; 5 yearly confirmation of this engagement to GTC Scotland.'[3]

Scotland is also committed to field-specific recognition. The policy discussed in this study awarded 'professional recognition' for teachers' expertise in SDE. To gain this recognition, registered teachers filled in an application form detailing a process of professional development and submitted it to the GTCS with a portfolio of documentary evidence. If successful, the award was noted on the register of teachers and announced in the magazine for Scotland's teachers. In some cases, there were award ceremonies.

To summarize the preceding sections: Teacher standards and award policies can reflect processes of neoliberal globalization; Scottish public school education is committed to such policies; and neoliberal globalization is often taken to be antithetical to SDE. It is therefore of interest that Scotland has an award policy that recognizes teachers for SDE. There follows a study of that policy.

Building the case: data generation

The case presented here developed reactively. A functional policy study (Ross 2011) was commissioned by the GTCS and WWF Scotland.[4] That study was independently extended and re-examined by the same researcher to provide the present critical case study. This study will report high-level interpretation from several data sources.

The following data from the original commissioned study were re-examined:

(1) In-depth interviews, with a total of eight teachers ($n = 8$) who achieved professional recognition for their work in SDE, each either in an individual interview ($n = 3$) or in one of two focus group interviews ($n = 5$). The sample interviewed could not be shown to be representative, being limited to all who agreed and were available in the project timeframe ($n = 8$ out of a total of 35 teachers who had been awarded professional recognition for SDE). All

the interviewed teachers were female, and all but one worked in primary schooling (with pupils aged 4–11 years old), from three urban, two suburban/mixed, and three rural communities. The smallest school represented had less than 5 pupils, and the largest primary school had approximately 500 pupils. All the interviews and focus group interviews were semi-structured and the same stem questions were used with all participants. These concerned the following: interviewees' SDE practices; their reflection upon and evaluation of their practices, including in terms of pupil outcomes; their role in spreading practice; their reasons for seeking recognition; and what consequences had arisen as a result of applying for, and receiving, recognition. The longest interview lasted 80 min, and the shortest was 40 min. All were video-recorded, and this record was used directly in analysis. Whether a teacher participated in an individual or focus group interview was regarded as immaterial. Although clearly different settings, the salience of interaction effects in focus group interviews depends on the purposes of the interview, moderator activity, and subsequent analysis (Morgan 2010). In this case, the moderator role was to ensure that each participant had the opportunity to respond to each question or point raised. Focus group interviews were originally planned for efficiency reasons, and individual interviews occurred because of the unavailability of participants for focus group interviews and were with the 3 participants from the most rural schools.

(2) These and other teachers' application forms ($n = 22$ out of a total of 35), which they had submitted to the GTCS in seeking professional recognition. The sample for the application form analysis could not be shown to be representative and was limited to all those who provided positive consent to having their application forms examined for the original study (the whole population was asked). The examined applications forms were from 2 male and 20 female teachers, all working in different schools, of which, 19 were primary schools and 3 were secondary schools, in 8 urban, 9 rural and 5 suburban/mixed school communities. One applicant's school was privately funded and one was a special school for pupils with severe, complex, and profound additional support needs.

The following data were generated as a part of the extended study:

(3) The written policy position of the policy-making bodies in relation to professional recognition, as represented by the GTCS's website and their public presentations on the policy, and the *Eco Schools Scotland* website[5] (the nature and relevance of this organization will be detailed below).

(4) Elite interviews with two policy actors ($n = 2$): the (then) manager of *Eco Schools Scotland* and the Education Advisor for the GTCS whose roles included professional recognition policy. These individual interviews were less formally structured and were audio-recorded. They explored the interviewees' understandings of the history of their organizations' involvement in the professional recognition for SDE policy, as well as their understandings of what the policy was supposed to achieve.

The distinction between the original and extended studies is highlighted above for two reasons. Firstly, the original study was commissioned, explorative, and inductive, whereas the critical re-analysis of the original study data and outputs, and the analysis of the extension study data, all of which produced the case below, was more deductive and explicitly focused on the exploration of neoliberal globalization and the policy context. Secondly, between the two studies, there was an incidental shift in the position of the researcher: from external evaluator (of the field-specific professional recognition policy) to policy insider (as an invited member of a GTCS-organized working group on a related issue). The case below was pieced together (Kincheloe 2001) with care for these shifts, but the handling of the subjectivities of both researcher and participants was inevitably, technically, and ethically complex (Ramaekers 2014). For these reasons, the study does not offer highly selective direct quotation and the case is told exclusively in the researcher's voice.

Telling the case (1): the professional teacher of SDE in policy

This section looks at the work that the policy and its authors performed in the construction of the professional teacher of SDE. The next section will look at how the teachers negotiated that concept themselves.

The professional recognition policy and the recognized teacher of SDE

According to the GTCS Education Advisor, the professional recognition policy was an attempt to modernize the teaching profession and to make it more flexible to change. However, she also positioned education policy-making in Scotland as being to some extent insulated from global drivers. The Scottish Government was interested in global conditions, but policy responses, including professional recognition, were developed relatively autonomously. The Education Minister would set up a committee comprising people who were fully or quasi-autonomous from Government and who had other commitments to a range of constituencies, including explicitly non-governmental representatives. The policy officer attributed significance to her own identity as a former teacher while acting as a GTCS Education Advisor on such committees.

The changes that the Education Advisor envisaged as necessitating the professional recognition policy included: first, a new loosening of Scottish school curriculum arrangements and a desire for distributed leadership in schooling (a devolution to all stakeholders, including classroom teachers, of responsibility for the on-going development of learning, curriculum, and pedagogy), both of which were rooted in a persistent decentralization of education governance in Scotland; and second, the need for interdisciplinary learning and the deconstruction of discipline-based 'silo mentalities'. This spoke to a desire to loosen commitments to traditional disciplines in order to be able to make new commitments to current priorities such as SDE.

The professional recognition application form itself represented the mechanisms for bringing about such change. It was based around documented teacher discussions with a line manager, the development of agreed actions to enhance various teacher attributes, the provision of evidence of these, and some program of learning, all of which were recorded and submitted with a folder of evidence to the GTCS in application for recognition.

From the GTCS policy perspective, then, the professional teacher of SDE was at least someone: who learned, adapted, achieved and took responsibility for so doing, individually; whose learning and achievement was marked by reference to accountability and evidence-checking; who therefore reported to a manager; and who understood the rationale for change, including that it challenged commitments to existing areas of expertise.

Eco Schools and the recognized teacher of SDE

A feature of the policy was the role of a non-governmental organization (NGO), *Eco Schools*, in the development of SDE as a category in which GTCS professional recognition could be gained. Just as the GTCS was engaged in policies that have worldwide parallels, *Eco Schools* claimed to be the largest sustainable schools program in the world and to have 11 million students taking part in 52 countries.[6] *Eco Schools* was managed internationally by the *Foundation for Environmental Education*, itself set up following the 1992 United Nations 'Earth Summit' in Rio de Janeiro and partly funded by corporate multinationals. In these senses, *Eco Schools* was a significantly international SDE policy. The *Eco Schools* model has been much studied (Henderson and Tilbury 2004; Mogensen and Mayer 2005; Boeve-de Pauw and Van Petegem 2011) including in Scotland (Pirrie et al. 2006). *Eco Schools'* Scottish operation claimed that Scotland was 'one of the leading countries in the world when it comes to Eco-Schools awards'.[7] *Eco Schools* programs were whole-school environmental management and learning processes, in which, some form of pupil council audited their school's environmental performance and planned and executed a series of actions for improvement. Typical areas for attention included litter, waste, school grounds, biodiversity, energy, and transport. By means of external inspection by a national license-holder, the school could achieve a range of award statuses including the 'Green Flag'.

Both *Eco Schools* and teacher reward polices in Scotland, then, might be regarded as effects of globalization. So, it is interesting that the interaction between *Eco Schools* and professional recognition policy in Scotland was strong. According to this study's interview with the then-manager of *Eco Schools Scotland*, it was her employees who first suggested to the GTCS that *Eco Schools* teachers were suitable for being recognized by a new category of professional recognition: SDE. It was her organization's network and publications that were responsible for nearly all the subsequent uptake of professional recognition in SDE, and their widely-circulated model of a completed application form was, in some detail, the basis for a number of the application forms that were examined in this study.

Although both GTCS and *Eco Schools Scotland* attributed importance to learning-based auditing and recognition systems, there was a central difference between the two policy-making organizations in their understandings of the purposes or merits of the policy. The work of *Eco Schools Scotland* was not particularly about teacher professionals, since it engaged directly with schools and pupils, but their manager thought that rewarding *Eco Schools* teachers using the GTCS policy was a good thing. The main reason for that was her view that professional recognition in SDE would result in schools and school managers taking SDE itself more seriously. This was because the field-specific award for teachers was in effect, also recognizing the field of SDE itself. This was a contrast with the GTCS policy's own discussion of a more fluid professionalism (above), where SDE appealed because it was interdisciplinary, challenged existing commitments and encouraged the teacher to deal with ever-changing realities, one of which was currently a need for SDE. Although the *Eco Schools* manager would not contest those, her own construction of teachers' professionalism included belonging to a stable field of educational endeavor, or a discipline, of SDE around which it might be possible to imagine an expert cohort and tradition of practice.

In summary of both these perspectives, the professional recognition of SDE policy itself included ambiguities concerning how the professional teacher of SDE was to be understood. As intended by GTCS, the policy incentivized lifelong learning and distributed leadership by individual teachers as a response to the changeability of conditions, whereas *Eco Schools Scotland* thought the policy usefully rewarded teachers for being defined by, and for belonging to, something more stable – a field or discipline of SDE.

Telling the case (2): the professionally recognized teacher of SDE, in person

This section will consider how participating teachers talked about their professional identities, to the extent that this understanding intersected with the policy of professional recognition for SDE. The two most striking aspects were: first, how they saw themselves less as incentivized to be individual achievers and more as networked into a wider profession with shared purposes; second, how they nonetheless saw themselves as managers and light-touch leaders of SDE activity in their schools, which *general* abilities set them apart from some of their colleagues more than did their expertise in SDE alone.

Professional recognition: of individuals or relationships?

The interviewed teachers were ambivalent about 'being recognized' individually, and this ambivalence has been discovered in relation to other award schemes for teachers (e.g. Mackenzie 2007). With one exception, they had been encouraged by others to apply for recognition. And (with a different exception) none had informed their colleagues that they had been recognized. Although many were quietly satisfied, all articulated modesty or said that they knew of other equally deserving teachers who had not applied for recognition. Moreover, the professionally recognized teachers defined a wide concept of their professionalism. This concept was less individual and more relational: All the participants identified with the idea of networks in explaining their engagement with SDE developments; those who had not moved on to other roles had hoped that professional recognition would be a means of identifying a group of experts in SDE to which they could belong; and in the focus group interviews discussion sometimes broke down into the sharing of contacts and ideas about SDE. All this begged the question: What could be the point of their participation in an individual recognition award scheme? There were two responses. The first was that recognition drew attention to the area of SDE with school management and this was a good thing, resulting in its being taken more seriously. The second was that in job applications or promotions, it would be a useful item on the applicants' curriculum vitae, though more as an indicator of effort and management/ leadership expertise rather than SDE expertise.

Therefore, in comparison with the negotiation of the professional teacher of SDE attempted by the GTCS policy (above), this small group of teachers appeared to identify with a network of disciplinary expertise rather than with individual incentive. This was more in keeping with the *Eco Schools Scotland* view that the professional recognition policy would help to recognize a field of SDE as much as a teacher. At the same time, though, the policy was understood by these teachers to identify a level of commitment beyond those of their colleagues, which included some commitment to management or leadership, in general, rather than of a field-specific kind, and accordingly conferred some individual competitive advantage in the teacher employment market.

Professional recognition: for SDE or for managing an(y) agenda?

The teachers also talked of their professionalism in ways that suggested the management of agendas. They referred to their roles in SDE as involving 'constantly improving', moving on, ensuring that initiatives 'spread' and 'embed' throughout the school. A picture emerged of light-touch, subtle, and sophisticated SDE leadership, and also one of constant movement, with new ideas being developed, or established ones being embedded further in the school community. They all recognized the significance of their engagement and enthusiasm as 'initiators' or 'doers', but in different ways their discussions went beyond this. One referred to tapping other people's enthusiasm and of getting others to 'sell' ideas; another of a distinction between leading rather than directing; and another of coming up with ideas that other people (pupils or staff) took forward. Several talked of school activities being pupil-led, energized, and initiated, as well as being prompted by outsiders. This distributed approach to action-learning initiatives is possibly characteristic of SDE, according to Kemmis and Mutton (2012), but for present purposes, the construction of the teacher as manager is of interest.

In addition, there was a sense that new ideas (such as plastic bottle greenhouses) were not particularly responses to new conditions in the environment or major evaluations of existing practices and instead were responses to the need to undertake change as part of the maintenance of the SDE agenda, or to keep moving more generally. The teachers discussed tentatively, if at all, any deep evaluation of SDE activities, and were consistently doubtful about the longevity of the effects of the activity on pupils (particularly when they left school). All but those teachers who were working at retirement age also talked of 'moving on', themselves, to headship (two had already done so) or to other areas of professional interest (at least two had obtained, or intended to obtain, professional recognition in other areas, such as science or assessment), or of developing other teachers who could take on some or all of their SDE leadership work.

Finally, with two exceptions, even those who professed some 'greenness' in their personal lives did not make strong connections between this and their school SDE leadership. They responded to the idea of 'activism' by associating it with their roles as initiator, motivator, or leader in the school institution, rather than in terms activism for the field of SDE or for the environment. Other researchers have noted tensions between various dimensions of teachers' professional and personal lives in the context of sustainability (e.g. Hill 2012). But the teachers interviewed in this study saw themselves as managing an educational agenda to some extent, and to that extent, correspondence between professional and personal commitments appeared to be less salient in general.

That conclusion somewhat contradicts the previous section's suggestion that the teachers understood themselves as belonging to the particular disciplinary field of SDE. The analysis of the policy in earlier sections has already shown some congruence with this account of being a professional manager, and that analysis too highlighted some of the contradictions between this and a commitment to the development of SDE as a discipline. Here, the teachers professed both a commitment to a field of SDE and network of experts, but also a managerial 'handling' or facilitation of the SDE agenda, potentially as one agenda among many. This is not to say that the policy caused these teachers' subjectivities and identifications, rather that similar negotiations of what it was to be a professional teacher of SDE were being undertaken at different sites in this case study.

Interpreting the case: professionalism, managerialism and globalization

The following sections explore these contradictions and argue that they arise from the negotiation of managerialism within educational professionalism. Moreover, it is argued that managerialism is a neoliberal technology and that the globalization of that technology demands its negotiation in any particular case, including the present case.

Neoliberalism and managerialism

Managerialism in public services, such as education, has been attributed to a mid- to late-twentieth century neoliberal political settlement that has since become orthodox in global education policy-making (Rizvi and Lingard 2010). A standard historical account of the development of that settlement in the UK is Clarke's and Newman's (1997) *The Managerial State: Power, politics and ideology in the remaking of social welfare*. They argued that specifically neoliberal (and neoconservative) political actors dismantled the bureaucratic-professional character of public service provision, not least to reduce costs in the face of increasingly fluid and global capital markets. Public service provision was encouraged to incorporate private-sector practices and assumptions: target-setting, indicators, and incentives for achievement and forms of decentralization, quasi-market arrangements, flexibility to changes in demand, and a consumer focus. Decentralization brought with it a further technology: 'the manager' as a central figure in the functioning of bureaucratic-professional contexts, including education contexts (Ball 2008). Managers and managerialism have therefore become a matter of interest in the educational literature (Apple 2008, Noordegraaf and de Wit 2012). The teacher professionalism literature often counterposes teacher professionalism with managerialism and related technologies (Darling-Hammond and McLaughlin 1995; Day 2002; Sachs 2003; Macdonald 2004). An extreme interpretation of managerialism by Ryan and Bourke (2013, 412) is that it 'sees teachers as unquestioning supporters and implementers of a competency-based, outcome-oriented pedagogy'.

Managerialism makes some sense of the contradictions that have been revealed in this study. The GTCS constructed the professional recognition policy as an individual incentive to develop and modernize teachers: for them to be more flexible and open to change and to respond to it by means of learning; for them to focus on public need and to challenge, rather than identify with, traditional disciplines and disciplinary groups; for them to individually take responsibility for change in a context of distributed leadership; for the process as shown by the application form to involve setting targets or agreed actions within a line-management process, and to provide evidence of these; for the possession of recognition to be thought by teachers to be relevant in a competitive labor market; and for that competitive advantage to be less about their commitment to SDE and more about their ability to manage such an agenda in schools.

However, no policy statement or participant in this study suggested that the recognized teachers of SDE were Ryan and Bourke's 'unquestioning supporters and implementers' (above); the relationship with managerialism was more subtle. Policy, policy-makers, and teachers were all involved in mediating the extent to which managerialism was part of being a professional teacher of SDE. The case revealed not only the teacher as subject *to* management, but also the teacher's subjectivity *as* manager – a more or less light-touch handler of the SDE agenda as opposed to a disciplinary expert committed to SDE. The tension here is exposed by Clarke's (2004, 36/37) argument that the particular knowledge used on problems by those in disciplinary groups is in contrast to the supposedly universalist, abstract rationality used by managers to produce decisions that both transcend and integrate such particularism. Therefore, 'the professional teachers of SDE', to the extent that they were managers of schools' SDE agendas, were engaged in professional purposes that were in some senses difficult to reconcile with their commitments to the particular discipline of SDE itself. Perhaps this was most evident in the ambiguities among: their work in the initiation and extension of SDE activities; the relative absence of deep evaluation of those activities' purposes and effects; their skepticism about the significance of those effects; and in most cases, the relative insignificance of any professed relationship between their professional lives and their personal engagements with sustainability. It is interesting to note, however, that despite these uncertainties, these teachers would all be identifiable as their schools' 'go to' SDE enthusiast.

Neoliberalism and globalization

The influence of neoliberal globalization on the public realm is often overstated (Clarke 2008). There is good evidence that policy discourses construct regimes of truth and that discourses of globalism can produce education policy convergence internationally (Ball 2008; Rizvi and Lingard 2010). But, such convergence is not by itself evidence of the centripetal ideological force implied by the phrase 'neoliberal globalization'. Highlighting a neoliberal technology in the present policy case does not prove that the policy or technology is subject to, or an effect of, globalization, even though the argument has been made that Scottish professional recognition of SDE (and for that matter its close relationship with *Eco Schools*), is representative of a wider and international set of policies.

However, the existence of tensions in policy-making and implementation, including in this case, might be understood as traces of engagement with, and resistance to, globalization. It is well-recognized that education policy technologies do not flow unhindered and unmediated from global to local or from place to place, and yet hindrance and mediation imply that policy is 'traveling' in at least some sense (Ozga and Jones 2006). There have been general challenges to sociological assumptions of global flow, 'liquid modernity' and spatial de-territorialization. In joining and summarizing those challenges, Robertson (2011) drew attention to the need to theorize the bordered nature of the social world in order to make sense of the realities of difference and social ordering. In her discussion, territories, borders, containers, and categories were socio-spatial but not necessarily national: The borders of 'public', 'profession', or 'western', for example, were the kinds of borders being re-negotiated under conditions of globalization. The border of 'professional teacher of SDE' has been under discussion here. Such borders are not static: Robertson refs to de- and re-bordering processes. These processes are defining features of globalization, and they are identifiable features of the present case.

The discourses in this study have been as much about re-bordering or insulating the concept of the professional teacher of SDE as they have been about its de-bordering or permeability to a globally circulating technology. This partial resistance in the education policy space has been shown in other Scottish studies, including in relation to managerialism (Reeves 2008; Grek et al. 2009). In this study, the GTCS policy-maker was explicit that the Scottish Government was in some respects focused on Scotland's international educational performance and on internationally circulating ideas about incentivizing teacher modernization through reward and recognition. But it was also made clear that education policy-making was delegated to committees of people with a range of identifications, and this was the case for the professional recognition policy. The formal policy-making institution, the GTCS, was an autonomous professional body. Beyond that, the professional recognition of teachers of SDE was suggested and near-solely promoted by a NGO, *Eco Schools Scotland*, holding a different construction of the professional teacher of SDE (albeit *Eco Schools Scotland* had its own global connections). Moreover, the take-up of professional recognition by teachers has been low, and those recognized have been a small minority of Scottish teachers who are *Eco Schools* coordinators let alone teachers of SDE. And the GTCS (since the study was conducted) has re-developed the policy model so that other providers, including other NGOs and higher education institutions, can be involved in validating various kinds of field-specific professional recognition. This is likely to lead to an expansion of the policy but also to a greater diversity of understandings and performances of the relationship between the professional teacher, in a particular field, and managerialism in general. Those diverse future understandings and performances in turn could be understood – like the discourses in this study – as border negotiations with neoliberal technologies.

Conclusion

The GTCS policy of recognizing teachers for their expertise in SDE – a policy that is representative of international trends – has been interpreted here as manifesting a process of negotiation with globally circulating technologies of neoliberalism. The potential field of reference of such interpretations can be extended. In Wesselink's and Wals' (2011) study of the perceived core competencies associated with the provision of environmental education in the Netherlands, they revealed that independent environmental education providers raised relatively few SDE/EE-specific competencies and rather more generic ones (such as customer- and results- orientation, which seem to the present author suggestive of the influence of the neoliberal settlement). These contrasted with Wesselink's and Wals' own careful analysis of how competencies could be understood, including in relation to the particularities of environmental education or sustainability. Some of the difference, they argued, can be explained by cultural contexts and trends. As with this study, then, their examples suggest that there is merit in examining the relationship between the technologies of neoliberalism and efforts to define, professionalize, or simply work in, the fields of SDE and environmental education. This study suggests identifying specific technologies and viewing policy and policy actors as engaged in processes of discursive border management. There must be value in exploring these relationships for those who are engaged in making them. The approach here revealed unfinished negotiations, and such incompleteness leaves greater agency for teachers and policy-makers than does either critical acceptance, or uncritical ignorance, of a global neoliberal hegemony.

Notes

1. Figures from 2010–2012, from http://www.scotland.gov.uk/Topics/Statistics/Browse/School-Education, accessed 5 May 2014.
2. http://www.gtcs.org.uk/home/home.aspx, accessed 5 May 2014.
3. http://www.gtcs.org.uk/professional-development/professional-update-what-do-i-need-to-know.aspx, accessed 5 May 2014.
4. WWF Scotland is part of the international WWF network that claims to be one of the world's most influential environmental organizations: http://scotland.wwf.org.uk/what_we_do/about_wwf_scotland/, accessed 5 May 2014.
5. http://www.keepscotlandbeautiful.org/sustainable-development-education/eco-schools, accessed 5 May 2014.
6. http://www.eco-schools.org/, accessed 5 May 2014.
7. Derek A. Robertson, Chief Executive, *Keep Scotland Beautiful* (http://www.ecoschools scotland.org/article.asp?nid=248, accessed 30 January 2012).

Notes on contributor

Hamish Ross is senior lecturer in Social Studies and Environmental Studies at The Moray House School of Education, University of Edinburgh. He would like to thank also the General Teaching Council for Scotland, WWF Scotland, and all those who agreed to participate in the study.

References

Andrews, H. A. 2011. "Supporting Quality Teachers with Recognition." *Australian Journal of Teacher Education* 36: 59–70.

Andrzejewski, J., M. P. Baltodano, and L. Symcox. 2009. *Social Justice, Peace, and Environmental Education: Transformative Standards*. New York: Routledge.

Apple, M. 2008. "Forward." In *Changing Teacher Professionalism: International Trends, Challenges and Ways Forward*, edited by S. Gewirtz, P. Mahony, I. Hextall, and A. Cribb, xiv–xvii. Abingdon: Routledge.

Ball, S. J. 2008. *The Education Debate: Policy and Politics in the Twenty-first Century*. Bristol: Policy Press.

Bassey, M. 2002. "Education Towards a Sustainable Society." *Management in Education (Education Publishing Worldwide Ltd)* 16: 12–15.

Bates, R. 2008. "Teacher Education in a Global Context: Towards a Defensible Theory of Teacher Education." *Journal of Education for Teaching* 34: 277–293.

Beck, J. 2008. "Governmental Professionalism: Re-professionalising or De-professionalising Teachers in England?" *British Journal of Educational Studies* 56: 119–143.

Bieler, D. 2012. "Possibilities for Achieving Social Justice Ends Through Standardized Means." *Teacher Education Quarterly* 39: 85–102.

Boeve-de Pauw, J., and P. Van Petegem. 2011. "The Effect of Flemish Eco-schools on Student Environmental Knowledge, Attitudes and Affect." *International Journal of Science Education* 33: 1513–1538.

Clarke, J. 2004. "Dissolving the Public Realm? The Logics and Limits of Neo-liberalism." *Journal of Social Policy* 33: 27–48.

Clarke, J. 2008. "Living With/in and Without Neo-liberalism." *Focaal* 51: 135–147.

Clarke, J., and J. Newman. 1997. *The Managerial State: Power, Politics and Ideology in the Remaking of Social Welfare*. London: Sage.

Collinson, V., E. Kozina, Y. Ä. Kate Lin, L. Ling, I. Matheson, L. Newcombe, and I. Zogla. 2009. "Professional Development for Teachers: A World of Change." *European Journal of Teacher Education* 32: 3–19.

Cutter-Mackenzie, A., B. Clarke, and P. Smith. 2008. "A Discussion Paper: The Development of Professional Teacher Standards in Environmental Education." *Australian Journal of Environmental Education* 24: 3–10.

Darling-Hammond, L., and M. W. Mclaughlin. 1995. "Policies that Support Professional Development in an Era of Reform." *Phi Delta Kappan* 76: 597–604.

Day, C. 2002. *Developing Teachers: The Challenges of Lifelong Learning*. London: Routledge.

Grek, S., M. Lawn, B. Lingard, J. Ozga, R. Rinne, C. Segerholm, and H. Simola. 2009. "National Policy Brokering and the Construction of the European Education Space in England, Sweden, Finland and Scotland." *Comparative Education* 45: 5–21.

Harvey, D. 2007. "Neoliberalism as Creative Destruction." *Annals of the American Academy of Political and Social Science* 610: 22–44.

Henderson, K., and D., Tilbury. 2004. *Whole-school Approaches to Sustainability: An International Review of Sustainable School Programs. Report Prepared by the Australian Research Institute in Education for Sustainability (ARIES) for the Department of the Environment and Heritage, Australian Government*. Sydney: Macquarie University.

Hill, A. 2012. "Developing Approaches to Outdoor Education that Promote Sustainability Education." *Australian Journal of Outdoor Education* 16: 15–27.

Ingvarson, L. 2010. "Recognising Accomplished Teachers in Australia: Where have We been? Where are We Heading?" *Australian Journal of Education* 54: 46–71.

Jickling, B., and A. E. J. Wals. 2008. "Globalization and Environmental Education: Looking Beyond Sustainable Development." *Journal of Curriculum Studies* 40: 1–21.

Kemmis, S., and R. Mutton. 2012. "Education for Sustainability (EfS): Practice and Practice Architectures." *Environmental Education Research* 18: 187–207.

Kincheloe, J. L. 2001. "Describing the Bricolage: Conceptualizing a New Rigor in Qualitative Research." *Qualitative Inquiry* 7: 679–692.

Ko, P.-Y., and B. Adamson. 2011. "Pedagogy and Human Dignity – The Special Rank Teacher in China Since 1978." *History of Education* 40: 371–389.

Kriewaldt, J. 2012. "Reorienting Teaching Standards: Learning from Lesson Study." *Asia-Pacific Journal of Teacher Education* 40: 31–41.

Larsen, M. A. 2010. "Troubling the Discourse of Teacher Centrality: A Comparative Perspective." *Journal of Education Policy* 25: 207–231.

Macdonald, A. 2004. "Collegiate or Compliant? Primary Teachers in Post-McCrone Scotland." *British Educational Research Journal* 30: 413–433.

Mackenzie, N. 2007. "Teaching Excellence Awards: An Apple for the Teacher?" *Australian Journal of Education* 51: 190–204.

Mogensen, F., and M. Mayer. 2005. *ECO-schools: Trends and Divergences*. Vienna: Austrian Federal Ministry of Education, Science and Culture.

Morgan, D. L. 2010. "Reconsidering the Role of Interaction in Analysing and Reporting Focus Groups." *Qualitative Health Research* 20: 718–722.

Noordegraaf, M., and B. De Wit. 2012. "Responses to Managerialism: How Management Pressures Affect Managerial Relations and Loyalties in Education." *Public Administration* 90: 957–973.

Obeidat, O. M., and S. M. Al-Hassan. 2009. "School-parent-community Partnerships: The Experience of Teachers who Received the Queen Rania Award for Excellence in Education in the Hashemite Kingdom of Jordan." *School Community Journal* 19: 119–136.

Ozga, J., and R. Jones. 2006. "Travelling and Embedded Policy: The Case of Knowledge Transfer." *Journal of Education Policy* 21: 1–17.

Pirrie, A., D. Elliot, F. Mcconnell, and J. E. Wilkinson. 2006. *Evaluation of Eco Schools Scotland. SCRE Research Report No. 124*. Glasgow: SCRE.

Ramaekers, S. 2014. "The Pursuit of Truth (s) in Educational Research." In *A Companion to Research in Education*, edited by A. D. Reid, E. P. Hart, and M. A. Peters, 51–60. Dordrecht: Springer.

Reeves, J. 2008. "Inventing the Chartered Teacher." In *Changing Teacher Professionalism: International Trends, Challenges and Ways Forward*, edited by S. Gewirtz, P. Mahony, I. Hextall, and A. Cribb, 106–116. Abingdon: Routledge.

Rizvi, R., and B. Lingard. 2010. *Globalizing Educational Policy*. London: Routledge.

Robertson, S. L. 2011. "The New Spatial Politics of (Re)bordering and (Re)ordering the State-education citizen Relation." *International Review of Education* 57: 277–297.

Ross, H. 2011. *Sustaining the Impact: Exploring Professional Recognition for Scottish Teachers of Sustainable Development Education. Research report for WWF Scotland and the General Teaching Council for Scotland.* Edinburgh: University of Edinburgh. Accessed May 5. 2014. http://edin.ac/1kx2fos

Ryan, M., and T. Bourke. 2013. "The Teacher as Reflexive Professional: Making Visible the Excluded Discourse in Teacher Standards." *Discourse: Studies in the Cultural Politics of Education* 34: 411–423.

Sachs, J. 2003. *The Activist Teaching Profession.* Buckingham: Open University Press.

Sclafani, S. 2009. *Evaluating and Rewarding the Quality of Teachers: International practices.* Paris: OECD Publishing.

Sterling, S. 2001. *Sustainable Education. Re-visioning Learning and Change.* Totnes: Green Books.

Thomas, S., and J. Kearney. 2008. "Teachers Working in Culturally Diverse Classrooms: Implications for the Development of Professional Standards and for Teacher Education." *Asia-Pacific Journal of Teacher Education* 36: 105–120.

Vaillant, D., and C. Rossel. 2012. "The Recognition of Effective Teaching in Latin America: Awards to Excellence." *Teacher Development* 16: 89–110.

Wesselink, R., and A. E. Wals. 2011. "Developing Competence Profiles for Educators in Environmental Education Organisations in the Netherlands." *Environmental Education Research* 17: 69–90.

Neoliberalism, new public management and the sustainable development agenda of higher education: history, contradictions and synergies

Sophie E.F. Bessant, Zoe P. Robinson and R. Mark Ormerod

Institute for the Environment, Physical Sciences and Applied Mathematics; School of Physical and Geographical Sciences, Keele University, Staffordshire, UK

This paper explores the ideological and the practical relationship between neoliberalism and New Public Management (NPM) and the sustainable development agenda of western higher education. Using the United Kingdom and specifically English universities as an example, it investigates the contradictions and the synergies between neoliberal and NPM ideologies and the pursuit and practice of the sustainability agenda, focusing in particular on education for sustainable development (ESD) and ESD research. This paper reveals a range of challenges and opportunities in respect of advancing sustainability in higher education, within the prevailing neoliberal context. It illustrates using examples how neoliberal and managerialist control mechanisms, which govern institutional, departmental and individual academic, as well as student behaviour, are working conversely to both drive and limit the sustainability education agenda. The case is made for further exploration of how 'nudging' and 'steering' mechanisms within English HE might provide further leverage for ESD developments in the near future, and the implications of this for sustainability educators.

The sustainable development and education for sustainable development agendas of western higher education

The concept of Sustainable Development (SD) and of education as imperative in the drive towards sustainability, were largely borne out of two key events: the World Commission on Environment and Development in 1987 and the UN Conference on Environment and Development in Rio de Janeiro, 1992 (Filho 2000). The sustainability movement within western Higher Education (HE) has emerged and gained pace over roughly the last 20 years and is now very much part of the global HE landscape. HE's fundamental responsibility towards sustainability is espoused on many grounds, including its critical role as a societal leader, future shaper and exemplar of best practice, its influence on local and national policy, and its role in educating the next generation of global citizens (van Weenen 2000; Corcoran and Wals 2004; Gough and Scott 2008).

Universities have tended to approach sustainability through four main realms of university activity, namely (1) sustainability-focused education and teaching; (2) sustainability-focused research; (3) campus operations and environmental management; and (4) community engagement around sustainability issues. Sustainability-focused education and teaching is commonly referred to as Education for Sustainable Development (ESD), emphasising its goal of contributing to a more sustainable future. Approaches to ESD within universities are philosophically and practically diverse, with different emphases, ranging from more formal curriculum-based ESD, to informal campus-based and student-led ESD projects, as well as interactive community-based sustainability learning. ESD has been integrated into university structures at disciplinary and interdisciplinary levels, through embedding sustainability within educational programme design and quality assurance and enhancement procedures, as well as specific sustainability-focused undergraduate and postgraduate degree courses and modules. A commonly used definition of ESD is as follows:

> Education for sustainable development is a vision of education that seeks to balance human and economic well-being with cultural traditions and respect for the earth's natural resources. ESD applies transdisciplinary educational methods and approaches to develop an ethic for lifelong learning, fosters respect for human needs that are compatible with sustainable use of natural resources and the needs of the planet and nurtures a sense of global solidarity. (UNESCO 2002, 1)

Many factors have culminated in an increasing focus on sustainability within English higher education, and more specifically ESD, which has gained increasing momentum over the last 5–10 years. Key drivers for change include *inter alia:*

- The United Nations Decade of Education for Sustainable Development (UNDESD) from 2005 to 2014, which arguably has provided momentum for some national-scale developments;
- The work of the Higher Education Academy (HEA), through their ESD thematic area since 2005, and their Green Academy change programme since 2011;
- The Higher Education Funding Council for England's (HEFCE) sustainable development 'strategic statement and action plan' published in 2005 and updated in 2009 (HEFCE 2005, 2009). The latest HEFCE sustainable development framework is currently being finalised. HEFCE funding has also been hugely important, e.g. the Revolving Green Fund and the Students' Green Fund;
- A growing number of sustainability organisations, communities of practice, benchmarking activities and awards, including the People and Planet Green League table of universities, the Green Gown Awards from the Environmental Association of Universities and Colleges and the Sustainability in Higher Education Developers (SHED-SHARE) network; and
- Increasing demand for sustainability from staff, students and local communities.

Although there are many developments taking place which are pushing ESD up the higher education agenda, many ESD practitioners in the UK and further afield believe that genuinely transformative ESD requires more radical and fundamental change, which goes beyond 'integrating', 'embedding' or 'mainstreaming' sustainability within HE. Calls have been made for a more transformative whole systems response which places sustainability at the heart of higher education's 'raison d'être' (Sterling 2013, 18): an epistemic and paradigmatic reorientation of universities towards sustainability. A distinction is drawn by these authors, between 'whole systems' cultural shifts and the sorts of sustainability advances which occur from *within* our current HE system as it stands, but which do not fundamentally change the make-up and ideology of the system itself (Cortese 2003; Ryan 2012; Blewitt 2013; Sterling 2013; Tilbury 2013; Jucker 2014).

The higher education system that we are working within in the UK is one characterised by the dominating political-governmental ideologies of Neoliberalism and New Public Management (NPM). Indeed, the forces currently shaping higher education globally are multiple and complex. Processes of globalisation, internationalisation, dynamic technological and social media interactions, commercialisation and corporatization have fundamentally changed our lives and the HE landscape. Along with the UK, countries such as the United States, Australia and New Zealand have also seen their HE systems significantly reoriented over the last thirty years, by the logic of neoliberalism. It is within this complex neoliberal system that sustainability educators have advanced and grown their work and will continue to do so in the near future.

Neoliberalism and NPM in the UK

Neoliberal ideology, most famously associated with the 1980s governments of Reagan and Thatcher, is based upon the principles of economic liberalisation and de-centralisation, including: free trade, open markets, privatisation, deregulation and a decrease in the welfare role played by state (Giroux 2002; Harvey 2007). Neoliberalism has been described as 'the defining political-economic paradigm of our time' and has been adopted by political parties of the centre, the traditional left and the right (McChesney 1998, 7). Ideologically, the coherence of the neoliberal doctrine continues to stimulate academic debate. Key debates centre on the ways in which governments that employ neoliberal tactics, i.e. marketisation and decentralisation, often also rely heavily upon measures of state dirigisme. These governments therefore portray seemingly paradoxical elements, as the state is simultaneously non-interventionist and decentralised in some realms, and highly interventionist and centralised in others, described as 'roll-back' and 'roll-out' neoliberalism (Gamble 1988; Peck and Tickell 2002; Graefe 2005).

Centralised state steering of the public sector within the neoliberal climate is commonly known as new public management (NPM) or new managerialism. NPM involves discourses of management derived from the private for-profit sector, being introduced into public services in the quest to modernise, reduce spending costs and improve 'efficiency, effectiveness and excellence' (Deem 2001, 10). NPM is characterised by the use of markets (and quasi markets) which drive competition between public sector providers; empowered entrepreneurial management; explicit standards, measures of performance, goal setting and quality assurance mechanisms; and a focus on outputs (Hood 1991; Gruening 2001; Deem and Brehony 2005; Ferlie, Musselin, and Andresani 2008). NPM may be thought of as an extrapolation of agency theory principles (the principal-agent problem) vested in neoliberal discourse (Goedegebuure and Hayden 2007), i.e. government (the principal) exerts control over the public sector (the agents) and ensures that public institutions move in desired policy directions, through using varying NPM mechanisms of control (Eisenhardt 1989; Williams 1997).

The effects of neoliberalism and NPM on higher education

Higher Education Institutions (HEIs) in the UK have been reformed and managed since the 1980s, through a complex mix of both decentralising and centralising processes, and the creation of markets and quasi markets (Williams 1997; Kogan and Hanney 2000; Middleton 2000). Quasi markets are essentially market mechanisms which operate in the public, rather than the private sector, and differ insofar as they are somewhat artificial, induced and regulated. In the quasi-market set-up of English HE, government purchases teaching and research services, from independent HE providers in competition with each other, via the non-departmental public body (NDPB), HEFCE, through the yearly block grant it provides to institutions (Dill 1997). University behaviour is steered as HEIs strive to reach particular performance levels with regard to research and to attract high numbers of (high quality) students (within allowed parameters) to maximise their income. In the last two years, the quasi market for teaching funding has shifted towards the student body, who now bring the majority of teaching funding into HEIs through significantly increased fees, although HEFCE continue to define the parameters, including the Student Number Control for each HEI, by which individual HEIs can recruit Home/EU students. This is discussed in more detail later in the paper.

'Real' markets also overlap with these quasi markets and include, for example, the market for external research funding from the UK Research Councils, the EU, and from business partnerships, or the market for recruitment of international students which is uncapped and represents a significant funding stream. In this highly competitive higher education set-up, universities are becoming evermore fiscally focused, businesslike and managerialist, and we are witnessing some huge transformations to the purpose, mission and framing of higher education. The changing direction of university strategic plans and policy priorities towards increased income generation, innovation, commercial enterprise, business engagement, and indeed, the advent of university 'corporate' plans highlight this change (Jary 2005; Marginson 2007; NEF 2008; Streeting and Wise 2009; McArthur 2011). The range of neoliberal and NPM impacts on HE are well documented in the literature and have been summarised in Table 1, with a focus on the UK/English HE context.

Education for the public good within the neoliberal university – paradox or possibility?

For many academics with an interest in the neoliberal and managerialist transformation of higher education, both from within the sustainability sector and beyond, these forces have often been viewed as antithetical to the purpose and responsibilities of higher education. Many have criticised HE for undermining its core values through choosing to uphold the neoliberal ethos and for the inevitable trade-offs faced with other values such as social justice, equity, environmental protection and ethical and democratic decision-making (Readings 1998; Saravanamuthu and Tinker 2002; Devaney and Weber 2003). In the 30th anniversary edition of his seminal work, 'Pedagogy of the Oppressed' (Freire 1970), Richard Shaull closes the book's foreword with the following:

Table 1. The effects of neoliberalism/NPM on higher education and characteristics of the 'new' twenty-first century model of HE.

General characteristics
- Universities are more businesslike and managerialist
- Focus on outputs, financial control, efficiency, value for money and strategic planning
- More interaction with businesses and the commercial and corporate sector
- Relationships and roles defined more in corporate terms, e.g. customers and service providers

Government funding and control mechanisms
- Increased transparency of government funding via formula funding mechanisms based on student numbers, discipline type and assessed research excellence
- Proliferation of accountability, quality assurance, audit processes, non-departmental public bodies (NDPBs)

Research and research funding
- Competition between HEIs for governmental research funds in a quality-related funding system
- Competition between HEIs for research funding from UK Research Councils, charities, the EU and business/industry partnerships
- Diversification of research funding to include more business/corporate funding partnerships
- Continued concentration of research funds from government in the highest performing institutions
- Marginalisation of research into fields which are recognised by rating systems and research funding bodies

Competition for students, student funding
- Competition for students between HEIs
- Drive to maintain student numbers and increase numbers in areas where this is possible (e.g. students with the grades A, B, B or better and postgraduates) and thus government teaching funding
- Drive to increase numbers of international students and associated revenues
- Reductions in unit resource of student funding from government
- Increases in student fees, from no fees in the early 1990s to ca. £1000 per year in 1997, to ca. £3000 per year in 2006 and up to £9000 per year in 2012

Academic staff
- Vice-Chancellors more akin to CEOs from the business world
- Pressure to compete for external research income from funding bodies and businesses
- Pressure to work on research projects outside of chosen field, to 'follow the money'
- Pressure to generate additional revenue streams, for example enterprise, CPD, new postgraduate courses and international partnerships
- More structured, monitored and managed regime than in the past
- Pressure to produce particular 'products' within ever tighter timescales with fewer resources
- Academics increasingly strategic about research collaborations and where work is published
- Staff appointments often based on research track record and potential rather than teaching capability
- Less genuine collegiality

References
Chandler, Barry, and Clark (2002), Giroux (2002), Mendivil (2002), Fridell (2004), Hill (2004), Archer (2008), Clegg (2008), Dowling (2008), Kolsaker (2008), Klenowski (2009), Reid (2009), Harland et al. (2010), McArthur (2011), Waitere et al. (2011)

> There is no such thing as a neutral education process. Education either functions as an instrument which is used to facilitate the integration of generations into the logic of the present system and bring about conformity to it, or it becomes the 'practice of freedom', the means by which men and women deal critically with reality and discover how to participate in the transformation of their world (Shaull 2000, 34).

Following from Freire's work, a leading group of critical pedagogy theorists in the UK have strongly championed seeking alternatives to the neoliberalizing university (Amsler et al. 2010). Critical pedagogy has been described as 'overtly political and critical of the status quo' and 'committed to progressive social and political change' (Crowther 2010, 16). Critical pedagogy theorists challenge us to rethink universities as radically democratic social and political institutions, to confront the monolithic nature of neoliberalism and to regain confidence in Marxist critiques of capitalism (Amsler et al. 2010; Cowden and Singh 2013). Brenner, Peck, and Theodore (2010) discuss several scenarios to counter neoliberalism in their paper 'After neoliberalism', and advocate, like many authors in the area of ESD, 'big picture' alternative frameworks, politics and economies for mobilising alternatives.

Critical pedagogy points of views are echoed in the works of many writers who seek to advance the public, socio-democratic and sustainability 'good' of higher education, arguing that if we operate *within* the paradigm we seek to shift, we are not only helping to sustain it, but are also compromising the radical potentialities of other emancipatory educations (Hall 2005; Naidoo and Jamieson 2005; Irwin 2007; Blewitt 2013; Jucker 2014). Indeed, ESD discourse has been described as fundamentally implicated as part and parcel of the neoliberal regime (Irwin 2007; Blewitt 2013). Jucker (2014, 38, 41) has noted, 'There is no real progress in the sense of the necessary paradigm change … ESD is only possible with a radical paradigm change'.

To counter these views, one could argue that English universities have responded in ways that are necessary to survive in the current climate and that they do not currently have the choice to opt out of the neoliberal regime. From an ESD perspective, advocating that nothing truly meaningful can be achieved within our HE system as it stands, negates the huge successes of the many innovative and life-changing educational transformations going on as a result of the growing ESD agenda. If examined practically and without supporting any one ideological stance, we believe that the prevailing neoliberal and managerialist regime in English HE has presented multiple opportunities for enhancing and progressing sustainability and ESD and that many sustainability advocates continue to exploit neoliberal and managerialist characteristics of universities to advance their work. On the other hand, we are also sympathetic to views that neoliberalism has tangibly stifled and contradicted the development of ESD in many ways and that more wholesale change of the system is certainly desirable. This paper continues by examining the political framing of higher education within the 'knowledge economy', student funding mechanisms and the 'student as consumer' rhetoric, quality assurance processes, quality-related research funding, and the relationship of these explicitly neoliberal and managerialist mechanisms to ESD. Examples from the UK and English HE systems are drawn upon throughout to demonstrate the contradictions and synergies present, before moving on to evaluate the implications of this for sustainability educators.

The political framing of higher education in the UK

There have been six different government departments responsible for higher education in the UK since the 1980s, which until 2007 were badged with 'education' in their title. In 2007, Brown's Labour government moved responsibility for HEIs to the Department for Innovation, Universities and Skills (DIUS), which was then merged into the Department for Business, Innovation & Skills (BIS) in 2009. Losing the terms 'education' and then 'universities' from departmental terminology raises fundamental questions for those actively concerned about the core purpose and underlying values of our HE system. Specifically, it implies that universities in the UK are being subsumed as a key supply-side component of the country's economic and business engine (Middleton 2000). The mission statement of BIS (2009), where university responsibilities reside, suggests this is so:

> The Department for Business, Innovation and skills (BIS) is the department for economic growth. The department invests in skills and education to promote trade, boost innovation and help people to start and grow a business.

McArthur's (2011) paper, 'Reconsidering the social and economic purposes of higher education' explores these critical issues in depth. She notes, 'Such a change suggests that higher education is primarily seen as a tool that contributes to the achievement of other primary goals – namely business, innovation and skills – rather than a priority in its own right' (McArthur 2011, 738). Higher education is no longer seen as an end in itself but the means to economic ends. Universities are increasingly being positioned as a key component of the 'knowledge society', in which education and research is primarily focused towards enhancing the economic prosperity of the country (Dill 1997; Mendivil 2002; Henkel 2007). In two of his early speeches as Secretary of State for BIS, Lord Mandleson made these priorities quite explicit as follows:

> I believe the logical home for university policy is in a new department whose core remit is investing in economic growth, investing in our future. Over the last decade or so our expectations of the HE system in delivering economic impact have risen sharply – and rightly … After students themselves, you [business] are the key clients of the higher skills system. (Mandleson 2009a, 2009b)

Using the phrase 'higher skills system' as opposed to 'higher education system' represents a deep shift in how the UK's leaders value and publicly represent what was once a system of higher learning and discovery (McArthur 2011). Although many educators agree that the 'ivory tower' view of universities is outdated, and that HEIs must demonstrate a broader societal role which addresses the many challenges of the twenty-first century, government's overriding focus on rebuilding the economy, and universities as implicated as part of this rebuild, does little to support universities who are attempting to holistically address societal, environmental and economic concerns. Sustainability advocates and educators would argue that this stance should be reformulated into a focus on the transition towards sustainable development and a sustainable green economy; a movement away from the primacy of neoliberalism (SDC 2004; Huckle 2008).

Higher education funding mechanisms, tuition fees and student consumers

In September 2012, a new HE funding system came into operation in England which very substantially reduced the teaching grant paid to universities by HEFCE and allowed universities to charge undergraduate students up to £9000 per year in tuition fees, an almost threefold rise from the previous maximum of £3290 per year. The government White Paper which accompanied this policy change, 'Higher Education: Students at the Heart of the System' (BIS 2011, 5) notes:

> The changes we are making to higher education funding will in turn drive a more responsive system. To be successful, institutions will have to appeal to prospective students and be respected by employers. Putting financial power into the hands of learners makes student choice meaningful.

The recent tuition fee hike, coupled with a growing emphasis on the development of 'employability skills' as a key goal of higher education programmes, is further stimulating competition between HE providers and encouraging students to view their education as a private economic investment focused on maximising future earnings (Giroux 2002; Harland et al. 2010). Whilst there is no doubt that securing a job after university is a hugely important and rightful concern for students, the growing 'student as consumer' and employability agenda may be seen as dangerous, as McArthur (2011, 743) has noted, 'it risks being complicit in students' understanding their identity mainly in terms of their exchange value in the world of work', rather than being based on other more humanistic, creative and ethical values which *can* (and arguably should) be developed at university (McCulloch 2009; McArthur 2011). In this sense, neoliberal agendas may significantly overwhelm values-building associated with sustainability within the student population.

Associated with these developments are potential changes to the types of subjects that students opt to study at university under enhanced fees regimes. As students become more focused on getting a financial return for their money, and universities become more anxious about securing student numbers (and related revenues), perceived poorer 'performing' subjects, in terms of student recruitment and graduate employment prospects, are more vulnerable to closure (Wolff 2010; Garner 2012). A real concern for sustainability educators here is that these sorts of changes could negatively impact upon the continued uptake of degree courses focusing on sustainability, which may be seen as 'soft', 'fuzzy' and not as explicitly linked with the typical graduate job market. Previous work in this area has shown that the average yearly intake for specific sustainability-focused undergraduate degrees in the UK is between 5 and 20, which means that they are vulnerable targets for closure in the efficiency-driven neoliberal market (Robinson and MacGregor 2011).

Conversely, a significantly growing discourse area in the ESD world involves drawing direct linkages and synergies between ESD and the student employability, skills and consumer rhetoric. To give a few examples from universities in England, Keele University offers a module to all first year students entitled: 'Greening Business: Employability and Sustainability', and Exeter University advertises a whole suite of 'SUSTAINability' modules through emphasis on students enhancing their employability skills by undertaking the modules. A Higher Education Academy (HEA) supported think tank report by Luna et al. (2012), 'Universities and the green economy: graduates for the future', has also discussed how universities in the UK, through the graduates they produce, might contribute towards shaping the growing 'green economy'. These sorts of linkages serve three key purposes: (1) they are practical way of championing sustainability education and literacy to the wider HE community, especially to staff and students who have a keen interest in employability issues, (2) they help to reinforce the importance that all graduates should be entering their careers with the ability to contextualise and action sustainability within their professions, and (3) they help to ensure that more graduates are prepared for jobs in specific environmental and sustainability sectors.

A significant advance to England's ESD movement has also recently been made possible, in part, by capitalising on the student consumer agenda, and the aforementioned government White Paper 'Higher Education: Students at the Heart of the System' (BIS 2011). The HEA and the National Union of Students (NUS) recently commissioned a series of surveys and corresponding reports over three years, reaching over 15,000 undergraduate students, entitled 'Student attitudes towards and skills for sustainable development'. The reports demonstrated that over 60% of students would like to learn more about sustainability and see sustainability covered as part of their university course (Drayson et al. 2013). The NUS were able to use these results to champion for increased sustainability-related funding from HEFCE, arguing along the lines: if students are at the heart of the system and their demands are important, then these reports demonstrate that they are demanding more sustainability exposure, and hence, this should be financially supported. This resulted in a £5 million grant from HEFCE in 2013 called the Students' Green Fund which is coordinated by the NUS and has funded 25 innovative student-led sustainability/ESD projects in HEIs in England.

Quality assurance agendas and ESD

As detailed in Table 1, quality assurance processes are a key mechanism of centralised NPM control over teaching and learning, which ensures that HEIs, 'as public institutions acting in the marketplace, remain accountable yet independent' (Ferlie, Musselin, and Andresani 2008; Reid 2009, 575). In England, quality assurance is governed by the Quality Assurance Agency (QAA) (in conjunction with the universities themselves), who carry out institutional reviews every six years. The remit of the QAA includes the definition and safeguarding of teaching/degree standards, as well as the production of subject benchmark statements. A recent HEFCE funded project, 'Leading Curriculum Change for Sustainability: Strategic Approaches to Quality Enhancement' (HEFCE 2012), was the first tangible attempt at moving towards linking sustainability education with national quality assurance and enhancement programmes. The QAA itself has also recently published its first sector-level cross-disciplinary guidance on incorporating ESD into formal university curricula. This attempt at symbiosis between ESD and quality assurance is working to enhance, promote and raise the profile of ESD at many different levels within universities, including encouraging engagement from the administrative centre of HEIs, which may ultimately lead to further mainstreaming of ESD.

ESD research – the impact of quality-related research funding

A quality-related research (QR) funding system was first introduced in the UK in the late 1980s to apportion funding for research between institutions, based upon the assessed quality and volume of an institution's research in different Units of Assessment (UoAs) (or subject areas). HEFCE carries out these 5–6 yearly research review processes, known formerly as the Research Assessment Exercise (RAE) and since 2012 the Research Excellence Framework (REF), and distributes research funds accordingly. The effect of this state-led managerialist instrument on general research drivers within institutions, on sustainability research, and on ESD research in particular, provides further insight into the contradictions and synergies between neoliberalism and NPM, and the sustainability activity of universities.

One impact of the RAE/REF systems has been the incentivisation of university staff to follow certain research directions at the expense of others in order to optimise QR funding and research rating esteem. Several studies have described the ways in which quality-related research exercises sustain environments which favour disciplinary over interdisciplinary research, short-term over long-term research, individual rather than group research, internationally applicable rather than nationally-relevant research, and which undervalue pedagogical research (Elton 2000; McNay 2003; Waitere et al. 2011). This has significant implications for ESD research which is often interdisciplinary, collaborative, and through its concern with the long-term impact of educational innovations on students' sustainability literacy and skills, longitudinal in nature. Much ESD research being produced in the UK is also nationally focussed and draws on specific institutional case studies, which potentially restricts how highly it can be rated in a system which gives much greater weighting to internationally significant research.

Although there has, as yet, been no systematic review of the impact of the RAE/REF systems on environmental/sustainability *education* research specifically, it is worth noting the lack of overt mention of the terms 'sustainable development', 'sustainability' and 'ESD' within the descriptors which detail the types of research accepted to the following UoAs: 'earth systems and environmental sciences', 'geography, environmental studies and archaeology', 'education' and 'social work and social policy'. Furthermore, ESD researchers come from a variety of background discipline areas and may be discouraged, actively or otherwise, from carrying out ESD research which is seen to detract from more conventional and rewarded research in their home discipline area. These pressures will no doubt impact upon staff choosing to bid for funding, undertake and submit for review ESD-related research projects. Which ultimately brings into question what value and esteem ESD research is currently afforded in our research system? Published research in this area is surely essential though, in order to understand the successes and challenges of the role of educating for a sustainable future, and to drive sustainability activity in institutions, as much ESD research follows an 'action research' methodology.

On the other hand, there are also examples from the quality-related research regime which are beneficial to the growth of sustainability and ESD research or have the potential to be in the near future. Under the new REF system, the *non-academic* 'impact' of research will now account for 20% of total mainstream QR funding which all submissions must demonstrate through selected case studies and an impact template. 'Impact' has been defined as follows: 'an effect on, change or benefit to the economy, society, culture, public policy or services, health, the environment or quality of life, beyond academia' (REF 2012). This potentially provides new scope for ESD research projects to be better valued in the REF context if they can demonstrate a range of beneficial non-academic impacts to different communities. There is also increasing national recognition of the value of interdisciplinary and multidisciplinary research in finding effective solutions to global societal challenges, as Research Councils UK (RCUK) have in recent years identified six multidisciplinary priority areas, five of which can be directly linked to SD: energy; global food security; global uncertainties; living with environmental change and lifelong health and well-being. The impact of these trends on supporting ESD research more specifically remains to be seen.

Concluding comments

Through this paper, we have attempted to explore some of the ideological and practical implications of the relationship between neoliberalism and managerialism in Western higher education, and the progress of sustainability education agendas. Whilst we support the continuing quest for reforms of educational models towards holistic and integrated sustainability education across all disciplines, and recognise the value of calls for paradigmatic reform of HE away from the dominant neoliberal, reductionist and corporate paradigm, we also recognise that there are myriad sustainability and ESD success stories to date within English HE and that these success stories continue to proliferate. There are evidently many different ways of working towards sustainability within our current, fundamentally neoliberal and managerialist, HE system. Thus, are we not contradicting ourselves if we say that nothing meaningful can be achieved within our existing system? Are we failing to celebrate all of the great work going on? Are we focusing on the negatives rather than the positives? Are we getting frustrated and disillusioned by the lack of systemic change? Are we being overly ideological and not practical and rational enough about the nature of change? Or by working within the neoliberal system, are we unwittingly continuing to support it?

Educating university students to critically engage with sustainability issues within their personal, academic and future professional lives, and equipping them with the skills to contribute towards a more sustainable future is urgent and imperative in light of the many social and environmental problems we face globally. One way of attempting to raise the profile and legitimacy of sustainability education and ESD research within the English HE system is for the agenda to be better represented and valued within the managerialist and market-led mechanisms and drivers which govern our academic systems and behaviours at the institutional, departmental and individual level. These mechanisms/drivers include *inter alia*, the distinctive academic reward systems of research quality assessment and promotion, improving reputation and status, incentivisation through funding and resource flows, and meeting the requirements of educational quality standards and benchmarks. By the same token, a key challenge is to interweave sustainability and ESD into instruments which publicly measure institutional performance and influence student choice of university and degree course, such as league tables and the National Student Survey, which provides satisfaction scores on students' university experiences.

It is neither possible nor desirable to exert directive 'one size fits all' sustainability policy on HEIs (Katayama and Gough 2008). Furthermore, enforcing/requiring change or employing sanctions is a notoriously bad way of attempting to change academic behaviour, and fundamentally will not result in the required engagement with the deeper ethical and values-based issues of sustainability and sustainability education that are required. However, the concept of 'steering' for sustainability (Ferlie, Musselin, and Andresani 2008; Broadbent, Laughlin, and Alwani-Starr 2010) and 'nudging' for sustainability (Thaler and Sunstein 2009) may provide some powerful and useful ideas for embedding sustainability into institutional structures and raising the profile of ESD, which would not only be beneficial for those currently working in this field, but could also make it easier, more desirable and more rewarding for academics across all disciplines to engage with this agenda. The following bodies all have the power to play a significant steering role in relation to sustainability education and ESD research in England: the Higher Education Funding Council for England (HEFCE), including the Research Excellence Framework (REF), the Quality Assurance Agency (QAA), Research Councils UK (RCUK), the Higher Education Academy (HEA), the National Union of Students (NUS), Universities UK ((UUK) who have thus far been rather silent in their support for ESD), as well as Unistats, who provide metrics data about university courses. Furthermore, individual institutions may deploy their own steering and nudging mechanisms to further ESD developments internally. Given the highly complex reality of higher education in England, we believe that ESD practitioners must strategically consider how to manage and progress their ESD work given the neoliberal contexts with which we are faced, to ensure that the current education system really does help us move towards a more sustainable future.

Notes on contributors

Sophie E.F. Bessant works as Sustainability Project Officer at Keele University and is a part-time PhD student. Sophie studied at The University of Nottingham from 2004 to 2008, graduating with a BSc Hons Degree in Geography and an MSc in Environmental Management. Sophie's PhD research focuses on the relationship between the sustainable development agenda of higher education in England and neoliberal and new public management political-economic influence within the sector.

Zoe P. Robinson is a Senior Lecturer in Environmental Science and Sustainability and Director of Education for Sustainability at Keele University, having started lecturing at Keele in 2004 following a period of time working in environmental consultancy. Zoe was awarded a National Teaching Fellowship by the Higher Education Academy in 2012 for her work contributing to the field of Education for Sustainability and Open Educational Resources. Zoe co-founded the environmental education group 'Science for Sustainability' in 2006 which has a nationally leading reputation and has won awards for its innovative work in engaging and educating young people and communities in environmental and sustainability issues.

R. Mark Ormerod has been Pro Vice-Chancellor (Research and Enterprise) at Keele University since August 2011, having previously been Head of the School of Physical and Geographical Sciences since its formation in 2005, and of the School of Chemistry and Physics. Professor Ormerod has been at Keele since 1992, when he was appointed to a Lectureship in Chemistry. Professor Ormerod's research interests centre on sustainable processes, in particular clean catalysis, sustainable materials chemistry, fuel cells and biogas conversion. Recently, he has extended his research interests to interdisciplinary research in sustainability including sustainable energy and lifestyles and education for sustainable development. Mark co-leads the 'Science for Sustainability' group.

References

Amsler, S., J. E. Canaan, S. Cowden, S. Motta, and G. Singh, eds. 2010. *Why Critical Pedagogy and Popular Education Matter Today. Higher Education Academy Subject Centre for Sociology, Anthropology and Politics*. [Online]. http://www.lulu.com/gb/en/shop/joyce-canaan/why-critical-pedagogy-and-popular-education-matter-today/paperback/product-6318961.html

Archer, L. 2008. "The New Neoliberal Subjects? Young/Er Academics' Constructions of Professional Identity." *Journal of Education Policy* 23 (3): 265–285.

BIS. 2009. *What We Do*. Department for Business, Innovation and Skills (BIS). [online]. https://www.gov.uk/government/organisations/department-for-business-innovation-skills.

BIS. 2011. *Higher Education: Students at the Heart of the System*. Department for Business, Innovation and Skills (BIS). [online]. http://discuss.bis.gov.uk/hereform/white-paper/.

Blewitt, J. 2013. "EfS: Contesting the Market Model of Higher Education." In *The Sustainable University: Progress and Prospects*, edited by S. Sterling, L. Maxey and H. Luna, 71–86. Abingdon: Routledge.

Brenner, N., J. Peck, and N. Theodore. 2010. "After Neoliberalization?" *Globalizations* 7 (3): 327–345.

Broadbent, J., R. Laughlin, and G. Alwani-Starr. 2010. "Steering for Sustainability." *Public Management Review* 12 (4): 461–473.

Chandler, J., J. Barry, and H. Clark. 2002. "Stressing Academe: The Wear and Tear of the New Public Management." *Human Relations* 55 (9): 1051–1069.

Clegg, S. 2008. "Academic Identities under Threat?" *British Educational Research Journal* 34 (3): 329–345.

Corcoran, P. B., and A. E. J. Wals. 2004. *Higher Education and the Challenge of Sustainability: Problematics, Promise and Practice*. Dordrecht: Kluwer Academic Publishers.

Cortese, A. D. 2003. "The Critical Role of Higher Education in Creating a Sustainable Future." *Planning for Higher Education* 31 (3): 15–22.

Cowden, S., and G. Singh. 2013. *Acts of Knowing: Critical Pedagogy in, against and beyond the University*. London: Bloomsbury.

Crowther, J. 2010. "Why Critical Pedagogy and Popular Education Matter." In *Why Critical Pedagogy and Popular Education Matter Today. Higher Education Academy Subject Centre for Sociology, Anthropology and Politics*, edited by S. Amsler, J. E. Canaan, S. Cowden, S. Motta, and G. Singh. [Online]. http://www.lulu.com/gb/en/shop/joyce-canaan/why-critical-pedagogy-and-popular-education-matter-today/paperback/product-6318961.html

Deem, R. 2001. "Globalisation, New Managerialism, Academic Capitalism and Entrepreneurialism in Universities: Is the Local Dimension Still Important?" *Comparative Education* 37 (1): 7–20.

Deem, R., and K. J. Brehony. 2005. "Management as Ideology: The Case of 'New Managerialism' in Higher Education." *Oxford Review of Education* 31 (2): 217–235.

Devaney, M., and W. Weber. 2003. "Abandoning the Public Good: How Universities Have Helped Privatize Higher Education." *Journal of Academic Ethics* 1: 175–179.

Dill, D. 1997. "Higher Education Markets and Public Policy." *Higher Education Policy* 10 (3–4): 167–185.

Dowling, R. 2008. "Geographies of Identity: Labouring in the 'Neoliberal' University." *Progress in Human Geography* 32 (6): 812–820.

Drayson, R., E. Bone, J. Agombar, and S. Kemp. 2013. "Student Attitudes towards and Skills for Sustainable Development." *Higher Education Academy*. [Online]. http://www.heacademy.ac.uk/assets/documents/sustainability/ESD_student_attitudes_2013_v4.pdf.

Eisenhardt, K. M. 1989. "Agency Theory: An Assessment and Review." *The Academy of Management Review* 14 (1): 57–74.

Elton, L. 2000. "The UK Research Assessment Exercise: Unintended Consequences." *Higher Education Quarterly* 54 (3): 274–283.

Ferlie, E., C. Musselin, and G. Andresani. 2008. "The Steering of Higher Education Systems: A Public Management Perspective." *Higher Education* 56: 325–348.

Filho, W. L. 2000. "Dealing with Misconceptions on the Concept of Sustainability." *International Journal of Sustainability in Higher Education* 1 (1): 9–19.

Freire, P. 1970. *Pedagogy of the Oppressed*. New York: Herder and Herder.

Fridell, G. 2004. "The University and the Moral Imperative of Fair Trade Coffee." *Journal of Academic Ethics* 2: 141–159.

Gamble, A. 1988. *The Free Economy and the Strong State: The Politics of Thatcherism*. London: Macmillan Education Ltd.

Garner, R. 2012. "University Challenge: Has the New Tuition-fees Regime Affected Students' Degree Choices?" *The Independent*. [Online]. http://www.independent.co.uk/news/education/higher/university-challenge-has-the-new-tuitionfees-regime-affected-students-degree-choices-8130995.html

Giroux, H. A. 2002. "Neoliberalism, Corporate Culture and the Promise of Higher Education: The University as a Democratic Public Sphere." *Harvard Educational Review* 72: 425–464.

Goedegebuure, L., and M. Hayden. 2007. "Overview: Governance in Higher Education – Concepts and Issues." *Higher Education Research & Development* 26 (1): 1–11.

Gough, S., and W. Scott. 2008. *Higher Education and Sustainable Development: Paradox and Possibility – Key Issues in Higher Education*. London: Routledge.

Graefe, P. 2005. "Roll-out Neoliberalism and the Social Economy." Draft paper prepared for: The Annual Meeting of the Canadian Political Science Association, University of Western Ontario, June 2, 2005. [Online]. www.cpsa-acsp.ca/papers-2005/graefe.pdf.

Gruening, G. 2001. "Origin and Theoretical Basis of New Public Management." *International Public Management Journal* 4: 1–25.

Hall, K. 2005. "Science, Globalization, and Educational Governance: The Political Rationalities of the New Managerialism." *Indiana Journal of Global Legal Studies* 12 (1). [Online]. http://repository.upenn.edu/cgi/viewcontent.cgi?article=1116&context=gse_pubs.

Harland, T., T. Tidswell, D. Everett, L. Hale, and N. Pickering. 2010. "Neoliberalism and the Academic as Critic and Conscience of Society." *Teaching in Higher Education* 15 (1): 85–96.

Harvey, D. A. 2007. *A Brief History of Neoliberalism*. Oxford: Oxford University Press.

HEFCE. 2005. "Sustainable Development in Higher Education." *Higher Education Funding Council for England*. [Online]. www.hefce.ac.uk.

HEFCE. 2009. "Sustainable Development in Higher Education: 2008 Update to Strategic Statement and Action Plan." *Higher Education Funding Council for England*. [Online]. www.hefce.ac.uk.

HEFCE. 2012. "Leading Curriculum Change for Sustainability: Strategic Approaches to Quality Enhancement." *Higher Education Funding Council for England*. [Online]. www.hefce.ac.uk.

Henkel, M. 2007. "Can Academic Autonomy Survive in the Knowledge Society? A Perspective from Britain." *Higher Education Research & Development* 26 (1): 87–99.

Hill, R. P. 2004. "The Socially-responsible University: Talking the Talk While Walking the Walk in the College of Business." *Journal of Academic Ethics* 2: 89–100.

Hood, C. 1991. "A Public Management for all Seasons?" *Public Administration* 69: 3–19.

Huckle, J. 2008. "An Analysis of New Labour's Policy on Education for Sustainable Development with Particular Reference to Socially Critical Approaches." *Environmental Education Research* 14 (1): 65–75.

Irwin, R. 2007. 'After Neoliberalism': Environmental Education to Education for Sustainability. Conference Presentation – Philosophy of Education Society of Australasia. [Online]. https://www.academia.edu/3123057/After_Neoliberalism_Environmental_Education_to_Education_for_Sustainability.

Jary, D. 2005. "UK Higher Education Policy and the 'Global Third Way'." *Policy and Politics* 33 (4): 637–655.

Jucker, R. 2014. *Do We Know What We Are Doing? Reflections on Learning, Knowledge, Economics, Community and Sustainability*. [Online]. http://rolfjucker.net/20140116_Do%20we%20know_incl%20Strachan_webversion.pdf.

Katayama, J., and S. Gough. 2008. "Developing Sustainable Development within the Higher Education Curriculum: Observations on the HEFCE Strategic Review." *Environmental Education Research* 14 (4): 413–422.

Klenowski, V. 2009. "Public Education Matters: Reclaiming Public Education for the Common Good in a Global Era." *The Australian Educational Researcher* 36 (1): 1–25.

Kogan, M., and S. Hanney. 2000. *Reforming Higher Education*. London: Jessica Kingsley Publishers.

Kolsaker, A. 2008. "Academic Professionalism in the Managerialist Era: A Study of English Universities." *Studies in Higher Education* 33 (5): 513–525.

Luna, et al. 2012. *Universities and the Green Economy: Graduates for the Future*. [Online]. http://www.heacademy.ac.uk/assets/documents/esd/Graduates_For_The_Future_Print_130812_1322.pdf.

Mandleson. 2009a. "Higher Education and Modern Life." Birkbeck University Lecture, London, July 27. [Online]. https://www.gov.uk/government/organisations/department-for-business-innovation-skills.

Mandleson. 2009b. "Higher Ambitions." CBI HE Conference, London, October 20. [Online]. https://www.gov.uk/government/organisations/department-for-business-innovation-skills.

Marginson, S. 2007. "University Mission and Identity for a Post Post-public Era." *Higher Education Research & Development* 26 (1): 117–131.

McArthur, J. 2011. "Reconsidering the Social and Economic Purposes of Higher Education." *Higher Education Research & Development* 30 (6): 737–749.

McChesney, R. W. 1998. "Introduction." In *Profit over People: Neoliberalism and Global Order*, edited by N. Chomsky, 7–19. New York: Seven Stories Press.

McCulloch, A. 2009. "The Student as Co-producer: Learning from Public Administration about the Student University Relationship." *Studies in Higher Education* 34 (2): 171–183.

McNay, I. 2003. "Assessing the Assessment: An Analysis of the UK Research Assessment Exercise, 2001, and Its Outcomes, with Special Reference to Research in Education." *Science and Public Policy* 30 (1): 47–54.

Mendivil, J. L. I. 2002. "The New Providers of Higher Education." *Higher Education Policy* 15: 353–364.

Middleton, C. 2000. "Models of State and Market in the Modernisation of Higher Education." *British Journal of Sociology of Education* 21 (4): 537–554.

Naidoo, R., and I. Jamieson. 2005. "Empowering Participants or Corroding Learning? Towards a Research Agenda on the Impact of Student Consumerism in Higher Education." *Journal of Education Policy* 20 (3): 267–281.

NEF. 2008. "University Challenge: Towards a Well-being Approach to Quality in Higher Education." *New Economics Foundation*. [Online]. http://www.healthyuniversities.ac.uk/uploads/files/qualitywellbeing_qaa.pdf.

Peck, J., and A. Tickell. 2002. "Neoliberalizing Space." *Antipode* 34 (3): 380–404.

Readings, B. 1998. *The University in Ruins*. Cambridge, MA: Harvard University Press.

REF. 2012. "The Research Excellence Framework: A Brief Guide for Research Users." *Research Excellence Framework*. [Online]. http://www.ref.ac.uk/media/ref/content/researchusers/REF%20guide.pdf.

Reid, I. C. 2009. "The Contradictory Managerialism of University Quality Assurance." *Journal of Education Policy* 24 (5): 575–593.

Robinson, Z., and MacGregor. 2011. "Making the Transition to Interdisciplinarity: Effective Strategies for Early Student Support." *Higher Education Academy*. [Online]. http://www.heacademy.ac.uk/assets/documents/sustainability/keele_interdisc_final.pdf.

Ryan, A. 2012. *Education for Sustainable Development and Holistic Curriculum Change: A Review and Guide*. [Online]. http://www.heacademy.ac.uk/assets/documents/esd/ESD_Artwork_050412_1324.pdf.

Saravanamuthu, K., and T. Tinker. 2002. "The University in the New Corporate World." *Critical Perspectives on Accounting* 13: 545–554.

SDC. 2004. "Shows Promise. but Must Try Harder." *Sustainable Development Commission* [Online]. http://www.sd-commission.org.uk/publications.php?id=72.

Shaull, R. 2000. "Foreword." In *Pedagogy of the Oppressed*, edited by P. Freire (1970), 29–34. 30th Anniversary Edition. New York: Continuum.

Sterling, S. 2013. "The Sustainable University: Challenge and Response." In *The Sustainable University: Progress and Prospects*, edited by S. Sterling, L. Maxey, and H. Luna, 17–50. Abingdon: Routledge.

Streeting, W., and G. Wise. 2009. "Rethinking the Values of Higher Education – Consumption, Partnership and Community?" *Quality Assurance Agency*. [Online]. www.qaa.ac.uk/students/studentengagement/undergraduate.pdf.

Thaler, R. H., and C. R. Sunstein. 2009. *Nudge: Improving Decisions about Health, Wealth and Happiness*. London: Penguin Books.

Tilbury, D. 2013. "Another World is Desirable: A Global Rebooting of Higher Education for Sustainable Development." In *The Sustainable University: Progress and Prospects*, edited by S. Sterling, L. Maxey, and H. Luna, 71–86. Abingdon: Routledge.

UNESCO. 2002. "Education for Sustainable Development Information Brief." *United Nations Educational, Scientific and Cultural Organisation*. [Online]. http://www.unesco.org/education/tlsf/extras/img/DESDbriefWhatisESD.pdf.

Waitere, H. J., J. Wright, M. Tremaine, S. Brown, and C. Pausé. 2011. "Choosing Whether to Resist or Reinforce the New Managerialism: The Impact of Performance-based Research Funding on Academic Identity." *Higher Education Research & Development* 30 (2): 205–217.

NEOLIBERALISM AND ENVIRONMENTAL EDUCATION

van Weenen, H. 2000. "Towards a Vision of a Sustainable University." *International Journal of Sustainability in Higher Education* 1 (1): 20–34.

Williams, G. 1997. "The Market Route to Mass Higher Education: British Experience 1979–1996." *Higher Education Policy* 10 (3–4): 275–289.

Wolff, J. 2010. "Why is Middlesex University Philosophy Department Closing?" *The Guardian*. [Online]. http://www.theguardian.com/education/2010/may/17/philosophy-closure-middlesex-university.

The promise and peril of the state in neoliberal times: implications for the critical environmental education movement in Brazil

Nicolas Stahelin[a], Inny Accioly[b] and Celso Sánchez[c]

[a]*International Educational Development, Teachers College, Columbia University, New York, NY, USA;* [b]*Graduate Program in Education, Federal University of Rio de Janeiro, Rio de Janeiro, Brazil;* [c]*Department of Didactics, Federal University of the State of Rio de Janeiro, Rio de Janeiro, Brazil*

> Neoliberal ideology has made an impact on environmental education (EE) policies and practices in Brazil. The EE in Family Agriculture Program, of national scope and administered by the Ministry of the Environment, seeks to promote sustainable development in rural areas, specifically through strategies focused on adult education and non-formal education aimed at small producers (family agriculture). This program reveals profound ideological contradictions between the critical and transformative rhetoric of public policy and the actual program structures and practices administered by the state in a dependent economy, which primarily serve to reinforce a capitalist mode of production marked by high environmental impact and deeply stratified class relations. In the neoliberal era, states intending to protect the environment through critical EE strategies suffer serious limitations due to their role as stewards of a globalized economy based on the supply of raw materials, high-impact land-use, and a cheap labor force.

Introduction

Brazil is an example of a nation that has advanced a national environmental education (EE) program designed around the precepts of critical EE, in explicit opposition to the now dominant paradigm of Education for Sustainable Development (ESD) propagated by UNESCO (Lima 2009). According to many observers, Brazil's EE discourse reflected in official documents, including EE policy and legislation, has been less influenced by the economic and technocentric approach of the dominant ESD paradigm, generally placing greater emphasis on the social and ethical dimensions of the environment, and more explicitly calling for strengthening critical pedagogical practices (Sauvé, Brunelle, and Berryman 2005). Yet, what can also be observed in Brazil is the co-optation of environmental discourse by big business and the ways in which the governance apparatus is mobilized to benefit domestic and transnational corporate interests, often in the form of public–private partnerships. This points to the perils that lie ahead for a critical EE movement facing the headwinds of a neoliberal climate in Brazil, where the state must grapple with powerful economic actors acting under the universal banner of sustainability.

In this article, we look at how neoliberal ideology has influenced EE practices in Brazil, focusing on the role of the state in mobilizing non-formal educational programs at the national level to promote rural sustainable development in family agriculture. Our analysis is based on Inny Accioly's (2013) recent case study of the EE in Family Agriculture Program (*Programa de Educacão Ambiental na Agricultura Familiar* [PEAAF], administered by the Ministry of the Environment, or MMA). This state-driven environmental educational initiative is important to examine because of its political–pedagogical implications, considering the way this program was affected by new environmental legislation forged by the close relationship between the agribusiness sector and Environment Committees of Congress. PEAAF highlights the role of the state and its complex dynamics with civil society when considering the effects of neoliberal ideology on EE. This analysis suggests that within Brazilian EE there are profound ideological contradictions between the transformative rhetoric of EE legislation and public policy, on the one hand, and the actual EE program structures and practices administered by the state on the other, which primarily serves to reinforce a capitalist mode of production highlighted by intensive land-use development and highly stratified class relations.

Neoliberalism, dependency theory, and the role of the state

Sustainable development presents an interesting phenomenon with which to examine the links between neoliberal ideology and EE, and the role of the state in either facilitating or interrupting these links. To address this matter, we engage the neoliberal turn in political-economic orthodoxy following David Harvey's definition of neoliberalism as 'a theory of political economic practices that proposes that human well-being can best be advanced by liberating individual entrepreneurial freedoms and skills within an institutional framework characterized by strong property rights, free markets, and free trade' (2005, 2). Neoliberalism in this sense is marked by an ideology that promotes this institutional framework as the most just and efficient organizing principle for the allocation of scarce resources for the welfare of society as a whole. Furthermore, in the realm of neoliberal governance mechanisms, the state has the role of setting up 'an institutional framework appropriate to such practices' (2). It is within this neoliberal institutional framework that we seek to understand the role of the state in promoting EE initiatives designed to foster sustainable development in the Brazilian rural sector. The focus of our analysis is on how state-driven EE initiatives, and associated processes of environmental legislation geared toward sustainable rural development in the Brazilian countryside, have absorbed and recently manifested key elements of neoliberalism.

The Marxist theoretical reference point of dependency theory (Fernandes 1972) is helpful here to highlight how this topic should be understood through the matrix of a global capitalist system. The maintenance of the capitalist mode of production has historically served to reproduce class inequalities both within nations and between nations across the north–south (core-periphery) divide. Accordingly, in the integration of national economies to global markets, we observe the transfer of surplus from dependent, the so-called 'Third World' nations to the elite in the core regions of the world economy, both in the form of profits as well as interests on debt (Harvey 2005; Amaral and Carcanholo 2009). The generation of this surplus in peripheral economies is due more to the hyper-exploitation of the labor force than to highly advanced levels of technology in production processes (Marini and Martins 2008). Therefore, to understand state-driven EE policies and practices aimed toward rural areas in Brazil it is necessary to situate the 'environmental question' within this nation's role as a dependent and semi-peripheral economy, whose rural labor force is hyper-exploited within the globally stratified division of labor. As such, we must treat the 'environmental question' as a profound social issue in which the exploitation of land and natural resources is inextricably linked to the exploitation of human labor and conflicts over access to land.

Harvey reminds us, furthermore, that the extraction of tribute from developing nations, associated with the international division of labor, is an 'old imperial practice,' but it has been pronounced in neoliberal times and has 'proven very helpful to the restoration of class power, particularly in the world's main financial centres' (2005, 74). This perspective places class conflict at the center of the environmental problematic, and makes the role of the state an important variable to examine in attempts to understand the contested nature of public EE initiatives. Along these lines, an important characteristic of neoliberalism that concerns us in our analysis is the objective to bring about the restoration (if not the initial formation) of class power. Neoliberalism according to Harvey is 'a political project to re-establish the conditions for capital accumulation and to restore the power of economic elites' (2005, 19). Our preoccupation is with how state-driven EE projects aimed at fostering sustainable development in the Brazilian countryside are mobilized to serve this purpose.

The role of the state is of central concern in this matter. Our approach to this question employs Gramsci's concept of the 'extended state,' which forms the conceptual basis upon which our interpretation of national political dynamics of education rests – and the dynamic upon which the PEAAF is inserted. The 'extended' state is composed of the conjunction of civil and political society with transnational articulations in the formation of policy. The polity of the state responsible for repression and coercion is entangled with elements of civil society that implicate the cultural–ideological mechanisms producing and maintaining hegemony (Buci-Glucksmann 1980). The 'extended state' in Gramsci's perspective is traversed by class conflict, forming a dialectical relationship between reproduction and transformation, the result of which cannot be predetermined. The struggle for ideological and cultural apparatus of hegemony is always a process of contestation. We must recognize that the struggle of the working class for control over public educational institutions and practices administered by the state puts pressure so that public resources may contribute to the formation and organization of this class according to its own interests. Yet, it is also true that the dominant class, having much more access to and control over the means of mass communication (and other institutions of cultural and ideological control), results in bourgeois class interests being absorbed harmoniously into the interests of the working class, constituting altogether the common interests of the national polity. The apparatus of hegemony for the ruling class is a powerful consensus builder, and public education initiatives form an important component of this apparatus.

Similarly, the state as a site of power struggle where both domination and resistance may take place is an established idea in critical studies of education (Carnoy and Levin 1985; Apple, Kenway, and Singh 2005). Through public educational institutions and practices, the state becomes not simply an arm of the ruling class, but 'an arena of conflict over the production of knowledge, ideology, and employment, a place where social movements try to meet their needs and business attempts to reproduce its hegemony' (1985, 50). In other words, both dominant and subjugated classes are going to try, and are variably able to, shape public education according to their needs. We argue that PEAAF, as a political–pedagogical project, reflects struggles over conceptions of agriculture, environment, and education waged in the arena of class conflict. Our primary interest is in understanding the internal contradictions of an EE project purported to be critical and participatory promoted by the state operating within the neoliberal framework of environmental governance.

Historical context of critical EE in Brazil

Although Brazilian EE has roots in conservationist legislations that go as far back as the nineteenth century, most observers see the beginning of its institutionalization at the federal level take place in 1973, when the military government established the Special Secretariat for the Environment (Carvalho 2008). For this reason, the character of Brazilian EE ideals in the present day need to be understood within the historical context of the extensive social movements for democratic change that took place during the transition from military to civilian rule, a time culminating in the mid-1980s known as *Abertura Política*.[1] Prior to this transition, EE in Brazil emphasized outdoor education, the teaching of ecology, and the preservation of natural areas when this did not interfere with the development agenda of a military regime more keen on appeasing global conservationist pressures than on responding to budding domestic environmental movements (Acslerad 2008). The political transformations of the 1980s, by empowering civil society, democratizing the state, and opening the public sphere to much wider participation by the citizenry, are a key factor explaining why EE in Brazil ultimately rooted its ethos in critical traditions.

On the heels of the *Abertura Polititica*, the growth of EE as a social and political project of national dimensions was driven by the state and civil society through extensive policy formulation. The legislative foundation for the strengthening of a national EE movement was established with the new constitution of 1988, of which article 225 states: 'All citizens have the right to an environment in ecological equilibrium, as a public good for common use and essential to a healthy quality of life, thus upon the state and the people the duty to defend it and preserve it for present and future generations' (our translation, Brasil 2003). Remarkably for a constitution, the mandate goes into much detail as to the role of the government: 'to uphold this right, it is incumbent upon the state to promote EE in all levels of schooling and the *conscientization* of the public for environmental preservation' (our translation, Brasil 2003). The constitutional mandate making the promotion and delivery of EE a responsibility of public authorities was a major victory for social movements that preceded this milestone. It led to a state-driven national system of EE provision that established its presence from the federal to municipal levels. This process included input from wide-ranging stakeholders in the private, public, and non-profits sectors across society, as well as from numerous regional and thematic networks of environmental educators, activists, and academics (Sánchez 2010).

The vision put forth by the *Carta Brasileira para Educação Ambiental* (Brazilian Charter for EE), produced by the networked EE movement that was also prominently engaged in Eco-92, delineated the vision and principles for a national EE program. This foundational document highlighted the importance of fostering critical thinking for local and planetary consciousness; of acknowledging the ideo-logical nature (not-neutral) of such education; of educating for active citizenship; of adopting holistic perspectives that affirm the necessity of interdisciplinarity for an adequate understanding of human–nature relationships; of social solidarity, respect for human rights, democratization, and multiculturalism; and of promoting wide political participation in the design and implementation of EE systems. Notably, overcoming the authoritarian legacy of the military regime, the *Carta Brasileira* called for 'the participation of communities directly and indirectly affected by envi-ronmental issues, in all instances, in the decision-making process regarding policies that shape EE initiatives' (our translation, MEC 1992).

The academy played a major role in the political effervescence of the times, laying a critical epistemological foundation for the mobilization of both civil society and the state around EE. Owing largely to popular education movements and the Freirean legacy of praxis and dialogical methods that emerged within a Latin American Marxist paradigm, the Brazilian EE movement took shape through an integrated socio-ecological approach to the environmental question, with a profound emancipa-tory perspective on human–nature relations, and strong concern for fundamental social transformation (Loureiro 2004). Identifying its critical epistemological roots, Carvalho (2008) contends that Brazilian EE ideals focus on nature not just as a ques-tion of natural resources, but also of cultural diversity, diverse livelihoods, identity and cultural rights, citizenship, and fundamentally as a matter of social justice.

In the present day, state-driven EE initiatives have continued this tradition, gen-erally flying the banner of critical EE. The notion of EE leading to the formation of citizen-subjects capable of critically reading socio-environmental realities and mobi-lizing collectively to intervene in transformative ways to overcome social injustice is quite central and well established in official environmental and pedagogical dis-course sanctioned by the state (Loureiro 2008). It is this common overarching iden-tity and tradition that allows the Brazilian EE field to resist the framework put forth by the UN Decade of ESD. From the Brazilian EE viewpoint, DESD is seen as a hegemonic construct attuned to the interests of northern high-income nations through its technocentrism, continued market orientation, and unshakable focus on universalized notions of progress normed according to standards of Western moder-nity that ignore cultural, socio-political, and biophysical diversity of other nations (Lima 2009).

This imagined overarching identity breaks down when we observe the field more carefully, as the evolution of Brazilian EE movement in the twenty years after the *Carta Brasileira* reveals divergent theoretical/methodological strands. Two promi-nent lineages should be mentioned here. One emphasized a Marxist approach to the role of the state and centrality of the public sphere in redressing the social asymme-tries of power and environmental injustices that are inherent to the capitalist politi-cal-economic system. This school of thought was mainly represented by the work of Jose Silva Quintas within IBAMA (the Brazilian Institute for the Environment and Renewable Natural Resources) and led to a model of EE known as *public environ-mental management education* (Quintas 2004). This model constitutes some of the earliest work on critical EE mobilized from within the state in Brazil, and Quintas' legacy can be found within the widespread institutionalization of this model within the legal framework for environmental licensing and regulation of industrial activity.

Another prominent lineage distanced itself from an orthodox Marxist reading of society, influenced instead by the post-structuralist Marxist dialectics of the

Frankfurt school and also inspired by Edgar Morin, Leonardo Boff, and others critically concerned with justice within a framework of complexity theory. The concept of Ecopedagogy, advanced by Moacir Gadotti and colleagues from the Paulo Freire Institute in São Paulo, was an early coalescence of these new inspirations, and was influential within a larger network of EE activists and academics that played key roles in Eco-92, the formulation of the *Treaty on Environmental Education for Sustainable Societies and Global Responsibility*, and the subsequent Earth Charter movement (Gadotti 1998; Kahn 2008). This school of thought remains very influential in the present day administrations of the General Coordinating Body of the National EE Policy (known as *OG-PNEA*) within in the Ministry of Education,[2] and the EE Directorship of the Ministry of the Environment[3] in Brasilia.

The variations in these two camps are based on different interpretations of Freirean political and pedagogical principles vis-a-vis Marxist conflict paradigms and post-foundational critical theories, even if they all locate themselves firmly within the broader camp of critical traditions. It appears that the banner of *critical* EE in Brazil is being flown as a catch-all category for conceptual and theoretical EE packages that actually diverge epistemologically and ideologically in important ways. This is most striking when noting the degree to which different strands of EE address (or do not address) the socio-ecological dialectics of Marxist thought through questions of power and social conflict (Trein 2012). The epistemological divergences that lie underneath the surface of the diverse critical tradition are causing ideological cleavages within the movement, and there is an emerging literature in the Brazilian academy attempting to map these divergences and understand its implications for practice (Layrargues 2012).

The theoretical divergences found in the lineages of Brazilian EE have methodological implications that translate into important differences on the ground. It is with this issue in mind that we present a case study of an EE program run out of the Ministry of the Environment, categorized as critical in theory but ultimately pragmatic and non-critical in practice when exercised through a state penetrated by the currents of neoliberalism. After all, Brazil is far from immune to neoliberal trends, so how do we reconcile the critical, emancipatory vision for EE with Brazil's reality as a peripheral (or semi-peripheral) economy, supplier of raw materials and cheap surplus labor for the centers of capital? Despite the transformative promise of the Brazilian EE movement, the co-optation of environmental discourse by big business, the ways in which the governance apparatus is mobilized across sectors to benefit corporate interests, and the institutionalization of EE through public–private partnerships often guided more by market-driven logics of neoliberal ideology than by grassroots struggles for social justice, all point to the perils that lie ahead for the critical EE movement in Brazil. The following section examines specific instances in which neoliberalism is making substantive inroads into Brazilian EE initiatives, paying particular attention to the state's relationship to the agribusiness sector.

EE in Family Agriculture Program: neoliberalism, the state, and 'civil society'

The Environmental Education Program in Family Agriculture (PEAAF), created and administered by the Environmental Education Directorate (DEA) of the Ministry of the Environment (MMA), seeks to foster sustainable practices in family agriculture and to promote sustainable natural resource management in rural areas, specifically through strategies focused on adult education and non-formal education. Among this program's central objectives, we find: (1) Contribute to rural sustainable development; (2) Support environmental regularization of rural properties in the family agriculture sector; and (3) Foster critical and participatory educational processes that promote education, capacity-building, communication, and social mobilization. Principles of social and environmental justice, democratic and participatory management, and plurality are prominent in the program's official literature. Among its directives, the program seeks to promote critical reflections on urban–rural and local–global relationships within the spirit of co-responsibility and solidarity. In these ways, PEAAF reflects the principles of critical EE espoused by the national EE agenda.

This program, we should note, was created through the Ministry of the Environment in response to ongoing demands by rural social movements, which consistently put forth the critique that EE provided by the public educational apparatus was weak or non-existent in rural areas. In Brazil, as we have explained above, the responsibility of the state to provide EE exists as a constitutional mandate. PEAAF was thus originally a social demand to address the real socio-environmental problems suffered by rural groups whose livelihoods consisted of small family agriculture (i.e. genetically modified crops, agro-toxins, megaprojects such as large highways or hydroelectric dams, etc.). In practice, however, the design and institutionalization of the program have been influenced by the neoliberal climate structuring the development of the Brazilian rural sector.

We focus the following critical examination of PEAAF and associated concerns on three examples that highlight how neoliberal ideology is guiding Brazilian state-driven EE initiatives: (a) The national EE context within which PEAAF is situated, where public–private partnerships and the corporate financing of environmental education administered by the state has become the norm; (b) the influence of the agribusiness sector in environmental legislation through campaign financing; and (c) the co-optation of principles of 'popular' participation that have resulted in pragmatic and non-critical forms of EE pedagogy being put into practice. In each of these examples, we find ways that the state, in the process of mobilizing EE programs, is actively involved in the reproduction of capitalist modes of production and deeply stratified class relations.

Corporate EE financing through public–private partnerships

We start with the national context of state-driven EE strategies implemented by the Ministry of the Environment, namely the National Environmental Education Program (PRONEA), within which PEAAF is inserted. Upon analysis of official literature produced by the Ministry about activities undertaken in PRONEA, we observed a recurrent referencing of partnerships between the Ministry and entities of 'civil society', a large part of which were representatives of the corporate sector. This is particularly the case with regard to financing and operationalization of EE programs, which points to the dearth of public resources allocated for this purpose at the national level. The development of national EE by way of these partnerships also points to the affinity that EE projects promoted by the Ministry have with the interests of the class that controls the means of production.

A striking example of a partnership between the MMA and the private sector, specifically in the EE of small rural producers, is the case of Bunge, a multinational corporation. The close relationship of the Bunge group with state and local governments is explained on its website. As a result of this partnership, in 2007, they produced a booklet called 'Environmental Responsibility in Agricultural Production'. This business conglomerate operates globally along the entire chain of food production, selling fertilizers to farmers and in turn buying their crops, then storing, moving, and processing them. Within the chain of production and distribution of Bunge, Brazil occupies the role of exporter of agricultural products, oilseed processor and flour mills. The activities of Bunge in Brazil are intensive with regard to the use of 'natural resources'. While 'supportive' of local farmers, any damage caused to the environment resulting from agricultural activities sponsored by the company would be the responsibility of individual farmers and not of Bunge; yet activities causing extensive environmental impacts are crucial to Bunge's bottom line. At the same time, Bunge sponsors and conducts courses, lectures and elaborate brochures on how to preserve nature and be 'environmentally responsible.'

If we can argue, as Wood has (2005), that the problem is not this or that corporation, but the actual capitalist system – with its economic compulsions for expansion – we can then conclude that the detrimental effects of this system cannot be eliminated by merely taming global corporations or making them more 'ethical', 'responsible' or 'socially conscious.' Not even the most benign or 'responsible' corporation can escape the automatic compulsions of capitalism to pursue the bottom line, for it has to follow the laws of the market and its responsibilities to shareholders in order to survive. This means inevitably putting profits above all other considerations, with its attendant destructive social and environmental consequences. Our interpretation of public–private partnerships suggests that the insistence of these groups to invest in EE assumes the purpose of disseminating values that legitimize corporate interests.

From this perspective, public–private partnerships in the financing of public EE initiatives exposes the ideological synergy between the state and the corporate sector, and give materiality to Gramsci's notion of an extended state where market-driven actors constitute a powerful segment of civil society. Harvey argues that such partnerships lie at the heart of neoliberalization, which sees a marked 'shift from government (state power on its own) to governance (a broader configuration of state and key elements in civil society)' (2005, 77). Neoliberal governance poses some difficult questions for public EE initiatives. What happens to information that is not of interest to the maintenance of corporate activity – i.e. information that may question or delegitimize the corporation's activities or hurt its credibility as a steward of the environment or promoter of the social good? Might EE projects financed and operationalized by the corporate sector, yet carrying the seal of the state, be contributing to the legitimization of continued capitalist accumulation – in other words, reinforcing social structures and economic activities that lead to continued environmental destruction and exploitation of the working classes? These questions reveal the profound contradictions that exist when neoliberal environmental governance meets public EE initiatives, where tensions arise between the public good and private interests.

Implications of campaign financing and the new Forest Code on EE

Tensions between the public good and private interests that may affect EE in the rural sector are also evident in electoral campaign financing and recent modifications to environmental legislation. Since 2009, when the creation of PEAAF was initiated by the Ministry, the process has been intimately connected to the tumultuous legislative process that led to the new Forest Code of 2012 (now-former federal law no. 4,771 of 1965). It is no coincidence that PEAAF, despite being debated and reformulated since 2009, is officially launched just a few days after the conflictive new Forest Code was approved in congress. As a result, PEAAF would now have to be based on the drastically different definitions and regulations encoded in the new environmental law.

The relevance of the new law to EE revolves around the importance of environmental codes of land tenure regularization, without which the participation in national and international markets is severely constrained for rural producers. EE, rural technical assistance, and training for rural producers had always been key components of this regularization process, which was generally aimed at family agriculture sector as 'special beneficiaries' of public assistance. As a result, the environmental component in the process of land tenure regularization had a fundamentally educational character prior to the new Forest Code.

The new Forest Code fundamentally changed this relationship between small rural producers and land tenure regularization that was so important to maintaining access to land. Environmental regulation of land tenure in the new law excludes most educational and training/professional development activities and is rather centered around managerial/administrative requirements such as the Rural Environmental Registry and the Environmental Reserve Quotas, which constitute 'a nominal land title representative of an area with existing primary or secondary (recovering) forest' to be recorded in 'commodity exchanges' or in systems of registration and financial liquidation of assets. The new Forest Code transforms the process of recuperating degraded areas into a monetized process with speculative value in a market, in turn making 'environmental regularization' expressed purely in financial and mercantilist values. In other words, in the new legislation, environmental regulation ceases to be an educational matter and becomes primarily a financial question. As Harvey affirmed succinctly, 'Neoliberalization has meant, in short, the financialization of everything' (2005, 33). From our perspective, EE in the rural sector in Brazil has not escaped this phenomenon.

Connecting back to Bunge, according to the educational booklet on environmental responsibility referenced above, 'Environmental regularization is the first step to have a chance to compete in the market ...'[4] The booklet goes on to describe the increasing number of requirements on production standards imposed by internal and external markets. In the context of the 'monopolization of territories' (Oliveira 2012), environmental regularization is mobilized as another form of coercion by commercial enterprises and industrial processing upon rural producers. To the extent that rural sustainable development is framed by environmental regularization laws designed to increase competitiveness in a global capitalist economy, we see PEAAF as an educational program molding family agriculture into a model of production more useful to capital.

The influence of agribusiness in the Brazilian process of environmental legislation exemplifies acutely the penetration of neoliberal ideology in ways that ultimately impacts practices of EE in the rural sector (Accioly and Sánchez 2012). By agribusiness, we refer not just to landowners, but rather to the complex industrialized agricultural sector in Latin America subordinated to the interests of financial capital (de Mendonça 2010). Members of ABAG (Brazilian Agribusiness Association) in fact include several banks, telecommunications companies, companies involved in the chemical industry and others. The extended state is again visible here in the way it establishes relationships with the corporate sector. This is a salient point when the latter finances the electoral campaigns of parliamentarians who, once elected, comply with a political agenda tightly synchronized with corporate interests, leading to key modifications in environmental legislation in ways that benefit the profit motive. As Harvey makes clear of neoliberal governance strategies, 'businesses and corporations not only collaborate intimately with state actors but even acquire a strong role in writing legislation, determining public policies, and setting regulatory frameworks (which are mainly advantageous to themselves)' (2005, 77). In Brazil, we see a perfect illustration of neoliberal governance through the articulations between agribusiness and the state in legislative processes (Accioly and Sánchez 2012).

Participation and pedagogical discourse in PEAAF

Given the larger policy and legislative context provided so far, what do we make of the 'critical, participatory, and dialogical educational processes' claimed in the PEAAF literature? In EE promoted by MMA and geared toward family agriculture, its primarily technical and pragmatic character can be observed, emphasizing the clarification of environmental legislations, the framing of the small agriculturalist into programs of environmental regularization of small rural properties, and the diffusion of 'successful initiatives' through the promotion of public–private 'partnerships' financed by the corporate sector. This type of EE, which neglects to debate the socio-environmental impacts of large-scale development projects, (such as PAC, *Programa Acelerado de Crescimento*,[5] or Accelerated Program for Growth), or the concrete modifications promoted by the reform of the Forest Code, is limited in its capacity to promote the critical reading of socio-environmental reality. What has remained out of the agenda in PEAAF is addressing the necessary context of class conflict, which presents itself in such pronounced fashion in the Brazilian countryside.

Participation, as conceptualized by PEAAF, has taken on different meanings along the process of designing and implementing the program. Initially, rural workers participated in negotiations around the program through meetings between staff members of the EE Department of the Ministry and rural workers' unions and social movements. The initial negotiations, where unions and social movements led a process of establishing criteria and resources for the mitigation of socio-environmental impacts resulting from the large-scale federal development projects, gave way to workshops where environmental issues were treated generically and decontextualized from local realities. Unions and social movements did not participate in setting the agenda of the workshops. They were not given prior access to the workshop programming once the agenda was set and had no recourse to changing the chosen topics for debate. Time for debate and discussion, in any case, was limited, with lectures and presentations by environmental technicians and other specialists predominating. As a result, the entities representing the interests of the rural working class gradually stopped participating in key decision-making meetings.

By self-referencing as a critical and participatory educational program, PEAAF re-signifies the concept of participation, so that what is prioritized is 'participation' by way of attendance of isolated individuals with no explicit ideological affiliations, without concrete decision-making powers, and fragmented into numerous groups – as opposed to the more substantive participation of the organized and oppressed masses, with concrete and unified agendas. In light of these observations, the notion of 'critical, participatory, and dialogical educational processes' claimed in the PEAAF literature risks becoming merely an educational slogan (Scheffler 1960). Prom our point of view, the discourse around 'critical, participatory, and dialogical' processes is intended to foster social adhesion, generating trust of the dominant model of development from society as a whole, and forging consensus around principles of sustainable development. This may be a form of consensus that reflects little of the ideals of the Freirean educational movements from which the ideas of critical, participatory, and dialogical education originates.

Along these lines, we see the promotion of a pedagogical practice that reduces environmental problems to mere technical–operational challenges, where environmental challenges are identified generically as a problem of human vs. nature, rather than as an outcome of specific power struggles between groups in society. In a macro-classification of the political–ideological tendencies found within the field of Brazilian EE (Layrargues and da Costa Lima 2011), the EE program described in this case could be categorized as 'pragmatic' (vs. 'critical'). According to Layrargues, in pragmatic EE initiatives, a lack of critical reflection derives from 'a belief in the neutrality of science and technology, which results in a superficial and apolitical perception of social relations and their interactions with the environment' (2012, 405). In this approach, class conflict is hidden as the social function of education is subordinated to the demands of capital, in effect demobilizing labor and strengthening the position of capital in the rural sector. In the Brazilian countryside, this is illustrated by the weakening of the traditional rural producer's lifestyle and livelihood, historically based on family agriculture practices. By stimulating the partnerships between the small producer and rural corporate enterprises, PEAAF strengthens the point of view of globalized agribusiness that is fundamentally geared toward the exportation of cash crops for global trade. In these partnerships between 'unequals', the problem of land conflicts and concentration of land among the few, which lies partly at the heart of an economic system with devastating social and environmental consequences, is left unaddressed.

Conclusion

The type of EE promoted by the Brazilian state, in the case of PEAAF, exemplifies a public educational program that originated as a victory of rural social movements, but became subsumed and co-opted by the dominant ideology and practices of neoliberal governance. In this instance of state intervention, solutions to a socio-environmental crisis that is the outcome of conflict between labor and capital are presented by pragmatic partnerships between these social forces. Promoting these partnerships between labor and capital in spite of ongoing land conflicts and environmental destruction reproduces an ideology that presupposes the end of class struggle and the demise of rural social movements. By masking class conflict deeply structured into the rural productive sector, and fostering the subordination of the working class to the interests of capital represented by globalized corporate agribusiness, PEAAF reinforces the ideology of consensus maintaining hegemony in a capitalist system. Instead of addressing social and environmental problems critically, so as to find locally based solutions to mitigate these impacts, the EE program ends up perpetuating the model of economic production that is at the root of social struggles and environmental devastation. This environmental ideology, framed by sustainability discourse mobilized in EE programs, is paradoxically both ecological and anti-ecological.

Juxtaposing the critical and transformative rhetoric of a state-driven EE program against the state's deep articulations with agribusiness in practice, we thus observe in a dependent economy (Fernandes 1972) a dramatic contradiction between the public defense and destruction of nature – environmentalism and anti-environmentalism acting as a complement of one another. More precisely: states seeking to protect the environment through critical EE strategies suffer serious limitations in the context of their own condition as stewards of a neoliberal economy based on the supply of raw materials, intensive land-use, and cheap labor force. The state in Brazil is still a platform with the potential to mobilize an alternative development paradigm according to the demands of social movements, but in the era of neoliberalization, it has been effectively used to advance the interests of capital and promote investments in unsustainable economic practices. In sum, the state needs to be understood as a contested space, displaying both promise and peril for critical EE practices in Brazil. Centrally in this contradiction, we find the mobilization of sustainability discourse as a vehicle for high-impact land-use development, and ultimately for the strengthening of dominant class power, in the era of globalized neoliberalism.

Notes

1. *Abertura política* refers to the process of democratization that took place between 1974 and 1985, when a long transition took place from military rule to the democratic 6th Republic.
2. *Coordenadoria-Geral de Educação Ambiental do Ministerio da Educação CG-EA/MEC.*
3. *Diretoria de Educação Ambiental do Ministerio do Meio Ambiente DEA/MMA.*
4. http://www.bunge.com.br/sustentabilidade/2008/port/download/cartilha_RA.pdf, accessed on May 22, 2013.
5. http://www.planejamento.gov.br/ministerio.asp?index=61&ler=s881.

Notes on contributors

Nicolas Stahelin is an EdD candidate in International Educational Development and Director of the Peace Corps Fellows teacher preparation program at Teachers College, Columbia University. His research examines the political ecology of critical environmental education initiatives in public schools of Rio de Janeiro, Brazil against the backdrop of the UNESCO Decade of Education for Sustainable Development.

Inny Accioly is a PhD student in Education at the Federal University of Rio de Janeiro (UFRJ), where she is a member of the *Laboratório de Investigações em Educação, Ambiente e Sociedade* (Research Laboratory on Education, Environment, and Society). She is a specialist in environmental education and technical advisor on environmental education in the Secretary of Environment of the State of Rio de Janeiro.

Celso Sánchez (PhD) is a Professor of Education in the Undergraduate and Graduate Programs in the Didactics Department at the Federal University of the State of Rio de Janeiro (UNIRIO), where he directs *GEASur: Grupo de Estudos em Educação Ambiental desde el Sur* (Research Group on Environmental Education from the South).

References

Accioly, I. B. 2013. "Ideário ambiental e luta de classes no campo: Análise crítica do programa de educação ambiental e agricultura familiar do Ministério do meio ambiente." [Environmental Ideology and Class Conflict in the Countryside: Critical Analysis of the Environmental Education and Family Agriculture Program of the Ministry of the Environment]. Dissertação de Mestrado,Universidade Federal do Rio de Janeiro, Faculdade de Educação.

Accioly, I., and C. Sánchez. 2012. "Antiecologismo no Congresso Nacional: o meio ambiente representado na Câmara dos Deputados e no Senado Federal [Anti-ecologism in the National Congress: Representation of the Environment in the Chamber of Deputies and Federal Senate]". *Desenvolvimento e Meio Ambiente* 25: 97–108.

Acslerad, H. 2008. "Grassroots Reframing of Environmental Struggles in Brazil." In *Environmental Justice in Latin America: Problems, Promise, and Practice*, edited by D. Carruthers, 75–97. Cambridge, MA: The MIT Press.

Amaral, M. S., and M. D. Carcanholo. 2009. "A superexploração do trabalho em economias periféricas dependentes [The Overexploitation of Labor in Peripheral and Dependent Economies]". *Revista Katálysis* 12 (2): 216–225.

Apple, M., J. Kenway, and M. Singh, eds. 2005. *Globalizing Education: Policies, Pedagogies, and Politics*. New York: Peter Lang.

Brasil. 2003. *Constituição da República Federativa do Brasil de 1988* [Constitution of 1988 of the Federative Republic of Brazil]. Brasilia: Presidência da República. Accessed June 15, 2013. http://www.planalto.gov.br/ccivil_03/Constituicao/Constituicao.htm

Buci-Glucksmann, C. 1980. *Gramsci and the State*. London: Lawrence and Wishart.

Carnoy, M., and H. Levin. 1985. *Schooling and Work in the Democratic State*. Stanford, CA: Stanford University Press.

Carvalho, I. S. M. 2008. "A educação ambiental no Brasil [Environmental Education in Brazil]". In *Salto para o futuro: Educação ambiental no Brasil*, 13–20. Brasilia: Ministério da Educação.

Fernandes, F. 1972. *Sociedade de classes e subdesenvolvimento* [Class Society and Under development]. Rio de Janeiro: Zahar Editores.

Gadotti, M. 1998. *Ecopedagogia e educação para a sustentabilidade* [Ecopedagogy and Education for Sustainability]. São Paulo: Instituto Paulo Freire. Accessed January 28, 2014. http://www.educacao.pr.gov.br/arquivos/File/det/palestra3_eco_educacao_sustentabi lidade_gadotti_1998.pdf

Harvey, D. 2005. *A Brief History of Neoliberalism*. Oxford: Oxford University Press.

Kahn, R. 2008. "From Education for Sustainable Development to Ecopedagogy: Sustaining Capitalism or Sustaining Life." *Green Theory and Praxis: The Journal of Ecopedagogy* 4 (1): 1–14.

Layrargues, P. P. 2012. "Para onde vai a educação ambiental? O cenário politico-ideológico da educação ambiental brasileira e os desafios de uma agenda política crítica contra-hegemônica [Where is Environmental Education Headed? The Political and Ideological Landscape of Brazilian Environmental Education and the Challenges of a Critical Counter-hegemonic Political Agenda]". *Revista Contemporânea de Educação* 14: 398–421.

Layrargues, P. P. and da Costa Lima, G. F. 2011. "Mapeando as macro-tendências político-pedagógicas da Educaço Ambiental contemporânea no Brasil [Mapping the Political and Pedagogical Macro-tendencies in Contemporary Brazilian Environmental Education]". Anais do VI Encontro Pesquisa em Educação Ambiental, Ribeirão Preto: USP.

Lima, G. F. 2009. "Educação ambiental crítica: do socioambientalismo às sociedades sustentáveis [Critical Environmental Education: From Socioenvironmentalism to Sustainable Societies]". *Educação e Pesquisa* 35 (1): 145–163.

Loureiro, C. F. 2004. "Educação ambiental transformadora [Transformative Environmental Education]". In *Identidades da educação ambiental brasileira*, edited by P. P. Layrargues, 65–84. Brasília: DEA/MMA.

Loureiro, C. F. 2008. "Proposta pedagogica: Educação ambiental no Brasil [Pedagogical Proposal: Environmental Education in Brazil]". In *Salto para o futuro: Educação ambiental no Brasil*, 3–12. Brasilia: Ministério da Educação.

Marini, R. M., and C. E. Martins. 2008. *América Latina, dependencia y globalización* [Latin America, Dependency, and Globalization]. Bogota: Siglo del Hombre Editores.

MEC. 1992. *Carta Brasileira para Educação Ambiental* [Brazilian Environmental Education Charter]. Rio de Janeiro: MEC. Accessed June 13, 2013. http://ambientes.ambientebrasil. com.br/educacao/artigos/carta_brasileira_para_educacao_ambiental_%28mec._rio-92%29. html

de Mendonça, S. R. 2010. *O patronato rural no Brasil recente (1964–1993)* [Rural Patronage in Recent Brazil (1964–1993)]. Rio de Janeiro: Editora UFRJ.

Oliveira, A. 2012. "A Mundialização da Agricultura Brasileira [The Globalization of Brazilian Agriculture]". In Anais do XII Colóquio Internacional de Geocrítica, Bogotá: Universidad Nacional de Colombia. 07 a 11 de maio de 2012.

Quintas, J. S. 2004. "Educação no processo de gestão ambiental: uma proposta de educação ambiental transformadora e emancipatória [Education in the Environmental Management Process: A Proposal for Transformative and Emancipating Environmental Education]". In *Identidades da educação ambiental brasileira*, edited by P. P. Layrargues, 113–140. Brasília: DEA/MMA.

Sánchez, C. 2010. "A educação ambiental como instituição: Uma perspectiva dos laços que nos unem [Environmental Education as an Institution: A Perspective on the Ties that Bind Us]." In *VI Fórum Brasileiro de Educação Ambiental: Participação, Cidadania e Educação Ambiental*, edited by D. Dib-Ferreira Reynier and J. Guerreiro, 132–146. Rio de Janeiro: IBG.

Sauvé, L., R. Brunelle, and T. Berryman. 2005. "Influence of the Globalized and Globalizing Sustainable Development Framework on National Policies Related to Environmental Education." *Policy Futures in Education* 3: 271–283.

Scheffler, I. 1960. *The Language of Education*. Springfield, IL: Thomas.

Trein, E. 2012. "A educação ambiental crítica: crítica de que? [Critical Environmental Education: Critical of What?]". *Revista contemporânea de educação* 14: 304–318.

Wood, E. M. 2005. *Empire of Capital*. London: Verso.

Towards a political ecology of education: the educational politics of scale in southern Pará, Brazil

David Meek

Department of Anthropology, University of Alabama, Tuscaloosa, AL, USA

Social movements have initiated both academic programs and disciplines. I present ethnographic data that I gathered during 17 months of fieldwork with the Brazilian Landless Workers' Movement (MST) in southeastern Pará, Brazil, to explore the MST's role in creating agroecological education opportunities. My analysis highlights three factors in southeastern Pará that initiate environmental education opportunities. First, activist professors are key players, serving as mediators between the state and social movements. Second, recurring events incubate environmental educational institutions and degree programs. Third, by collaborating with institutionalized education, movements are able to develop their own radical educational spaces. These three factors result in a gradual anti-neoliberal transformation in southeastern Pará's rural educational opportunities. I develop a theoretical perspective of the political ecology of education to understand the relations between these three factors and educational change. By drawing attention to the educational politics of scale, I help advance theories of environmental education in a neoliberal age.

Introduction

Social movements are challenging neoliberalism's dual vision of education and environmental resources as a market system of privatized services (McCarthy and Prudham 2004; Mein 2009). Social movements institutionalize critical environmental learning as part of a larger anti-neoliberal project. Yet, how and why do social movements institutionalize critical environmental education in the very neoliberal educational system? I address this larger question by exploring the following three sub-questions:

(1) How do social movements access political programs and financial resources?
(2) What facilitates the evolution of innovative educational institutions?
(3) How can institutionalized education help movements train their members?

In this article, I begin constructing a theoretical framework to attend to these questions, which synthesizes insights from political ecology and the political economy of education.

Political ecology is an interdisciplinary sub-field that explores the relationships between environmental change and political, economic, and social processes (Bryant 1992; Greenberg and Park 1994; Robbins 2004). Political ecology can be contrasted with classic ecology, which apolitically explores relationships between organisms and their surroundings (Biersack and Greenberg 2006). Scholarship in the political economy of education, meanwhile, analyzes the relationships between political policies and the funding of educational programs (Elmore 1984; Carnoy 1985; Torres and Schugurensky 2002; Mitchell and Mitchell 2003).

As Roderick Neumann indicates in the opening to *Making Political Ecology*, 'The environment and how we acquire, disseminate, and legitimate knowledge about it are highly politicized, reflective of relations of power, and contested' (Neumann 2005, 1). Yet, despite this clear articulation of the relations between the politics of knowledge and the environment, there lacks a *political ecology of education*. In defining a political ecology of education, I expand on two traditional definitions of political ecology. The first is a synthesis 'of political economy, with its insistence on the need to link the distribution of power with productive activity and ecological analysis ...' (Greenberg and Park 1994, 6). Secondly, I draw upon the definition of political ecology as 'the study of interdependence among political units and of interrelationships between political units and their environment' (Hempel 1996, 150). Synthesizing these conceptions, I define a *political ecology of education* as a framework for understanding how the reciprocal relations between political economic forces influence pedagogical opportunities – from tacit to formal learning – affecting the production, dissemination, and contestation of environmental knowledge at various interconnected scales. It also affords the possibility to explore downstream effects on access and control over natural resources, interactions with cultural landscape, as well as local conceptions of nature–society relationships.

I apply this nascent political ecology of education framework to a case study of the Brazilian Landless Workers' Movement (*O Movimento dos Trabalhadores Rurais Sem Terra* or MST), an agrarian social movement that has institutionalized critical environmental education. First, I unpack the concept of *scale*. I then provide a short background on the MST. I then present research results in three sections, each of which examines one of the questions posed above. I collected these data during 17 months of ethnographic fieldwork, involving participant-observation and semi-structured interviews, between 2009–2013 in a variety of MST settlements and educational spaces in southern Pará, Brazil. I accounted for response bias due to my subject position as ethnographer by triangulation, verifying data when results became redundant (Luhrmann 2006).

The educational politics of scale

There remains little agreement on how to operationalize the term *scale* (Marston et al. 2005, 16). I employ a combination of a *hierarchical* and a *horizontal* conception of scale. A *hierarchical* vision of scale is a nested set of territorial units, ranging from the global to the body (Brenner 2005, 9). *Horizontal* scale, by contrast, is a network that transgresses boundaries (Leitner 2004, 237). I integrate these two scalar lenses within the political ecology of education perspective to help explore the implications of what I term the *educational politics of scale*. My conception of an educational politics of scale draws upon previous scholarship of "'educational scales' as the spatial and temporal orders generated as pupils and teachers move and are moved through educational systems" (Nespor 2004, 309, see also McKenzie 2012). I build upon Nespor's understanding of scale as networked by emphasizing how the interconnections between multiple sites of political economy and social contest structure the production of educational opportunities for environmental learning.

I understand the *educational* politics of scale as concerned with the spatial character of educational policy and action. Similar to Cox (1998), one might draw upon the educational politics of scale to ask, for example, whether anti-neoliberal educational actions are inherently local, regional, national, or international? Similarly, where can one geographically position the public policies that fund anti-neoliberal educational initiatives? By addressing these questions, I demonstrate that the educational politics of scale are central to a political ecology of education, and its analysis of how interrelations between political policy, economic resources, and educational action affect environmental knowledge production.

Case study: the Brazilian landless workers' movement

The Brazilian Landless Workers' Movement (MST) is widely recognized as the most successful agrarian social movement in Brazil (Wolford 2010). MST members occupy what they perceive as unused agricultural land and pressure the government to take the land and create a community, known as an agrarian reform settlement. Two foci within the MST are locally relevant education and agroecology.

The MST has a complicated relationship with the state in terms of education provision. The MST believes that education within settlements is the state's responsibility. Yet, the MST also believes these schools' curricula should incorporate the movement's ideals and principles. The MST seeks to create culturally relevant curricula through its vocal position in an umbrella movement for education reform known as *Educação do Campo*.[1]

The *Educação do Campo* movement is a major force in shaping rural education in agrarian reform settlements. The *Educação do Campo* movement is a movement of movements, 'defined by its demands for quality and free education from infancy through university, and the construction of a distinctly rural school that is guided by a vision of rural development, which is based in social justice, agricultural cooperation, environmental respect, and the valuing of rural culture (Munarim 2008, 61)'. This movement has helped shape Brazilian educational policy toward locally relevant rural education as opposed to homogenous national programs that do not attend to local diversity in geography, culture, and history (Comilo and Brandão 2010; Breitenbach 2011).

Agroecology, which is the integration of ecological principles into sustainable agricultural systems (Gliessman 2006), is another main focus of the MST and larger *Educação do Campo* movement's educational agendas. The MST's ideological and material engagement with agroecology can be tracked to its role within the international umbrella peasant movement *La Via Campesina (LVC)* (Wittman 2009). Agroecology is employed by the MST as a tool opposed to industrial agriculture, and its conventional focus on environmentally damaging export crops, instead promoting agricultural sustainability (Altieri and Toledo 2011; Rosset and Martinez-Torres 2012).

The contest between neoliberal and anti-neoliberal education in Brazil

Brazilian universities are key battlegrounds between neoliberalism and anti-neoliberalism. The formation of the Brazilian higher education system, particularly its agronomy programs, was interlinked with large-scale agribusiness and international financing. During the 1940s, the American International Association for Economic Development, funded by the Rockefeller foundation, founded university agronomy training programs that trained extension agents to transform rural producers from purportedly backward agricultural practices to modern ones based in advanced technology and industry (Callou et al. 2008). These programs increasingly focused on large-scale, technical and capital-intensive agriculture. During the 1980s, with the fall of the Brazilian dictatorship, civil society began to critique the increasingly 'American organizational model of a rational, capitalist university-enterprise focused on productivity' (Orso 2007, 79 in Carvalho and Mendes 2011, 133). However, the three successive national governments of Fernando Collor de Melo (1990–02), Itamar Franco (1992–03), and Fernando Henrique Cardoso (1995–8 and 1999–2002) put into place the neoliberal educational policies of the World Bank, which included privatization and outsourcing of university activity (Segundo 2005). As Chauí notes, the university became characterized 'as a service provider to private companies' (2001, 35–36 in Carvalho and Mendes 2011, 134).

Against this neoliberal backdrop, the MST has helped advance rural universities focus on *educação do campo*. In 1998, the MST and other social movements that comprise the larger *Educação do Campo* movement began challenging the market logic of education policy by advocating the creation of the National Program for Education in Agrarian Reform (PRONERA). PRONERA provides funding to support secondary and post-secondary courses for inhabitants of agrarian reform settlements. I see PRONERA as exemplary of an anti-neoliberal educational policy, because its programs do not further privatize, but instead strengthen existing state educational institutions and seek to train students to attend to local social and environmental justice needs rather than those of the market system.

I now turn to explore the interplay between the opportunities and constraints facing the MST's anti-neoliberal educational initiatives in the southeastern portion of the state of Pará. The educational institutions I analyze are the Federal University of Pará (UFPA), the Rural Marabá Campus of the Federal Technical Institute of Pará (IFPA-CRMB), and the Agroecological Institute of Latin America-Amazonia branch (IALA). The IFPA and UFPA are regional federal educational institutions' while the IALA is a social movement educational space. I focus on two MST educational programs that revolve around critical environmental learning. The first is a graduate certificate program entitled 'The Agrarian Question, Agroecology, and *Educação do Campo*,' which is a PRONERA course offered in partnership between the UFPA and IALA. The second is a vocational high-school program in agroecology that takes place at the IFPA-CRMB. Both involve critical place-based learning activities.[2] The only students who can participate in these PRONERA programs are inhabitants of agrarian reform settlements. Frequently, the students chosen to attend these PRONERA programs are the most politically active members of their communities.

How do the region's social movements access political programs and financial resources?

Two signs frame the entrance to the Federal Institute of Pará, Rural Campus of Marabá (IFPA-CRMB). The first indicates the amount of governmental investment in the campus's construction. The second shows the MST flag and reads *Educação do Campo* – Our Right – The State's Obligation. These signs' juxtaposition points to the ongoing struggle necessary to secure state resources for rural education.

On a Saturday in November 2012, a community forum is taking place at the IFPA-CRMB. The forum won't start for some time, and so Helix, a student in the program, offers to show me some of the students' experimental agroecology projects. We enter a garden area and find a tarp-covered piece of ground. A trellis with a PVC pipe surrounds it. This, Helix proudly tells me, is a biogas generator. 'We just finished it, so no gas yet, but it would come out here,' he points at a valve. 'We bring the food waste from the school and mix it with manure, drop it under the tarp and let biodegradation do its work. When methane rises, the tarp will billow, and the only byproducts will be rich compost and a liquid that is high in nutrients.' Impressed, I turn around and find Marcos Aurelio, Helix's agroecology teacher, bending down in some bushes. Seeing Helix and me, he calls us over. In his agroecology class they'll be talking about nitrogen fixation, and Marcos wants to show his class an example of rhizomes. 'I want to show them how rhizomes look like. It can't just be in theory, it needs to be in practice as well. The students need to be able to see and feel the rhizomes. He reaches down and pulls up a plant, gently fingering its roots. This will do.' We walk back toward the auditorium and come to an area where beans are planted in amongst the grass. Marcos remarks 'We're doing research on these beans, looking at them as a method of combating the pasture grass. Rather than burning, farmers can plant beans, which not only give food, but also provide nitrogen to the soil. Early results look promising.' Heading towards the cafeteria where the presentations will take place, I reflect on how divergent these experiential agroecological learning opportunities are from the traditional educational system that reproduces a conception of high-input agriculture.

In the auditorium, the director of the IFPA-CRMB is giving a presentation to an assembled group of parents. A summary of the budget of the school's agroecology high-school program is projected on the wall. The director provides context for these figures by describing the ongoing struggles, victories, and setbacks that occur in the process of securing the state's promised education funding. The audience erupts into applause as the director concludes his presentation with a picture of him hugging Brazilian president Dilma Rouseff. 'That was just three days ago in Brasíla!' he smiles. The image in combination with the director's account of trials, struggles, and partial victories keeping the campus fiscally solvent paints a clear picture: The administration and faculty are directly linked to the seat of power and will traverse geopolitical scales in order to pressure the government for the resources needed. Negotiating these educational politics of scale is essential to obtain the political and financial resources needed to continue the dual projects of advancing locally relevant education and the creation of agroecological education opportunities.

The UFPA is another site of anti-neoliberal action that is resulting in the creation of critical environmental education opportunities. The case of Gemeson Brito, below, illustrates how activists working within the university are crucial for motivating and sustaining PRONERA's activity. With his black coconut ring symbolizing his commitment to emancipatory social change, and MST movement shirt, Gemeson Brito contrasts from most high-level university administrators. Brito has directed nearly all of the region's PRONERA courses. When asked about the political economy of PRONERA, Brito responded, 'PRONERA only agrees to fund courses that have an involvement with a University or an educational institution, and social movements. And why is it this way?' he asked, rhetorically. 'Because, the program was designed by the social movements themselves... But it's very unstable, because it is open to the evaluation of the *Ministerio Publico*, and the accusations of the *Bancado Ruralista* [a right-wing land owners' lobby group].' He goes on to explain,

> There was a crisis in which there was a congressional inquiry of the MST. They were going to evaluate government projects that finance the MST's projects. The first program that was analyzed was PRONERA, and almost two years went by without being able to liberate any monies, or almost any funding.

Brito's evaluation of PRONERA's political economy highlights two important points concerning the educational politics of scale. First, Brito draws attention to the role of a horizontally scaled social movement in molding the funding networks that influence local education. Social movements helped develop PRONERA in order to fund *partnerships* between themselves and universities. Additionally, Brito underscores the vertically scaled political economy of education: whereas the congressional inquiry into the MST's finances was at a national level, the experience of financial instability was inherently local.

Brito goes on to discuss the linkages between bureaucracy, financial instability, and the everyday resistance of activist professors. When asked what his daily life is like as a coordinator of these PRONERA programs, Gemeson sighs, takes off his wire rim glasses to rub his eyes, and continues, 'In a variety of ways you simply have [long pause] ....to struggle, because you have to get involved. If you were just to send a memo requesting funds to be made available it can easily be forgotten.' Brito continues, 'So if you don't pick up the phone and call, and insist, and question – *so many times* I've had to personally go to INCRA, you understand? Because sometimes to get access to a [financial] installment you need to get approval at five levels.' Brito concludes:

> So you send in the protocol, but the thing doesn't move forward in the nice way that it should, and so you call and they say, 'Oh, it's stopped at the first level,' and so you go there personally: 'What's the problem?'.... 'Oh, it's missing this document, you need to correct this or that,' and so you need to exert this additional force, because if you don't these things take too long, you lose the window of time. There is an activist force, in the sense that you need to force the bureaucracy to function.

Brito's persistence is more than simply following up on his administrative responsibilities. His persistence is emblematic of quotidian forms of resistance (Scott 1987). Studies of such resistance, particularly among institutional activists negotiating bureaucracy (Katzenstein 1998; Moore 1999; Raeburn 2004; Arthur 2009; Banaszak 2010), highlight the importance of simple tactics such as picking up the phone.

Much like Gemeson Brito, Marcio de Souza's life is intertwined with education and activism. Marcio is a teacher in the IFPA-CRMB's vocational agroecology program. Marcio is a long-time member of various social movements and is extensively involved with PRONERA courses. He describes the accretion of educational opportunities in this area as an organic process arising from sheer need in the early 2000s.

> The first course was in literacy, and then it was like, 'How can you have literacy training without teachers' education?' So then there was teachers' education. 'Okay, so you've got teachers' education, well how can you not have a technical course?' So the technical course was the first in Brazil, but then we said 'Okay, you've got a technical course, how can you not have a university level course?' So then we got a university

level program in agronomy and rural education. And then we asked ourselves, 'How can you have a university level program without a post-graduate program?' It was in this way that it kept developing in the region.

Marcio's perspective underscores how the relationality between educational scales is constitutive of gradual change. The creation of educational opportunities at various institutional scales – from high-school to university to graduate certificate to continuing education – enabled the 'the vertical integration of courses,' as another professor described it. The metaphor of 'vertical integration' is a tactical deployment of the educational politics of scale, as the combination of local projects evidence regional change. The piecemeal manner that anti-neoliberal movements and their interlocutors advance specific projects is, therefore, one way they articulate a counter-hegemonic vision of education within the larger hegemonic neoliberal system. The educational politics of scale constitute the examples of the director of the IFPA-CRMB's trip to Brasilia, the financial instability of PRONERA funds, and Souza's description of the vertical integration of rural education courses. From a political ecology of education perspective, institutional activists' negotiation of the educational politics of scale is a key factor in the production of critical environmental education opportunities.

What facilitates the evolution of innovative educational institutions in southern Pará?

Spaces of dialog are instrumental to creating anti-neoliberal environmental education opportunities. Spaces that have an intended educational objective and whose purpose is to encourage critical dialog with the ultimate goal of actualizing emancipatory social change are termed dialogic spaces (Rule 2004, 320). As Eduardo, an activist professor who directs the agroecology certificate program at the UFPA, describes, debate is a key strategy for creating change within the University:

> Our orientation and partnership with the social movements is clear. You begin to occupy the university with debates, with actions, with videos, with week-long activities, which is part of our strategy ... when you're bringing all this in, there's no way that the university can turn its back on it...you enable the reflection on what other forms the university can take.

Eduardo is explicit: Both social movements and faculty seek to physically and ideologically occupy the university through the debates and activities they host. These debates are, according to Eduardo, used to integrate and legitimate the demands of activists from social movements in the university's public consciousness. These dialogic spaces have a trickle-up scalar effect. Although they started at a small scale, they caused a transformational process at the larger scale of the university itself.

Indeed, the origination of the Rural Campus of Marabá (IFPA-CRMB) grew out of the scalar politics of dialogic spaces. All professors I spoke with emphasized how this agroecological school arose from a series of debates and associated activism that took place at the Regional Forum of *Educação do Campo* (FREC) in 2005, 2009, and 2011, consisting of seminars, plenaries, debates, and workshops.

The importance of the FREC to both the origination, and continued development, of the CRMB, is sustained by having a FREC representative on the CRMB advisory board. Jean Luc is the FREC representative. A 75-year-old French agronomist, educator, and activist who worked in the region for the last 30 years, Jean Luc has only a handful of remaining teeth, evidencing that his life in the *campo* was not much different than the peasants with whom he works. When I ask Jean Luc to help me understand FREC's role in the region, he tells me:

> the Rural Campus of Marabá is the product of a dialog that was created by the FREC. The FREC brought together the diverse institutions and movements that are working in the region – and from there created a debate that led to the creation of the Rural Campus of Marabá.

The CRMB is the only federally funded and managed agroecological technical institute within an MST settlement in Brazil. This achievement exemplifies a national scale change in the form of a space for radical education within the federal technical institute system. Employing a political ecology of education lens, the constitutive nature of the FREC and the various debates in the university draw attention to how the reciprocal relations between the spaces and scales of debate created the CRMB and a transformed university, providing new opportunities for critical environmental education to students from agrarian reform settlements.

How can institutionalized rural education help movements train their members?

In Pará, institutionalized rural education is facilitating the construction of radical education spaces that are intended to augment the MST's reach in providing agroecological education to its members. Take, for instance, the concluding section of the UFPA graduate certificate course in 'The Agrarian Question, Agroecology, and *Educação do Campo.'* This event was a three-day seminar in December 2012 hosted at the Agroecological Institute of Latin America (IALA), located in another MST settlement. MST leaders and University professors organized this event as an opportunity to strategize the development of this institute as a Pan-Amazonian center for radical agroecological training. Fifty MST and educator activists travelled from the Pan-Amazonian region to discuss how IALA can achieve its mission to be a space for agroecological convergence.

A state MST leader, Andreia, takes the microphone on the second day and launches into a polemic: 'The seminar, from yesterday, to today, to tomorrow, is a process for us to reflect about the necessity for the construction of a project, and the construction of a strategy.' Andreia both goads and grounds the presenters:

> One of the things that we've discussed through the weekend is that all that we've done at IALA up until this moment isn't sufficient to achieve what we've wished for, or for what we've been challenged to do... and for this we have the saying.

Her voice slows and she speaks the next words like a mantra: 'the IALA is a process of construction that is...' and the crowd collectively finish for her, 'continual.' During a break between sessions, Dayze, a dedicated MST activist, the long-time director of IALA, and a student about to graduate from the certificate program, reflects on the collaboration of the nascent IALA with the certificate program, noting that:

> We began with the certificate because it was the only type of course that we could develop with the University, and because *then* it is easier to access other types of training programs, whether at the level of certificate or even at the high-school level. In addition, offering the certificate gives you a certain liberty to include in the course curriculum themes that help us to engage not only with the course itself, but to think about the challenge of the construction of IALA, what is it that IALA should be?

Dayze's sentiments, and the context in which they were given (namely, at a seminar weekend of a University course hosted in a radical agroecological institute) show that leaders within the MST strategically designed courses that would facilitate the creation of University partnerships. Lastly, Dayze explains that the freedom built into course helps develop the institute itself; in other words, there is a scalar feedback loop between the IALA and the creation of the course. Similar to Marcio's description of 'vertical integration,' IALA is being constructed through an iterative scalar process, where scale is understood as educational, in terms of variety of course offerings, and both horizontally and vertically geographic, as exemplified by its course offerings that brought together students and activist intellectuals from across the Pan-Amazonian region.

In two ways, the concluding section of the graduate certificate course evidence how the politics of educational scale provide insight into the political ecology of education. First, recursive debates arose at IALA as students presented their research projects on agroecological production challenges in the region, leading to discussions about how IALA could better reach not only the region's 500 settlements, but also the countless other rural communities in the Pan-Amazonian basin. These discussions were intended to create educational opportunities at vertically and horizontally interconnected geographic scales – from the local to the regional, national, and international. This scaling out was inherently horizontal, as the *regional* leaders of the MST, a *national*-level Brazilian movement, advanced the agroecological aims of the *international*, umbrella social movement *LVC*. Second, financial resources from the vertically scaled national PRONERA program enabled a horizontally scaled convergence as dozens of MST members, activist professors, and renowned academics converged in this MST settlement to debate the future of its evolving agroecological educational space. The certificate program was funded by the national-level PRONERA program and was explicitly designed to facilitate the construction of an anti-neoliberal educational space that would attend to the needs of various vertical and horizontal scales. It achieved this by embracing the politics of scale and drawing upon a national vertically scaled program to bring together horizontally scaled local, regional, national, and international activists and intellectuals. The political ecology of education lens draws attention to the importance of iterative relations between scale, political economy, and the creation of critical environmental learning opportunities at educational institutions, such as those described here between IALA and the UFPA.

Conclusions

In this article, I proposed a theoretical framework for explicating the political ecology of education of educational institutions in Pará. The educational politics of scale are integral to this perspective and offer a way of understanding how economics, policy, power, and resistance influence both vertically and horizontally scaled opportunities for environmental knowledge production. I drew upon the political ecology of education framework to answer three main questions related to the evolution of opportunities for critical environmental education in southern Pará, Brazil.

How do the region's social movements access political programs and financial resources? As my results illustrate, institutional partnerships, and the activists that directed them, were key players in creating new rural educational opportunities. This draws attention to how both 'local neoliberalisms' (Peck and Tickell 2002) and local anti-neoliberalisms are imbricated within wider networks. The contest between neoliberal and anti-neoliberal tactics – between funding and blockage – produces *heartlands*, such as the capital of Brasília where policies are formed and disputed, and the *zones of extension*, such as rural Amazonia where they are implemented (Peck and Tickell 2002). Additionally, the amalgamation of new program across the region constitutes gradual change. Paying attention to these scalar politics makes it difficult to trace historical points of origination and larger geographical trajectories of change (Steiner-Khamsi 2004). As they conglomerate, the existence of anti-neoliberal educational opportunities begins to take on the omnipresent and unquestionable nature of neoliberalism (Hursh 2007; Ferguson 2009).

What facilitates the evolution of innovative educational institutions in southeastern Pará? Eduardo's narrative highlighted how the UFPA faculty strategically held debates and activities to bring about a transformative discussion at the university level. Directing the focus to the incubation of institutions, Jean Luc's vignette provided a third example by pinpointing the FREC as the originating point of the CRMB. By exploring the relations between scale, space, and environmental learning, a political ecology of education lens showed how dialogic spaces affect the production of critical environmental education opportunities.

How does institutionalized education help social movements train their members? The IALA narrative highlighted how IALA was able to benefit from PRONERA funding by forging a University partnership, starting it on a perceived road toward expanded radical education provision at various educational scales. The results from IALA, when seen from political ecology of education perspective, demonstrate that the MST fostered a unique feedback loop between the graduate certificate program and the construction of IALA, harnessing the resources and opportunities afforded by institutionalized rural education.

These three questions, and the analyses presented along with them, collectively highlight a central conclusion: by creating anti-neoliberal educational opportunities at various institutional scales, inter-institutional networks of MST and professor activists have fomented a regional transformation in agroecological education opportunities currently taking place in southern Pará. This gradual swell is occurring on various planes. The educational politics of scale were exemplified by 'vertically integrated' courses, educational spaces, such as IALA that attend to Pan-Amazonian educational needs, and spaces of debate that led to the origination of the CRMB and a transformed university. This sea change is also pedagogical – based in an anti-neoliberal paradigm of education, known as *educação do campo*. Part and parcel of each of these facets are political and economic processes.

The political ecology of education perspective emphasizes the importance of power, resistance, and economics in mediating the construction of interconnected scales of agroecological education opportunities. Whereas three ostensibly separate questions guided this article, from the political ecology of education perspective, they are part of a broader question about the relations between political and economic processes and changes in critical environmental education opportunities. This vantage point understands environmental education opportunities as a product of power, resistance, and scale. Future studies are needed to further develop both the theoretical implications and practical utility of a political ecology of education lens, bringing into focus the often messy scalar relations between politics, economy, education, and ecology.

Acknowledgements

This research was supported by the National Science Foundation Doctoral Dissertation Improvement Grant [BCS-1060888]; Social Science Research Council's International Dissertation Research Fellowship; Fulbright Foundation Fellowship. Pilot research in 2009 was funded by the University of Georgia's Dean's award; Melissa Hague award; and Tinker award. Additional field research in 2013 was supported by the University of Georgia's Wilson Center Foundation.

Funding

This research was supported by the National Science Foundation Doctoral Dissertation Improvement Grant [BCS-1060888]; Social Science Research Council's International Dissertation Research Fellowship; Fulbright Foundation Fellowship. Pilot research in 2009 was funded by the University of Georgia's Dean's award; Melissa Hague award; and Tinker award. Additional field research in 2013 was supported by the University of Georgia's Wilson Center Foundation.

Notes

1. I capitalize *Educação do Campo* when referring to the education reform movement; otherwise, the phrase refers to locally relevant pedagogy.
2. Space constraints preclude extended discussion of the content of these programs; in this manuscript, I focus on the origination of these critical environmental education opportunities and the institutions that offer them.

Notes on contributor

David Meek is currently an instructor of anthropology at the University of Alabama. His research interests surround the intersection of sustainable agriculture, critical environmental education and social movements. He has published on this research in *The Journal of Peasant Studies, Antipode, Environment and Society: Advances in Research, Studies in the Education of Adults, Journal of Sustainability Education* among other journals.

References

Altieri, Miguel, and Victor Toledo. 2011. "The Agroecological Revolution in Latin America: Rescuing Nature, Ensuring Food Sovereignty and Empowering Peasants." *Journal of Peasant Studies* 38 (3): 587–612.

Arthur, Mikaila Mariel Lemonik. 2009. "Thinking Outside the Master's House: New Knowledge Movements and the Emergence of Academic Disciplines." *Social Movement Studies* 8 (1): 73–87.

Banaszak, Lee Ann. 2010. *The Women's Movement Inside and Outside the State.* New York: Cambridge University Press.

Biersack, Alleta, and James B. Greenberg. 2006. *Reimagining Political Ecology.* Durham: Duke University Press.

Breitenbach, Fabiane Vanessa. 2011. "A Educação do Campo no Brasil: uma História que se Escreve entre Avanços e Retrocessos [Educação do Campo: A History that is Written between Advances and Setbacks]." *Espaço Academico* 11 (121): 116–123.

Brenner, Neil. 2005. *New State Spaces: Urban Governance and the Rescaling of Statehood.* New York: Oxford University Press.

Bryant, Raymond L. 1992. "Political Ecology – An Emerging Research Agenda in Third-World Studies." *Political Geography* 11: 12–36.

Callou, Angelo Brás Fernandes, Maria Luiza Lins e Silva Pires, Maria Rosário F. Andrade Leitão, and Maria Salett Tauk Santos. 2008. "O estado da arte do ensino da extensão rural no Brasil [The State of the Art in the Teaching of Rural Extension in Brazil]." *Revista Extensão Rural* 15 (16): 84–116.

Carnoy, Martin. 1985. "The Political Economy of Education." *International Social Science Journal* 37 (2): 157–173.

Chauí, Marilena. 2001. *Escritos sobre a Universidade* [Writings about the University]. Sao Paulo: Editora Unesp.

Comilo, da Silva Maria Edi, and Elias Canuto Brandão. 1998. "Educação do Campo: A Mística como Pedagogia dos Gestos no MST [Educação do Campo: Mística as a Pedagogy of Gestures in the MST]." *Revista Eletrônica de Educação* 6.

Cox, Kevin R. 1998. "Spaces of Dependence, Spaces of Engagement and the Politics of Scale, Or: Looking for Local Politics." *Political Geography* 17 (1): 1–23.

Elmore, Richard F. 1984. "The Political Economy of State Influence." *Education and Urban Society* 16 (2): 125–144.

Ferguson, James. 2009. "The Uses of Neoliberalism." *Antipode* 41: 166–184.

Gliessman, Stephen R. 2006. *Agroecology: The Ecology of Sustainable Food Systems*. London: CRC.

Greenberg, James B., and Thomas K. Park. 1994. "Political Ecology." *Journal of Political Ecology* 1 (1): 1–12.

Hempel, Lamont C. 1996. *Environmental Governance: The Global Challenge*. New York: Island Press.

Hursh, David. 2007. "Assessing No Child Left Behind and the Rise of Neoliberal Education Policies." *American Educational Research Journal* 44 (3): 493–518.

Katzenstein, Mary Fainsod. 1998. "Stepsisters: Feminist Movement Activism in Different Institutional Spaces." In *The Social Movement Society: Contentious Politics for a New Century*, edited by David Meyer and Sidney Tarrow, 195–216. Lanham: Rowman & Littlefield.

Leitner, Helga. 2004. "The Politics of Scale and Networks of Spatial Connectivity: Transnational Interurban Networks and the Rescaling of Political Governance." In *Scale and Geographic Inquiry*, edited by Eric Sheppard and Robert B. McMaster, 236–256. New York: John Wiley and Sons.

Luhrmann, Tanya M. 2006. "Subjectivity." *Anthropological Theory* 6 (3): 345–361.

Marston, Sallie A., John Paul I. Jones, and Keith Woodward. 2005. "Human Geography Without Scale." *Transactions of the Institute of British Geographers* 30 (4): 416–432.

McCarthy, James, and Scott Prudham. 2004. "Neoliberal Nature and the Nature of Neoliberalism." *Geoforum* 35: 275–283.

McKenzie, Marcia. 2012. "Education for Y'all: Global Neoliberalism and the Case for a Politics of Scale in Sustainability Education Policy." *Policy Futures in Education* 10 (2): 165–178.

Mein, Erika. 2009. "Literacy, Knowledge Production, and Grassroots Civil Society: Constructing Critical Responses to Neoliberal Dominance." *Anthropology & Education Quarterly* 40 (4): 350–368.

Mitchell, Douglas, and Ross Mitchell. 2003. "The Political Economy of Education Policy: The Case of Class Size Reduction." *Peabody Journal of Education* 78 (4): 120–152.

Moore, Kelly. 1999. "Political Protest and Institutional Change: The Anti-Vietnam war Movement and American Science." In *How Social Movements Matter*, edited by Marcio Giugni, Douglas McAdam, and Charles Tilly, 97–120. Minneapolis, MN: University of Minnesota Press.

Munarim, Antonio. 2008. "Trajetória do movimento nacional de educação do campo no Brasil [Trajectory of the National Movement of educação do campo in Brazil]." *Educação* Jan/Abr, 57–72.

Nespor, Jan. 2004. "Educational Scale-making." *Pedagogy, Culture & Society* 12 (3): 309–326.

Neumann, Roderick P. 2005. *Making Political Ecology*. London: Hodder Arnold.

Orso, Paulino. 2007. "A Reforma Universitaria dos Anos de 1960 [University reform in the 1960s]." In *Orso*, edited by Paulino Educação, 63–84. Campinas: Autores Associados.

Peck, Jamie, and Adam Tickell. 2002. "Neoliberalizing Space." *Antipode* 34 (3): 380–404.

Raeburn, Nicole C. 2004. *Changing Corporate America from Inside Out: Lesbian and Gay Workplace Rights*. Minneapolis: University of Minnesota Press.

Robbins, Paul. 2004. *Political Ecology: A Critical Introduction*. Malden: Blackwell Pub.

Rosset, Peter, and Maria E. Martinez-Torres. 2012. "Rural Social Movements and Agroecology: Context, Theory, and Process." *Ecology and Society* 17 (3). http://dx.doi.org/10.5751/ES-05000-170317.

Rule, Peter. 2004. "Dialogic Spaces: Adult Education Projects and Social Engagement." *International Journal of Lifelong Education* 23 (4): 319–334.

Scott, James C. 1987. *Weapons of the Weak: Everyday Forms of Peasant Resistance.* Newhaven: Yale University Press.

Segundo, Maria das Dores. 2005. "O Banco Mundial e suas Implicacoes na Politica de Financiamento da Educacao Basica do Brasil: O Fundef no Centro do Debate [The World Bank and the Implications of Education Financing Policies in Brazil. The FUNDEF at the Center of the Debate]." Doctoral Thesis (Education), Fortaleza: Universidade Federal do Ceara.

Steiner-Khamsi, Gita, ed. 2004. *The Global Politics of Educational Borrowing and Lending.* New York: Teachers College Press.

Torres, Carlos A., and Daniel Schugurensky. 2002. "The Political Economy of Higher Education in the Era of Neoliberal Globalization: Latin America in Comparative Perspective." *Higher Education* 43 (4): 429–455.

Wittman, Hannah. 2009. "Reframing Agrarian Citizenship: Land, Life and Power in Brazil." *Journal of Rural Studies* 25: 120–130.

Wolford, Wendy. 2010. *This Land is Ours Now: Social Mobilization and the Meanings of Land in Brazil.* Durham: Duke University Press.

Against neoliberal pedagogies of plants and people: mapping actor networks of biocapital in learning gardens

Clayton Pierce

Education, Culture, & Society Department, University of Utah, Salt Lake City, UT, USA

This paper attempts to answer this question: what should ecoliteracy mean in a biocapitalist society? The author situates his analysis of this question within the general context of the neoliberal reconstruction of education in the US. Specifically, focus is given to the shared model of governmentality GE food industries and education policies both utilize to manage life in the field and classroom – one where optimizing the value of plants and people for 'flat world' economic competition is the defining goal. Given this landscape, I suggest that what some environmental educators have called 'ecological literacy' or 'critical ecoliteracy' must now include a dimension that rejects the ways both human and nonhumans are progressively being implicated into biocapitalist enterprises. I offer an example of how biocapitalist industries educate market understandings of life by looking at how the GE food industry's educational projects attempt to teach students and the public to think of nature *and* themselves as entrepreneurial actors. In the final section, I provide an example from my research using actor network theory in learning gardens as a way to develop a theory and practice of ecoliteracy that is capable of identifying and resisting the ways both human and nonhuman life are being captured and reconstructed within biocapitalist development ventures.

Introduction: ecoliteracy in biocapitalist society

Over the past few years, the field of environmental education (EE) has begun to develop strong connections between socioecological crises and the radical neoliberal restructuring projects that have taken hold of the public education system in the US (Gruenewald and Manteaw 2007; Jickling and Wals 2008; Kahn 2010; Hursh and Henderson 2011; Martusewicz 2011). What this path-breaking work in the field of EE has made clear is that thinking about socio-ecological crises and neoliberal models of schooling separately is tantamount to talking about fire without smoke. Thought of in this way, the expansion of the charter school system, merit pay protocols, and new-fangled measurement devices such as value-added metrics attached to policies like Race to the Top are not dissimilar to free market responses to ecological crises. The governing of crises like deforestation and 'drop out factory' schools in neoliberal society are met with similar ways of thinking about people and plants as mismanaged forms of life.

States, transnational corporations, and governmental agencies (and NGO's) govern socio-ecological crises such as global climate change and famine through market responses such as 'clean coal,' carbon emissions trading, or biotech food products such as Golden Rice (GE rice that carries beta carotene) that purport to offer a sustainable and healthy food sources for the poor 'developing world.' Within the intersection of these two neoliberal developmental zones, schools and nature, how should the field of EE respond to neoliberal governing strategies that understand life in each domain as fixable only through radical free market experiments?

This paper argues that for the field of EE to respond effectively in socio-ecological environments increasingly being shaped through neoliberal governing strategies, life in schools and the natural world must be wrestled away from 'flat world' visionaries and their developmental policies (Friedman 2007; Darling-Hammond 2010). Educational reform designed around an image of students and teachers as entrepreneurial actors or human capital machines, for instance, looks a lot like the processes transnational corporations, such as Monsanto, utilize to capture biological life throughout the earth's biosphere (Peters 2005; Simons 2006). Both are treated as potential sites of market valuation: one in a race to out-educate the rest of the world and the other to feed the frenzied growth of Big Agra and Pharma (Pierce 2013). Overlapping terms such as loss of productivity, value-added metrics, merit pay, and teacher, school, and student ratings, for instance, are all part of an expanding neoliberal lexicon that can perhaps best be described as indices concerned with optimizing life for free market competition within educational and economic zones of recovery. What has clearly emerged over the past 30 years is a distinct model of neoliberal governmentality of education where, through state and corporate strategies and practices, schools are increasingly in the business of disciplining and regulating the nation's educational resources (as human capital stock) in order to maximize potential for high-yield crops of twenty-first century skilled students.

Given this landscape, I suggest that what some environmental educators have called 'ecological literacy' (Orr 1991; Stone and Barlow 2005) or 'critical ecoliteracy' (Gruenewald 2003, 2008; Kahn 2010) must now include a dimension that focuses on the ways the vital capacities of both human and nonhumans are progressively being implicated into biocapitalist enterprises. In this paper, I argue that one way the field of EE can respond to the neoliberal restructuring of schools and nature is to calibrate ecoliteracy to the emergent systems for governing life that are unique to biocapitalist society. Analyses of biocapitalism began in the work of feminist theorists and anthropologists of science who first described how previously unreachable biological realms of both human and nonhuman life have been integrated through new scientific fields such as the genetic sciences into capitalist productive and exchange relations (Shiva 1999; Waldby 2000; Franklin 2003; Sunder Rajan 2006). With a focus on how life (bios) is being captured and remade into market forms in neoliberal societies, biocapitalism also helps elucidate how human and biotic populations have come under more sophisticated forms of control. In other words, I am using biocapitalism in a way that 'extends Foucault's concept of *biopolitics,* that practice of governance that brought "life and its mechanisms into the realm of explicit calculations"' (Foucault 1978, 143 [Quoted in Helmreich 2008, 464]). I am also in agreement with Stephan Helmreich (2008) who points out how

> [t]heorists of biocapital [who] posit that such calculations no longer organize only state, national, or colonial governance, but also increasingly format economic enterprises that take as their object the creation, from biotic material and information, of value, markets, wealth, and profit. The biological entities that inhabit this landscape are also no longer only individuals and populations – the twin poles of Foucault's biopower – but also cells, molecules, genomes, and genes. (464)

Therefore, conceptualized within a biocapitalist framework, I argue that ecoliteracy needs to encompass not only 'learning to read the landscape, acknowledge and appreciate human and nonhuman otherness, and discover our at-homeness [which] can only happen if our understandings of literacy and human development include these themes' (Gruenewald 2003, 40). Ecoliteracy also needs to take into account the ways humans and nonhumans in the classroom and GE crop field are being similarly defined and valued through neoliberal governing strategies in a biocapitalist society.

The first section of the paper starts rethinking ecoliteracy in a biocapitalist society by turning to the recent work on bioprospecting, which provides an instructive framework in which to better understand what takes place when corporations and states privatize nature in their search for forms of life to capitalize. In particular, I utilize Agrawal's (2005) concept of 'environmentality,' because it helps to illuminate how subjectivities (individual habits, desires, and values about nature) in bioprospecting zones are formed in spaces being shaped through neoliberal governing strategies of development. The historical and ethnographic research on bioprospecting reveals how the biotechnological mode of production that the genetic food and pharmaceutical industries are built upon have two qualities that are important to look at for thinking about what ecoliteracy means in a biocapitalist society. First, GE food companies only grow by identifying and extracting vitality from existing forms of life in the natural world. Second, in order to operate, bioprospecting zones need to establish a type of environmentality in these sites in order to teach subjects an ethical relation with nature and nonhumans based on their potential economic value as genetic reservoirs for biocapitalist production. Bioprospecting, in short, is an important example of how the neoliberalization of nature is not only achieved through land acquisition, but also through teaching subjects how to think about nature.

In the second section of the article, I analyze an example from the biotech food industry's educational project, the Council for Biotechnology Information's (CBI) activity book. In analyzing the discourses of the educational enterprises of the biotech food industry, I focus on the characteristics of what Jasanoff (2005a) has called the civic epistemology undergirding GE food corporations' model of public pedagogy. In drawing out the specific qualities of the civic epistemology associated with the GE food industry, I focus on how it proscribes a particular neoliberal characterization of nature *and* the global poor. Foundational to the epistemological framework of biotech food industries' public pedagogy, is a salvationary ethos that normalizes a view of the natural world as a site where the productive limits need to be pushed in order to create new, life-saving genetically reconfigured food commodities. Here, I argue, we must think of the civic epistemology promoted through the CBI's educational project as constructing a type of environmentality, where the goal is 'the simultaneous redefinition of the environment and the subject as such redefinition is accomplished through the means of political economy. In this sense, it refers to the concurrent processes of regulation and subject making that underpin all efforts to institute new technologies of government' (Agrawal 2005, 23–24).

In the final section, I turn to learning gardens as a site to develop critical ecological literacies rooted in an alternative epistemological framework. Drawing on my work with junior high students, pre-service and in-service teachers, and community members, I show how creating actor network maps that follow the webs of relation associated with nonhuman actors such as plants can provide an alternative model for learning about plants and human relations with them. In doing so, I have developed three general framing devices to guide students/communities in research on a particular plant chosen to grow in the school garden: origin, movement, and current hegemonic form (or what food products does your plant appear in today?). By mapping the actor relations associated with plants such as maize (corn), a highly educative picture of one of the most important food staples of the Americas comes into frame. Moving from its original bioregion in Mesoamerica (Oaxacan highlands) where thousands of varieties of corn once existed, to spreading across the Americas through human migration and trade routes, its most prominent form is now radiated throughout the industrial food base of the US in its various genetic reconstructed identities.

Mapping actor networks of plants in learning gardens, I argue, also builds off critical place-based education's goal to cultivate ecological thinking that can respond to questions and crises particular to biocapitalist society. For instance, 'should ... the genetic diversity in ecosystems and agriculture be conserved in an era of mass extinction and biotechnology,' or 'should constitutional rights be conserved as governments and corporations devise new methods of surveillance and manipulation' (Gruenewald 2008, 319)? In a moment when plant DNA material is an intellectual property right and transnational governing structures are redistributing place, land, and biome through the circuits of biocapital, EE needs to develop effective ways of thinking and resisting this vision of life on the planet. Within such a context, creating and using actor network maps in learning garden settings can call into question some of the more insidious 'methods of surveillance and manipulation' that are being applied to both educational subjects and GE crops in neoliberal society. The production of food and education under neoliberal forms of governmentality, both perhaps best described as bioprospecting ventures, indeed signal a serious challenge to environmental educators. One of EE's challenges in the neoliberal moment is the need to establish a model of ecoliteracy that connects how the monocropping of people and plants in the field and school are part of the same governing rationality that guides neoliberal society and its endless drive to extract more value from increasing numbers of living things on this planet.

Bioprospecting: mining value from people and plants

In her illuminating research in one of the most active bioprospecting regions on earth, Southern Mexico, Cori Hayden has argued that one of the most important discursive strategies used to legitimize bioprospecting is the transformation of the natural world into an economic framework couched in the language of biodiversity conservation (Hayden 2003). Hayden argues that shifting the regulatory discourse about nature from an explicit colonial framework to a free market system where biodiversity is protected through trade is important, because it allowed *and* legitimated a massive market expansion into the earth's biosphere. As Hayden (2003) points out, 'for advocates of bioprospecting as a conservation strategy, biodiversity's secret to survival is its promise to "pay for itself" – a magical sleight of hand that is carried off by its newly heightened status as potentially lucrative raw material for the drug, biotechnology, and agrochemical industries' (54). Hayden's analysis of the manner in which bioprospecting has been framed as a type of free market regulatory practice for conserving the earth's biosphere also highlights one of the primary qualities of neoliberal environmentality: the best way to regulate and optimize the potential latent value of life (both human and nonhuman) is to subject it to free market disciplining and security mechanisms. Hayden's research on bioprospecting as it relates to developing a model of critical ecoliteracy in biocapitalist society is, however, particularly important in how environmentality involves teaching subjects to think of themselves and nature as entrepreneurial actors. Understanding what kind of social and political environment is simultaneously being constructed through the neoliberal environmentality associated with bioprospecting projects in nature, in other words, also helps underscore how individuals and groups are *taught* extractive and promissory values about the natural world and its ecosystems.

One of the strengths of Hayden's research on bioprospecting, which is particularly relevant to constructing a model of ecoliteracy in a biocapitalist society, is how it maps the assemblage of actors involved in bioprospecting ventures (i.e. pharmaceutical companies, university scientists, indigenous communities, multiple states and their legal systems, venture capitalists, and so on). Hayden's mapping of how pharmaceutical companies and a chain of other actors construct a network of power in order to locate and extract plant material from Southern Mexico provides a striking example of how bioprospecting involves developing a social space, where 'conservation' discourses and practices attempt to teach a market ethic of self-care to individuals and communities. Describing this pedagogical dimension of the bioprospecting network Hayden states:

> The notions of compensation within discussions of indigenous intellectual property rights emphasize that indigenous 'interests' (i.e. claims) in biodiversity axiomatically exist (indigenous peoples have an interest in their knowledge and thus should be compensated for it). When framed as a conservation strategy, bioprospecting comes to us as a mode of *creating interest* in biodiversity in the first place. In this vein, the goal of prospecting agreements is to turn often-conflicting parties – developing nations, indigenous or local communities, the pharmaceutical and agrochemical industries – into mutually dependent 'investors,' by actively producing one piece of shared ground: that each has something tangible to gain from the sustainable management of biodiversity … The production of interest in biodiversity thus depends heavily on the presumption of a self-interested, maximizing actor – a rural plant collector, members of a community, a researcher, a representative of a national government, even, in some ways, a pharmaceutical company – who will respond appropriately (rationally) to biodiversity's newly attributed and articulated value. (61)

One of the most important underlying features of this type of neoliberal environmentality associated with bioprospecting, as Hayden points out above, is the subject formation of an entrepreneurial self. Making subjects within bioprospecting zones hinges on corporate-state partnerships' ability to articulate market pedagogies aimed at teaching individuals and groups how to value themselves *and* nature. Getting people to think of medicinal plants or their knowledge of such plants as exchangeable and maximizeable values on the market, in other words, is an important and understudied educational dimension built into bioprospecting ventures.

Yet bioprospecting, as indigenous scholar and activist Harry (2006) points out, also represents a form of 'biocolonialism' since much of the biological material of interest to bioprospecting actors exist within regions in or near indigenous lands and communities. In this sense, the educational projects associated with bioprospecting sites are not dissimilar to American Indian boarding school practices in the US that attempted to 'kill the Indian, save the man' (Churchill 2004). What is at stake, and what incentive sharing structures such as those Hayden's work captures, is also about acquiring and transforming alternative indigenous value frameworks and knowledge systems with nature that exist in bioprospecting zones into market-friendly ones. Harry and other indigenous scholars and activists' struggles against biocolonialism reflect yet another important feature of the pedagogical dimension of neoliberal environmentality, namely, that bioprospecting is part of a larger biocolonial project that requires a kind of cultural and biological death of the indigenous in order to realize market value from life. As Harry puts it

> the profit motive in genetic research makes indigenous peoples even more vulnerable to exploitation and to attitudes of racism, dehumanization, and oppression. Nearly everything that we hold collectively and value as peoples is at risk of appropriation and subject to the new global market in genetic resources, including Indigenous foods, medicines, and even our traditional knowledge developed and passed down from generation to generation over millennia. (72)

In Hayden's and Harry's respective analyses of bioprospecting, what emerges is a picture of an incentivized field of action created to guide the conduct of actors involved in bioprospecting projects. However, there is also a second intent, a 'productive destruction ethic' that requires the appropriation and acquisition of not just the biological material of plants, but also the place-based subjectivities and cultural worldview of a particular bioregion where potentially valuable biomaterial exists.

Here, we have arrived at what I consider to be one of the most pernicious aspects inherent to neoliberal models of environmentality represented in this case in the practice of bioprospecting. While many have pointed to the ways the genetic food and pharmaceutical industries have enclosed nature at the genetic level (Shiva 1999), few have pointed to the equally problematic *educative* enterprises of subject formation in sites controlled and regulated through neoliberal environmentalities. That is, it is one thing to arrange for the structural relations by which bioprospecting actors can extract value from nature, it is another to create and maintain institutional and political networks of power that are actively seeking to teach people and communities that the healthiest and most rational ethical relation one can have with nature is to understand and value it as a potential storehouse of economic (and thus personal) value.

The educational dimension of bioprospecting enterprises provides an important governing strategy for corporations such as Monsanto and Syngenta. Specifically, setting into place market incentive structures is an attempt to naturalize entrepreneurial discourses and practices within 'developing' world populations. Indeed, biocapitalist corporations recognize that inventing ways to turn genetic material into economic value also includes a type of 'inventiveness [that has] more to do with manipulating society than manipulating genes: it was more about social control, in other words, than about controlling unruly nature' (Jasanoff 2005b, 189). Sheila Jasanoff's incisive characterization of Syngenta's dual types of inventiveness (genetic engineering and social control for societal acceptance of biotechnological products such as Golden Rice) highlights one of the most prevalent strategies of social control associated with bioprospecting and is one I am suggesting needs to be better understood in the field of EE to develop counter ecological literacies that are resistant to existing neoliberal environmentalities. In order to begin to develop eco-logical literacies of resistance within the field of EE appropriate for a biocapitalist society, it is necessary to look at how exactly neoliberal environmentalities fuse humans and nonhumans into a shared field of action governed by free market ratio-nalities and practices. As the analysis of bioprospecting has shown, nature's privati-zation requires subjects who see themselves and the ecosystems they live in as potential economic value. If this is the case, where can we look to better understand how such identity construction comes into being in other educational spaces being shaped by biocapitalist actors?

Learning about life through a biotech civic epistemology

As a front group for the world's leading agrochemical and genetic engineering food companies such as Monsanto, Dow Agro Sciences, Dupont, Bayer CropScience, and Syngenta, the CBI's educational material provides a rich example of how (a) neoliberal environmentality functions pedagogically and (b) what type of subjectiv-ity corporate actors are attempting to produce in classroom settings amenable to the GE food industry's market objectives. My approach to delineating the kind of neoliberal environmentality operating through the CBI's lesson plan is to focus on the particular knowledge regime (rationality) that frames the workbook and the practices it calls the subject (student) to perform.

In order to see how the CBI's workbook is connected to larger governing strategies interested in promoting biocapitalism, I look at how biotechnology is legit-imated through a specific knowledge regime that carries with it a specific pedagogi-cal purpose. This educative intent, I argue, centers on the goal of normalizing the view that gene manipulation in organisms is part of a broader global scientific effort to improve the condition of human and nonhuman life around the globe. CBI's workbook begins by establishing a knowledge regime through the figure of the sci-entist who is invested with biotechnological power over nature. Students learn, for instance, that biotechnology 'is a tool that uses biology to make new products. For example, agricultural biotechnology is a precise way to make seeds with special qualities. These seeds will allow farmers to grow plants that are more nutritious, more resistant to pests and more productive. Biotechnology is a tool for looking clo-ser at nature to find solutions that improve the health of the Earth and its people' (CBI 2012, 2). The expert, however, who is capable of 'us[ing] biology to make new products' is situated in a privileged position, because, through biotechnology, the scientist is granted access 'to look closer at genes and make improvements on them' (3). What I am suggesting the CBI workbook is teaching, at the level of a dis-cursive truth, is that biocapitalist knowledge of nature is ultimately emancipatory in that it helps free nature and humans from their natural limitations. In this sense, it also contains an underlying pedagogical goal to naturalize biotechnological expertise as capable of optimizing nature as well as human life. In other words, genetic engi-neers in the workbook embody a rationality that normalizes actions 'to study how plants grow and how they react to the environment. As a result, scientists can now insert a specific gene into a plant that will help it adapt to its environment, make it more pest resistant, or even make it more nutritious' (CBI 2012, 3). Here, students learn the important lesson that control over plant genes also equals greater population health (or an increase in its productive capacities).

With scientists portrayed as the expert who engender biotech knowledge, farmers are cast in the practical role of the biotech truth regime encapsulated in the CBI workbook. From a strategic standpoint, it is important to recognize how the knowledge regime of the biotech food industry and its expert gatekeepers (scientists) are constructed in the workbook in relation to who receives the benefits of their triumphs. Farmers, in other words, are strategically situated in the workbook as actors used to help codify the pedagogical message of CBI. For example, as students engage the workbook, they learn that 'weeds can be a problem for farmers too. Weeds crowd out farm crops and rob them of water, light and nutrients they need to grow. Many farmers plow their fields to destroy these weeds, but plowing can cause soil erosion. Thanks to biotechnology, a farmer can manage the weeds without having to plow. This saves energy as well as the soil! Giving farmers more choices to control harmful bugs and weeds helps their farms and the environment' (CBI 2012, 8). Here, students are subtly taught that market choices developed through GE food companies' biotechnological breakthroughs provide a salvationary tool for food producers and their consumers. In the competitive industrial growing field where weeds (a negative value) and commodity crops (value added) exist in an antagonistic state, students are taught that biotech solutions offer farmers a way to 'control' nature by maximizing its free market value, while also augmenting the farmer's own entrepreneurial abilities.

Built into CBI's construction of the relationship between the biotech expert, farmer, and nature is also an important notion of freedom particular to neoliberal narratives surrounding science/technology and economic progress in neoliberal society. Freedom, put differently, only makes sense in the workbook if it is interpreted through a free market definition, where the farmer is cast as a consumer of biotech goods that helps him/her achieve a maximum amount of surplus value from their crop. From a related standpoint, the biotech expert is depicted as a producer of knowledge and tools that allow for the recoding of nature into new marketable commodities that can achieve yet unrealized value. What the CBI workbook embodies is a distinct model of neoliberal environmentality that attempts to teach subjects, through the knowledge regime of biotech science, a manner of conduct that is framed within a defined range of 'free' acts consistent with free market social realities. Here, we can see that one of the important issues at stake within the CBI's model of environmentality is an epistemological vision of the very grounds on which human and natural life are understood and valued. Such an epistemological standpoint, however, is not only limited to biotech industry's forays into the classroom. It is part of a broader biotech civic epistemology that has been constructed by biotech actors to teach the public how to think about biotech goods as promissory solutions to deeply rooted social and ecological problems.

While the CBI workbook is certainly one explicit example of many from the GE food industry's pedagogical enterprises, it also needs to be situated within the larger constellation of public pedagogies (also known as 'consumer outreach,' 'health education campaigns,' or 'voter awareness campaigns' as in the case of proposition 37 in California) produced by biocapitalist actors in general. Part of developing an appropriate ecoliteracy for biocapitalist society thus depends on finding alternative epistemological ground from which to think and act. One that is capable of creating healthier and more just relations between human and nonhuman actors.

Ecoliteracy in a biocapitalist age: actor network epistemologies of resistance

In this final section, I want to focus on how an alternative civic epistemology might be constructed around GE food controversies within educational spaces. Specifically, I am concerned here with what a model of ecoliteracy would look like that facilitates epistemic starting points for rejecting the ways life is being capitalized upon (both humans and nonhumans) by biocapitalist industries. Yet beginning to answer this question also points to an important challenge facing the field EE in the neoliberal moment. Namely, as David Gruenewald (now Greenwood) has pointed out in his work, one central problem the field of EE has faced under increasing neoliberal pressures on schools is that the translation of transformative goals tends to get diluted and domesticated when set within content area goals and testing/standardizing regimes mandated through federal governing structures such as NCLB and now Race to the Top (Gruenewald 2004; Gruenewald and Manteaw 2007; Kahn 2010). Given the dominant 'teaching to the test' culture that has accompanied budgetary and other privatization assaults on public schools, many of the critical positions that environmental and sustainability education promote are left out of the curriculum entirely (or, at best, EE concerns are sanitized through consumer and market friendly veneers). Within the seemingly permanent temporality of economic crisis shaping neoliberal school reform in the US, it is increasingly important for EE to develop ways (or counter-strategies) to bridge socio-ecological problems in communities with diverse learning contexts – both within and outside of the classroom. For example, Hursh et al. (2011) provide an interdisciplinary model for rooting ecoliteracy in community problems by teaching school-age children about local environmental health risks such as polluted air, water, and food. Within the context of outdoor/ adventure education, Marcia McKenzie has also pointed in her research how nontraditional educational spaces can create alternative ethics of care between individuals and local ecologies (McKenzie and Blenkinsop 2006).

Building from existing models such as these and others such as Ferreira's (2013) work using a 'history of the present' approach to look at how environmental citizenship is governed in society, I suggest that ecoliteracy also needs to be capable of resisting *and* reshaping dominant networks of power that frame how subjects think of themselves and nature in a biocapitalist age. It is imperative, I think, that the field of EE takes a leading role in delineating an alternative educational model for producing resistive environmental subjects to the emerging problems posed to communities and ecologies in biocapitalist arrangements of society. The research I have conducted with communities, students, and teachers in learning gardens offers a generative example of how such a model of ecoliteracy can be rooted in an alternative civic epistemology that prepares and empowers individuals and groups in socio-ecological settings increasingly being populated by biocapitalist actors.

One approach I have implemented as a practice of ecoliteracy attuned to the ways humans and nonhumans are enrolled in GE actor networks has been through the use of learning garden that forefront food justice concerns in communities. Specifically, I have drawn upon actor network theory to develop ecoliteracies for understanding and critically interpreting GE food controversies by utilizing a plant actor from the garden as a tether point for exploring the constellation of other actors that coproduce how its existence is understood and constructed by students and their community more broadly. Dilafruz Williams and Jonathan Brown's work on learning gardens has shown, for example, how gardens can help create educational practices and experiences that move away from modern industrial understandings of education and the inherently unsustainable principals they are built upon. Learning gardens for Williams and Brown (2012) offer an alternative to the

> homogenization [that] weakens ecosystems and social systems, whereas diversity strengthens them through building complex networks of interdependence. At the present, the homogenization of curriculum emphasizes the industrial quality of schools in which the critical importance of context is erased. The production and transmission of knowledge is divided spatially, socially, and temporarily from society and removed from the local human and biotic communities in which schools physically exist (Smith and Greenwood 2008 [Referenced in Williams and Brown]). (7)

I see actor network theory approaches with learning gardens as one way to start mapping the ways homogenization obscures networks of interdependence as well – especially those networks (such as GE food assemblages) that construct unsustainable and exploitative forms of interdependence.

In constructing an actor network approach to use in learning gardens, I have drawn upon Latour's (2004, 2005) work on what he has called 'object oriented democracy.' I find the concept of an 'object oriented democracy' useful, because it allows learning to take place through the mapping of plant actors to the network of power relations from local place-based settings to global, transnational ones. It is from an actor network perspective that I argue an appropriate civic epistemology can be developed for reconstructing how communities and individuals understand and are involved in public controversies such as the ones orbiting the introduction of GE food into society.

An object-oriented democracy for Latour includes the following: (a) a politics no longer limited to humans and incorporates the many issues to which they are attached; (b) is one where objects become things, that is, when matters of fact give way to their complicated entanglements and become matters of concern and (c) where assembling is no longer done under the already existing globe or dome of some earlier tradition of building virtual parliaments (Latour 2005, 41). The primary goal behind a politics guided by what Latour calls an object-oriented democracy (and actor network theory more generally) is to move away from modern explanations of social and natural phenomena that rely on scientific experts to mediate public problems, while also simultaneously reinforcing the view that nature and culture exist as two neatly separated domains: one to be studied by scientists and the other ordered through the political interests of various competing parties. Instead, in his development of actor network theory, Latour has argued that in order to better understand something like the Golden Rice controversy (a GE rice crop designed to produce high levels of beta carotene and solve malnutrition illnesses such as blindness in 'developing' world poor populations), communities (or collectives) need to construct a democratic politics, where nonhumans are granted agency in a way that includes their social existence as part of a collective decision-making process as opposed to one governed in a hierarchical and undemocratic manner. In the diagram adapted from Latour (2004) below, we can see what such an epistemological shift means for Latour.

The left side of Figure 1 represents the current way a controversy such as Golden Rice is managed and regulated as a public problem: a nonhuman actor (a GE rice product) is created in Syngenta's laboratory by scientists; it is then set loose into a multitude of rice fields in Manila; meanwhile, the human and ecological risks associated with the unknown consequences of the rice are mediated through biotech food experts and the assemblage of corporate-state actors pushing for its adoption as

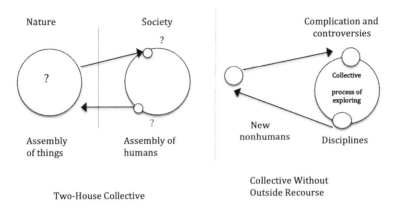

Figure 1. Epistemic models of ecoliteracy in biocapitalist society.

a staple food crop in the 'developing world;' and finally, the public is educated about the GE product through a civic epistemology that grants ultimate power to Syngenta et. al and the governing structures that have been established to ensure these undemocratic relations with their product. There are at least two hidden power relations in this example of Golden Rice plugged into the figure above that I want to emphasize before I turn to the right side of the figure and use an example from my work in learning gardens. The first power relation obscured in the scenario above is generated from how Golden Rice is cleansed from its birthplace (a GE laboratory), since it is epistemologically treated as a part of nature (indicated by the bifurcating line between 'society' and 'nature' in Figure 1 and not its true identity as a nature/culture hybrid). Second, the public's political recourse to the Golden Rice controversy is governed through powerful biotech knowledge regimes that ban the newly created nonhuman from truly entering into a common (and more democratic) political relationship with humans. That is, the ethical/political condition of Golden Rice is upheld as a property relation (which also reinforces the objectification of nature) that is created through genetic manipulation and the potential future value such a nonhuman represents to its powerful stakeholders.

The left side of Figure 1, when considering the nonhuman actor Golden Rice, also represents how neoliberal environmentality is maintained through a civic epistemology that designates sovereign power to biotech scientists and the assemblage of invested actors connected to their valuable nonhuman product. On the left side of the diagram, in other words, it is only the scientist and the powerful assemblage of Syngenta/Monsanto/GF and international intellectual property legal apparatuses that ultimately speaks on behalf of nonhumans. This is despite the fact that Golden Rice does not exist in some objective realm of nature only discernible by experts, but rather as an admixture of humans, GE food corporations, rice genes and beta-carotene, developing world agricultural communities, health experts, international/state courts, gene splicing technology/software, and so on. On this side of the figure, humans learn that GE controversies and debates, the politics of nonhumans, can only take place in the terms established by the nondemocratic assemblage governing public understanding of Golden Rice. Now let us turn to an alternative epistemic arrangement that is not built around these knowledge/power relations undergirding the neoliberal environmentality embodied in the GE food industry's civic epistemology.

Democratic lessons from plants in learning gardens

Phase I: plant origins

My research and work with seventh and eighth grade students, teachers, and communities using learning gardens is an ongoing pedagogical experiment that situates food controversies such as GE corn (or Golden Rice) on the right side of the diagram. In designing research projects with students/communities, I have created three phases to guide collective research on plants. The first phase (the first month of the semester) of actor network research uses learning gardens as a platform to focus on plant histories, while rooting inquiry within the collective concerns, histories, and needs of students and their community. At the beginning of each semester-long research project, students and families are asked to identify plants they use on a regular basis in their food preparation at home and would like to grow in the garden (families often have experience and knowledge with growing/harvesting plants). One of the recurring plants chosen by students and families to grow and research over the past five years has been corn (maize) as it is central to the diet and culture of the particular community I have worked, which consists largely of Latino/a students, a growing number of refugee students from a variety of African countries, as well as a smaller amount of white students. In this first phase of research, students focus inquiry on the historical/cultural origins of corn, including identifying and describing the home bioregion of corn in Mesoamerica (Oaxacan highlands), discovering how much genetic diversity exists among natural corn plants in its home bioregion, and the amount of diverse agricultural practices associated with the history of corn production in its original bioregion. During this phase of the actor network research, knowledge of corn is also incorporated from elders and other community members who are willing to share knowledge and cultural relations with plants that are associated with events such as blessing ceremonies. What is important in this initial phase is that students are able to construct their own lines of inquiry that help situate the nonhuman agency of corn within accurate and diverse historical, political, and place-based knowledge systems associated with different (or similar) cultural relationships with corn.

Phase II: actor movement

The second phase of my actor network research with students focuses on how corn (in this case) migrated from Mesoamerica to other parts of the globe. Priming research on the mapping of movement of the actor corn, students are posed these framing questions: how did corn first move from Mesoamerica to different parts of the continent?; what modes of transportation were used?; and finally, what major event(s) transformed the scale and cultivation practices of this actor's role as a food source? One of the most important recurring findings uncovered during this phase of research on corn's movement is the watershed moment when the plant became an industrial food commodity in the early part of the twentieth century in the US. In tracing the industrialization of corn, students also learn that from the mid 1990s, genetic manipulation marked another transitional moment in the life of corn as genetic control of the plant allowed biotech and chemical companies to monopolize the conditions of its production and consumption. Collective research projects also connect how agricultural laws in the US promote monocropping practices, the dead marine ecological zone in the Mississippi River delta, and the destruction of small, place-based farming practices. At this point in the research, students usually begin to see an actor network map of corn emerging that started with local, place-based practices, and knowledge systems in the diverse bioregions of Southern Mexico to one highly regulated by powerful corporations and legal systems put into place to protect and standardize the industrial system of food production. Students also learn that the dominant way humans relate to corn today is through a dizzying array of food and nonfood products.

Phase III: Current hegemonic forms, or, where does corn show up in our lives today?

The final phase of research concluded in the latter part of the semester frames student inquiry around an investigation into the existing forms corn takes in the US industrial food system. In the first week of this research phase, students are asked to make a list with their families of the types of food they eat that either is made from corn or contains it as an ingredient. Students generate examples such as tortillas, chips, bread, or tamale masa (tamale dough) that are used as reference points to start discussions at home. Once students have created a data list of corn food from home (and the school cafeteria), the next step in the research is to expand inquiry on these foods by collecting data at local grocery stores that focuses on identifying how many food products are involved with the actor of corn.

There are multiple methods for conducting this type of food research with students and communities. One is to arrange a field trip to the nearest grocery store to the school, where many students families' shop and organize an aisle-by-aisle assessment of the food evidence using ingredient lists on products. One can also simulate grocery store aisles using smart or whiteboards, where basic items are discussed and their ingredients are researched on the internet. The purpose of this phase of actor network research is to have students develop a literacy of corn as a keystone food product to the industrial food system in the US. That is, once students map and sort the data collected of foods containing a corn product a highly networked web of food and human relations is revealed that creates starting points for discussion and debate around issues such as monocropping, chemical-based agriculture, type II diabetes, GE food, food justice/sovereignty, and many more. For instance, tracing corn in food products teaches students that the plant or derivations of it appears in foods as diverse as beef products, soda, condiments such as mustard and ketchup, juice, candy, bread, dairy products, salad dressing, and so on. From this actor network map focused on food, a connection is drawn between monocrop fields and monofoods as well as other important network relations such as how agricultural legislation affects food production in the US.

As indicated above, the goal of each phase of actor network research is to develop and experiment toward a model of ecoliteracy capable of reading and critically interpreting the diversity of actors involved in something as seemingly uncomplicated and mundane as corn. More specifically, I see actor network research situated in learning gardens as a site in which to develop an alternative civic epistemology to the GE food industry's pedagogical model. What's more, actor network approaches to studying controversies such as GE food products provide a space where an alternative subject formation can occur by rooting learning in place-based and collective sites of inquiry that begin with an understanding that nonhumans are coconstructive to our socio-ecological realities and, as such, should be part of a democratic politics of nature. Now, returning to the right side of diagram 1, with the example of actor network research I have provided, we can see how to develop, through an alternative epistemic arrangement, an ecoliteracy critical to GE food pedagogies (Figure 2).

One of the crucial effects such an epistemic shift provides is that it allows for experimentation toward an alternative civic epistemology in which to understand GE food controversies. As a collective process of inquiry that frames the knowledge of a host of community and school actors (community elders/family members, teachers, students, pre-service and in-service teachers, and university graduate students and professors) in horizontal instead of hierarchical relation, biotech knowledge regimes, as a consequence, are decentered as the expert field of knowledge GE food controversies governing public understanding. Instead what a collective, coproductive, and multicentered model of knowledge production allows is the reshaping of research around the actor network of GE corn that applies a ground-up approach that is *both* more accurate (in that it actually takes seriously GE corn as an actor and not a natural object to be shepherded away from public involvement by an expert) and inverts the power relations associated with biotech educational enterprises. For instance, recall the model of environmentality that the CBI workbook utilizes for imbuing a particular ethic of self-care that normalizes the privatization of nature as a desirable and economically rational mindset. Actor network research in learning gardens, by contrast, epistemologically rejects these knowledge/power relations as undemocratic and obstructive to a community-based decision-making processes around how people choose to learn about food and its agency. Knowledge of food and its relations to communities and bodies should start from the soil of the learning garden and not from the petri dish of a genetic laboratory.

This shift in knowledge production using a network civic epistemology provides a potential shift in how subjects conduct themselves in relation to GE food controversies within society and their own communities. Instead of classrooms, communities, and educational subjects being framed as a deficit population by the educational enterprises of the GE food industry, groups lacking not just the skills but also salvationary belief in biotech food as a beneficial market solution to social and economic problems, collective actor network research projects on GE food (and other GE

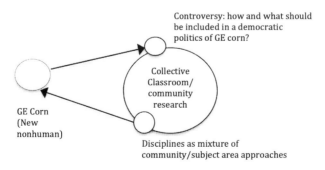

Figure 2. Alternative epistemological model to learn about biocapital actors.

actors) have the potential to facilitate an ethic of self-care that develops in a resistive power relation to the GE industry's model of environmentality. Therefore, an important result of mapping GE food controversies with educational collectives in learning gardens is the production of alternative habits, desires, and values between food and bodies. Mapping GE corn within actor network epistemological framework can teach individuals and groups how the plant's political life is being held hostage by corporate and governmental groups intent on controlling the terms by which their nonhuman actors are understood in our socio-ecological realities *and* what relationship they will have to our bodies.

Ultimately, I am suggesting that actor network research in learning gardens can be a productive site for developing critical ecoliteracies that can point to an alternative model of environmental subject/citizen that rejects biocapitalist constructions of how to understand and relate to market configurations of life. One of most effective ways to decenter the environmentality model associated with the GE food industry's educational projects is to counter-educate an alternative ethic of self-care in individuals and communities that does not begin with an understanding of plants as investible and optimizeable commodities. Yet such an ethic of self-care can be also be extended to broader understandings of how life is being produced in biocapitalist society, not just life in the garden but also in the classroom. What we can also learn from an actor network civic epistemology is how the GE food industry's environmentality shares many of the same characteristics of the life-controlling technologies that accompany the neoliberal restructuring of education in the US.

Another important benefit of learning from a plant about the ways its life processes have been enlisted into the productive projects of biocapitalist corporations such as Monsanto and Syngenta is the cognitive connection that can be made to how educational lives are also being constructed by educational testing experts and measurement devices into things like value-added units or human capital investments.

It is not a coincidence, for example, that the Bill and Melinda Gates Foundation (GF) is the biggest funder of Golden Rice research and application in the developing world and also the largest financial backer for developing and using value-added metrics in the classroom through their Measures of Effective Teaching Project. Just as the GF agricultural projects in the developing world seek to optimize 'developing world' life for the future labor and consumption needs of expanding markets through GE food projects like golden rice, the GF development and proselytizing of value-added measurement tools as the most innovative way to evaluate and sort twenty-first century student crops in the US shares the same neoliberal vision: to optimize the economic value of life. In a recent *Wall Street Journal*, editorial Bill Gates ties these two development zones together nicely:

> An innovation – whether it's a new vaccine or an improved seed – can't have an impact unless it reaches the people who benefit from it. We need innovations in measurement to find new, effective ways to deliver those tools and services to the clinics, family farms, and classrooms that need them. I've found many examples of how measurement is making a difference over the past year – from a school in Colorado to a health outpost in rural Ethiopia. (Gates 2013)

Here, we can see another strength of actor network mapping as a tool for challenging emergent types of neoliberal governmentalities over life that have become prominent in biocapitalist society. Biocapitalism does not just include the lives of the flora and fauna of the natural world that are being targeted by powerful new technologies of control able to penetrate into the genetic building blocks of life. Within an actor network epistemological landscape, educational measurement tools and testing devices designed to assess and shape the value of the educational population in the US can also be placed in their proper genealogical relation alongside (or in some cases within) similar actor assemblages such as those constituting the nonhuman actor of Golden Rice. In this sense, I am arguing that actor network research as a practice of cognitive resistance to neoliberal governmentality over life also provides a type of epistemological scaffolding to multiple sets of technological apparatuses currently designed to target different segments (or species) of life on the planet – both human and nonhuman. Developing an ecoliteracy model attentive to biocapitalist regimes and practices through actor network mapping can, thus, also deepen connections between what Richard Kahn (Kahn 2010; Fassbinder, Nocella, and Kahn 2012) has called 'collective cognitive practice' in socio-ecological movements and educational settings. Actor network maps created by students, in this sense, can become entry points for connecting, for example, concerns of food justice movements that are similarly struggling to redefine communities' relationship to food. Making links that create cognitive synergy between educational spaces trying to resist the management and regulation of life within the industrial food *and* school systems can reorient ecoliteracy in ways that are attentive to biocapitalist economic arrangements that are now defining the horizon of both learning and eating. Ecoliteracy in the biocapitalist age should involve making connections from vertical relations with life to horizontal ones rooted in communities and movements already struggling to do so. Mapping networks of biocapitalist power and their unhealthy and unjust demands they make on life is one way to help facilitate these connections.

Notes on contributor

Clayton Pierce is an assistant professor in the Education, Culture, & Society department at the University of Utah. His research and community-engaged scholarship is interested in ecological literacy, genetically engineered food, neoliberal school contexts and policy, and developing ways to use community gardens as a site of community praxis and learning.

References

Agrawal, A. 2005. *Environmentality: Technologies of Government and the Making of Subjects*. Durham, NC: Duke University Press.
CBI (Council for Biotechnology Information). 2012. *Look Closer at Biotechnology*. http://www.whybiotech.com/resources/Kids-Biotech-Basics-Activity-Book.pdf.
Churchill, W. 2004. *Kill the Indian, Save the Man: The Genocidal Impact of American Indian Residential Schools*. San Francisco, CA: City Lights Publishers.
Darling-Hammond, L. 2010. *The Flat World and Education: How America's Commitment to Equity will Determine Our Future*. New York: Teachers College Press.
Fassbinder, S. D., A. J. Nocella III, and R. Kahn, eds. 2012. *Greening the Academy: Ecopedagogy Through the Liberal Arts*. Rotterdam: Sense.
Ferreira, Jo-Anne. 2013. "Transformation, Empowerment, and the Governing of Environmental Conduct: Insights to be Gained from a 'History of the Present Approach'." In *International Handbook of Research on Environmental Education*, edited by R. B. Stevenson, M. Brody, J. Dillon, and A. Wals, 63–68. New York: Routledge.
Foucault, M. 1978. *The History of Sexuality Volume I: An Introduction*. Translated by R. Hurley. New York: Vintage Books.

Franklin, S. 2003. "Ethical Biocapital: New Strategies of Cell Culture." In *Remaking Life and Death: Toward an Anthropology of the Biosciences*, edited by S. Franklin and M. Lock, 97–128. Santa Fe, NM: School of American Research Press.

Friedman, T. 2007. *The World is Flat 3.0: A Brief History of the Twenty-first Century.* New York: Picador.

Gates, B. 2013. "My Plan to Fix the World's Biggest Problems." *The Wall Street Journal.* http://online.wsj.com/news/articles/SB10001424127887323539804578261780648285770.

Gruenewald, D. 2003. "At Home with the Other: Reclaiming the Ecological Roots of Development and Literacy." *The Journal of Environmental Education* 35 (1): 33–43.

Gruenewald, D. 2004. "A Foucauldian Analysis of Environmental Education: Toward the Socioecological Challenge of the Earth Charter." *Curriculum Inquiry* 34 (1): 71–107.

Gruenewald, D. 2008. "The Best of Both Worlds: A Critical Pedagogy of Place." *Environmental Education Researcher* 14 (3): 308–324.

Gruenewald, D., and B. O. Manteaw. 2007. "Oil and Water Still: How No Child Left Behind Limits and Distorts Environmental Education in US Schools." *Environmental Education Research* 13 (2): 171–188.

Harry, D. 2006. "High-Tech Invasion: Biocolonialism." In *Paradigm Wars: Indigenous Peoples' Resistance to Globalization*, edited by J. Mander and V. Tauli-Corpuz, 71–80. San Francisco, CA: Sierra Club Books.

Hayden, C. 2003. *When Nature Goes Public: The Making and Unmaking of Bioprospecting in Mexico*. Princeton, NJ: Princeton University Press.

Helmreich, S. 2008. "Species of Biocapital." *Science as Culture* 17 (4): 463–478.

Hursh, D., and J. A. Henderson. 2011. "Contesting Global Neoliberalism and Creating Alternative Futures." *Discourse: Studies in the Cultural Politics of Education* 32 (2): 171–185.

Hursh, D. W., C. A. Martina, H. B. Davis, and M. A. Trush. 2011. *Teaching Environmental Health to Children: An Interdisciplinary Approach*. New York: Springer.

Jasanoff, S. 2005a. *Designs on Nature: Science and Democracy in Europe and the United States*. Princeton, NJ: Princeton University Press.

Jasanoff, S. 2005b. "Let Them Eat Cake: GM Foods and the Democratic Imagination." In *Science and Citizens: Globalization and the Challenge of Engagement*, edited by M. Leach, I. Scoones, and B. Wynne, 183–198. New York: Zed Books.

Jickling, B., and Arjen E. J. Wals. 2008. "Globalization and Environmental Education: Looking Beyond Sustainable Development." *Journal of Curriculum Studies* 40 (1): 1–21.

Kahn, R. 2010. *Critical Pedagogy, Ecoliteracy, and Planetary Crisis: The Ecopedagogy Movement*. New York: Peter Lang.

Latour, B. 2004. *Politics of Nature: How to Bring the Sciences into Democracy*. Translated by Catherine Porter. Cambridge, MA: Harvard University Press.

Latour, B. 2005. "From Realpolitik to Dingpolitik: Or How to Make Things Public." In *Making Things Public: Atmospheres of Democracy*, edited by B. Latour and P. Weibel, 14–41. Cambridge, MA: MIT Press.

Martusewicz, R. A. 2011. "Musings on Two Worlds: Local Self-determination in the Shadow of NeoLiberal 'Opportunities' in Jamaica and Detroit." *Educational Studies* 47 (5): 415–418.

McKenzie, M., and S. Blenkinsop. 2006. "An Ethic of Care and Educational Practice." *Journal of Adventure Education and Outdoor Learning* 6 (2): 91–105.

Orr, D. 1991. *Ecological Literacy: Education and the Transition to a Postmodern World*. Albany, NY: State University of New York Press.

Peters, M. 2005. "The New Prudentialism in Education: Actuarial Rationality and the Entrepreneurial Self." *Educational Theory* 55 (2): 123–137.

Pierce, C. 2013. *Education in the Age of Biocapitalism: Optimizing Educational Life for a Flat World*. New York: Palgrave Macmillan.

Shiva, V. 1999. *Biopiracy: The Plunder of Nature and Knowledge*. Boston, MA: South End Press.

Simons, M. 2006. "Learning as Investment: Notes on Governmentality and Biopolitics." *Educational Philosophy and Theory* 38 (4): 523–540.

Smith, G., and D. Gruenewald. 2008. *Place-based Education in a Global Age*. New York: Routlege.

Stone, M. K., and Z. Barlow. 2005. *Ecological Literacy: Educating Our Children for a Sustainable World*. San Francisco, CA: Sierra Club Books.

Sunder Rajan, K. 2006. *Biocapital*. Durham, NC: Duke University Press.

Waldby, C. 2000. *The Visible Human Project*. New York: Routledge.

Williams, D., and J. D. Brown. 2012. *Learning Gardens and Sustainability Education: Bringing Schools and Community to Life*. New York: Routledge.

Community organizing, schools, and the right to the city

Gregory A. Smith

Graduate School of Education and Counseling, Lewis & Clark College, Portland, OR, USA

> One of the central tenets of the neoliberal world view is that there is no alternative to market-based societies with their focus on competition, individualism, and the abandonment of social safety nets and environmental protections. This vision has become the new common sense. As neoliberal policies and practices have spread across the planet, communities and regions have been turned into winners and losers with seemingly little voice in the matter. Alternatives, however, are in fact being invented in places that have been most victimized by this process. Much can be learned from them. Non-formal and formal educators in Detroit, Michigan and Roxbury, Massachusetts are demonstrating how young people can become participants in efforts to resist this vision and join with their communities in inventing solutions that promise to be healthier for human beings and the natural world.

Reclaiming the right to the city

In February 2013, the North Dakota Study Group, an informal collection of progressive educators who have been meeting on an annual basis since the 1970s, broke its long-standing tradition of assembling for three days in Chicago to gather in Detroit to see and hear about ways local residents there are responding to what former US Labor Secretary Robert Reich is now calling 'the war against the poor and the middle class' (Kornbluth 2014). Three years earlier, Grace Lee Boggs, the now 99-year-old philosopher and civil rights activist, met with the group in Chicago. Her presence was electrifying, and people were interested in learning more. Boggs and activists associated with the organization named after her and her late husband have been at the center of some of the most creative and hopeful initiatives in a city that is generally portrayed in the media as the poster child of political and economic mismanagement. Examples of their efforts can be found in the 2012 film, *We Are Not Ghosts* (Dworkin and Young 2012). Boggs frequently speaks about the critical nature of our time 'on the clock of the universe,' and the way the combination of environmental and social crises of the twenty-first century is necessitating an evolution to new patterns of thinking and acting. She calls for the emergence of 'solutionaries,' people able not only to reject and resist but to imagine and create new institutions needed to replace the failing structures of late capitalism (Boggs 2011).

NEOLIBERALISM AND ENVIRONMENTAL EDUCATION

The need for these new institutions is palpable in Detroit. Long before the rise of neoliberal policies in the 1980s with their rejection of the fifty-year consensus in the West that governments could successfully enact social policies that benefit their least advantaged citizens, the city had been experiencing the consequences of deindustrialization, automation, and racism. Hailed as the bastion of democracy in the years following World War II, the city was one of the primary engines for US economic redevelopment in the 1950s. It was also one of the places where Black Americans, no longer needed to pick Southern cotton, migrated to find work in the city's automobile factories. While residential red-lining limited Blacks to living in the city, Detroit's white residents began fleeing to newly constructed suburbs. Eventually the factories left the city with many moving initially to the South and then out of the country altogether in pursuit of lower labor costs. The result has been a gradual and then more rapid depopulation of the city from a high of nearly two million in the 1950s to its current 750,000. The city's distress is at least in part tied to declining revenues and its inability to support public services and infrastructure once underwritten by one and a half times as many people (Howell 2013).

Essentially abandoned by mainstream institutions, Detroit's remaining residents, the great majority Black, were largely left to fend for themselves in neighborhoods where abandoned houses were allowed to decay or burn as public services were curtailed or cut off. In time, groups of people began to see opportunities where others saw only destruction (Boggs 2011; Bowers and Martusewicz 2006). It was these experiments and their educational potential that drew the North Dakota Study Group to the city. Hundreds of people, for example, have transformed empty lots into community gardens and urban farms with the intent of providing vegetables and fruit for families otherwise consigned to live in a 'food desert.' Farmer's markets set up to sell these products provided opportunities for small-scale entrepreneurs as well as informal public gatherings. New businesses like bakeries or bike repair shops created meaningful jobs for individuals otherwise cut off from economic possibilities that had long ago moved to the suburbs. Artists and media savvy youth joined with one another to create alternative stories about the city infused with vision and hopefulness. One young rap artist who calls herself Invincible well represents the spirit of this group. And innovative educators stepped into the gaps left by closed schools to create programs aimed at teaching pregnant and mothering teens how to become urban farmers (Catherine Ferguson Academy) or at affirming elementary school students' African roots (Nsoroma). These people were claiming their 'right to the city' and their capacity to reimagine its space in ways that benefit those who remain there.

The concept of 'right to the city' was initially developed by the French philosopher and sociologist Henri LeFebrve in the 1960s and has been defined more recently by geographer David Harvey in the following way:

> The right to the city is far more than the individual liberty to access urban resources: it is a right to change ourselves by changing the city. It is, moreover, a common rather than an individual right since this transformation inevitably depends upon the exercise of a collective power to reshape the processes of urbanization. The freedom to make and remake our cities and ourselves is, I want to argue, one of the most precious yet most neglected of our human rights. (Harvey 2008, 23)

Exercising the right to the city is fundamentally an exercise in democracy. What until recently has been encouraging in Detroit is the way the voices and energies of people generally ignored by political power holders have been engaged in a process of imagining a different kind of city, a city that works for nature and for citizens too often denied access to resources or possibilities. It was the enactment of these possibilities that drew the US Social Forum to Detroit in 2010 as a place where average citizens were creating a more sustainable and just world.

Neoliberal structural adjustments

This emergence of grassroots democracy and community action, however, has in the past decade entered into a competition with another vision of urban renewal and experimentation that is now threatening to overwhelm and displace the work of Detroit's longstanding residents. This is a vision that is being enacted in other major cities in the United States, as well, where neighborhoods once inhabited by primarily black and brown people are being reclaimed by white investors and corporations interested in remaking the city in their own image. In Chicago, for example, this has entailed the elimination of low-cost housing opportunities in the inner city, the closing of schools, and the gentrification of neighborhoods that then become financially out-of-reach for lower income families (Lipman 2011). In Detroit, this situation seems even more extreme as a result of the loss of nearly 1/3 of its housing stock and the reversion to open fields and vacant lots of residential properties throughout the city. In early 2013, the Republican governor of Michigan appointed Kevyn Orr to serve as emergency manager. Acting without the consent of elected representatives of the city, Orr filed a Chapter 9 bankruptcy petition that if accepted could result in the slashing of health care and pensions owed to public workers, the privatization of vital city services, the sale of public lands including the Belle Isle Park, and the auctioning of masterpieces from the Detroit Museum of Art (Howell 2013). With regard to education, the appointment of an emergency manager for the Detroit Public Schools drew upon the same game plan used after Hurricane Katrina in New Orleans that resulted in the replacement of public schools by charter schools coupled with the elimination of union protections and seniority for teachers formerly employed by the public system (Pedroni 2011). This process in the fall of 2013 did allow for the creation of a new K-8 school under the auspices of the Boggs Center, but as of this writing, it has also resulted in the closing of the Nsoroma School mentioned earlier and the loss of teachers whose work had been instrumental to the success of the Catherine Ferguson Academy.

What is being seen in Detroit is a process of structural adjustment associated with the neoliberal vision of economists such as Frederick Hayek (1960) and Milton Friedman (1952, 1962), a vision that asserts that self-regulating markets provide a more certain route to economic prosperity and political freedom than governmental initiatives aimed at equitably distributing the fruits of production or controlling economic activities that threaten human or environmental harm. Neoliberalism stands in opposition to the forms of collectivist planning encountered in socialist and communist nations as well as the Keynesian-inspired social and economic interventions encountered throughout the West in the aftermath of the Great Depression. The enactment of these policies involves the paring back of governmental services, reducing regulations that inhibit corporate flexibility and free trade, and privatizing formerly public services. Drawing upon Bowles and Gintis' analysis (1986), Hursh and Henderson (2011) assert that 'the global push for neoliberalism is a response to the democratically achieved gains by workers, women, and people of color after

World War II in which they were able to extend their personal and political rights for education, housing, health, workplace safety and the right to vote' (173). Since the 1970s, these policies have been enforced as a condition for loans from the International Monetary Fund and World Bank in countries such as Chile, Poland, and Argentina (Klein 2008) and have often been linked to declining democratic participation if not outright dictatorship.

Now that similar policies are being actively applied to the American context, a fundamental dilemma for US educators concerned about social justice, equity, and environmental sustainability is whether schools here in any way can challenge or mitigate these processes. Given the wealth of those who support this set of policy agendas and their ability to shape public opinion through the media, it is easy to despair about the capacity of common citizens to participate in any form of successful resistance. At the same time, it seems critical to realize that no human created system is impregnable or immortal, even capitalism, and that a failure to engage in the exploration of alternatives inevitably reinforces that status quo. Could any learning experiences help young people gain at least some of the skills needed to successfully claim their 'right to the city' and become the solutionaries so needed in this period of economic, political, and environmental challenge and uncertainty. Finding potential answers to that question is what brought the North Dakota Study Group to Detroit.

Teaching youth and young adults to become solutionaries

During the first day of the 2013 February conference, the 170 meeting participants divided into a dozen groups and then traveled to different organizations striving to challenge the common neoliberal assertion that 'there is no alternative' to a world dominated by the competitive individualism and environmental exploitation associated with free-market policies. The level of success of these organizations is mixed, as the closing of the Nsoroma School in the months since our visit demonstrates, and their efforts often seemed miniscule in the face of so much urban deterioration and the economic and political forces arrayed against them. Despite this, the energy and commitment of people we met stand as a testament to the power of human cooperation and collective action, the unknown factor in any set of circumstances that makes it impossible to predict future developments with confidence. Myself and eight or nine other people chose to spend the afternoon at the East Michigan Environmental Action Council (EMEAC) with a small collection of youth and adults committed to addressing food security and environmental justice issues. Our three hours at EMEAC suggested the potential of integrating community organizing skills into the content and pedagogy of social studies or environmental education courses encountered in middle and high schools with the aim of preparing young people to preserve, restore, and reshape their own neighborhoods and communities in ways that match the interests and desires of their current residents.

EMEAC is located in the Cass Corridor Neighborhood, close to downtown and Wayne State University. The Cass Corridor Neighborhood has been the site of a grassroots redevelopment effort for more than a decade and is the home of the Avalon Bakery, one of the better known of Detroit's cooperatively owned businesses. In 2011, EMEAC moved into buildings previously owned by the city's Unitarian Church including the sanctuary, meeting and classroom spaces, and an adjoining timber baron's mansion built in the late 1800s. Now called the Cass

Corridor Commons, the building's 44,000 square feet served as the staging site for the 2010 US Social Forum meetings in Detroit. Fresh from the bakery just three blocks away, we were met in the women's parlor of the mansion by Charity Hicks, the Food Justice Taskforce Coordinator. Hicks works with local environmental and food justice organizers for two-thirds of her time and as a national food policy advocate through the Jesse Smith Noyes Foundation in Washington, DC for the remainder. She introduced us to Will Copeland, one of EMEAC's community organizers, and a group of young people in their late teens and twenties; Charity then took a back seat until the conclusion of our visit.

Copeland spoke about the value of engaging young people in the process of issue analysis and action, and the way that skills associated with this work are often ignored by the educational establishment. He then turned the first hour of our afternoon at EMEAC over to two members of the Young Educators Alliance (YEA), Anthony and Odessa, who ran us through the kinds of group exercises they share with their fellow citizens. Will moved to a back table where he said he would serve as their coach.

Anthony and Odessa directed our attention to signs located in the center of the room's four walls that created a grid between two sets of polarities: unity/division and power/powerlessness. They then asked us and a growing number of young people who joined us throughout the afternoon to respond to different questions by locating ourselves at a place in the room that best matched our experience. The first question asked about how we perceived our relationship with our own community. The questions moved on to the way we had experienced dealing with different community issues. After each question, a few people were asked to explain why they had positioned themselves in the way they had. The final question involved our relationship with the police in our own communities. Anthony and Odessa were surprised that so many of us primarily White adults either stood in the middle of the room or in the sector that combined division and powerlessness. As we went through this active and dialogical process, I could imagine the conversations that might emerge among adolescents and young adults given the opportunity to reflect on these and similar topics.

After this warm-up exercise, Anthony and Odessa introduced us to an activity aimed at 'unearthing the invisible capital of community.' The aim of this process was to identify central issues we were facing that were preventing us from living the lives we wanted to live, the resources we possessed to potentially deal with these issues, and our vision of how things could be different. Since all of us were educators, they asked us to focus on school related challenges.

Their first question was: What are we up against? People in our group identified school closings, the growing number of for-profit charter schools, the underfunding of public education, standardized testing, high dropout rates, segregation, the isolation of schools from their communities, and poor science teaching. When asked the second question – What resources do we have? – people pointed to our ancestors, local youth and adults, social media, the collective wisdom of the broader community, social justice and cultural organizations, our ability to vote, and the other people we knew in the North Dakota Study Group. The final questions directed our attention to what we wanted to build. We generated a broad set of responses. These included engaged communities and students, a fair and adequate school funding system, a new definition of education, youth organizing aimed at building power and resistance, moving from an education that forces students to adapt to society to one that results in a society responsive to youth, and learning experiences that are hands-on and that encourage students to be bold and action-oriented.

Our experience matched well the description of the central purpose of the YEA, which is to bring youth together 'to identify issues in their environment and work collectively on solutions, using their creativity and personal insight.' The YEA aims to help young people 'learn to identify injustices, place them in a historical context, and propose alternatives that involve community input, community organizing, and advocacy' (EMEAC no date). One of the intentions of environmental education from the Tbilisi Declaration on has been to cultivate citizen involvement with regard to environmental stewardship and advocacy. Rarely, however, are young people regularly provided with opportunities to address collectively the kinds of environmental issues facing them in their own communities.[1] The YEA is inducting youth into exactly the kinds of dialogues and skill sets required to become citizen activists.

The day after our visit to the Cass Corridor Commons, for example, members of the YEA orchestrated a daylong workshop called Feed One/Teach One that focused on the issue of gentrification in different parts of the city and the impact this was having on Detroit's primarily low-income and Black residents. This has become an especially vital issue after the Detroit City Council in December 2012 approved the purchase of 140 acres of abandoned but now city-owned property by an investor named John Hantz who intends to turn this property into what he has called the 'world's largest urban farm' (MacMillan 2012). Hantz has also stated that over and beyond his interest in creating a hardwood tree farm in the middle of the city, his primary goal is to create land scarcity in an effort to inflate property values (Yakini 2012). Such an effort undercuts the emergence of citizen-created gardens and farmers' markets aimed at giving the city's current residents some level of control over their own food security as well as access to small-scale economic opportunities. Members of the YEA are seeking to exercise their 'right to the city' by finding ways to bring new residents into already existing neighborhoods without displacing others and developing approaches to make these neighborhoods more comfortable for everyone, a vision that is at once inclusive and equitable. If enacted, it could serve as a model for a very different future from the one currently being created in Chicago where gentrification and school closures are actively driving black and brown residents from the city.

Following these activities, high school students from the Detroit Institute of Technology participated in a presentation about another EMEAC project that involves transforming ugly schoolyards into places of beauty. This project is one element of EMEAC's Greener School Initiative that engages students from across grade levels in curricular and extra-curricular programs that focus on community gardening, environmental justice, and health. Working with a volunteer landscape architect who had in her earlier career been employed as an environmental educator, students from the Detroit Institute of Technology submitted a design to EMEAC's Ugliest Schoolyard Contest. Winners receive a $10,000 grant from the Kellogg Foundation to fund their plans. After studying their neighborhood and then assessing its assets and social and ecological problems, students at the DIT created a project aimed at remediating toxic soils by planting sunflowers outside the school's front doors. In the process, they drew upon support from their science, social studies, and math teachers. They also gained the interest and labor of additional people from the community and the school. Given its unique local characteristics, projects like this go far beyond the constraining prescriptions of the standardized curricula favored by neoliberal educational reformers that tend to focus on knowledge and issues that have little to do with young people's lived experience and that are aimed primarily at preparing successful students to leave their communities rather than contribute to them.[2]

Tension and contradiction in visions for renewal

Despite its positive elements, this project exemplifies one of the contradictions faced by many non-profits in a place like Detroit: accepting money from foundations whose projects may be at cross-purposes with one another. While supporting EMEAC as well as a new school associated with the Boggs Center, the Michigan-based Kellogg Foundation also invests millions of dollars in the neoliberal inspired effort to transform Detroit's public schools into charter schools (Pedroni 2011). Erik Olin Wright's discussion about social transformation in *Envisioning Real Utopias* (2010) may help situate EMEAC's decision to accept money from this organization. Wright lays out three options for social change: ruptural transformation, interstitial transformation, and symbiotic transformation. Ruptural transformations involve major shifts in political leadership and power along the lines of what occurred during Arab Spring. Wright argues that changes of this nature are unlikely in most developed nations, although in Detroit returning authority to the city council and eliminating the role of the emergency manager would be a move in this direction. Interstitial transformations involve finding ways to create new 'utopian' organizations and ways of doing things in the spaces that exist within current systems and institutions. The increasingly widespread emergence of businesses cooperatively owned and run by workers would be an example of this kind of transformation, as would the emergence of grassroots urban agriculture in Detroit. Symbiotic transformations are initiatives that both address the needs of current mainstream institutions but also those of a more equitable and just world. EMEAC's ugliest schoolyard contest can be viewed as a symbiotic transformation as it engenders among students a deeper sense of community responsibility and efficacy as well as educational engagement, the latter goal being one ascribed to by at least some neoliberal educational reformers, as well. People in Detroit are attempting to address social transformation at all of these levels.

Our final twenty minutes at EMEAC included a tour of the facility led by Charity Hicks. What was most striking was our visit to the strategy room where chart paper filled with the results of earlier community discussions covered the walls. Topics ranged from solar energy and climate change to pollution cleanups and food security. Especially impressive was a chart that displayed the names of powerful individuals who could be counted on to support or resist environmental and social justice initiatives, including a list of those on the fence between these two positions who might be swayed one way or the other. Also posted were the names of organizations and unorganized populations of people who could be turned to or developed as allies and the names of those local environmental organizations that most often sided with corporate rather than community-inspired and driven initiatives. All of this pointed to the degree to which the experience of people at EMEAC is informed with a kind of political acumen and analysis rare in public schools.

NEOLIBERALISM AND ENVIRONMENTAL EDUCATION

Public schools as sites for community organizing, dialogue, and action

A decade ago, Gruenewald (2003) argued in a widely cited article, 'The Best of Both Worlds: A Critical Pedagogy of Place,' that preparing young people to deal with contemporary environmental, economic, political, and cultural challenges should include two central foci: (1) educational opportunities to critique institutions, policies, and practices that result in the exploitation and domination of human and more-than-human communities, what he called *decolonization*; and (2) opportunities to engage in work that would contribute to the restoration of the health of these communities, something he referred to as *reinhabitation*. Such an agenda would place the depredations associated with neoliberalism and the generally unquestioned values of competitive individualism, profit, and economic growth at the heart of the educational enterprise, something that runs counter to the historic tendency of schools to avoid political controversy. As Stevenson (1987) has pointed out since the late 1980s, this avoidance of controversy has been a dilemma for environmental educators from the beginning. In order to maintain their apparent neutrality, schools tend to discourage the forms of advocacy encountered at an institution like the Eastern Michigan Environmental Action Council while at the same time leading children and youth to accept dominant cultural beliefs and values simply by not acknowledging alternative perspectives.

Fortunately, many public school teachers have been able to teach against this particular grain and demonstrate how the kinds of experiences young people are gaining at EMEAC can be introduced into the classroom. One that I am most familiar with took place at the Greater Egleston Community High School (GECHS) in Boston. For a number of years, science teacher Elaine Senechal (2008) taught an environmental justice course that addressed Gruenewald's two domains of decolonization and reinhabitation. She was able to do this in part because of her partnership with a local non-profit organization called Alternatives for Community and Environment (ACE). While attending ACE meetings to discover potential projects for her students, Senechal met two youth developers who were willing to join her class on Fridays to teach students how to become community organizers. They brought to a public school the skills that Will Copeland in Detroit is bringing to young people in an outside-of-school setting. The results were striking.

At the outset, students helped public health agencies publicize concerns about air quality in Roxbury where diesel traffic was seemingly contributing to high rates of asthma. Their efforts resulted in new funding that allowed Roxbury public health agencies to purchase air-monitoring equipment that in time proved that particulate levels in students' home neighborhoods were higher than any other community in the state. Students also helped write and distribute a survey to local residents about asthma, as well as, create a system for communicating whether air quality on a given day was safe or dangerous. With these experiences under their belt, students were ready to help ACE staff when they discovered an unenforced Boston city ordinance that restricted the amount of time vehicles could idle at one location. They began an anti-idling campaign that consisted of organizing public meetings, demonstrations, testifying before the Boston City Council, and regular interaction with the press. After several years, this work resulted in the enforcement of the anti-idling ordinance and a judicial ruling that required Boston's bus company to both obey the law and convert its vehicles to natural gas.

Senechal's course immersed students in learning and work that exemplified powerful forms of decolonization and reinhabitation. Much of this was accomplished because of her decision to reach out and collaborate with a local advocacy organization where community organizers and youth developers possessed the skills my colleagues and I saw being enacted in Detroit. Rather than simply accommodating themselves to the way low-income and non-white populations across the United States have been victimized by public and private policies that locate polluting industries and activities as well as toxic waste dumps in politically and economically marginalized communities, students at the GECHS were being given experiences that showed them their capacity to analyze and then act to correct discriminatory practices, a central element in their own decolonization. In this process, they began to see themselves as actors capable of challenging social injustices not merely as individual voters but as members of collective organizations composed of people from diverse backgrounds. Staff at ACE, for example, were largely White; students at the high school were primarily Black and Latino.

Simply by improving air quality, students were contributing to the reinhabitation of their own region. Senechal, however, did not stop there. In addition to involving her students in a long-term air quality action project, she also engaged them in the reclamation of a piece of property immediately across the street from the school. When she initially interviewed for a job at the GECHS, she couldn't help but notice the weed and trash filled lot that would have greeted students each day they came to classes. She thought of how dispiriting this lot with its overshadowing billboard must be for them and determined that if she were hired, she would make sure that it changed. She was hired, and over a three-year period she was able to work with her students to design a park and gain the permission and funding required to build it. Now a 'peace park,' its murals, plantings, and benches have become a site for community and cultural gatherings. The billboard still stands, but what had been an eyesore has become a source of community pride, sending a message about human vitality and creativity very similar to the message sent by the school gardens constructed by students, their teachers, and EMEAC volunteers in Detroit. This is reinhabitation in action. Students at the GECHS learned that they possessed the agency to both protest and create. They were becoming the 'solutionaries' Grace Lee Boggs has sought to engender in Detroit.

Fortunately, educators throughout the United States, and world, are addressing similar issues in different ways. They are called by many names: environmental educators, ecojustice educators, social justice educators, place- and community-based educators, sustainability educators, or advocates for critical pedagogy or ecopedagogy. Their efforts, however, are being increasingly constrained by curriculum reforms that dictate exactly what should be taught and when. Recent research in Australia demonstrated to me that many teachers no longer feel they have the time to do much more than just prepare for the multiple choice tests that are treated as the ultimate measure of their students' progress and their own effectiveness. A narrowing definition of pedagogy to activities dominated by memorization and rote learning, especially in schools that serve economically disadvantaged students (Ladson-Billings 2009), is also driving out learning predicated on inquiry, exploration, and service, exactly the kinds of experiences that lead to engagement and long-term interest and involvement. In their recent volume about writing instruction in the United States, Applebee and Langer (2013) bemoan these trends and the way they lead educators to neglect the development of students' capacity to think and reflect. Although these pressures are severe, I still regularly encounter in the United States and elsewhere inspired and courageous teachers who are able to engage in transformative educational work in the interstitial spaces they are able to locate within their schools. This work is not easy and is almost always fragile and threatened, but it exists, much as the fragile and threatened reforms in Detroit exist and point to the possibility of a more humane, just, and environmentally prudent world.

EMEAC and the GECHS: takeaways

What are lessons that can be taken from EMEAC and the GECHS that might more widely inform the work of social studies or environmental educators concerned about addressing the impact of neoliberalism on the human and more-than-human communities that support us? The first is that educators need to start learning from and collaborating with community organizers. Especially given the constraints schools now find themselves under given the pressures of the standards and account-ability movement as well as fiscally strapped school budgets, thinking beyond cur-ricular and testing requirements has become increasingly difficult for many teachers. Few teachers, as well, possess either the knowledge of local issues or the political savvy to effectively address difficult community challenges. People who work for organizations like EMEAC have this knowledge and these skills and are often eager to find ways to gain access to young people who can help them with their work. If it is impossible to fit such concerns into the regular curriculum, projects like those in Boston and Detroit can also be tied to after-school classes or clubs, providing an opportunity for interested young people to direct their talents and energies to com-munity needs (for an example of this see Chapter 7 about Wausau, Wisconsin in Putnam and Feldstein 2003).

The second lesson that can be taken from these efforts is that school learning, if we are serious about preparing the young to become citizens, needs to consist of something beyond the academic content typically encountered in most classrooms. A well-functioning democracy requires much more than the willingness to seek information about pressing local issues and then the casting of a vote. If our commu-nities are to truly become sites of engaged and responsible participation, young peo-ple need to be taught how to effect changes required to improve our common life and protect and preserve the natural resources and systems upon which human well-being depends. Elites have rarely welcomed such participation, so the absence of what might be called authentic citizen education in the United States is not a sur-prise. But in an era where large political and economic institutions seem less and less able or willing to address fundamental human and ecological needs, it seems imperative that the cultivation of democratic skills and the desire to make use of them become a primary concern of educators – environmental and otherwise.

The third lesson is that young people who have had learning experiences like these come to develop a remarkable level of responsibility, self-confidence, and political sophistication. As one of Elaine Senechal's students observed after partici-pating in the environmental justice class:

> I am proud of my accomplishments in environmental justice this trimester. Most impor-tantly, I have been able to gain confidence to speak in front of large groups of people. Before presenting to the City Council I was very nervous. But after watching them and

my classmates somewhat debate I realized they are regular people just like my family, my teachers, and my friends, and I should not be nervous when it comes to speaking my mind. (Senechal 2008, 100)

Both Anthony and Odessa demonstrated a similar confidence and clarity of expression in their work with my colleagues and me during our time at EMEAC on that February afternoon. They did not seem like young kids whose primary job in most classrooms is to remain quiet and take in what their teachers have to say. They instead are learning to be facilitators of the kind of Freirian dialogue I associate with consciousness raising and political empowerment. Knowing that they use the same skills and processes with their peers as well as older residents of Detroit gives me faith that a growing number of people in this city will have the opportunity to explore difficult questions and imagine possible solutions in ways similar to what we encountered while under their guidance. Young people long to be placed in positions where they can hone competencies that are valued by others, especially their elders. Imagine what our communities could be like if all children and youth were provided with comparable opportunities to engage in democratic practice and decision-making and were inducted into the practice of civic involvement from an early age in the same way they are taught to play baseball or soccer now. Doing so would require political leaders willing to both listen to and be seen by the next generation, a process that at least for some could lead to greater transparency as well as compassion as they consider the ways they might be judged by their own children and grandchildren.

Imagination and the right to the city

At the 2010 US Social Forum in Detroit, historical sociologist Immanuel Wallerstein participated in a panel discussion with Grace Lee Boggs (Boggs and Wallerstein 2010). In his talk, he spoke of the way that world systems like capitalism or feudalism have limited life spans and eventually fail. He asserted that capitalism is now in a process of decline, that economic and political elites realize this, and that they are creating a new system aimed at taking its place while maintaining their power and privilege. To some extent, the consolidation of wealth in the hands of fewer and fewer people, the erosion of democratic practice at all levels in the United States, and the increase in state surveillance all may be part of the transition they are imagining. During liminal periods like our own, however, Wallerstein argued that no one can predict the outcome and that small local actions can potentially influence the shape of whatever new system comes into being after capitalism.

It is for this reason that the work of young activists in places like Detroit or Boston and the educational processes that support them seem worthy of our attention. On one hand, their effort to imagine a city that includes rather than rejects them and their families and neighbors seems both naïve and ineffectual in the face of wealthy investors and power holders who want to reclaim the city as an urban center that benefits current elites. On the other hand, what people in Detroit are creating now could thirty years from the present become an exemplar for urban renewal in other economically gutted cities in both the developed and developing world. In his new book *The World We Made: Alex McKay's Story from 2050* (2014), British environmentalist Jonathan Porritt imagines what might happen if humanity were to marry currently available technologies to an economy predicated on sharing and cooperation. In it, he includes a section about Detroit that has been able to both rebuild itself as an urban center but also grow its emerging community gardens into a highly productive agricultural sector. Keeping such visions in our minds and the minds of the young may be one of the most critical things we can do to resist the impact of neoliberalism. The small moves of the brave and persistent residents of Detroit help nourish these dreams for us all.

Notes

1. An important exception to this assertion can be found in the process of issue analysis advocated by Cheak, Volk, and Hungerford (2002) and described in detail in their 2002 study of research projects conducted by students at the Aka'ula School on Molokai.
2. Michael Corbett's (2007) volume, *Learning to Leave: The Irony of Schooling in a Coastal Community*, describes the way schooling prepares rural students for occupational opportunities that don't exist in their own communities. The same can be said of students growing up in impoverished urban neighborhoods for whom school success often requires moving elsewhere if they hope to pursue higher education and their vocational ambitions.

Notes on contributor

Gregory A. Smith is a professor in the Graduate School of Education and Counseling at Lewis & Clark College in Portland, Oregon, USA. His two most recent books are *Place-based Education in the Global Age: Local Diversity* (co-edited with David Gruenewald and published by Taylor & Francis) and *Place- and Community-based Education in Schools* (co-written with David Sobel and published by Routledge).

References

Applebee, A., and J. Langer. 2013. *Writing Instruction That Works: Proven Methods for Middle and High School Classrooms*. New York: Teachers College Press.

Boggs, G. (with Kurashige, S.). 2011. *The Next American Revolution: Sustainable Activism for the Twenty-first Century*. Berkeley: University of California Press.

Boggs, G., and I. Wallerstein. 2010. *A Conversation. U.S. Social Forum, Detroit, June 24, 2010*. Detroit, MI: Boggs Center to Nurture Community Leadership.

Bowers, C. (with Martusewicz, R.). 2006. "Revitalizing the Commons of the African-American Communities in Detroit." In *Revitalizing the Commons: Cultural and Educational Sites of Resistance and Affirmation*, edited by C. Bowers, 47–84. Lanham, MD: Lexington.

Bowles, S., and H. Gintis. 1986. *Democracy and Capitalism: Property, Community, and the Contradictions of Modern Thought*. New York: Basic Books.

Cheak, M., T. Volk, and H. Hungerford. 2002. *Molokai: An Investment in Children, the Community, and the Environment*. Carbondale, IL: Center for Instruction, Staff Development, and Evaluation.

Corbett, M. 2007. *Learning to Leave: The Irony of Schooling in a Coastal Community*. Black Point, NS: Fernwood.

Dworkin, M., and M. Young. 2012. *We are Not Ghosts*. Oley, PA: Bullfrog Films.

East Michigan Environmental Action Council. no date. *Young Educators Alliance Pamphlet*. Detroit, MI: East Michigan Environmental Action Council.

Friedman, M. 1952. *Essays on Positive Economics*. Chicago, IL: University of Chicago Press.

Friedman, M. 1962. *Capitalism and Freedom*. Chicago, IL: University of Chicago Press.

Gruenewald, David. 2003. "The Best of Both Worlds: A Critical Pedagogy of Place." *Educational Researcher* 32 (4): 3–12.

Harvey, D. 2008. "The Right to the City." *New Left Review* 53: 23–40.

Hayek, F. 1960. *The Constitution of Liberty*. Chicago, IL: University of Chicago Press.

Howell, S. 2013. "Bankrupting Democracy." *OpenDemocracy*, November 18. Accessed January 10, 2014. http://www.opendemocracy.net/print/76985

Hursh, D., and J. Henderson. 2011. "Contesting Global Neoliberalism and Creating Alternative Futures." *Discourse: Studies in the Cultural Politics of Education* 32 (2): 171–185.

Klein, N. 2008. *Shock Doctrine: The Rise of Disaster Capitalism*. New York: Picador.

Kornbluth, J. 2014. *Inequality for All*. Beverly Hills, CA: Anchor Bay Entertainment/Starz.

Ladson-Billings, G. 2009. "Race Still Matters: Critical Race Theory in Education." In *The Routledge Handbook of Critical Education*, edited by M. Apple, W. Au, and A. Gandin, 110–123. New York: Routledge.

Lipman, P. 2011. *The New Political Economy of Urban Education: Neoliberalism, Race and the Right to the City*. New York: Routledge.

MacMillan, L. 2012. "Vast Land Deal Divides Detroit." *New York Times*, February 24, 2013. http://green.blogs.nytimes.com/2012/12/10/vast-land-deal-divides-detroit/.

Pedroni, T. 2011. "Urban Shrinkage as a Performance of Whiteness: Neoliberal Urban Restructuring, Education, and Racial Containment in the Post-industrial, Global Niche City." *Discourse: Studies in the Cultural Politics of Education* 32 (2): 203–215.

Porritt, J. 2014. *The World We Made: Alex McKay's Story from 2050*. London: Phaidon.

Putnam, R., and L. Feldstein. 2003. *Better Together: Restoring the American Community*. New York: Simon & Schuster.

Senechal, E. 2008. "Environmental Justice in Egleston Square." In *Place-based Education in the Global Age: Local Diversity*, edited by D. Gruenewald and G. Smith, 85–112. New York: Taylor & Francis.

Stevenson, R. 1987. "Schooling and Environmental Education: Contradictions in Purpose and Practice." In *Environmental Education: Practice and Possibility*, edited by I. Robottom, 69–82. Geelong, VIC: Deakin University.

Wright, E. 2010. *Envisioning Real Utopias*. London: Verso.

Yakini, M. 2012. "Ill-conceived Hantz Farms Land Deal Should be Dropped." *Michigan Citizen*, February 22, 2013. http://michigancitizen.com/ill-conceived-hantz-farms-land-deal-should-be-dropped/.

The UN Decade of Education for Sustainable Development: business as usual in the end

John Huckle[a] and Arjen E.J. Wals[b,c]

[a]Bedford, UK; [b]Wageningen University, Wageningen, The Netherlands; [c]Department of Pedagogical, Curricular and Professional Studies, University of Gothenburg, Gothenburg, Sweden

An analysis of the literature supporting the UN Decade of Education for Sustainable Development and a sample of its key products suggests that it failed to acknowledge or challenge neoliberalism as a hegemonic force blocking transitions towards genuine sustainability. The authors argue that the rationale for the Decade was idealistic and that global education for sustainability citizenship provides a more realistic focus for such an initiative. They anchor such education in appropriate social theory, outline its four dimensions and use these to review four key products from the Decade, before suggesting remedial measures to render ESD a more effective vehicle for promoting democratic global governance and sustainability.

Introduction

In 2002, the UN General Assembly adopted a resolution that called for a Decade of Education for Sustainable Development (DESD 2005–2014). The ESD Section of UNESCO would act as the Secretariat for the DESD, offering oversight and advice and coordinating the efforts of member states, UN agencies and other groups. The Decade aimed 'to integrate the values inherent in sustainable development into all aspects of learning to encourage changes in behaviour that allow for a more sustainable and just society for all' (UNESCO 2005a).

Readers seeking an overview of DESD might consult the following documents: *The Decade at a Glance* (UNESCO 2005a); *The International Implementation Scheme for the Decade in Brief* (UNESCO 2005b); a mid-decade review (Wals 2009); *The Bonn Declaration* (UNESCO 2009); and the comprehensive report on DESD *Shaping the Education of Tomorrow* (Wals 2012). These documents suggest that the discourse guiding the Decade was essentially reformist acknowledging mounting global problems and suggesting that shifts in values, lifestyles and policy within prevailing forms of society, will be sufficient to put global society on a sustainable path. The 'basic vision of ESD is a world where everyone has the opportunity to benefit from education and learn the values, behaviour and lifestyles required for a sustainable future and for positive societal transformation' (DESD 2014). Yet, while there is adequate analysis of what such values, behaviour and lifestyles should involve (notably through the influence of *The Earth Charter* – see below), there is too little attention to power, politics and citizenship; the ways in which neoliberalism has made the adoption of sustainable behaviours and lifestyles less likely; what alternative forms of social and environmental relations (political economy) would aid their realization; and whether students should consider liberal and radical views of social change alongside the reformist, and sometimes idealist views reflected in the literature of DESD (Huckle 2012).

Our article starts with the case for a genuinely critical and transformative ESD as envisioned in the document *The Education We Need for the World We Want* (TEWN). In an attempt to anchor this vision in appropriate social theory, it then examines the emerging theory and practice of what we term global education for sustainability citizenship (GESC). Four dimensions of such education are outlined together with their implications for curriculum content and pedagogy at the level of secondary or high school students.

The focus then shifts to the UN and UNESCO and their potential to promote sustainable development and GESC. Our central argument is that the Decade represents 'business as usual in the end' since the majority of those who determined its rationale and developed educational projects and programmes under its umbrella failed through inadequate guidance, misplaced idealism or the censoring of more critical ideas and content, to face up to current global realities. This argument is supported by an analysis of four DESD publications that may influence school teachers and teacher educators working in the mature economies of the West. These are evaluated against the four dimensions of GESC considered earlier in the article, before a final section looks beyond the Decade to ways in which a more critical and transformative ESD may develop in the future.

The Education We Need for the World We Want

At the time of Rio+20 in 2012, a working group on education produced a paper, TEWN (Rio+20 Education Group 2012), for the People's Summit that ran in parallel with the official summit. The group's members included the International Council for Adult Education; the World Education Forum; the Latin American Council of Adult Education; and others representing the educational interests of civil society. The paper analysed the challenges posed by the global crisis; set out an educational agenda in response to these challenges; and commented on the likelihood that Rio+20 would adopt this agenda.

The authors regard the crisis as not only one of 'financial capital in its neoliberal phase' with its attendant economic, social and environmental impacts, but also one of 'greater magnitude' linked to prevailing forms of development and underdevelopment that lead to 'global exhaustion' and prompt social movements seeking radical alternatives. A key cause of the crisis is a global political order, in which there is 'no international democratic space for taking decisions on issues that are of global dimensions and (have) differential impacts at the local level', and, in which the interests of some states, corporations and banks, 'under the interests of capital', weaken the scope for 'multilateral, collective decision-making'. Faced with a crisis that denies basic human rights and increases environmental and social injustice, social movements around the world are reflecting and acting on new institutional forms of democracy and citizenship. They are rejecting the economic analysis of the crisis adopted by multilateral financial organizations that leads to policies of structural adjustment, reduced public expenditure, cuts to welfare and austerity for the majority, and are demanding greater economic, political and cultural democracy. Central to these demands are new forms of global citizenship that offer the prospect of social and environmental justice for all.

Turning to education, the authors remind us that the global crisis is also a crisis of education. This continues to be restructured in most parts of the world to better reproduce workers, consumers and citizens who meet the needs of neoliberal capitalism. Educational institutions have largely given up 'training people capable of thinking about important political, environmental, economic and social issues of global order' and reflecting and acting on radical alternatives. There is an urgent need to restore a 'civic pedagogy' that 'rescues the notion of education as a human right' that can 'open the eyes to the democratization of societies', and 'train critical citizenship' in ways that 'establish bonds' with social movements. The critical understanding of 'contested meanings' or discourses is a central part of such education, as is the testing of knowledge through real or simulated involvement in issues facing communities variously affected by neoliberal globalization. What is needed is a 'critical and transformative education that respects human rights and those of the whole community of life to which humans belong, and specifically promotes the right to citizen participation in decision-making spaces' such as those that shape the prospects of more sustainable forms of development.

With regard to the Rio+20 summit, the authors of TEWN argue that along with other social movements, the education movement should defend education as a fundamental human right that is central to citizens' powers to transform current patterns of production, consumption and distribution in order to achieve greater environmental and social justice. They fear the summit will merely be 'an opportunity for 'greening the capitalist exit from the crisis', for 'humanizing it' and 'appealing to the social and environmental responsibility of companies'. Capitalism's responsibility for the crisis is likely to be 'erased' and opportunities to launch radically new ways of thinking and living based on a 'truly democratic social order' are likely to be overlooked.

Anchoring a critical and transformative ESD in appropriate social theory

If key causes of the global crisis are the prevailing geopolitical order and lack of global governance, together with a lack of 'civic pedagogy', as the authors of TEWN maintain, then global citizenship education should lie at the heart of an international initiative on ESD, such as DESD. This premise leads us to suggest combining the emerging theory and practice of sustainability or sustainable citizenship with that of ecopedagogy and global citizenship education. The resulting concept of GESC can offer an appropriate perspective from which to review the weaknesses of the Decade as revealed in some of its key products, and to suggest remedial measures.

Ecopedagogy (Gadotti 2008; Kahn 2008, 2010) combines the critical pedagogy of Paulo Freire with a future-orientated ecological politics, and involves teachers and students carrying out projects in the classroom and community that open spaces for dialogue that allows critical analysis of the discourses surrounding sustainability (OSDEM 2013). They cooperatively reflect on their understandings of the world, recognize false understandings (ideology and hegemony) and act to validate discourse that appears to offer a more truthful interpretation of reality and the ways in which it might be transformed (Hursh and Henderson 2011; Walsh 2009).

There are alternative approaches to global citizenship education and GESC as we outline it, draws on what Shultz (2007) terms radical and transformationalist approaches, and on cosmopolitan global education, environmental global education and global critical justice education as outlined by Gaudelli and Heilman (2009).

A sustainability citizen is one who displays 'pro-sustainability behaviour, in public and private, driven by a belief in fairness of the distribution of environmental goods, in participation, and in the co-creation of sustainability policy' (Dobson 2011, 10). Bullen and Whitehead (2005) explain that sustainable citizenship represents a paradigm for post industrial living that disrupts the spatial parameters and temporal scope of conventional citizenship and raises important questions about the material constitution of the citizen. It requires citizens to exercise responsibilities to distant people and places and past and future generations, and to commit themselves to ecologism (Smith 1998) to the extent that they are required to exercise care or stewardship for non-human nature. It enlarges the public sphere in which citizenship is conceived and practiced to include the environment; embraces the private sphere of citizens' lifestyles and consumption patterns; and is relational in the sense that it requires a keen awareness of the connections, which exist between social actions, economic practices and environmental processes.

Van Poeck, Vandenabeele, and Bruyninckx (2013) argue that while Jickling and Wals (2007) distinguish three approaches to ESD ('Big Brother ESD', 'Feel Good ESD' and 'Enabling Thought and Action'), the theory and practice of their favoured approach ('Enabling Thought and Action') would be strengthened by drawing on contemporary accounts of sustainable citizenship. These employ the concept of ecological footprints to suggest a post-cosmopolitan form of ecological citizenship (Dobson 2003); extend notions of liberal environmental citizenship by regarding citizenship as a site of struggle, where 'the limits of established rights are (re)defined and (re) affirmed' (Gilbert and Phillips 2003); and draw on civic republican approaches to citizenship to suggest that sustainability citizenship is a form of resistance citizenship existing within and as a corrective to unsustainable development (Barry 2005).

Van Poeck and her co-authors suggest the emerging multidimensional view of sustainability citizenship has potential to enrich ESD by providing insights into its overlapping scale, ethical, relational and political dimensions. While these dimensions might be labelled differently, we will follow their labelling and consider the dimensions with reference to GESC at the secondary or high school level.

Delivering GESC's four dimensions through ecopedagogy

The *scale dimension* of GESC can be considered foundational as it introduces students to global society and the ways in which personal and collective decisions have impacts on distant human and non-human others. Ecological footprints provide an appropriate starting point, encouraging students to consider issues of justice and the desirability of sustainability citizenship. They should learn about structures of power and the processes at work in the capitalist world economy; the rise of neoliberalism and its social, environmental and cultural impacts; and the contemporary 'crisis' and the need for more sustainable forms of development. Such development requires public/collective as well as private/individual actions, and students should recognize that a focus purely on individuals' values and lifestyles serves to depoliticize and privatize a very political and public issue, and thereby contributes to the reproduction of the status quo.

The *ethical dimension* requires students to recognize sustainability as a normative notion and to consider how such principles as those set out in the Earth Charter might enable the development of a global society based on respect for nature, universal human rights, economic justice and a culture of peace. Students should consider their own behaviour, and that of others, in relation of issues of justice/injustice; right/wrong; rights/obligations; and sustainability/unsustainability; as they engage with issues through values education strategies that pace their moral development. The impact of neoliberalism and associated individualization and financialization (Lapavitsas 2013) should be acknowledged, as once idealistic young people are now more inclined to think only of themselves and to evaluate everything in purely monetary terms. Case studies of individuals and communities who live in ways that reflect Earth Charter principles are clearly desirable.

The *relational dimension* focuses on the social construction of such concepts, as sustainability and citizenship, and requires students to understand that whilst there is widespread acceptance of Earth Charter principles amongst civil society organisations around the world, sustainability and citizenship can be based in other values and interests. They should be introduced to the notion of discourse as:

> a shared way of apprehending the world. Embedded in language, it enables those who subscribe to it to interpret bits of information and put them together into coherent stories or accounts. Each discourse rests on assumptions, judgements, and contentions that provide the basic terms for analysis, debates, agreements and disagreements, in the environmental area no less than elsewhere. (Dryzek 1997, 8)

Media education should enable students to appreciate that discourse pervades the home, classroom and community and shapes their understanding (along with our misunderstanding and ignorance) of global society, globalization, global governance and sustainable development. As far as older secondary/high school students are concerned, they should consider discourses of globalization such as those outlined by Held and McGrew (2002); environmental discourses as outlined by Dryzek (1997); the politics of sustainable development as mapped by Hopwood, Mellor, and O'Brien (2005); and the forms of democracy and sustainability citizenship that might give expression to Earth Charter principles. Links to social movements and school students in other parts of the world, via social media, should enable them to understand how concepts of sustainability and citizenship are changing under the influence of such movements, and how dialogue across space can engender global solidarity.

Finally, the *political dimension* focuses on issues of social and environmental justice first raised when considering ecological footprints. Students should explore issues of the environment and development in ways that reveal structural causes and consider reformist and radical solutions. The ideas and policies of governments, corporations, political parties, NGOs and social movements should be related to the discourses mentioned above, and real or simulated participation in real sustainability issues should be used to further develop the knowledge, skills and values that contribute to sustainable citizenship. Key to such citizenship are issues of global governance and the fact that there is no 'international democratic space', in which global citizens can co-determine more sustainable futures for their communities. Clearly students need to be introduced to the history of international governance (Mazower 2012), governance challenges in the wake of neoliberalism (Calhoun and Derluguian 2011) and the kinds of global democracy that may allow and encourage sustainability citizenship (Held 1996; Monbiot 2003; Smith and Pangsapa 2008).

Harris (2014) reminds us that neoliberal capitalism 'needs the big centralised state to clear its way and enforce its insanities'. Alongside new forms of democratic global governance, students should be introduced to new forms of localism and radical democracy, as being pioneered by social movement such as Occupy (Graeber 2013) and the Transition Movement (Hopkins 2013). Place-based pedagogies (Gruenewald and Smith 2008) thus contribute to the political dimension, allowing students to consider the social and ecological wellbeing of the places they inhabit, and their role in shaping and nurturing their identity.

The role of the UN and UNESCO in supporting global sustainability citizenship education

What prospect is there that the UN through its agency UNESCO, will promote GESC? Answering this question should start by recognizing that the UN General Assembly is an assembly of nation states, not an assembly of the world's citizens. It cannot represent their common interests in sustainable development because the interests of the most powerful states are closely aligned with those of global capital. In addition, the principle of state sovereignty, embedded within such agreements as the Rio Declaration (Elliott 1998), undermines agreement and action on such issues as climate change. Ultimate power lies with the five permanent members of the Security Council for by exercising their veto, they can overrule measures approved by the General Assembly and prevent reform of the UN constitution. Mazower (2012) reviews the changing fortunes of the UN within the recent history of global capitalism, while Park, Conca, and Finger (2008) attribute the failure of the 1992 Rio Earth Summit and its Agenda 21 to inadequate institutional support and economic resources; an improperly focussed vision that overlooked the needs of the poor; and the adoption of a model of development based on the institutionalization of incremental efficiency improvements or ecological modernization that failed to question capitalist industrialization (Park, Conca, and Finger 2008). The Rio+20 Summit in 2012 proved incapable of renewing the global agenda of sustainability politics as the authors of TEWN feared (EuroMemo Group 2013; Monbiot 2012). As a result, politicians and others, including proponents of ESD both within and outside UNESCO, now put increasing faith in the greening of capitalism or the green economy (Brand 2012; UNHLP 2013).

UNESCO is a specialized agency of the UN whose purpose is to contribute to peace and security by promoting international collaboration through education, science and culture in order to further universal respect for justice, the rule of law and human rights along with the fundamental freedom proclaimed in the UN Charter. Learning to Live Together (LTLT) is an ongoing UNESCO-supported educational framework, in which 'citizenship education in the twenty-first century can comfortably anchor itself' (UNESCO Bangkok 2014) that advocates pedagogy to foster, amongst other outcomes, sustainable development, social cohesion and dialogue amongst people. Two related global education initiatives led by UNESCO are Education for International Understanding (EIU) and DESD. Early in the Decade, UNESCO's then Director of the Division for the Promotion of Quality Education wrote an article linking global citizenship to the four key values identified in the DESD implementation scheme (Pigozzi 2006). Given UNESCO's recognition of the overlap of LTLT, EIU and DESD, it is somewhat surprising that global citizenship education has remained somewhat marginal to the literature of the Decade.

UNESCO and UNEP jointly held their first intergovernmental conference on environmental education (EE) in Tbilisi in 1977, which followed an international workshop on EE held in Belgrade, in 1975. Upon (re)reading the Tbilisi declaration and the Belgrade charter, it becomes clear that the language used almost 40 years ago was much more explicit than that associated with DESD, when referring to the global economic and political order and the need for change:

> Policies aimed at maximising economic output without regard to its consequences on society and on the resources available for improving the quality of life must be questioned. (UNESCO-UNEP 1975, 2)

> Environmental education has a role to play in developing a sense of responsibility and solidarity among countries and regions as the foundation for a new international order which will guarantee the conservation and improvement of the environment. (UNESCO-UNEP 1978, 25)

The countries of the South were at that time calling for a new international order, but the US subsequently subverted these calls and used the turn to neoliberalism to impose a new American international economic order using the IMF and structural adjustment in this process (Mazower 2012). With the shift to the right amongst global elites, and the associated attacks on democracy and socially critical education, critical forms of EE and later ESD were marginalised, and the focus increasingly shifted to values, behaviour and lifestyles, rather than power, politics and citizenship. This leads Selby and Kagawa to conclude that ESD is

> the latest and thickest manifestation of the 'closing circle' of policy-driven EE. Characterised by definitional haziness, a tendency to blur rather than lay bare inconsistencies and incompatibilities, and a cosy but ill considered association with the globalization agenda, the field has allowed the neoliberal marketplace worldview into the circle so the mainstream ESD tacitly embraces economic growth and an instrumentalist and managerial view of nature that goes hand in glove with an emphasis on the technical and tangible rather than the axiological and intangible (Selby and Kagawa 2010, 37 [also see Selby and Kagawa 2014]).

Consequently, it is not surprising that we find no references to Tbilisi or to EE in general within the history of ESD presented in the so-called abridged version of the last monitoring and evaluation report of the DESD (UNESCO 2012). Nor is it perhaps surprising that DESD staff excluded comments from some key informants from the final report (Wals 2012) during its editing, on the grounds of obtaining a geographically balanced range of sources. One such comment raised the impact of neoliberalism on government policy:

> No transformative approach has been allowed, just tweaking. Education remains a political ball. It continues to be ad hoc, small scale and without a clear mandate that [ESD] has to happen. Mainstream education won't do it unless they are told they have to. Mainstream education has been habituated to directives from government, so some ESD is under the radar if it is happening. Economic growth continues to dominate everything with little reflection about the values and thinking that got us to where we are today. (Unpublished quote from the UN DESD Global Monitoring Data Set, Key Informant Survey, Sustainable Schools Alliance, United Kingdom)

Analysing DESD products against GESC dimensions

Our argument that UNESCO has trimmed and tamed DESD so that it does not challenge neoliberalism and fails to develop GESC, can best be further advanced by examining some of its key publications. We have selected four that can be considered to be aimed at teachers in the secondary/high school sector and those concerned with their professional education. We acknowledge that all of these were written or are available in English by authors, whose cultural backgrounds are perhaps too similar, and that ideally we should consider a greater range of more diverse sources. Nevertheless, the evaluation of these publications, against the four dimensions of GESC, raises some important issues.

The ESD Lens. (UNESCO/Fien and Parker 2010, http://unesdoc.unesco.org/images/0019/001908/190898e.pdf)

The ESD Lens (ESDL) (Fien and Parker 2010) is a set of 13 review tools to enable policy-makers and practitioners to reorient education, particularly in the formal sector, towards sustainable development. An initiative of the DESD uses the lens metaphor to encourage users to 'look again with new eyes' at current educational provision. The review tools are grouped into four modules (planning and preparing the Lens review; reviewing national policy; reviewing quality learning outcomes; and reviewing practice) and are addressed to a variety of potential users.

The strengths and weaknesses of ESDL can be seen by considering the first two review tools that seek to build a common understanding of ESD and encourage integrative learning. Users are encouraged to view ESD in an integrated context and are provided with a short history of sustainable development together with a list of its sample concepts (UNESCO 2002). Neither the integrated context of ESD, nor the history of sustainable development is adequately related to real-world political economy. Users are given few insights into the structural causes of unsustainable development; the politics of sustainable development; and the contested meanings and significance of such concepts as global equity and justice or democracy and civic participation within different discourses. They are told that 'the industrial revolution introduced a model of growth and development that has led to mass exploitation of resources and degradation of life-support systems' (ibid, 17), and that global challenges 'require a re-orientation of economic thinking and practice and cultural change' (ibid, 18), but nowhere is there mention or analysis of global capitalism, associated forms of global governance or reformist and radical alternatives.

This neglect of the political dimension of ESD is compounded by review tool two. There are brief mentions of global citizenship and the capacity to envision alternatives in the introduction to integrative learning (ibid, 23), but the tool consists largely of a table outlining key curriculum knowledge, skills and attitudes and values under each of the four pillars of sustainable development (society, environment, economy and culture). The problem here is lack of detailed specification. Without further exploration and referencing, what are users to make of such content as: 'how societies work and change' (knowledge of society); 'knowledge of the relationship between environment, society, culture and economy, and its impacts on ecosystems and ecosystem services' (knowledge of environment); or 'different economic models' (knowledge of economy)? There is much in this table, and in other tools, that prompts attention to the ethical, scale and relational dimensions of ESD, but users deserve more realistic guidance on the politics of education and sustainable development and how this can best be accommodated within an ESD that fosters GESC.

YouthXChange. (Loprieno et al. 2006/UNESCO-UNEP 2008 2nd edition, http://unesdoc.unesco.org/images/0015/001587/158700e.pdf)

YouthXchange (YXC) (Loprieno et al. 2006; UNESCO-UNEP 2008), is a training kit on sustainable lifestyles, developed by UNESCO and UNEP that encourages young people to reflect on their personal consumption behaviours, assumptions and experiences in ways that enable them to 'analyse global and personal patterns, causes and impacts of consumption and to unfold the ethical dimension of reducing the social and ecological impacts of human productive activities at global and local levels' (Heiss and Marras 2009, 182). It consists of: a website (http://www.youthx change.net/main/home.asp), a training manual translated into 18 languages, a project team and a network of partner organizations around the world. The website provides access to the manual and team and to curriculum resources arranged in nine 'rooms' than span three levels of consumption: individual; friends and family; and the community at large. A further three areas of the website provide utilities to aid learning, opportunities to participate in the project and links to YXC worldwide partners. Page 9 of the manual links YXC to the DESD claims that it is 'at the heart of this UN initiative'.

As regards, the dimension of scale YXC acknowledges that personal consumer decisions have widespread consequences and that the private and public spheres are linked, but it echoes neoliberalism in privileging private/individual actions over public/collective actions. It is stronger on the ethical dimension linking consumer behaviour to issues of social justice; acknowledging that sustainability is a normative notion; and providing rich material for values education. YXC has given attention to learning from and with communities elsewhere in the world (the relational dimension), but its focus on sustainable consumption within prevailing forms of political economy may limit real cross-cultural dialogue on alternative meanings of sustainability and citizenship.

As regards, the political dimension of GESC, YXC fails to link unsustainable consumption to the structures and processes that shape consumer capitalism and deprive many of environmental and social justice. The focus is on the role of the global consumer/citizen in persuading governments, regulatory institutions, NGOs and business to take action (see page 11), but the materials give little attention to barriers to change (the power of economic, political and cultural elites); the limitations of its dominant discourse of ecological modernization (Dryzek 1997; Warner 2010); and the economics and politics of radical alternatives. The social belonging room acknowledges that at 'local and global levels civil society is organising itself and networking to move towards a more tolerant and inclusive world', but the case studies in the 'citizens corner' fail to reflect the real breadth and vitality of global civil society or its record in opposing neoliberalism and urging new forms of consumption, citizenship and global governance (see for example Hopkins 2013; World Social Forum 2013).

As regards, the dimension of scale YXC acknowledges that personal consumer decisions have widespread consequences and that the private and public spheres are linked, but it echoes neoliberalism in privileging private/individual actions over public/collective actions. It is stronger on the ethical dimension linking consumer behaviour to issues of social justice; acknowledging that sustainability is a normative notion; and providing rich material for values education. YXC has given attention to learning from and with communities elsewhere in the world (the relational dimension), but its focus on sustainable consumption within prevailing forms of political economy may limit real cross-cultural dialogue on alternative meanings of sustainability and citizenship.

ESD: An expert review of processes and learning. (Tilbury 2011, http://unesdoc.une sco.org/images/0019/001914/191442e pdf)

The Expert Review of Processes and Learning (Tilbury 2011), a component of the UN DESD's monitoring and evaluation scheme seeks clarification on: (a) commonly accepted learning processes that are aligned with ESD and should be promoted through ESD activities and (b) ESD and related learning opportunities that contribute to sustainable development (Tilbury 2011).

From the review it is quite clear that the ethical dimension is rather weak, if not absent, in most of the documents and cases reviewed. One case refers to 'inter-generational justice/fairness; intra-generational justice/fairness; and fair relations between humans and nature' (ibid, 82), but without providing much guidance as to how to develop such justice/fairness.

With respect to the political dimension, the 13 case studies reviewed suggest 'a wide range of contributions through ESD to economic, environmental, social (including cultural) and educational change' (ibid, 9). However, in the documents and cases reviewed political change does not appear to be emphasized. There are references to 'empowerment' of change agents, 'capacity-building for economic change', and, in one case, 'change of government' (ibid, 45), but such references lack any critical analysis of: why things are the way they are, what keeps them from changing, what kind of change or transition might be needed, and how to go about making such change in practice. The report observes that '… increasingly, notions of building social capital or capacity for "transition" feature prominently in the goals of ESD programmes. The notion of "transition" considers the need for social adaptation to address current and future socioeconomic and environmental realities' (ibid, 45). This will prompt some readers to wonder why social adaptation is the preferred mode of change, and why there is so much emphasis on personal empowerment and agency, and so little attention to the power of collectives and social movements to bring about change.

Box 4.3 on page 47–50 summarizes the key findings of the case study analysis in terms of the contributions of ESD to economic change which unwillingly perhaps takes current neoliberal principles and routines for granted, thereby essentially affirming them. The box reveals an emphasis on improving resource efficiency, reducing costs, employability and supporting local and regional economies, all of which can be accommodated within current hegemonic neoliberalist economic mod-els and principles. The box does identify 'new economic models' as a topic case studies might allude to, yet only one of the 13 cases reviewed does so: Learning for Social Entrepreneurship in Egypt (case 5.4). Clearly, even in this case a focus or belief in financial competitiveness in itself is not challenged, but is rather seen as a given that can be harmonized with social justice.

Finally, the review does show that many of the case studies seek to link the glo-bal and the local in terms of how what happens elsewhere affects us, and how what we do here affects people – mostly people … – elsewhere. But they do not seem to challenge globalization as a homogenizing force steering humanity towards a singu-lar perspective on what constitutes well-being (e.g. being a flexible worker, being food secure, having purchasing power to purchase goods at any time of the day, anywhere in the world). Instead, as one case illustrates, it is suggested that: '… strat-egies [are] incorporated … to resist globalization's negative challenges and to take advantage of its constructive potential to forge models of personal and communal development based on lifestyles that are peaceful, democratic, and sustainable' (ibid, 87). At the same time the power of localization as illustrated by, for example, the emergence of transition towns seems to remain unnoticed in the documents and cases reviewed.

> Teaching a sustainable lifestyle with the Earth Charter. (Vilela de Araujo et al. 2005, http://www.earthcharter.nl/upload/cms/230_Teachers_guidebook.pdf)

The Earth Charter, first proposed at the Earth Summit in 1992 and launched in 2002 after widespread discussion and debate throughout global civil society, offers 16 principles for building a global society based on respect for nature; universal human rights; economic justice; and a culture of peace (Earth Charter Initiative 2013). Teaching a Sustainable Lifestyle with the Earth Charter (Vilela de Araujo et al. 2005) is a manual for basic education that focuses on dimensions of sustainable development that are not generally well covered in other DESD-related guidance documents: the ethical, spiritual, cultural and political dimensions. On page 5 it is stated that 'In order to achieve sustainable development, we must remember that ... economic development does not take environmental impacts, social relationships or democratic processes into consideration.' This suggests there is a tension, if not an incompatibility, between these two developments (capitalist development and sustainable development), whereas most ESD documents appear to suggest that eco-logical modernization or the greening of capitalism can result in a balance between them (i.e. balancing People–Planet–Profit).

The manual appears to be critical of globalization and consumerism and the life-styles they engender. 'Latin American countries have lost some of their identity and roots, because they have underappreciated their own culture. Globalization has nota-bly exacerbated this phenomenon, as it tends to homogenize cultures and generate a loss of cultural identity' (ibid, 24). Becoming critical of globalization is an explicit learning goal, as is an ability to distinguish between development from a 'consumer-istic' point of view and development from a 'sustainable development' perspective, which according to the manual looks toward the future with care and respect and takes responsibility for the wise use of natural resources.

Questions relating to whether students should consider liberal and radical views of social change alongside the reformist and sometimes idealist views reflected in the literature of DESD, are not raised in the manual. Instead, students are invited to start their own organic garden, join a political party or participate in a range of other activities that may contribute to 'sustainable lifestyles'. Avoidance of political econ-omy and real alternatives is further illustrated by a list of easier-said-than-done actions people can take to 'avoid' the problems of climate change: avoid burning vegetation, decrease petroleum use, use clean technology and renewable energy, avoid deforestation, and 'use our cars less, because they produce contaminant gases which increase the greenhouse effect, acid rain and smog. Therefore, the less we use our cars, the healthier our planet' (ibid, 55).

As far as the scale dimension is concerned, the Earth Charter itself acknowledges that 'We are at once citizens of different nations and of one world in which the local and global are linked.' Principle 6c states that we need to 'Ensure that decision-making addresses the cumulative, long-term, indirect, long distance, and global con-sequences of human activities.' In the teaching with the Earth Chart manual, the scale dimension is addressed mainly by introducing Wackernagel's ecological footprint concept. Students are encouraged to explore their own lifestyles using this concept. The ecological footprint can be seen as a valuable educational tool and as a way into the political dimension of SD, as long as the limitations of the tool are also acknowledged. As Lenzen and Muray (2003) note the tool does, for instance, not reveal where impacts really occur or unveil much about the nature and severity of lifestyle impacts. A critical use of the ecological footprint could unwillingly contribute to a false consciousness engendered by ideology and hegemony, while leaving existing structures of power intact.

Arguable, the Earth Charter itself places much emphasis on the relational dimension. However, the teaching manual to go along with the Earth Charter remains rather vague about how the advocated 'universal responsibility', 'human solidarity' and 'humility regarding the human place in nature' can be developed in practical ways in everyday life. As such the link between ethics and citizenship and guidance in the realization of counter hegemonic values in public life is rather weak.

Beyond DESD

Our analysis of these four products of DESD suggests that it amounted to 'business as usual in the end' as far as challenging neoliberalism and encouraging GESC are concerned. Given this weakness, what is the way forward? Firstly, we should acknowledge the potential for greater synergy between UNESCO's international education initiatives and the prospect that such events as the forum on global citizenship education, held in Bangkok in December 2013, may lead to GESC being given a stronger profile within UNESCO's advocacy and promotion of ESD. Those readers with influence within UNESCO may be able to advance this agenda. Latin-America was strongly represented in the working group that wrote TEWN and it is here, where the dual power of social movements and progressive political parties is pioneering new forms of sustainability citizenship (Guardiola-Rivera 2010) that we should perhaps look for inspiration and guidance on ecopedagogy and GESC.

Secondly we should acknowledge that while there are signs of recovery in the world economy, analysts predict 'a larger scale version of an Occupy Wall Street type movement will begin by the end of 2014' (Thibodeau 2013) largely because machines are replacing middle-class workers in high cost, specialized jobs, and the young are becoming a 'jilted generation' denied the jobs, housing and pensions their parents took for granted (Howker and Malik 2013). Protest continues to 'kick off' around the world (Mason 2013) and ESD can assist the transition from neoliberalism by giving the voices of protest a considered hearing within our curriculum and pedagogy. This will involve defending GESC and 'civic pedagogy' against those who continue to promote a neoliberal version of global citizenship education (Shultz 2007).

Thirdly, we should draw strength from a socially critical tradition in EE and ESD that continues to develop ecopedagogy using new insights provided by social theorists such as Harvey (2010), Castells (2012) and Wright (2010). Ultimately, global sustainability requires a directly elected world parliament that can hold international powers to account; give global citizens and opportunity to influence decisions; and accelerate the realization of Earth Charter principles (Monbiot 2003). There is much that GESC and a reformulated ESD might do to hasten its arrival.

Notes on contributors

John Huckle is a geographical and environmental educator who taught at De Montfort and London South Bank Universities. His website is at http://john.huckle.org.uk.

Arjen E.J. Wals is a professor and UNESCO chair in social learning and sustainable development at Wageningen University in The Netherlands. He also is an Adjunct Faculty member of Cornell's Department of Natural Resources and a visiting Professor at Gothenburg University. His blog can be found at: www.transformativelearning.nl.

References

Barry, J. 2005. "Resistance is Fertile: From Environmental to Sustainability Citizenship." In *Environmental Citizenship: Getting from Here to There?*, edited by D. Bell and A. Dobson, 21–48. Shandong: MIT Press.

Brand, U. 2012. "Green Economy – The Next Oxymoron?" *GAIA* 21 (1): 28–32. http://www.openscience4sustainability.at/wp-content/uploads/2012/06/GAIA-2012_brand_green-econ omy.pdf.

Bullen, A., and M. Whitehead. 2005. "Negotiating the Networks of Space, Time and Substance: A Geographical Perspective on the Sustainable Citizen." *Citizenship Studies* 9 (5): 499–516.

Calhoun, C., and G. Derluguian, eds. 2011. *The Deepening Crisis: Governance Challenges After Neoliberalism*. New York: NYUP.

Castells, M. 2012. *Networks of Outrage and Hope: Social Movements in the Internet Age*. Cambridge: Polity.

DESD (Decade of Education for Sustainable Development). 2014. http://www.desd.org/About%20ESD.htm.

Dobson, A. 2003. *Citizenship and the Environment*. Oxford: OUP.

Dobson, A. 2011. *Sustainability Citizenship*. London: Greenhouse.

Dryzek, J. 1997. *The Politics of the Earth: Environmental Discourses*. Oxford: OUP.

Earth Charter Initiative. 2015. http://www.earthcharterinaction.org/download/about_the_Initia tive_history_2t.pdf.

Elliott, L. 1998. *The Global Politics of the Environment*. London: Macmillan.

EuroMemo Group. 2013. *EuroMemorandum 2013*. http://www.euromemo.eu/euromemoran dum/euromemorandum_2013/index.html

Fien, J., and J. Parker. 2010. *Education for Sustainable Development Lens: A Policy and Practice Review Tool*. Paris: UNESCO. http://unesdoc.unesco.org/images/0019/001908/190898e.pdf.

Gadotti, M. 2008. "What We Need to Learn to Save the Planet." *Journal of Education for Sustainable Development* 2 (1): 21–30.

Gaudelli, W., and E. Heilman. 2009. "Reconceptualizing Geography as Democratic Global Citizenship Education." *Teachers College Record* 111 (11): 2647–2677.

Gilbert, L., and C. Phillips. 2003. "Practices of Urban Environmental Citizenships: Rights to the City and Rights to Nature in Toronto." *Citizenship Studies* 7 (3): 313–330.

Graeber, D. 2013. *The Democracy Project: A History, a Crisis, a Movement*. London: Allen Lane.

Gruenewald, D. A., and G. A. Smith. 2008. *Place-based Education in the Global Age*. New York: Erlbaum.

Guardiola-Rivera, O. 2010. *What if Latin America Ruled the World?* London: Bloomsbury.

Harris, J. 2014. *The Left is Too Silent on the Clunking Fist of State Power*. http://www.the guardian.com/commentisfree/2014/jan/05/left-silent-state-power-government-market.

Harvey, D. 2010. *The Enigma of Capital and the Crises of Capitalism*. London: Profile Books.

Heiss, J., and I. Marras. 2009. "Educating and Engaging Youth in Sustainable Consumption: YouthXchange Programme." In *Young People, Education and Sustainable Development: Exploring Principles, Perspectives and Praxis*, edited by P. B. Corcoran and P. M. Osano, 181–190. Wageningen: Wageningen Academic Publishers.

Held, D. 1996. *Democracy and the Global Order: From the Modern State to Cosmopolitan Governance*. Cambridge: Polity Press.

Held, D., and A. McGrew. 2002. *Globalization/Anti-Globalization*. Cambridge: Polity.

Hopkins, R. 2013. *The Power of Just Doing Stuff*. Cambridge: Transition Books.

Hopwood, B., M. Mellor, and G. O'Brien. 2005. "Sustainable Development: Mapping Different Approaches." *Sustainable Development* 13 (1): 38–52. doi:10.1002/sd.244.

Howker, E., and S. Malik. 2013. *Jilted Generation: How Britain Has Bankrupted Its Youth*. London: Icon Books.

Huckle, J. 2012. "Towards Greater Realism in Learning for Sustainability." In *Learning for Sustainability in Times of Accelerating Change*, edited by A. E. J. Wals and P. B. Corcoran, 35–48. Wageningen: Wageningen Academic Publishers.

Hursh, D. W., and J. A. Henderson. 2011. "Contesting Global Neoliberalism and Creating Alternative Futures." *Discourse Studies in the Cultural Politics of Education* 32 (2): 171–185.

Jickling, B., and A. E. J. Wals. 2007. "Globalization and Environmental Education: Looking Beyond Sustainable Development." *Journal of Curriculum Studies* 40 (1): 1–21.

Kahn, R. 2008. "From Education for Sustainable Development to Ecopedagogy: Sustaining Capitalism or Sustaining Life?" *Green Theory and Praxis* 4 (1): 1–14.

Kahn, R. 2010. *Critical Pedagogy, Ecoliteracy and the Planetary Crisis: The Ecopedagogy Movement*. New York: Peter Lang.

Lapavitsas, C. 2013. *Financialisation in Crisis*. Leiden: Brill Publishers.

Lenzen, M., and S. A. Murray. 2003. *Ecological Footprints – Issues and Trends*. http://www.isa.org.usyd.edu.au/publications/documents/Ecological_Footprint_Issues_and_Trends.pdf.

Loprieno, P. L., M. Bhatt, and P. Williams. 2006. *YouthXchange: The Guide*. Paris: UNESCO/UNEP.

Mason, P. 2013. *Why It's Still Kicking off Everywhere: The New Global Revolutions*. London: Verso.

Mazower, M. 2012. *Governing the World: The History of an Idea*. London: Penguin Books.

Monbiot, G. 2003. *The Age of Consent: A Manifesto for a New World Order*. London: Harper Perennial.

Monbiot, G. 2012. *The Mendacity of Hope*. http://www.monbiot.com/2012/06/18/the-mendacity-of-hope/.

OSDEM (Open Spaces for Dialogue and Enquiry Methodology). 2013. http://www.osdemethodology.org.uk/.

Park, J., K. Conca, and M. Finger, eds. 2008. *The Crisis of Global Environmental Governance*. London: Routledge.

Pigozzi, M. J. 2006. "A UNESCO View of Global Citizenship Education." *Educational Review* 58 (1): 1–4.

Rio+20 Education Group. 2012. *The Education We Need for the World We Want*. http://rio20.net/en/propuestas/the-education-we-need-for-the-world-we-want/.

Selby, D., and F. Kagawa. 2010. "Runaway Climate Change as Challenge to the 'Closing Circle' of Education for Sustainable Development." *Journal of Education for Sustainable Development* 4 (1): 37–50.

Selby, D., and F. Kagawa, eds. 2014. *Sustainability Frontiers: Critical and Transformative Voices from the Borderlands of Sustainability Education*. Opladen: Barbara Budrich Publishing.

Shultz, L. 2007. "Educating for Global Citizenship: Conflicting Agendas and Understandings." *The Alberta Journal of Educational Research* 53 (3): 248–258.

Smith, M. 1998. *Ecologism, Towards Ecological Citizenship*. Buckingham: Open University Press.

Smith, M., and P. Pangsapa. 2008. *Environment and Citizenship: Integrating Justice, Responsibility and Civic Engagement*. London: Zed Books.

Thibodeau, P. 2013. "Gartner's Dark Vision for Tech Jobs." *Computer World*. Accessed October 10, 2013. www.computerworld.com/s/article/9243138/Gartner_s_dark_vision_for_tech_jobs

Tilbury, D. 2011. *Education for Sustainable Development: An Expert Review of Processes and Learning*. Paris: UNESCO. http://unesdoc.unesco.org/images/0019/001914/191442e.pdf.

UNESCO. 2002. *Education for Sustainability, from Rio to Johannesburg: Lessons Learnt from a Decade of Commitment*. Paris: UNESCO.

UNESCO. 2005a. *The DESD at a Glance*. Paris: UNESCO. http://unesdoc.unesco.org/images/0014/001416/141629e.pdf.

UNESCO. 2005b. *International Implementation Scheme*. Paris: UNESCO. http://unesdoc.unesco.org/images/0014/001486/148654E.pdf.

NEOLIBERALISM AND ENVIRONMENTAL EDUCATION

UNESCO. 2009. *Bonn Declaration of the World Conference on Education for Sustainable Development*. Paris: UNESCO. http://www.esd-world-conference-2009.org/fileadmin/download/ESD2009_BonnDeclaration080409.pdf.

UNESCO. 2012. *Shaping the Education of Tomorrow – Abridged Version*. Paris: UNESCO. http://unesdoc.unesco.org/images/0021/002166/216606e.pdf.

UNESCO Bangkok. 2014. *Teacher Education and Training in the Asia-Pacific Region*. http://www.unescobkk.org/?id=11455.

UNESCO-UNEP. 1975. The Belgrade Charter on Environmental Education – Adopted by the UNESCO-UNEP. International Environmental Workshop held in Belgrade, October 13–22, 1975. unesdoc.unesco.org/images/0001/000177/017772eb.pdf.

UNESCO-UNEP. 2008. *YouthXchange: The Guide*. 2nd ed. Paris: UNESCO/UNEP. http://www.youthxchange.net/main/english-guide.asp.

UNESCO-UNEP. 1978. *The Tbilisi Declaration of the Intergovernmental Conference on Environmental Education*, Tbilisi, October 14–26, 1977, Final Report. Paris: UNESCO/UNEP. http://unesdoc.unesco.org/images/0003/000327/032763eo.pdf.

UNHLP (United Nations High Level Panel on the Post 2015 Development Agenda). 2013. *A New Global Partnership: Eradicate Poverty and Transform Economies Through Sustainable Development*. http://www.un.org/sg/management/pdf/HLP_P2015_Report.pdf.

Van Poeck, K., J. Vandenabeele, and H. Bruyninckx. 2013. *Sustainable Citizenship and Education*. https://lirias.kuleuven.be/bitstream/123456789/329860/1/Paper_081_Katrien VanPoeck.pdf.

Vilela de Araujo, M., E. R. Ramirez, L. H. Rojas, and C. B. Lobo. 2005. *Teaching Sustainable Lifestyle with the Earth Charter: Guideline for Second Cycle Teachers of Basic General Education*. San Jose, CA: Earth Charter Initiative. http://www.earthcharter.nl/upload/cms/230_Teachers_guidebook.pdf.

Wals, A. E. J. 2009. *Review of Contexts and Structures for Education for Sustainable Development*. Paris: UNESCO. http://unesdoc.unesco.org/images/0018/001849/184944e.pdf.

Wals, A. E. J. 2012. *Shaping the Education of Tomorrow – Full Length Report*. Paris: UNESCO. http://unesdoc.unesco.org/images/0021/002164/216472e.pdf.

Walsh, J. 2009. "The Critical Role of Discourse in Education for Democracy." *Journal for Critical Education Policy Studies* 6 (2): 54–76.

Warner, R. 2010. "Ecological Modernisation Theory: Towards a Critical Ecopolitics of Change?" *Environmental Politics* 19 (4): 538–556.

World Social Forum. 2013. http://www.fsm2013.org/en.

Wright, E. O. 2010. *Envisioning Real Utopias*. London: Verso.

Index

ABAG (Brazilian Agribusiness Association) 143–4
Abertura Política 138, 146
access to political programmes and financial resources 152–5, 157–8
actor movement 173–4
actor networks 165, 170–7
Agenda 21 198
agendas, management of 112–13
'Agrarian Question...' course 152, 156–7
agribusiness 143–4, 145
agriculture, urban 13, 53–66
Agroecological Institute of Latin America - Amazonia branch (IALA) 152, 156–7, 158
agroecology 151; vocational high-school programme 152–3, 154–5
agro-food (agriculture and food system) 53–4, 64; alternative food networks (AFNs) 54, 55–6, 63
air quality action project 187–8
alternative economic spaces 64
alternative food networks (AFNs) 54, 55–6, 63
Alternatives for Community and Environment (ACE) 187, 188
American Corrections Association (ACA) 70
American International Association for Economic Development 152
anti-essentialist approach 64
anti-neoliberal education 14, 151–8

Bakker, K. 84–5
Ball, S.J. 12
Bangkok forum on global citizenship education 204
Barrett, M. 99
bats 46
beans 153
Beck, U. 26
Belgrade charter 199
Berry, W. 3
Bill and Melinda Gates Foundation (GF) 176
biocapitalism 162–79
biocolonialism 166–7
biodiversity conservation 165–6

biopolitics 75, 163
biopower 70
bioprospecting 164, 165–8
biotech civic epistemology 164, 168–9; *see also* genetically engineered (GE) food industry
Blay-Palmer, A. 56
Block, F. 2, 3
Blumstein, D.T. 41
Boggs, G.L. 180
borders 114–15
Boston 187–8
Brazil: constitution of 1988 138; critical environmental education 14, 135–48; Environmental Education in Family Agriculture Program 14, 136, 138, 140–6; historical context of critical EE 138–40; Landless Workers' Movement 14, 149–61
Brenner, N. 28, 63
Brito, G. 153–4
Brooklyn urban agriculture programme 53, 54, 56–64
Brown, J. 170–1
Brown, M.Y. 88–9
Bruyninckx, H. 196
Bunge group 141–2, 143

campaign financing 142–4
Canada 30–3
capitalism 84–5; decline of 190; global capitalist system 136–7
carceral geography 73–4
carceral political ecology 73–4, 75
Carta Brasileira para Educação Ambiental 138–9
Cass Corridor Commons 183–5
Catherine Ferguson Academy 181, 182
Chicago 182, 185
Chicago University 5
cities: right to the city 14–15, 180–92; urban agriculture youth programmes 13, 53–66; urban environmental education 13, 80–91
citizen-subjects 95–6
citizenship: environmental 13, 92–104; sustainability *see* global education for sustainability citizenship

209

INDEX

civic epistemology: alternative 170–7; biotech
164, 168–9
civic pedagogy 195, 204
civil society 137; neoliberalism, the state and in
Brazil 140–6; *see also* social movements
Clarke, J. 113
class conflict 137–8, 144, 145
climate change 6
Codd, J. 6
coercion 24–5
collective cognitive practice 177
colonization 81, 89; *see also* decolonization
Columbia University 14
commodification 9, 10
common sense: appropriating the common
sense of environmental education 85–7;
neoliberalization of 82–5
communicative travel 25
community engagement 59–60
community forum 153
community organizing 14–15, 180–92
competencies 115
competition 24–5, 27–8; for students 123
conservation 44–5; bioprospecting as
biodiversity conservation 165–6
consumption 11, 101; food consumption
choices 61–2; reducing 93–4
context 26; of decision-making 100
Cooper, M. 9–10
Copeland, W. 184
core competencies 115
core and periphery 136–7
corn (maize) 165, 173–6
corporations 5; corporate financing 141–2
corporeal travel 25
Costanza, R. 46
Council for Biotechnology Information (CBI)
workbook 164, 168–9, 175
creative destruction 55
crises 10, 163; global crisis 7, 194–5
critical consciousness 98–100
critical environmental education 14, 135–48
critical geography 84
critical pedagogy 122–4
critical and transformative ESD 195–6
Cronon, W. 82
current hegemonic forms 174
curriculum reforms 170, 188–9

Dauverne, P. 9
de Souza, M. 154–5
debates 155–6
de-bordering processes 114–15
Decade of Education for Sustainable
Development (DESD) 15, 120, 139, 193–207
decision-making context 100
decolonization 89, 187–8
deep neoliberalisms 55

Department for Business, Innovation and Skills
(BIS) 125
dependency theory 136–8
depoliticization of policy-making processes
29–30
deregulation 3, 84, 182
despair work 88–9
Detroit 14–15, 180, 181–2, 183–6, 190–1
Detroit Institute of Technology 185
developmental readiness 100
Dewey, J. 3
dialogic spaces 155–6
disciplinary governmentality 45
discourse 197; dominant discourses 99;
ecologically modern discourses 28–9;
pedagogical 144–5
dissensus 35
diverse economies 64
dominant discourses 99
Donald, B. 56
Dryzek, J. 197

Earth Charter 197, 203–4
Earth Charter movement 140
Earth Institute 14
East Michigan Environmental Action Council
(EMEAC) 183–6, 187, 189–90
Eco Schools 110–11
Eco Schools Scotland 110, 111, 115
Eco-92 140
ecobiopolitics 69, 72, 75, 76; environmental
knowledge and prison ecobiopolitics 72–4
ecohealth 72
ecoliteracy 162–79
ecological footprints 196, 203–4
ecological readiness 100
ecologically modern discourses 28–9
economic sustainability 31–2
ecopedagogy 140, 195; delivering GESC's four
dimensions through 196–8
eco-prisons 70–2
ecosystem services 9, 13, 42, 46–7
ecotherapy 72
ecotourism 12–13, 40–52; neoliberalization in
ecotourism education 45–7
ecotourist gaze 43–5
'Edible School Yard' program 55
Educação do Campo movement 151, 152
Education for International Understanding
(EIU) 198
education policy mobility 12, 21–39
education reforms 8–9, 163, 170
education for sustainable development (ESD)
135; agenda of higher education 14, 119–34;
critical and transformative 195–6; ESD
research 127–9; teacher reward policy 13–14,
105–18; UN Decade of ESD 15, 120, 139,
193–207

INDEX

educational measurement tools 8–9, 176–7
educational politics of scale 150–1, 154, 155, 157, 158
employability agenda 126–7
emulation 24–5
entrepreneurial self 166
entrepreneurship 62, 95
environmental citizenship 13, 92–104
Environmental Education in Family Agriculture Program (PEAAF) 14, 136, 138, 140–6
environmental knowledge 72–4
environmental regularization 143
Environmental Reserve Quotas 143
environmental subjects 45
environmental sustainability 31–2
environmentality 45, 164, 169
ESDL: An Expert Review of Processes and Learning 202–3
ESD Lens (ESDL) 200
ethic of self-care 176
ethical dimension of GESC 197, 199–204
Eurocentrism 43
evolution of innovative educational institutions 155–6, 158
Exeter University 126
exploitation 71
extended state 137, 142, 144

Federal Technical Institute of Pará - Rural Marabá Campus (IFPA-CRMB) 152–3, 154–5, 155–6, 158
Federal University of Pará (UFPA) 152, 153–4, 155, 156, 158
Feed One/Teach One workshop 185
Fien, J. 200
financial resources: campaign financing 142–4; corporate financing 141–2; social movements' access to 152–5, 157–8; *see also* funding of higher education
fiscal austerity 84
focus group interviews 107–8
food: agro-food 53–4, 64; alternative food networks (AFNs) 54, 55–6, 63; consumption choices 61–2; urban agriculture youth programmes and education about 60–2
food industry 14, 162–79
Forest Code 142–4
Foucault, M. 44, 45, 67, 73, 75, 163
Foundation for Environmental Education 110
Francis, Pope 6–7
FREC 155–6, 158
freedom 169
Freire, P. 98
Friedman, M. 5, 182
funding of higher education 122, 123, 125–6, 127–9

Gadotti, M. 140
Gallagher, B.E. 70–1
Gates, B. 176
Gates Foundation (GF) 176
General Teaching Council for Scotland (GTCS) 107, 109, 110, 111, 113, 115
genetically engineered (GE) food industry 164–5, 168–77; GE food controversies 170, 171–2, 173, 175–6
gentrification 185
global capitalist system 136–7
global conservation movement 44
global crisis 7, 194–5
global education for sustainability citizenship (GESC) 15, 194, 195–204; analysing DESD products against dimensions of 199–204; delivering the four dimensions through ecopedagogy 196–8; role of UN and UNESCO in supporting 198–9
global governance 197–8
global political communities 100–1
globalization 23, 114–15
Golden Rice 171–2, 176
governance 142, 144; global 197–8
government/state funding: higher education 122, 123, 125–6; social movements' access to 152–5, 157–8
governmentality 8, 45; neoliberal 45, 163
governments 5; *see also* state
Gramsci, A. 137
Great Depression 4
Greater Egleston Community High School (GECHS) 187–8, 189–90
Green Academy programme 120
green economy 198
green lifestyle movements 96
green prison movement 70–2
Greener School Initiative 185
Gruenewald, D.A. 72, 88, 170, 187
Guthman, J. 56

habilitation 72
Hantz, J. 185
Harry, D. 166–7
Harvey, D. 54, 136–7, 144, 181
Hayden, C. 165–6
Hayek, F.A. 4, 5, 6, 7, 182
heartlands 158
hegemony 137–8; current hegemonic forms 174
Helmreich, S. 163–4
Henderson, J. 83
Heynen, N. 83–4
Hicks, C. 184, 186
hierarchical scale 150, 154, 157
higher education (HE) 14, 119–34; effects of neoliberalism and NPM 122, 123; political framing of in the UK 125

INDEX

Higher Education: Students at the Heart of the System 126
Higher Education Academy (HEA) 120, 127, 130
Higher Education Funding Council for England (HEFCE) 120, 122, 125, 127, 130
higher skills system 125
horizontal scale 150, 154, 157
Howells, R.E. 47
Hursh, D.W. 83
hybridization 83–4

IBAMA 139
IFPA-CRMB 152–3, 154–5, 155–6, 158
imaginative travel 25
incarceration rates 68
individuals 5–6, 43–4; decision-making context 100; professional recognition policy 111–12; shift of responsibility from the state to 95–8; urban agriculture and individual effort 61–3
innovative educational institutions, evolution of 155–6, 158
Inside-Out Prison Exchange Program 76
institutional greenwashing 33
institutionalized rural education 156–7, 158
intellectual labour 25–6
International Monetary Fund 183, 199
interstitial transformation 186
interviews 58, 107–8
Irwin, R. 30

Jasanoff, S. 167
Judt, T. 4

Kagawa, F. 199
Keele University 126
Kellogg Foundation 186
knowledge, environmental 72–4
knowledge regime 168–9, 172
knowledge society 125

labour: intellectual 25–6; prison 71, 75–6
land tenure regularization 143
Landless Workers' Movement (MST) 14, 149–61
Latour, B. 171
Lave, R. 75
leadership development 60
learning, policy 24–5
learning gardens 165, 170–7
Learning to Live Together (LTLT) 198
LeFebvre, H. 181
Lemke, T. 75
Leopold, A. 80, 86
liberalism 4; social democratic 4–5, 7
liminal experience 44
Lister, J. 9
local alternatives 55–6, 62, 64

Loprieno, P.L. 200–1
Louv, R. 47

Macy, J. 88–9
maize (corn) 165, 173–6
management of agendas 112–13
managerialism 13–14, 105–18; neoliberalism and 113–14; *see also* new public management (NPM)
Mandelson, Lord 125
markets 2, 4, 6, 7, 163, 182; biodiversity conservation 165–6; CBI workbook 169; higher education in the UK 122
Marxism 139–40
McArthur, J. 125
McCann, E. 29–30
Measures of Effective Teaching Project 176–7
Mesoamerica 173
methodological cosmopolitanism 26
methodology 34–5
Millennium Ecosystem Assessment 46
Ministry of the Environment (MMA) 140, 141–2
mobility turn 23–7; *see also* policy mobility
Monsanto 167
Mont Pelerin Society 5
more-than-human/modern neo-liberal continuum for wilderness 86–7
MST 14, 149–61
multi-stakeholder commitment approach 69–70

National Environmental Education Program (PRONEA) 141
National Institute of Corrections 69, 70
National Program for Education in Agrarian Reform (PRONERA) 152–8
National Union of Students (NUS) 127, 130
nature deficit disorder 47–8
neoliberal citizen-subjects 95–6
neoliberal governmentality 45, 163
neoliberal science regimes 75–6
neoliberalism 2–3, 4–8; and environmental education 8–10
neoliberalization 22, 54–5, 142; of common sense 82–5; in ecotourism education 45–7; and mobile policies 27–8; urban agriculture and the (re)production of 61–3
Netherlands, the 115
networks 25; professional recognition 111–12
Neumann, R. 150
New Ecological Paradigm Scale 71
new public management (NPM) 27–8; neoliberalism and in the UK 121–2; and the sustainable development agenda of higher education 14, 119–34; *see also* managerialism
Newman, J. 113

INDEX

Next Generation Science Standards 1
Norquist, G. 5
North Dakota Study Group 180, 181, 183
Nsoroma School 181, 182, 183
nudging mechanisms 129–30
NUS 127, 130

object oriented democracy 171
Olssen, M. 6
O'Neill, A.-M. 6
Ontario 84
oppression 89
Orr, K. 182
Osborne, T. 25–6

Pará, southeastern 14, 149–61
Parker, J. 200
participant observation 57
participation 144–5
PEAAF 14, 136, 138, 140–6
peace park project 188
Peck, J. 23, 24–5, 28
pedagogical discourse 144–5
penal state 68
physical movement 25
place-based education 80–1, 88
plants: in learning gardens 173–7; origins 173
policy enactment 34
policy mobility 12, 21–39
policy models 28
policy title terminology 31
policy transfer-diffusion 23–5
political ecology 76, 150; carceral 73–4, 75; of education 14, 149–61
political organizing training 63
political programmes, access to 152–5, 157–8
politics: and environmental education 1–2, 10–11; neoliberalism as a political project 2–3, 8; political dimension of GESC 197–8, 199–204
Porritt, J. 190–1
post-secondary education policy 12, 21–39
pragmatic EE initiatives 145
prison labour 71, 75–6
prisons 13, 67–79
private sphere 96–8
privatization 84, 182; of education 27–8
productive destruction ethic 167
professional recognition policy 107, 109–15
professionalism 13–14, 105–18
PRONEA 141
PRONERA 152–8
protest movements 204
Prudham, S. 84
public environmental management education 139
public good, education for 122–4
public–private partnerships 141–2

public services 113; neoliberal structural adjustments 182
public sphere 96–8

Quality Assurance Agency (QAA) 127, 130
quality assurance agendas 127
quality-related (QR) research funding 127–9
quasi markets 122
Quintas, J.S. 139
quotidian forms of resistance 154

RAE 127–8
RCUK 128–9, 130
readiness, ecological 100
Reagan, R. 5, 121
rebirth 72
re-bordering processes 114–15
recognized teacher of SDE 109–13
reduce-reuse-recycle 10
REF 127–9, 130
Regional Forum of *Educação do Campo* (FREC) 155–6, 158
regularization 143
reinhabitation 89, 187–8
relational dimension of GESC 197, 199–204
re-regulation 3, 5, 84
Research Assessment Exercise (RAE) 127–8
Research Councils UK (RCUK) 128–9, 130
Research Excellence Framework (REF) 127–9, 130
research funding 122, 123, 127–9
resilience theory 9–10
resistance: actor network epistemologies of 170–2; quotidian forms 154
rhizomes 153
right to the city 14–15, 180–92
Rio Earth Summit 119, 198
Rio+20 Education Group 194–5
Rio+20 Summit 198
Robertson, S.L. 114–15
romanticism 86
Roosevelt, F.D. 4–5
Root, E. 42
Roxbury 187
ruptural transformation 186
Rural Environmental Registry 143
rural workers' unions 144

Sachs, J. 14
Saylan, C. 41
scale: dimension of GESC 196, 199–204; educational politics of 150–1, 154, 155, 157, 158; horizontal and hierarchical 150, 154, 157
Scerri, A. 97
schools: community organizing and the right to the city 14–15, 180–92; developing environmental citizenship 13, 92–104

213

INDEX

Scotland 105–18
Selby, D. 199
self-care, ethic of 176
Senechal, E. 187–8
Shaull, R. 122–4
Smith, M. 82
Sobel, D. 100
social adhesion 145
social change, options for 186
social control 167–8
social democratic liberalism 4–5, 7
social justice science education 13, 92–104
social movements 144, 204; access to political programmes and financial resources 152–5, 157–8; Landless Workers' Movement 14, 149–61; *see also* civil society
social naturalism 6
social sustainability 31–2
soft skills 60
solutionaries 180, 188; teaching youth and young adults to become 183–6
Somers, M. 2, 3
southeastern Pará, Brazil 14, 149–61
Special Secretariat for the Environment 138
stakeholder theory 44; multi-stakeholder commitment approach 69–70
standards, teaching 106–7
state 3, 4, 5, 7–8; extended 137, 142, 144; funding *see* government/state funding; neoliberalism, civil society and in Brazil 140–6; neoliberalism, dependency theory and the role of 136–8; penal 68; shift of responsibility to the individual 95–8
state sovereignty 198
steering mechanisms 129–30
Stevenson, R.B. 1, 41, 42
Stiglitz, J. 7
Story of Stuff, The 93
structural adjustment 182–3, 199
Student Number Control 122
students: competition for 123; as consumers 125–7; funding 123, 125–6, 127
Students' Green Fund 127
subjectivation 75
subjugated knowledges 73
sustainability 9; in the education policy of post-secondary institutions 30–3; policy mobility and reimagining 12, 21–39; three pillars model 12, 31–2, 33; twinning and mobility of neoliberalism and in education policy 28–30
'Sustainability 101' curriculum 69
sustainability citizenship *see* global education for sustainability citizenship
Sustainability in Prisons Project (SPP) 13, 68–76
sustainability science 13, 67–79
sustainable development education *see* education for sustainable development (ESD)

symbiotic transformation 186
Syngenta 167

Tbilisi declaration 199
teacher reward policy 13–14, 105–18
teaching standards 106–7
Teaching a Sustainable Lifestyle with the Earth Charter 203–4
'teaching to the test' culture 170
TEEB (The Economics of Ecosystems and Biodiversity) initiative 46
Temenos, C. 29–30
Thatcher, M. 5, 121
The Education We Need for the World We Want (TEWN) 194–5
Theodore, N. 28, 63
three pillar model of sustainability 12, 31–2, 33
Tilbury, D. 202–3
transformation 72; options for social change 186
transformative standards 106–7
transnational food industry 14, 162–79
Treaty on Environmental Education for Sustainable Societies and Global Responsibility 140
tuition fees 125–6

UFPA 152, 153–4, 155, 156, 158
ugliest schoolyard contest 185, 186
UNEP 199
UNESCO 135, 204; role in supporting GESC 198–9
unions 144
United Kingdom (UK) 119–34; neoliberalism and NPM 121–2
United Nations (UN): Conference on Environment and Development (Rio Earth Summit) 119, 198; Decade of Education for Sustainable Development (DESD) 15, 120, 139, 193–207; role in supporting GESC 198–9
United States (US) 1, 4–5; AFNs 54, 55–6; community organizing, schools and the right to the city 14–15, 180–92; ecoliteracy 162–79; environmental citizenship education 93–5; incarceration rates 68; Sustainability in Prisons Project 13, 68–76; urban youth agriculture programmes 53, 54, 56–64
universities *see* higher education
upper-middle-class cultural perspective 43–4
urban agriculture youth programmes 13, 53–66
urban environmental education 13, 80–91
urbanization 85–6
Urry, J. 44
US Social Forum 182, 190

Van Poeck, K. 196
Vandenabeele, J. 196

INDEX

variation in neoliberalism 27
vehicular ideas 12, 21, 22, 23, 29–30, 32
vertical integration of courses 155
vertical scale 150, 154, 157
Vilela de Araujo, M. 203
virtual travel 25
visions for renewal 186
vocational agroecology program 152–3, 154–5

Wacquant, L. 68, 71, 73
Walker, J. 9–10
Wallerstein, I. 190
Wals, A.E. 115
Washington State Department of Corrections (DOC) 69, 70
We Are Not Ghosts 180
weeds 169
Wesselink, R. 115

Whitmarsh, L. 100
wilderness: in cities 81–2, 86, 89–90; continuum 86–7; ecotourism 43–4
wildness 82, 87
Williams, D. 170–1
workshops 13, 80–1, 85–7
World Bank 152, 183
World Commission on Environment and Development 119
world parliament 204
Wright, E.O. 186

Young Educators Alliance (YEA) 184–5
youth urban agriculture programmes 13, 53–66
YouthXChange (YXC) 200–1

zones of extension 158